The Salmon Fly

Faithfully yours
Geo. M. Kelson

The Salmon Fly

How To Dress It and How To Use It.

by

George M. Kelson

The Classics of Salmon Fishing

John Culler & Sons

The Classics of Salmon Fishing

The Salmon Fly by George M. Kelson
The Ristigouche and Its Salmon Fishing by Dean Sage
Autumns on the Spey by A.B. Knox
Jones Guide to Norway by Frederic Tolfrey
Halcyon by Henry Wade
Days and Nights of Salmon Fishing on the Tweed by William Scrope
A Book on Angling by Francis Francis
Salmon & Sea Trout by Herbert Maxwell
The Erne, Its Legends & Fly Fishing by Henry Newland
A Book of the Salmon by Ephemera
Blacker's Art of Fly Making by William W. Blacker
Salmonia by Sir Humphry Davis
Northern Memories by Richard Franck
The Sportsman in Canada by Frederic Tolfrey
The Rod and the Line by Hewett Weatley
The American Angler's Book by Thaddeus Norris
On River Angling for Salmon and Trout by John Younger
How to Tie Salmon Flies by Captain J.H. Hale
By Hook and by Crook by Fraser Sandeman
Salmon Fishing on the Grand Cascapedia by Edmund W. Davis
Salmon Fishing by John James Hardy
How to Dress Salmon Flies by T.E. Pryce-Tennatt
Salmon Fishing by Eric Tavener
Atlantic Salmon Fishing by Charles Phair

Dedication

The Classics of Salmon Fishing is dedicated to Paul Schmookler, outstanding fly tier, fisherman, publisher, historian and all-around good friend.

This volume designed by Wendy L. Trubia
Printed in the United States of America.
ISBN 1-887269-00-2

JOHN CULLER & SONS
P.O. BOX 1227, CAMDEN, SC 29020
(800) 861-9188

Introduction

George Kelson is perhaps the greatest enthusiast in the history of fly-fishing for salmon, and certainly one of the most important figures in that history. This, his *magnum opus*, is almost certainly the most important book ever written on the salmon-fly and on fly-fishing for salmon, though to call it the bible of either is to oversimplify the matter, and in fact there is no single book that merits either such title. To understand why this is the case, and the true importance of the book, we should understand something of the nature of the man, and the condition of the sport when he assembled the book. I say "assembled" rather that "wrote" because most of what is here had appeared in his earlier columns, particularly in *Land and Water.*

The book was published in 1895 (the date on the title page), or perhaps very early 1896 – in any case, this is a Centennial Edition. If in 1895 Kelson had assembled his articles and columns from the previous two decades, pruned and edited them, and published them in edited form, he might well have created the bible for salmon-fly-fishing, as of the mid-1890's. In any case, if Kelson had done all this editing and pruning, rather than rushing his book into print, he would not have been Kelson. He was an enthusiast, a controversialist, a promoter, and quite thoroughly incapable of pruning and editing his own work.

George Mortimer Kelson was born on December 8, 1835, the son of a surgeon who had apparently at one time held an appointment to the Prince Regent. He claimed descent from the Mortimers, though his precise relation to the ancient family is uncertain. So far as I know, he attended neither public school nor university – he was a distinguished cricketer, but I have found no record of his playing for any school, college, or university, nor is he listed among the graduates of any that have been checked.

His uncle, Colonel Charles Kelson, served as a subaltern under Major James Browne in Canada, at the time Frederic Tolfrey was a young member of the Governor's staff there, but despite the connexion with Browne and Tolfrey, fly-fishing for salmon was not the sport at which George Kelson first achieved public distinction. In his twenties and thirties he was indeed best known as a cricketer, playing for Kent and in 1863 in the All-England match of the Gentlemen against the Players (he was a Gentleman – that is, an amateur). He was once 164 not out for Kent, and another time scored centuries in three successive matches. (There is no even approximate equivalent in games or sports in the United States, but 164 not out in a County match would be about as common as hitting four home runs in a Major League game.) At his death in 1920, at the age of 84, he was still remembered as a cricketer, and his obituary appeared in *Wisden's*.

He had given up his career as a cricketer sometime after his marriage (1864), as his family grew, though he was playing into the 1870's, and at least one Bank Holiday club match in the 1880's. (His wife, by the way, was a Miss Herbert, but I am unable to suggest her connexion, if any, to that Henry Herbert better known as Frank Forester.) He rode with several hunts (including the Old Surrey), was a champion distance swimmer, played a notable match at billiards, and might generally have been considered a sportsman quite a while before he became famous as a salmon-fly enthusiast. His fame as an authority on the salmon fly owed something to his tireless self-promotion, but it was not only himself that he promoted. If he had done nothing else, he would still have earned our gratitude for moving fly-fishing for salmon to center stage in English sport.

Before Kelson, the salmon fly was largely the province of Welshmen like Francis Francis (né Francis Morgan – but I am told that I am exaggerating his Welshness), or Major John Popkin Traherne, or Scotsmen like Jock Scott (the laird or the ghillie), or (particularly) Irishmen like Major Browne or Edward Fitzgibbon ('Ephemera'). The gaudy fly to which Kelson was especially attracted had its origins in the West of Ireland, and of course Kelson's connexions through his uncle with Major James Browne would make an Irish tinge to his flies unsurprising – though not necessarily a West of Ireland tinge. Kelson's attributions as to the invention of certain salmon-flies are sometimes tendentious and not infrequently wrong – perhaps out of loyalty to friends and family –, but he may in such cases have meant only that a particular form of a given pattern could be so attributed. In any case, he was severely taken to task for his errors (if such they were) by Marston and others, and taking him to task is not my purpose here.

In appearance and strength as well as manner he was not unlike Conan Doyle's Professor Challenger, though in colour rufous rather than swart. He was something of a pocket Hercules, below average height, immensely strong in the shoulders, strong in the legs, a bristling sort of man, and perhaps even, like Challenger, a bit of a bully. Also like Challenger, he was never wrong in his own eyes. It is important to remember that he was a comparative outsider in the kind of society where salmon-fishing was then a favorite sport (which may explain his pride in the friendship of such men as General Beresford): in this character as an outsider he was almost the exact antithesis of his slightly younger contemporary, Sir Herbert Maxwell. It may be that this character, combined with his pugnaciousness and self-promotion, and his occasional inaccuracies, was not conducive to popularity either for himself or his book. Indeed, the book was published by Kelson himself, not by a commercial publisher.

A discussion of the reasons for this would involve an analysis of the role played by R. Bright Marston, Kelson's critic and opponent and scion of the Marston of Sampson Low, Marston & Co. That, in turn, would involve a discussion of Captain Hale's *How To Tie Salmon Flies* (1892), published by Marston, with its borrowings from Kelson's articles and columns. And that would more properly appear in an introduction to Hale, which will also appear in this series. Suffice it to say here that Hale's patterns bear a quite suspicious resemblance to those Kelson had published, being in general identical with the occasional substitution of black tying silk for black ostrich herl on the head. And on our more immediate subject, suffice it to say that Hale's book provided Kelson with a new grievance against Marston.

But *The Salmon Fly* was nonetheless published, thereby standing as a beacon for future generations. Though reading the prose has a certain quality of swimming upstream to it, nonetheless, the book was and is necessary to any library on fly-fishing for salmon. Eventually, of course, in the 1960s and 1970s, the future generations rediscovered it: it was scarce and expensive, and it was indispensable, and it was reprinted. The Angler's and Shooter's Press of Goshen, Connecticut, published a reprint edition in 1979, nor is our volume the only reprint edition bruited since. If it had not been there to be rediscovered, it is at least arguable that the recent revival of interest in the classic days of Victorian salmon-fishing would never have occurred. Even more important, of course, if Kelson had never existed, it is at least arguable that the classic days of Victorian salmon-fishing themselves would never have occurred.

Perhaps a word here on the distinguishing characteristics of the Victorian salmon fly would not be out of place. The prodigality of the Victorian salmon fly, its use of scores of feathers from birds that were rare even then, and exotic to Britain but not to her far-flung Empire and dependancies, can be considered an Imperial statement. Kelson was not the only authority who "Imperialised" the Irish gaudy fly, but he did it more extensively than most: his own creations, if they err at all, err in the direction of prodigality. His publication of Major Traherne's patterns, so magnificently executed and photographed in Paul Schmookler's recent book, *The Salmon Flies of Major John Popkin Traherne* (Millis MA, 1993), was of a part with this taste for the brilliant and the exotic, indeed for the Imperial.

There are parts of *The Salmon Fly* which remind me of parodies by the late Stephen Potter (*Gamesmanship, Lifemanship,* and their ilk), particularly the correct method and incorrect method of gaffing (on pp. 423-424) – perhaps because the Potter books are in part parodies of Victorian books on how to play cricket, and Kelson wrote a "how-to" book on fly-fishing something on the model of "how-to" books on cricket. Or perhaps that is too fanciful an analysis. In any case, the real problems with the work do not lie occasional self-parody or even constant self-promotion, though they are related to them.

The real problems are at least three in number. First, the book, despite being fifteen years in the making, seems hastily thrown together: some flies which could well have been included – and on which Kelson had written – are not included, and some are included that have to recommend them nothing much except that Kelson had an example at hand. Second, nearly one third of the flies in *The Salmon Fly* are Kelson's own (which probably explains why he had an example at hand), and of the others an inordinate number seem to be attributed to professional tiers with whom Kelson was friendly – notably James Wright of Sprouston, but there are a number of others. Third, like certain German philosophers, Kelson found it necessary to invent his own terminology, particularly in his discussion of casting techniques, a process conducive neither to easy comprehension nor to passing on his undoubted skill in fly-fishing for salmon. And, a possible fourth problem, sections in the latter part of the book are rather like a catalogue of Kelson-approved products.

In his defence, it should be said that Kelson published the book more hurriedly than he might have because Marston had given him a new grievance (or that is how I read it), and neither patience nor turning the other cheek were among Kelson's primary virtues. It should be said also that Kelson was, after all, a major inventor of patterns, and that James Wright of Sprouston (for example) was an important tier of flies and deserved most of the attention given him – if not all the attributions. And it should be said that Kelson's invented terminology was not created to rival someone else's, but was pretty much first in the field, so that if it too errs in prodigality, it may be only because later fly-fishers could not see the differences underlying Kelson's distinctions, because they did not share his *expertise.* (It is true that I, for one, would not care to hazard my personal safety by trying the Governor's cast, nor would anyone else, so far as I know, except Kelson – but this reflects an unnecessary prodigality in invention, rather than in taxonomy.) Kelson also codified the terminology for describing salmon flies, for which anyone interested in the subject owes him an immense debt of gratitude: not all his terminological excursions were awry. As to the Kelson-approved products, this was after all a "how-to" book, and they must certainly have been of more immediate interest to his readers in 1895-96 than they are to us now.

There are 251 flies whose patterns are given in *The Salmon Fly,* though only 239 are listed and described in the section on patterns: the rest appear in the text, or only in the plates. (I take this division to betray a haste in compilation.) Of the total more than 70 are attributed to Kelson himself, and roughly an equal number attributed to various professionals – among them Wright, William Brown of Aberdeen, William Garden of Aberdeen, Farlow, Malloch, James Enright of Castle Connell, John Bernard of London, Holbrow, William Turnbull of Edinburgh, Nicol McNicol of Reay (Thurso), and perhaps Davie Murray (to name only those with several flies each). Of other sportsmen, only Major Traherne, Major "Glen" Grant, John Jewhurst of Kent, and the Rev. A. Williams (three Usk flies) have three or more, and one sportswoman, Mrs. Courtney. A number of sportsmen are credited with a single fly, most often one bearing the sportsman's name, and frequently one quite well-known, like the Popham or the Childers. The ghillie Jock Scott (1817-1893) is credited with the Jock Scott. We may know more on this subject now than Kelson knew a century ago, but we are not to picture him with a reference library to consult when he was writing *The Salmon Fly:* what he did was to seek information from those he fished with or who tied his flies or supplied his tackle and other gear, and generally be content with that. After all, he was indeed writing a "how-to-do-it" (or rather a "how-I-do-it") book, not an historical treatise. Though his attributions and his attitude seem to me a trifle cavalier, and his whole manner pompous (with a slight touch of the huckster), I may be over-critical.

Kelson seems to have believed there was one best fly to be used on each water in each possible condition of water, of wind, of light, of weather, and each permutation and combination of these. Unfortunately, the great work in which he set out the scientific principles on which his selection was based never appeared, leaving the critical (or perhaps over-critical) reader with an impression of higgledy-piggledy *dicta* overlaid with pseudo-science. Moreover, his categorization of casting techniques may be less than entirely useful as a result of the vagaries of his writing style and of his idiosyncratic nomenclature – though here much may be forgiven to one who was largely first in the field.

The book is oddly illustrated. The plates of salmon flies seem to have an artificial regularity to the flies, reflecting a kind of engineer's abstract impressionism – not the artist's but the author's concept of the essence of the fly. The pictures of anglers by L.E. Lawrence include several at best only tangentially involved with the text, though they may have something to do with his casing taxonomy. The portrait of Major Grant ("Glen Grant") and his wife accompanying the discussion of Spey-casting may be justified by Major Grant's prowess in Spey-casting, mentioned in the text (with a letter from Major Grant). It is possible that the portrait of Mr. Henry J. Davis accompanying the discussion of wind-casting serves to identify the "quite a young Angler" on the upper Wye whose achievement at wind-casting Kelson notes on the following page (p. 352). But once again, even if this explains the inclusion of the pictures, it does not explain it very well, and certainly the book as a whole hangs together rather too loosely for our modern taste.

And yet, we must not forget that Kelson was the reigning expert on salmon flies and a remarkably successful fly-fisher. And however much we cavil at its imperfections, *The Salmon Fly* is indeed his *magnum opus*.

There have been better illustrations of salmon flies before and since, better-written books on salmon-fishing before and since, improvements in equipment (and quite a bit of the book is taken up with choosing equipment), but if we are looking for the salmon-fisher's *vade mecum,* rather than his bible, this is pretty much our only candidate. It is far from perfect, even as Kelson was, and it is not even as good a book as he could have made it, but it is the best we have. And in promoting fly-fishing for salmon, Kelson was the best we have ever had.

It was not quite his last word. The columns and articles went on, and there were the thirty-two *Land and Water* salmon-fly cards, with text, published in 1902, the year which also saw his *Tips,* like *The Salmon Fly* privately printed, containing six additional flies and perhaps deserving republication. (The cards have been reprinted in the Flyfisher's Classics series, but for reasons best known to the publisher without the text.) Kelson's later years were clouded by his controversy with Marston, which antedated *The Salmon Fly* but received new impetus from it, and which culminated in the "Little Inky Boy" affair of 1907-08. New claimants to the title of the bible of fly-fishing for salmon came, and largely went. The fashion in salmon flies changed as the British Empire changed: Kelson outlived his time and his fishing fame. When he died, *The Times* published an obituary praising him as a cricketer and not even mentioning his salmon-fishing or his salmon-flies, and *The Field* published the same obituary.

He should have been better remembered.

Jared C. Lobdell
Harrisburg, Pennsylvania
Candlemas
February, 1995

CONTENTS.

INDEX.

WYMAN & SONS, LIMITED,
PRINTERS,
CARTER LANE, DOCTORS' COMMONS,
LONDON, ENGLAND.

COLOURED PLATES.

PREFACE.

THIS book is published "by request." It aims at filling up a gap in angling literature, and is designed to stamp out the common fallacy that no one can learn how to make a fly "from written instructions." In truth, I know of no volume on the subject at all sufficiently clear, instructive or exhaustive.

In illustration of the leading statement I may perhaps be allowed to quote the following from amongst many similar requests made to me :—"I envy your being able to tie such flies," says a well-known Angler, in a letter dated 1888, "Tell me how you get the silk body so even. . . . You certainly turn out the best fly I ever saw and I hope some day to see you at work. Why do you not write a plain, concise, little book on the subject? Think over this." So I thought over it.

Onerous editorial duties stood in the way of my accepting many such written and oral promptings, but finally a friend's offer of assistance induced me to assume the task. I acknowledge my great obligations to the late Mr. A. H. Gribble for the part he was able to take in the mechanical details of fly-"tying," for, as his Mentor, I have, I believe, been able to achieve a success in fly-dressing with novices in a way that has not hitherto been compassed. During the progress of instruction in the art of "dressing," for which other than personal lessons have seemed inadequate, the opportunity was carefully taken to make notes in detail of the measurements, manipulation and methods employed to avoid or lessen the obstructions in the novice's road to excellence. The notes were all new to my friend; for me they had an unexpected value; and whoever, from practice through long years, has eyes to observe, and fingers to make short work of the *minutiæ* of fly-"tying," will readily understand that without them I must have failed to appreciate and make due provision for many little ensnaring but exasperating difficulties that lie in wait for the learner.

An adept's familiarity with an art may lead him to contemn, if not overlook, many little matters that make it impossible to the uninitiated. And as this fact was gradually brought to my mind, it opened a wide view of the task before me and laid bare a long vista of minor particulars needful to explain, if I would guide others of less experience than myself.

I have, however, not been deterred by that view, nor ceased to keep to my first intention to produce an *original* manual, useful to refer to on practical matters, which have not suitably, certainly not similarly, been dealt with by previous writers. I may seem now and then over didactic, but any veteran who may honour my text by reading it, will easily forgive me, when remembering that I write also for the novice in Salmon-capture. If, in wading through deep and undefined problems, I seem to be tediously slow and unentertaining, it will be without any profession to avoid dryness. I foreswear, for the purpose of these pages, all that may be hurriedly gathered from the Catalogues of our leading "fishing-tackle" makers. My programme embraces so much that is technical and mechanical that I should rather endeavour to please by instructing, than to instruct by pleasing. A *Vade mecum* as light in weight and writing as may be, a "handbook" full of information, direct, reliable, condensed, and strictly intent on business, is what I wish to offer to the public.

Although it may not be considered satisfactory that such a course should have been deemed necessary, I have ventured, with all due deference, quietly to point out where our technical expressions and principles have been misunderstood and misapplied. The gravity of the position is thoroughly realised. But in such an undertaking there may be very considerable advantages, and that seems to render the responsibility unavoidable. In any case I am animated by one feeling, and one feeling only; and that is by a real and natural desire to explain the true sense of my own special terms, which, unfortunately, have been sadly diverted in recent literature from their original meaning. So wide and opposite have been the ideas conveyed, that Anglers above the average have been hindered from doing justice to themselves by inability to understand them. This being the case, it may be gently hinted that the drawing of false conclusions from just principles has been no less injurious to the unenlightened than the untold evil of drawing just conclusions from false principles.

Not the least important measure in connection with my own improvements in "tackle," is that which refers to the Patent Lever Winch. This article, I can promise, will make a vast difference in anyone's annual fishing record. But I should wish to state that I derive no pecuniary gain from praising it, or, in fact, from the sale of any tackle associated with my name.

As many of our standard flies are not generally known, and as the dresser frequently goes wrong, both as to their colour and material, a long list of them is given in Chapter IV., and each pattern is precisely described for the dresser's guidance. In order that the collection may be readily consulted, the flies are alphabetically arranged. With a few exceptions, the name of the inventor is published, together with the rivers wherein I have known each fly to kill the most fish. And it is presumed that this list, including, as it does, not only "general," but "special," standards, will prove useful to the whole body of Salmon-fishermen.

Being naturally desirous of enlisting on behalf of my views and methods every circumstance that can lend them weight, I freely own to the confidence inspired by the honour done me in making me a Juror at the Fisheries Exhibition of 1883, and by the unstinted appreciation accorded to a small case of Salmon-flies exhibited by me there. The same case of flies won me the first prize both at Berlin and Norwich, at which places I was not disqualified by office from exhibiting as a competitor. Nor can I leave unrecorded the appreciation of Fishermen generally, which I have enjoyed during the whole time of my connection with the press both as contributor and as Editor.

How far my success as a Fisherman has been due to inheritance from generations of Salmon-anglers, is a question outside the scope of such a book as this; but I should like its pages to record some words in memory of my late Father and Grandfather, to whom I owe my earliest and much subsequent information on matters pertaining to the sport.

As a conclusion to these prefatory observations I have convincing evidence that the diligent application of my methods and directions suffices for the education of an accomplished "fly-dresser." The case of my friend Mr. Gribble is sufficient example; and it emboldens me greatly in submitting this book to the supreme judgment and test of brother Salmon-anglers.

It would be unbecoming to anticipate criticism. We all perceive how nearly impossible it is that persons should feel and think alike upon the subject of fish and fish-capture; and although fixed as are my own views, I should indeed be sorry to decry the opinions of those who differ from me. A similar moderation is all I claim of them. Good Anglers are notably good fellows, and will judge fairly of what I give them—practical lessons in a high art, the result of accurate observations during the varied and full life of an enthusiastic Salmon-angler.

That my work may be helpful to my brothers in the pursuit of our fascinating sport is my deeply founded hope. *Hope!* the mother of *Success*, when the companion in *Practice*. Her rays enable one to penetrate the mysteries of either the darkest pool, or water beaten into the whitest foam. She conjures up to the imagination of her charge the vision of future triumph, gladdens the heart of all, and forces many a seeming impossibility to give way to ultimate victory.

G. M. K.

CHAPTER I.

INTRODUCTORY.

"The principles which art involves, science evolves . . . . Art in its entire stages is anterior to science—it may afterwards borrow aid from it."

WHEWELL.

IN the present practice of Salmon-fishing there is great need of "system." It may be said, "We don't want 'system.' We are quite content with things as we find them, as long as we get our pleasure out of them." But such a speech will carry at least one fallacy. People get a certain pleasure out of whist, who know very little more about it than not to revoke, and perhaps not to trump their partner's trick; but that is no reason why the game should not be a serious study to others, books written on its laws and problems, and a high mental exercise enjoyed in its practice.

Speaking for myself—and I know I represent the opinion of many—as one who has all his life been an ardent devotee of Salmon-fishing and a close observer of everything relating to it, I cannot subscribe to the creed which proclaims that when "system" comes in at the door, "fun" flies out of the window. On the contrary, I have long been convinced, and have said so in the London Press, that lack of "system" means proportionate loss of sport and pleasure.

The man, for example, who owes his success in fishing to "the straight tip in flies" imparted by some expert, would incontestably have gained for himself vastly higher gratification, not to speak of any claim to praise, had he been his own "tipster," *i.e.*, had he possessed certain *systematic* knowledge.

With reference to this general statement, it may be said that principles engendered in truth are indestructible things, and, like hardy plants, grow wherever you take them: whereas mere "rules-of-thumb" have but the lowest vitality and will not survive transplantation. Possessed of the former, the Fisherman is equipped with knowledge applicable for new ground and for new conditions. The untried, indeed, just stimulates his skill and enhances his pleasure. But "rules-of-thumb," whatever returns they may yield within the limits of familiar waters and ordinary conditions, generally prove, elsewhere and otherwise, a source of perplexity, delusion, or helpless dependence on others.

To the remark that a good deal of this book might appear to some to wear the garb of "rule-of-thumb," the reply is, that it must be so with regard to much that is technical and mechanical. Yet even here the dry bones may become clothed with living texture, when their reason and purpose are given with them; when, in other words, we fall back on the underlying principles.

In advocating "system," I must guard against the supposition that I am about to offer a complete scheme of Salmon-fishing. All I can do is to point to the need of some further light, and offer my modest contribution at whatever its worth may be. Dare I hope that it may be the *nucleus* for the valuable experience of other Anglers and the seedling of a great consistent "system"?

A *complete* "system" is probably beyond any man's power, and is certainly beyond my own. I must, therefore, warn those who would put my doctrines to the proof, that they must adopt my practice in its entirety. This caution applies emphatically to the style of rod I recommend. As I make clear hereafter, "casting" is not performed by the rod alone, but by the rod and line taken together. So that to use such a rod with any other "tackle" than that described as best suited to it (I am not referring to the back-line), can only end in failure to display its good qualities and its utmost powers.

To plead for "science" in Salmon-angling is to plead for "system" (system in knowledge as well as system in action), for science is but another name for *systematised knowledge*. In vain will some, even of our older hands, ejaculate "Blow 'science' in fishing!" The concentrated blast of all the Fishermen that have ever flogged water could not blow science out of Salmon-*catching*, for it is absolutely *there*, involved it may be, but *there*, and the very essence of the sport itself. Let such objectors remember the story of the gentleman in one of Molière's plays who suddenly discovers that he has been talking prose all his life without knowing it. The real matter for decision is, Shall your knowledge be confused, undigested, vague, or badly stowed? or, shall it be methodical, organised, precise, and always ready to hand? Behind each art lies a corresponding *science*, and the art of Salmon-angling clearly has *its* science; though, for the most part, it still waits to be evolved. Let the science be elaborated by all means, and fully compacted. How much of it he will have, each man can settle for himself. You may plunge into it up to the neck out of pure love of the thing, or you may have no more than that sprinkling, which even mediocrity needs. But for their own sakes, I pray Salmon-fishers to look upon "science" as their friend, and not as a bugbear.

How are we going to get at this science? By the orthodox route. Where is it? In all seriousness it is hard to find, and the guide-posts are few and often misleading. Facts obtained or obtainable, observation, experiment, will serve us; and if we exercise our brains to collect, compare, classify, and generalise, we shall soon tread on the heels of those advanced laws and principles which we wish to apply in adapting our means to the ends we have in view.

In the wide field of *observation* there is much to be gathered. Every Fisherman can contribute help here without entering upon the more austere operations of "science." The more facts, the safer the induction. It should, however, be noted that observation is of value in proportion as it is accurate; and that really accurate observations are not so common as might be thought. Eminent scientists have testified how difficult it is even for a man of superior intelligence, to keep distinct what he *actually* sees from what he *thinks* he sees. (A man in a fog appears bigger than he is; a fish in the water is not in the place in which he seems to be.) It is so very easy to see what agrees with one's own preconceived ideas.

Even where verification is easy and the matter of observation within the grasp of one's hand, observation may be wanting in care—a statement which I will illustrate, not from the spacious field of nature, but from the smaller sphere of an Editor's experience.

A few years ago, a Fisherman came into my office on some angling business. Not knowing me by sight, he got into a discussion on Salmon-flies, and presently declared:—"I don't believe in Kelson's flies" (meaning those figured in "*Land and Water*"). He added:—"The wings are a deal too heavy and have too much stuff in them." In confirmation he produced from his pocket-book a fly, shewing what he considered a fair amount of "wing" for the Usk, a river which then wanted a "heavy" wing. On comparing this fly with the original pattern, which the critic had pronounced to be over bulky in the wing, he was soon compelled to confess himself mistaken. It was seen that, after all, my flies were constructed with less wing-material than his, and that the difference in appearance was due to the way in which the material was disposed. In my patterns each component strip of fibre in the wing was displayed to view in fan-like expansion, whilst in his fly one half at least of its constituents were hidden by the other half, the strips being compressed into an untidy bunch. It was also evident that this local authority was unacquainted with the principle, that the bulk of wing in a given pattern is variable according to the river, or even according to different parts of the same river, as well as in relation to weather and the condition of the water. Unfortunately this case is a typical one.

Exactitude is needed in applying our principles, *i.e.*, in adapting our means to the ends in view. Having clearly and definitely before our eye what those ends are and what they demand, we should not relax our efforts until we have mastered the means that best satisfy those demands. In this connection let me show what I mean, by reference to the most simple of all operations (fully explained in Chapter III.) in making "floss-silk" bodied flies, viz.: the waxing of the silk. What is the object here? Evidently to manage the waxing (1) without soiling the fingers; (2) without breaking the silk, or weakening it by letting it untwist, or by rubbing it too hard; (3) without getting too much wax on so as to quite spoil the floss-silk which covers it. Now, in spite of the fact that there is for doing this a method so simple that the dullest novice could follow it successfully, cobblers' wax is often condemned because of the trouble caused in using it.

There are pre-eminently three matters in which I believe Salmon-anglers would reap much benefit from "system." (1) The style of rod. (2) The modes of "casting." (3) The construction and choice of flies. In the first and third of these especially the principles we have mastered by observation and experiment have yet to be applied far more fully than is ordinarily the case, and with far stricter regard to the precise objects in view. In the following Chapters I have sought not only to point out the road to success, but also to move some little way along that road. The Chapter on the "Rod" does not call for preliminary comment here; and as to the modes of "casting," illustrated and described in Chapter VII., I would only remark that, as their efficiency depends on obedience to certain primary laws of mechanics, the directions for making each "cast" should be minutely followed. Failure to accomplish them will ensue, not because some peculiar "knack" or "dodge" has remained undisclosed, but because *some rational condition remains unfulfilled.* To see precisely, and at first sight, what has to be done, greatly helps a man towards the right way of doing it. In such a thing as learning by book-instruction how to "cast," it is necessary that not only the "WHY" and the "WHEREFORE" should be explained, but also the "HOW." And this I have striven to do in the following pages.

It is in the choice of flies that so much yet remains to be done in the way of observation and experiment. Here for the most part we have to make our own science, before we can apply it. The facts we must build on are the *habits* and *tastes* of the Salmon, as affected by the variety of his natural surroundings, the predisposition he evinces for certain shades of colour and certain types of flies, the variations of water and weather, and above all by the mischief brought about by the preceding efforts of Fishermen destitute of all practical knowledge.

Men call Salmon "capricious"; but is not the term a cover for their own ignorance about the habits of the fish and the flies they show them, rather than the truthful representation of facts? No one has proved wanton inconsistency on the part of the fish. We may depend on it, that Salmon instinctively and undeviatingly act according to certain predispositions, obey fixed natural laws, and are never troubled with "intellectual" originality, even of a rudimentary type. If he is as immovable as the rock of the river-bed to-day, and then gives himself away to the artless lure of the rawest novice on the morrow, depend upon it, there is an underlying cause, which it were more profitable to seek for, than to cover up with the convenient term "caprice."

In the choice of flies and the method of making and using them, the improvements of recent times have been patent and far-reaching.

When we come to analyze what a fly really is, we must associate ourselves with that reform in fishing which opposes much "received opinion;" and our attitude is justified by unmistakable and undeniable evidence. As a sample of the experiences on which I found some of my views against "received opinion," here is a narrative which may not be altogether uninteresting. It dates from 1849, when I commenced my earliest investigations on the river Darenth.

The late Sir P. D——, my father, and Mr. J. G. C——, had been discussing at Halstead Place the question of rod-material, and of trying a new kind of wood purchased by the latter of these gentlemen for making ram-rods. In a few days, by the valuable help of Mr. C——, himself a first-class workman, I turned out an 11 ft. 6 in. green-heart Trout-rod. On testing it, we soon found that we could cover with it more water than with the rods of hickory which we had been accustomed to use. Presently below the saw-mill our attention was drawn to a Pike of about 5 lbs. weight, lying close to a barrier of wood-work forming the upright side of a sheep-wash.

As some one about that time—Mr. Jewhurst, I believe, the inventor of one of our best standard flies—had created a stir in the district by killing one of these fish with a "Butcher," I, having no other means at hand to secure it, dressed a similar pattern and caught the Pike with it.

"What on earth," said my father, "did the fish take that fly for? Get under the water and see what it is like."

Little indeed did I dream of the benefits which this inspection would lead to. But it was not until after some half-dozen trials that I succeeded in getting a good view of the fly. The bed of the river at the sheep-wash was muddy, and I could not stay under water long enough for it to clear; I was also unaccustomed to the business and could not manage to lie still, nor avoid stirring up the mud. "All I can tell you is," I said, at last, "that it looks just like a living fly working its legs and wings."

Our curiosity being greatly excited, the experiment was rehearsed elsewhere.

Of all the places I have tried thus, the best and the worst was the one particular pond at Bradbourne Vale (then the property of Mr. Hughes). It was best, because its bed was not muddy, whilst the water itself was brighter than the proverbial gin. It was worst, because the water was icy cold. There, nevertheless, I practised year after year, and notes of my observations were taken by some of the interested parties who generally attended the entertainment. The penalty I paid for my under-water investigations was a slight deafness, which affects me still.

We came to the conclusion, that the stiller the surface of the water, the more favourable it is for inspection: that the brighter the day, so long as the sun is not in the background, the more clearly can the details and the conduct of the fly-materials be scrutinised: that, however seemingly still the water may be, there is always a movement in some part of the fly: also that, to the human eye, a dark fly shows best on a dark day, whilst in bright weather the fly of many colours is more easily and more minutely distinguishable. But this was not all. I benefited further, for it taught me the grand lesson not to "play" long-hackled patterns which, of themselves, unassisted by rod-action, assume a life-like motion even in the quietest water possible. I also learnt that a person talking on the bank can be heard by another under water. Whether a fish can so hear, is a question.

There is information here, without doubt, that can be turned to practical good in Salmon-fishing. I hope the few deductions that I was enabled to draw from these experiments will be found useful, as being sound, so far as they go. To them I owe many a success, and this especially induces me to submit them to my readers with confidence. The system I wish to exemplify is, to all intents and purposes, based on some practice that is at once consistent and intelligible. The trial has been in many a struggle for the day's "top score" on Association waters which I no longer fish, sometimes for any score at all when low, vapid water and bright sun have given full scope for testing every kind of theory.

Punch has depicted some theorist baffled to the verge of desperation, finally throwing his collection of flies, book and all, into the "Catch." Then there is the numerous school of sportsmen, whose guiding doctrine is, "Some days, you know, you can't keep fish off the hook, and some days they won't look at the best fly in your book or anybody else's." A dummy clock face with painted hands is periodically right—twice in twenty-four hours; and such people have the solace of occasional success, though its recurrence is generally at long intervals. It is true that, at times, nothing avails to tempt fish, but then these barren times are very much fewer for the systematic Fisherman than for the novice; were it otherwise, there would be no *raison d'etre* for this book. In short, I hold that the advantages of the "systematic" Angler are surprisingly pronounced. Even a few good working principles are needful to justify any assurance of success.

The ability to "dress" a fly, even fairly well, enhances the pleasure of Salmon fishing to a degree truly inconceivable to the uninitiated. "Fly-dressing," in itself a pleasant art, is an accomplishment that must very often contribute to sport otherwise unattainable; and there are many occasions when it proves to be the actual determining condition of any sport at all, for it is no uncommon experience that a fish which has refused a boxful of "likelies" has, in the end been lured to his doom by a fly hastily dressed at the river's side to meet the exigencies of the moment. Somewhere or other, I forget where, I have read an ill-founded but unimportant sneer at the possibility of doing such a thing; but I have myself succeeded in this way many and many a time. It is no exaggeration of words to say that I have dressed hundreds of flies *al fresco* and with admirable results in their use as an immediate consequence.

There is no necessity to burden one-self with any great bulk of materials, in order to command a far larger scope in size and in pattern of fly than that afforded by the most corpulent of fly-books. Not unfrequently, be it remembered, a small deduction from, or addition to, a wing turns the scale (and scales) in the Angler's favour.

For the less ambitious, even a theoretical knowledge of the methods adopted by our best artists, such as I trust may be gathered from this book, is, I can assure them, no mean advantage. It endows a man with critical ability—which means, that the critic is enabled to tell a good fly from a bad one when he sees it—and supplies the power not only to detect and reject bad materials and faulty construction, but to know precisely what is wanted, as well as to convey accurate instructions to the "fly-dresser."

When a friend inquires what description of fly it was the critic lost in the big fish below, identification can scarcely be easy when he replies :—"Well, don't you know, it was a darkish kind of thing with blue at one end and legs of a sort of speckle, and then there was some metal stuff round the woolly part, and a feather like a spray of gold for a top-knot"; and such a description is not a caricature of common river-side speech. But without going so low down in the scale of ignorance, there is a large class of Fishermen who can only just distinguish what is meant to be a "Jock Scott" from what is meant to be a "Durham Ranger," or a putative "Butcher" from a putative "Blue Doctor"; for certain flies bear unmistakably distinctive marks. But there the knowledge stops. The particular specimens may yet exhibit such a departure from the original composition, yes, even in important features, as to seriously impair their efficiency. A little more technical knowledge would avoid this.

For those, however, who "dress" their own flies, the pleasure of banking an extra sulky Salmon, from whose jaw they proceed with all tenderness to extract the product of their own skill in fur and feathers, attains its full height, *when the pattern of the fly is also their own invention*. All the conditions of the occasion have been studied—light, wind, weather, water, and nature of the "catch"; the size, the amount of "show," and degree of mobility that should answer have been determined. And then comes success to crown the patient and deft manipulation, which clothed the hook from one's own original idea, and which awakens a new and gratifying faith in one's calculation and judgment.

Surely it is worth considering that by this delicate and fascinating art, the pleasures of fishing are extended over a longer period of the year. They begin, not at the opening of the season on the river-bank, but weeks before, at the best lighted window of the "den" or library, saving many a man from the task of "killing time." No wise man reads directly after lunch, for reading then sends the blood to the head, when it is required below. But "dressing" a fly will generally be found no enemy to digestion and goes well with a chat, and perhaps even with a pipe.

And "fly-dressing" employs faculties besides those used in fishing. In addition to the keen eye and ready hand, the persistent observation, the care, endurance, courage, and patience required by open-air practice, those other qualities are called into play, the training of which establishes for Salmon-fishing a true kinship with the Fine Arts, and supplies as much of mental and moral discipline as may fairly be looked for in what we are accustomed to designate "rational amusement." The "fly-dresser" finds room for the utmost nicety of calculation in arrangement and adaptation, as well as a field for the exercise of the imagination in realizing symmetry, proportion, mobility, and colour-harmony. In short, we have here a well-bred hobby not unworthy the attention of the greatest amongst us who are fishers, whether Divines or Statesmen, Doctors or Lawyers, Poets, Painters, or Philosophers.

Having thus adduced some reasons why the *piscator ad unguem* (I use the term advisedly) should "dress," or at least know how to "dress," his own flies, I may well introduce an observation once made by a keen man of the world. It embodies, I believe, the experience of most people who are qualified to judge of the specific mental influence of fly-fishing for Salmon and Trout. Fly-fishing has the power to bring sure and unbroken relief to the jaded mind, with thorough oblivion to all else but the sport itself. Its very nature seems to compel the entire attention. As a consequence, therefore, the more we lay ourselves out for this pastime, the greater will be the benefit derived from it, in the original and best sense, a *recreative* agent. This consideration obviously gives fresh life to my praise of "fly-dressing" as a complement to "fly-fishing." Anyone can imagine himself under the following circumstances :—

Breakfast despatched and the fishing news carefully digested, you have seated yourself at that little table in the window, looking river-wards, in a capital light. Your box of materials is on a chair beside you, and two or three of its trays out before you on the table. . . . . . Water a bit higher than you thought, eh? Haven't exactly the thing you want?—(puff! puff! capital smoking mixture this!)—No, these "Jocks" are just two sizes too small. And that one?—Don't like the yellow of it—too orangey, Turkey strips not pure white-pointed, "Jungle" not bright enough. Ah! twist—butt—floss—oval-tinsel—Toucan—topping and Crow! Now then. And so you get to happy, hopeful work, looking up at intervals to relieve the eye by a moment's change of focus and to get an inspiring glance at the noble stream below!

Where are your "notices of motion," your Committees and Division-bills now? Where the mortgages, the conveyances, the briefs? Where script and share-lists, bills and notes of hand? And what has become of your prescriptions and mighty harassings, the daily rounds of fever and mental worries? And where are those "editorials," that daily pile of letters, that waste-basket, and so forth? Faded away—all of them—out of sight and mind too, thank goodness! Smoke and din and dull routine, head-ache and heart-ache, are all clean gone, and in their place have come the calm and charm of meadow and purple moor, of ruffled "catch," deep gliding pool and foaming rapid; of birds and of humming insects buzzing among the wild flowers and fresh undergrowth. Your mind has just enough spontaneous energy to keep pace with the bodily forces in healthful pleasure, and to enjoy the anxious labour of dressing or choosing the fly that shall presently stir up a full fifteen minutes' glorious excitement and yield material for oft-told tales and life-long reminiscences. What do not those men *lose* who do not fish? And as to fly-making—well, by that engaging occupation, apart from all practical considerations, many men have been imbued with a fascination which has since brightened too many dull days of their life.

Any apology for the possibly tedious fulness of detail inseparable from really genuine instruction on such a technical subject as "fly-dressing" it would be too illogical to offer. Clearness in this case is impossible without amplitude of detail; an orderly system in progress from stage to stage, as indispensable as in Euclid's "Elements." But let the learner take courage. When first he learns the method and has mastered the preliminaries in detail, it will not be long before he will boldly attack the most elaborate patterns and venture with enthusiasm upon the artistic expression of his own fancies in all the kaleidoscopic possibilities of fur and feather, floss and pigs-wool.

As a conclusion to the disappointing instructions of many guide books for "fly-dressers" the student is advised that, as the art, after all, cannot really be learnt from books, he should resort to some professional "tier" to teach him. This suggests the probability that the writer of the guide, however expert he otherwise may be, has felt himself on thin ice in the practical knowledge of this department, or at least in the ability to communicate it to others. It may be added that the better class Salmon-fly of to-day is an altogether different product from that of forty years ago, and, as a work of art, an incomparably superior one. No high technical knowledge is needed, for example, to discern the contrast in artistic excellence and working adaptation to purpose between the few standard flies as illustrated in *Land and Water* (under my departmental Editorship) and the flies depicted in certain older works on angling. The contrast is most striking in the symmetrical proportions, the arrangement of the wings, the distribution of material generally, and in strength and neatness of finish particularly.

Blacker was, in his day, a champion "dresser," but it would have been a case of almost incredible stagnation if the art he helped so much to promote had made no progress since his time. It would be very unlike what has in many a river happened to the fish. They have changed, or been made to change, their tastes. As for Blacker's book on "Fly-tying," it is, as regards Salmon-flies, practically useless for present day instruction in the *modus operandi*, and is only valuable as a literary curiosity.

In his "Book on Angling" it is clear that my valued friend and colleague, the late Mr. Francis Francis, scarcely makes a serious attempt at any complete instruction in this matter. Certain it is that from the directions there given alone, no novice could learn to dress a fly that any tackle-maker of repute would care to place in his shop window. And it is simple truth to declare that in a work unequalled to this day as a complete synopsis of angling, and as such reaping the reward of unabated popularity, the chapter on Salmon-fly dressing is, by far, the least valuable in his book.

No pupil was more apt, none more attentive. But the enthusiasm which led him to accomplish with mathematical precision the neatest victories over Mayflies and Quilled-gnats, scarcely extended itself into the regions of high art in Salmon-fly dressing. "Yours," he would say to me, "is the result of imagination and judgment: mine a hobby to indulge in without much effort; and it gratifies my taste, if it tries my eyes."

To pass to a kindred topic, Mr. Francis has undoubtedly rendered immense service to Salmon-fishermen, by gathering from the various rivers, at evident cost of time and labour, the large collection of patterns that fill so many pages of his treatise. Here is a record of facts, a trustworthy account of the local patterns, district, and personal favourites reigning when the collection was made, and a certain number of them still retain their sway. Any Angler, with the "Book on Angling" in his hand, may be sure of selecting for a given river patterns, that had, once upon a time, and in some cases still have, the sanction of local tradition and past favour. Whether the same authority enables him to provide adequately for a change of taste on the part of the fish is quite another matter. Such changes do occur, sometimes (but not often), in Nature's own mysterious way, sometimes (indeed very frequently) in consequence of too much familiarity with baits, or even with foreign flies introduced by new-comers—men who are not content with local faiths and "rules of thumb." Such rules are too rigid to meet the change. There is your list of flies; your only variety in them lies in the matter of size. If large and medium, and small flies of those patterns fail, you must either resort to the enterprising men for their patterns, or invent better ones yourself. That is to say, you must forsake tradition for invention, and "rule of thumb" for principles of some sort, because your list teaches that the highest preference of your fish has not been hit on, and that it fails to provide for a palate that has become dainty through untoward water or weather, or has been educated up to a different bill of fare.

Let me not be misapprehended. I wish especially to attribute its full value to this great collection of fly patterns. But what I advocate most earnestly, is the logical step forward from all such data, if only from the simple fact that so many of the feathers we employ now are far more suited to the object in view. The Angler who takes this step will soon train and use his own powers of observation and judgment. Practice and experiment on his part will then breed confidence, and confidence will bring for him marked improvement in capacity and all round proficiency.

Now it is manifest that in all collections of patterns yet offered in print—and Mr. Francis's is, perhaps, the most complete of any—we have little else than the bare patterns to guide us. There is not sufficient induction from them; no comparison, analysis, classification, made of them, either in themselves, or with direct regard to the natural characters of the rivers to which groups of flies are severally assigned. Whilst the features of many of the flies described as used on certain rivers in times gone by are strongly marked enough to base a classification on, and perhaps to enable some advance towards general principles, yet it seems to me, that the local use has so frequently been governed by mere accident, whim, and fashion, and so entirely without attempt at rational process or systematic observation, that I would prefer, and I recommend, *original experiment based on general principles, with a deferential side-glance at the traditions of the elders.*

It is evident that any practice relying solely on such lists of flies, however time-honoured, must, as unscientific, sooner or later be found valueless to some extent, and hopelessly so in the face of any such enlightened competition as must be met on the more open fisheries.

In certain flies, leading conditions common to several localities have been happily filled, and so we have such standard general patterns as "Jock Scott," "Silver Grey," and "Blue Doctor." But it is clear that the demands of the *unusual* and complicated conditions in hard-fished waters could not be thus uncerimoniously chanced on, and to meet these, we need, not the standard *general* patterns, but the standard *specials*, *e.g.*, the "Variegated Sun-fly," "Blue Boyne," "Red Pirate," "Bo-Peep," "Silver Spectre," &c., &c.

Complicated conditions, and the discovery of the best means and methods of mastering them will cost many observations, careful record, and much thought, but the measure of success already known to follow such investigation lifts the Angler far above any blind or groping reliance on the best traditions of the past. Is it not notorious that in several of our rivers the fish have been educated to persistently snub old patterns in favour of new? And is it not indeed an achievement to present to the fish a fly that he then and there prefers to your rival's—to have yourself made the attraction so strong, as to establish, more or less permanently, a decided taste in the fish, so that he refuses other flies, *to wait for yours!*

In mentioning, just now, the names of a few standard patterns, I might have added, with regard to the results brought about by the special use of Sun-flies, that I have evidence, nay, the strongest proof, of what may be accomplished from systematised knowledge.

What, in the name of sport, would our forefathers think Salmon angling had come to, could we tell them of the great results that have been achieved altogether without periods of much trouble, while fishing in the brightest sunshine! They first taught us, it is true, to use bright flies in bright weather and so on; but they themselves never failed to reel up in the daytime under a cloudless canopy of blue, nor ever dreamed of sport with such a pattern as the "Variegated Sun-fly," which, by the way, has more than filled the promise of its youth.

It is happy for us latter-day Anglers that the "specials" came into existence, that they still live, and that they afford so many proofs of their own masterful vitality in those very times when all other flies fail. Our knowledge in the matter of these, at any rate, is "methodical, organised, precise, and always ready to hand"; and I put forward my own portion of the work with great confidence.

CHAPTER II.

Salmon-flies: Their Kinds, Qualities and Materials.

"*Oft expectation fails, and most oft there where most it promises.*"
Shakespeare.

DESCRIPTION AND CLASSIFICATION.

An orderly and uniform method of description being essential to progress in all technical matters, there can be no need to vindicate my attempt to supply this, with regard to Salmon-flies and their dressings. Happily, in this case, the reformer has only to contend against a certain amount of disorder and confusion.

The advantage of always describing a fly in the successive order of its parts, and of always using the same names for the same things, is obvious. We often encounter in print, and elsewhere, a departure from this wholesome principle, and this can only be attributed to the absence hitherto of any general practice, based on the requirements of convenience and consistency. I hope that the diagram given opposite, in which a typical fly is explained in regular succession of detail, will be found of service in satisfying these requirements. The names adopted by me are those now in general use amongst Anglers and tackle-makers, and the order followed is (practically) that of the actual process of dressing.

The benefit derived from following this order is, that with a minimum of strain on the memory, even without practice in dressing, an orderly formula can be impressed on the mind—a formula applicable to any fly, and in such a way that its composition can easily be retained in the mind's eye and reproduced at pleasure. Further, this formula is a valuable aid to the memory in the successive operations of fly-dressing; the value being in direct ratio to the elaboration of the pattern in hand.

Those who fix this simple scheme in their minds, will not find, on finishing a fly, that they have left out the body hackle or one of the "butts"; nor that, in sending to a friend the description of some murderous favourite, they will have written it in such complicated detail as to defy every attempt at reproducing it either in imagination or in material. *Order* is nature's first law, and it is certainly that of every good Salmon-angler.

ANALYTICAL DIAGRAM, illustrating parts and proportions of a Salmon-Fly.

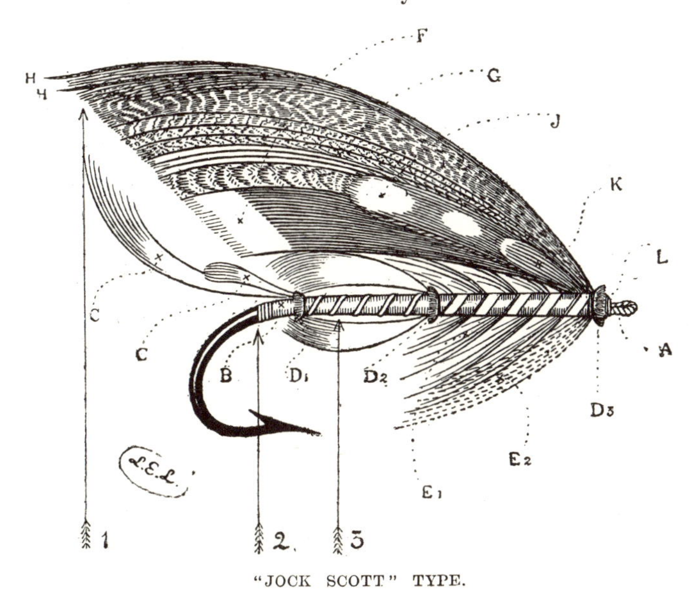

"JOCK SCOTT" TYPE.

EXPLANATION.

A. *Gut loop.*

B. *Tag:* here in two sections—silver twist, succeeded by floss silk.

CC. *Tail.* Of a topping and an Indian crow feather.

D1, D2, D3. "*Butts.*" Between D1 (tail-butt) and D3 (head-butt) lies the *Body*, divided in this type of fly into two sections by D2 (section-butt), each section having 5 *Ribs* of tinsel ; D2 is here preceded (in order of construction) by Toucan feathers above and below.

E. *Hackle.* Here distinguished as the "*Upper section hackle.*" When wound over nearly the whole length of the body it is termed the "*Body hackle.*"

E2. *Throat-hackle,* usually written "Throat."

F. *Under-wing.* Here of "white-tipped" Turkey.

G. *Over Wing,* in most flies capped with a "topping."

HH. *Horns.* J. *Sides.* K. *Cheeks.* L. *Head.*

1. Is a line showing a proper length of tail and wing beyond the hook-bend.

2. Indicates the place of the first coil of the *tag* relatively to the *hook-barb*, the barb supplying the best guide to the eye in the initial operation of tying on the "tag" material.

3. Indicates the place on the hook-*shank* (relatively to the hook-*point*), at which the ends of the *gut loop* should terminate, leaving the *gap*, for adjustment (particularised in Chap. III.).

This figure is intended also to give the student a general idea of the due proportions and symmetry of a good fly, as a whole, and in its parts severally.

In dressing, the terms "headwards" and "tailwards" mean towards right and left respectively, as seen in the plate.

The terms "bend of the hook," "point of the hook," "point of the barb," "barb-junction," &c., explain themselves on inspection. By a *mane* —a common term in Ireland—is understood a tuft of mohair introduced at some place on the body after the manner of the upper group of Toucan feathers seen in the plate in rear of section-butt D2. But as this means of ornamentation is not considered favourable, I shall leave the subject alone for a while.

In classifying his flies the Salmon-angler stands at a disadvantage as compared with the Trout-fisher. The latter has a basis of classification ready made for him by Nature. His path is already trodden smooth for him by the entomologist, so that in following his principle of imitation, he has but to study the habits and habitats, the times and seasons, that distinguish the several natural classes represented by his "duns" and "spinners," his "midges" and "gnats," his "sedges" and "palmers"; ephemeridæ, Phryganeidæ, and so forth. The Salmon-angler, on the contrary, has, as a rule (exceptions are duly recorded in this book), to fall back on an artificial classification. He betakes himself to nature only on rare, but notable, occasions. So in truth his principle is a matter of less consequence to him generally, though it is undeniably both of use and interest.

Of the possible principles of classification only two will commend themselves to our consideration, a division according to "bodies," or a division according to "wings." I choose the latter for the following reasons:—firstly, because there is as much variety of construction in that part as in any other; secondly, that there is also a variety in this part dictated by local taste—in man, or fish, or both—and finally, that the wings are a "leading article" in the matter of fly dressing.

There is, however, a considerable variety in bodies, not only as regards quantity and kind of material, but also as regards the disposition of the latter with reference to proportion and colour; witness the plain fur or silk body, the "Jock Scott" body, the "Butcher" body, and that of the "Popham"—all distinct types. The wing, however, seems on the whole to afford the simplest and best fundamental division. I am unaware of any previous attempt at such a classification, and therefore, unaided by the light of earlier exploration, I offer with all due diffidence the following simple scheme, as the best I have been able to devise:—

A. FLIES.

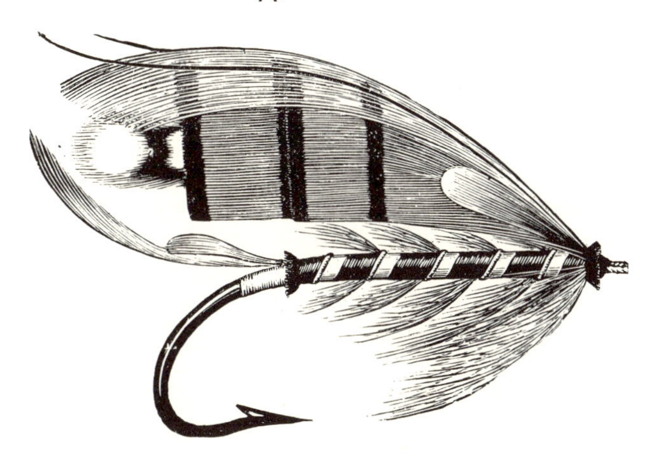

WHOLE FEATHER WINGED—"BLACK RANGER."

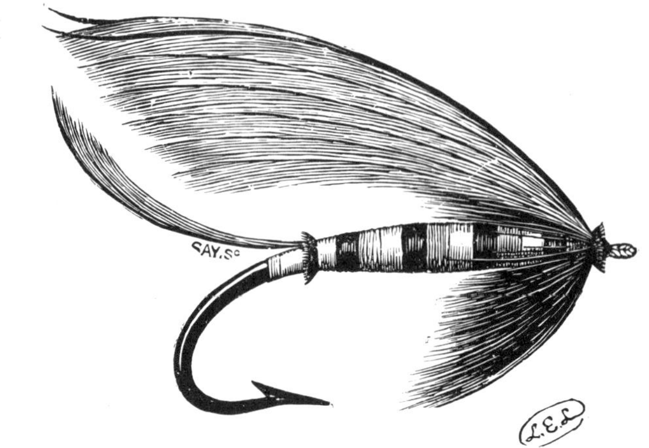

TOPPING WINGED—A "VARIEGATED SUN FLY."

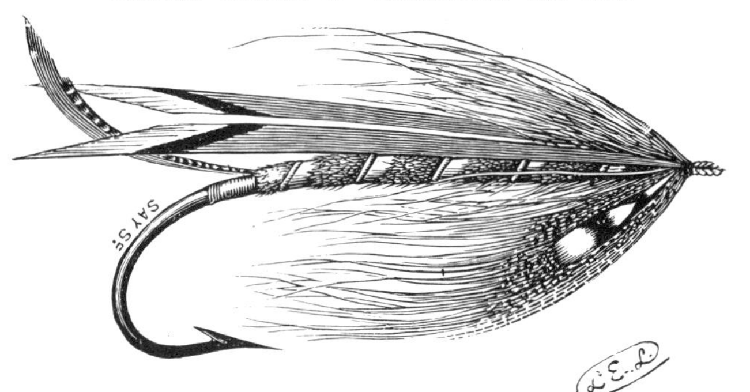

STRIP WINGED—"THE DUNT."

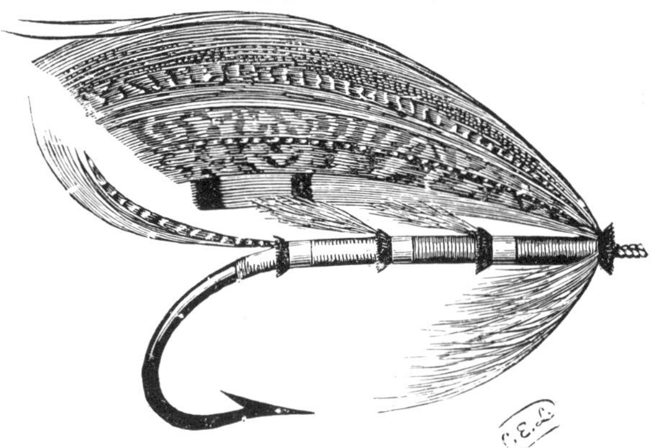

BUILT WINGED OF MARRIED STRIPS—"BEACONSFIELD."

MIXED WINGED OF FIBRES—"INSTRUCTION FLY."
Illustrated in Chapter III., No. 2.

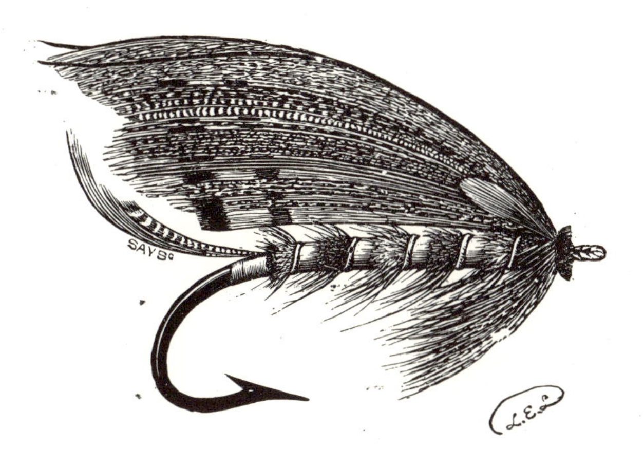

ANY COMBINATION OF THE ABOVE—"THE BUTCHER."

B.—GRUBS.

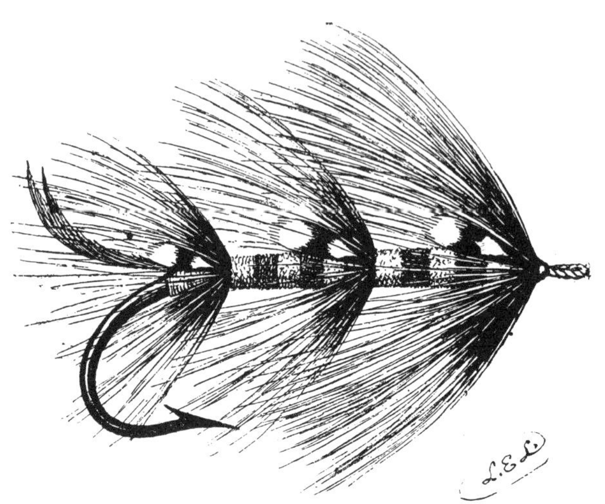

WINGLESS PATTERNS—"THE JUNGLE HORNET."

There is no need to explain in detail what is meant by "*Whole feather*" *wings*. Each wing is composed of one or more whole feathers of some such bird as the Macaw. Their stiffness makes them invaluable for crooked going, or for swirly catches, where the ordinary mobile "mixed" wings become a shapeless mass of huddled fibres, and have no chance whatever of playing alluringly.

"*Topping*" *wings* are made entirely of Golden Pheasant "toppings," from four to eight being used according to circumstances and size of hook. They are very effective in bright weather and clear water, and especially so in sunshine, but four on one river may be equal to six on another.

In the "*Strip-winged*" fly each entire wing consists of a single strip of feather generally taken from the tail-feather of some large bird. Wings of this kind may be set on to lie close to each other, or to lie apart at a considerable angle, as seen in "The Dunt." On the Aberdeenshire Dee and elsewhere in Scotland these wings are still in vogue, but on other rivers—the Usk, for instance—they are rapidly yielding ground to the vastly superior "built" and "mixed" wings.

"*Built Wings*" —built up of strips of feather "married," are, perhaps, the most difficult to construct and set on satisfactorily, but they are very telling in their proper place and time—as telling on the fish as they appear, when skilfully arranged, to the artistic eye. The Angler who aims at enduring success cannot do without them. The most successful of this type of fly are those known as *decided* patterns—*i.e.*, flies containing two or three or more distinct colours in the body and corresponding colours in the wings and even in the tail. They are specially useful at the beginning and end of the season, or, at other times in high water, when a striking pattern is temporarily wanted. As a rule, they are more successful in flowing streams than in quiet pools.

"*Mixed wings*," composed of single fibres, are easily set on by an improved method, and are very effective in the water. It stands to reason that they must be the most mobile of all wings. They are specially suited to sluggish pools and unruffled waters, and may be varied and beautified indefinitely according to the judgment and taste of the dresser. For personal use I tie a large majority of wings in this fashion, and can give them unreserved commendation.

"*Grubs*" or "apterous" patterns in many places are found to be o great service, particularly when pools have been over thrashed with "winged" flies. They are supposed to represent caterpillars and other crawling insects which frequent the river bank or bed. Every Salmon-fly should have its grub, and every Fisherman should use them. On some rivers—the Usk, for instance, where (long before the "Glow-worm" I introduced the "Trois-temps"—they have become the favourite patterns of most men. On the Spey they remained unknown until recent years.

"Cheeked" with a point of Jungle at each hackle, after the style of the "Jungle Hornet" (whether fur, silk, or chenille be used for the body), Grubs, as soon as winter ceases to chill the "lap of May," do great execution amongst shy fish.

NECESSARY QUALITIES.

Symmetry, Colour, &c.—For the highest standard of sport, Salmon-flies should possess certain qualities and characteristics. Season, locality, &c., fix the limits of their relative bearing and importance.

At times Salmon will take anything, at times nothing. In a fever of excitement the King of Fish will exercise his royal jaw upon a thing it were an outrage to call a Salmon fly. A one-sided, wobbling, hydrocephalic bunch of incongruous feathers. Nay, this same whimsical despot has been known to bring destruction upon himself and discomfiture on all theory and calculation by fixing his momentary affections upon a single Jay or Jungle feather tied anyhow on a big bare hook! Only a few years since, I believe in '83, a well-known Fisherman, passing from pool to pool at Ringwood, and dangling his crude fly in the stream as he hurried along, hooked, in eighteen inches of water, and successfully landed, a forty-two pound fresh-run fish. "Hi Regan" tells me of another, caught in the upper Moy with a field daisy, impaled on a small hook. And there are many living witnesses to these crowning instances of a Salmon's fastidiousness. Fishing the Earn one sulky day in '87, I saw within six feet of me a Salmon working up a gravelled shallow. Several flies had previously been tried in vain. The last, made by a novice, having just lost its Mandarin-drake wings, was lying on the bed of the river, for the purpose of keeping the gut in order, whilst I whipped up another like it. On nearing the rude hook—it was but little else—the Salmon came about a yard out of his way, picked it up and made off down stream at a flying pace. I soon got in command of him, and went home carrying 11 lbs. more than I started with.

But fishing is no more the mere "catching" of fish, than is cricket mere smashing down wickets by chance, or billiards mere "knocking three balls about on a table covered with green baize."

Strength and symmetry are necessary qualities in every Salmon-fly, especially for waters harbouring shy fish, where bait-fishing* does not defeat the whole thing. As for *strength*, first, we must obviously be prepared for the worst. The battle may last for hours and its issue must depend in a great measure on the strength of the fly. So then, first, let the hook be of the best make and well tested beforehand. There is a vast difference in barbs, which fact anyone may easily study with profit to himself, by submitting to scrutiny, under an ordinary magnifying lens,

* People exist who fancy that this way of ruining a river for fly-fishing involves a *puzzling* question And yet we are rapidly approaching the end of the nineteenth century!

the first dozen hooks he comes across. The test is, of course, best performed on hooks all of one size. Many are rendered worthless by too deep an incision of the barbing knife into the hook-wire. In others the barb and the hook point are needlessly long. Again, the second bend of the hook, *i.e.*, the part of the bend nearest the point of the hook, is where a long experience has shown more hooks fail than in any other part. Correct temper, more than amount of metal there, is the best security against weakness. Sometimes, however, the bend of the hook itself is altogether too narrow, in which case the hook may neither catch hold, nor hold when it catches.

That the *whipping of gut-loop to hook* should be efficient and the whole fly strongly put together is evident; but neatness and symmetry are often somewhat lost in trying to secure strength.

Too much or too thick material is used in the item of tying-silk especially, and too little attention is paid to tapering the ends of the loop and placing the tying-silk closely and evenly upon them. Put in a spiral form, or with some coils over others, and the fly falls to pieces in no time.

We must remember that the strain of the fish is borne by the hook and gut. The measure of the strength required in the other parts of the fly is the wear and tear of casting, of playing it in the water, and of the fish's jaws. In actual experience the student will be astonished to find with what little tying-silk, *skilfully used* and of the *right sort*, a fly will wear to the very end of the life of its constituent materials. And this is the never failing reward of dressing after a proper method and with proper materials.

How often can one take a purchased fly and twist the wings, almost without effort, right round to the body! Yet this test may be pressed too far; for whilst it is possible to so tightly and firmly compact a fly that the very fibres of the wing shall first give way, such a degree of compacted strength is by no means requisite in a well-tied fly. It is enough if, after an ordinary amount of pressure, you find that the wings set on by the method described in this book still hold their position.

By "symmetry," I mean proportion of *shape*, and to some extent of *material*. This quality is essential in a good fly. Even in "Exaggerations," though in them, as the name implies, we seem to set aside some of our usual notions of symmetry, we must retain that general proportion of shape, without which the fly would not fish properly. This consideration supplies the key to what is meant by "symmetry" as a general quality. Symmetry is sought, not for mere beauty of appearance, but for its value as an element of allurement. We want balance of part in a fly, so that it shall pose in the water and not loll about—so that it shall advance and retire when required to do so steadily and gracefully, like a finished dancer, and not pitch like a vessel in a head wind, plunge like a rocking-horse, or hang on one side (it should not, in fact, *hang* at all) from increasing weakness at the juncture with the line. We do not want it to wobble; or, as in the case of extra long gut-loops and all sorts of metal loops,* to take upon itself the performance of any movement which we cannot provide for or control at our pleasure. A "skirting" fly, too —*i.e.*, one that from an overgrown head sheds in its train a stream of subaqueous bubbles of light—is an abomination, for "skirting" means scaring.

All these things, good and bad, depend on "symmetry." *For the greatest success, every element of attraction that has been selected should be displayed to the fish.* This can only be ensured in a fly that fishes properly when in the water, and a fly fishes properly only when dressed properly and mounted properly. Each feather, each strip, and each fibre must keep its place and show itself there, as the wings, in all alluring naturalness of manner, expand and close in regular order. What is the use of my putting red and blue Swan, Teal, and Canadian Duck in my wings if the fly "rides" so badly or wobbles so much, that a sombre strip of Turkey or Bustard covers these brightening constituents, and hides them from the ever watchful eye that so dotes on a "bit of blue" or speckly black and white?

No; if your fly is not symmetrical it will not obey you, and if all your tackle does not obey your brain, art and science are banished from your sport. Away goes *skill*—in comes *chance!* You may put your wings, for example, in the constraining embrace of two strips of feather with a "topping" above, and two good sides of Jungle-fowl below, but all this will not avail to keep the rebels in order under water. The tail,

* N.B.—"Metal loops" signifies eyed hooks.

bunchy and crookedly set on, acts like a helm put hard a-port, one wing has twice as much stuff in it as the other, and so "wobble," "wobble" goes your fly. The body, moreover, has just twice as much fur in it as it ought to have, and so the fly will not fish deep. The head is enormous, and whenever the current is strong enough, produces the fatal string of beads or bubbles of light. The gut loop is defective, it is too long and a hinge is formed at the point of junction with the hook, to help the fly to plunge and rock. The attachment of the single gut to the loop is incorrectly managed, and the wings turn towards one side against stream, and towards the other side down stream. But I shall have occasion to treat fully with these matters hereafter.

A *gradual tapering* of the body finds its prototype in nature and is subservient to the good working qualities just discussed.

A *graceful arching* of the entire wing is not only an element of symmetry, but also helpful to mobility—the quality which follows symmetry in order of importance. It is evident that this arching not only assists towards the general animation of the wing, but by its form helps, to a certain extent, in keeping the play within bounds and especially within the same plane of action. For not only do feathers, set on to curve rightly, resist tendency to side-play and maintain the play in one direction, or, as is said, in one plane, and so all get a fair chance of display in the order of the intended harmony of colour, but they also resist tendency to play too far aloft and away from each other. The wing maintains its character in all respects in full unbroken integrity. To this ruling many may take exception. I well remember giving a highly-finished fly to a friend who, declaring it "only fit for a glass case" instantly rubbed the feathers the wrong way. I then inquired if he thought "that sort of finishing touch would make much difference." "All in the world," he confidently replied, as he "firmly believed in the roughest looking patterns." "Then you had better not mount that one," said I, but I followed this up with :—"Directly the stream catches it all the feathers will be washed back into their original position." (He used it.)

The *mobility* of a fly is mainly determined by the roughness of the water, the method of working the rod, and the construction of the fly itself. It is obvious that in turbulent, rough-and-tumble waters, a wing *must*, if it is to preserve any consistency at all, be made of stiffer and stouter feathers or fibres than those which would hold their own well enough in quieter reaches. But apart from this, a certain degree of movement is absolutely essential to liveliness in a fly, and this movement is the result of the current coming in contact with it. The movement will vary with the strength of the stream or with the amount of "play" put into the rod-top by the Fisherman. Obviously also, the more mobile the wings, hackle and tail—for it is these parts which are concerned in the question—the greater the effect produced on them by either of the ministering agencies mentioned. Therefore, to get the same amount of life-like motion out of our flies under differing conditions, we must consider, (1) the state of the water; (2) whether, on the whole, the place to be fished is rough or quiet, and (3) whether our business is to work the rod-top much or little. The motion given to the fly by a steady and regular movement of the rod, is far more effectual, when practicable, than the "hops" and "skips" resulting either from the effect of swirly waters, or from the rod being worked in a clumsy, harum-scarum manner.

I have said enough, I think, on this point, to enable the student to work out for himself every rider to the problem. It need only be further remarked that, generally speaking, the smaller the fly, the more mobile in proportion should be the hackles and wing-materials. Of these, should the flies be very small, the best hackles are the most transparent ones without any "list" at all; and the best feathers for the wings are the finest in texture, always excepting "Horns," "Sides" and golden toppings. For the sake of clearness and order in these remarks we must confine our discussion to *colour*, simply as a quality of the fly considered by itself and without reference to the actual circumstances which will ultimately govern the Anglers' choice in using it. A simple principle guides us here. Uniformity of means is essential to obtaining uniformity of results under invariable conditions. If we have found success under certain given conditions, our aim must be to restore those conditions, as far as they are within our control. We cannot command rain, or sunshine, or cloud; but in this or that combination of nature's varying moods, we can resort to the employment of those means which have already proved trustworthy. Ah! there's the rub, for one day last year I "headed the list" by aid of a certain fly, and to-day by reference to my diary, I recognise an absolute repetition of the conditions which prevailed on the "red letter day." The state of things at bankside seems to have gone back just twelve months. And the fish? they are there too; and yet our fly, of the same size exactly, displays his harmonious contrasts in vain. Up with him! Take him in hand—"What's the matter, eh?" Looking in our box, there buried at the very bottom actually lies the hero—tooth ragged, but not by tooth of time—the very conqueror of that memorial day. Laid beside the undefaced imposter he reveals just one point of discrepancy. "Can it be that?"—the body of the hero bedecked with *blue* characteristics, the body of the failure with *red!* Three minutes will confirm the truth of our suspicion . . . the scarred veteran once more *buries his barb deep in the jaws of a sixteen pounder.*

We put on the right colour, and colour has done it. And where is the surprise?

As a matter of course the dye-pot is often employed to bring Nature up to the requirements of certain pools.

In dressing his patterns, then, it is manifestly most important that the student should secure by some means, *precision* in colour, let alone *combination* of colour. That colour in a fly should be good and true is a statement few will be likely to challenge. The student can best secure this in daylight by means of contrast. Those, however, whose sense of colour is weak must rely on the eye of a friend or on the opinion of a responsible dealer.

That all dyed colours should be fast, and otherwise free from fault, is evidently needful; but a certain slow and limited fading—"toning down," we might call it at its best—comes inevitably with the lapse of time. Nor is it altogether unwelcome, for, when there is no sun to spoil our complexions, fish frequently reject a new fly for a somewhat faded specimen of the identical pattern.

Natural feathers, besides those dipped in dye, are subject to this toning down. Some suffer more than others, whilst the Golden Bird of Paradise and the leading tail-feathers of an old, healthy Macaw enjoy immunity from the ravages of time and dirty water.

At the prominent parts of the ordinary (general standard) fly where light can freely pass through, viz.: the tail, hackles, and upper outline of the wing, translucent feathers are better at times than those which are opaque ; the superiority of the former consisting in colour radiated all round, and this we see in greater extension when looking through them. They are, therefore, far preferable for places where the sun can shine through the fly-material. (Of course, it is not necessary always to use special flies when the sun shines.) Opaque feathers can be seen by reflected light only; semi-transparent feathers often by both reflected and refracted light.

The location and distribution of colour give scope for study as a matter of taste on the part of the fish. The usual fly-dressing traditions of colour demand that when the body of a fly is parti-coloured, the lightest colour shall be at the tail-section. One prominent exception is found in "Benchill"—the first and best invention of Malloch. The head section of this "successful creation," to quote early criticism, "being of light sky blue, tradition is reversed."

Then as to distribution, the general character of the fly has to be consulted, and the laws of colour enter to warn us that an equal division of any two colours in a fly by no means leads to a necessarily harmonious result. For instance, a smaller portion of blue or of yellow, in opposition to a larger one of yellow or blue, may establish a harmonious combination much more apparent than two exactly equal portions of these colours. We must decide, in view of general effect, what colours shall go side by side, and how much of each, in proportion to the whole. There is a harmony of *balance* and a harmony of *contrast*. The alteration of the colour of the silk of the "tag" will often strongly effect the appearance of the whole fly, especially when viewed from the fish's usual point of view—from the rear.

The kind and amount of tinsel, gold or silver, put on a fly materially modifies the effect of its colours—as a rule, enriching and stimulating that effect. Black Ostrich herl as a butt, aids definition and enhances colour, especially yellow, *vide* "Jock Scott."

Despite the advance made in dyes and dyeing, and in the substitution of certain naturals, to wit, Chatterer for Kingfisher, it must by no means escape the memory that a fly thoroughly wet exhibits to both man and fish far different colouring from that of its dry state; and that, in this regard, certain dyed silks suffer very much in comparison with others. Bad results in the silks themselves can only be detected and avoided by the test of experiment. However, Pearsall & Co. (who, through personal influence and direction, brought out our matchless Gossamer tying-silk) have, at length, effectually overcome all difficulty; not only are their body-silks perfect in quality, but the dyes are perfect also.

In forming the body of a fly one defect is commonly due, not to the silk itself, but to an undue economy of the material. A certain thickness of silken layer in such work is absolutely requisite, to prevent extra discolouration of its surface by the effect of cobblers' wax, however sparingly the latter has been applied to the tying-silk beneath. This wax, if used in its pure state, though productive of some slight trouble to the novice, has special virtues. It must on no account be messed about with any mixture whatever, and, except at the head of the fly, must not be varnished.

As my name has been publicly connected with a table of Standard Colours, it may be expected that I shall have something to say here on purity of colour and nomenclature as well. It has been suggested, and with much reason, that a practical code of colours might be constructed on a natural basis instead of an artificial one. Amongst other advantages, a natural code would easily win favour and would not be subject to change: for "lemon," "red plum," "yellow," "apple-green," "violet," "primrose," "orange," and the like (supplied by common and unvarying natural objects) need only such supplementary epithets for skilled hands as "medium," "light," and "very light," "dark," and "very dark." But to meet a fly-dresser's want for some accurate and fixed expressions of colour, indeed, to secure absolute precision all over the world, our best means seem to consist in a correct arrangement of lettering on a copy of a solar spectrum.

To this idea I have not given enough study to be able to attempt any system at present; besides, the expense is too much for me. But to give it an airing here may help to do a real service to the Salmon-angling world generally.

Having discussed at some length the chief qualities which should be looked for in a good fly, we come next to the subject of the materials.

The Hook. Enough has already been said about the need of strength in this item. The simplest method of testing strength and temper is, to stick the point of the hook into a piece of soft deal and give two or three short tugs in a direction at right angles with the shank, so as to make the hook-curve gape, noting closely whether or not the hook, on release, springs at once back to its original shape without bend or break of any part. If the hook is over-tempered, it will break; if too soft, remain bent. No hook should be used for fly-tying until it has been tested and its barb and point carefully examined. In the case of blunt points let not the file be used, but the waste basket instead. Economy here is a mistake and is invariably attended with disappointment.

With regard to its shape, our purpose being to hook and hold fish, I have ground for preferring, for general purposes, the modern "Limerick" to all other kinds. I had the original shape improved, because, in practice, an alteration seemed to me to be urgently needed. A slight, very slight, outward (not lateral) tendency of the point gives increase of penetration and grip, and makes the hook work into the flesh deeper and deeper during an "engagement." These particulars are put mildly, but the reader may place implicit reliance on the fact that the hook in our picture excels all others, as the moon outshines the minor stars, the truth of which dictum, however, would be completely upset by the erroneous theories which have crept, goodness knows on what grounds, into this subject at one time or another.

THE IMPROVED LIMERICK HOOK.

When the point of the "Improved Limerick," which deviates vertically from the shank, comes in contact with a fish's mouth, the "line of

Plate 1

The Black Ranger

The Infallible

Britannia

Jock Scott

The Champion

The Black Dose

pull" and the angle of impact are certainly *not* parallel; that is to say, the line of *pull* does *not* coincide at the time of striking with the direction of the force applied. Hence the remarkable popularity and unlimited success of this particular design.

In striking fish, the hook, being in a vertical position, the point thus shaped obviously takes a slight downward course, and this provides us with ample proof that the chances of *hooking and holding* are augmented, if not actually redoubled. Herein lies the secret—a secret not infrequently unfolded to us in every-day working experience.

As to the questions concerning "angles" of impact, "coincidence of line of pull," and "directions of force applied," they involve considerations too tedious—perhaps too deep—for these pages, and I shall pass them by without further words; but knowledge derived from experiment and careful daily observation in my own practice will justify an endeavour to clear up several doubtful questions.

Now the maximum of metal consistent with the living powers of the fly is not only an element of its strength, but also helps us to fish deep, and admits of a more plentiful dressing in proportion to the size of the hook; a by no means "despicable advantage," where the local tastes of the fish have to be consulted. A real gain arising from this extra strength promptly reveals itself in a contest with a "grubbing"* fish. I certainly prefer stout hooks where flies are heavily dressed—on the Tweed or Usk for instance; but where fish are as shy as Thames Trout, and quite as well educated as the Salmon in the Lee, I often find myself using fine hooks. Of these, for the North, the best, in my opinion, are the long-shanked, hammered hooks—*i.e.*, those with flattened sides, as sold at Winchester by Holland. Their chief merits consist in the increased depth of bend, and superior manufacture.

The shank end of our hook tapers fairly well to a point, chiefly in order to get a small head to a fly, whilst the increase of flexibility gained by this taper obviously establishes a more harmonious, and, therefore, a more lasting, connection between the supple gut-loop and the rigid metal shank.

* When hooked through or near a bone, a fish "grubs"—tries to disengage itself by knocking the hook against boulders.

Perhaps, however, I should just remark that some years ago there appeared a statement in a well-known work on angling, which has been read far and wide, to the effect that, in striking a fish, the "line of pull" *ought to coincide with the direction of the force applied!* So plainly did the writer state his ideas, and so convincingly did he express himself about the matter that the worst* hook of all was introduced by somebody or other, and strongly recommended by him.

Hardly any statement could have been more injurious to Fishermen than this. The "line of pull" has *no* such meaning, as I intend now to demonstrate.

On fastening the moistened "cast" to the gut-loop, which we know is best placed *under* the shank of the hook, the Angler takes about a foot of the attached gut in his right hand, and, whilst holding the bend of the hook in his left, gives a few firm tugs so as to fasten the knot in the position whereby the trace (or cast) shall work as straight as possible *in a true line with the shank.* This is what is meant by the "pull," which, in reality, is an expression as well as a scheme of my own. The Angler next proceeds to test his work in the water—to play the fly in front of him, in order to see that it swims properly; for it may yet fail to fish straight, and so require his further attention. The reader may well understand that some little time would elapse before the hook, improperly mounted—that is, *crookedly* mounted—could work itself, by the strain put on it in casting, into the position which would give it the best chance to penetrate properly. If "the pull" were in a direct line of the *point* of the hook, in striking the fish the point would be apt only to scrape the skin; at any rate, it would be more liable to do so than to work into the flesh.

But I have not quite done with the matter yet.

In the foregoing engraving we see, so far as my experience extends, the *perfection* of a hook. In our mind's eye we easily observe what happens when the fly is well mounted and the tackle arranged and attached as

* I allude to the hook having a turned-up metal eye, with its point turning *towards* the shank—turning *inwards,* in other words. It is "worst" because (1) it see-saws when "played" in the water, instead of advancing and retreating in a perfectly straight line. (2) Because if it should hook a fish, the subsequent strain of the rod tends to bring the point *out* instead of sending it *in* deeper.

described elsewhere—that is to say, we realise not only the extreme likelihood of the hook catching hold, but also the ease with which the point of it works deeper and deeper during a fight with a fish, for the barb works as a wedge to imbed it. Such evidence is, to the unbiassed mind, irresistible.

Of course, writers take their own views and inculcate their own ideas of the hooks they themselves fancy. But men, now-a-days, want *facts* not *fancies*, and we must all stand shoulder to shoulder in defence of the former, otherwise this branch of my subject might just as well have been left unwritten.

I hope that I seldom find fault without just cause; but when the mania for eyed hooks broke out afresh I pointed out their faults, and persistently maintained that they never could and never would become popular. I predicted and published my opinion as to what would happen

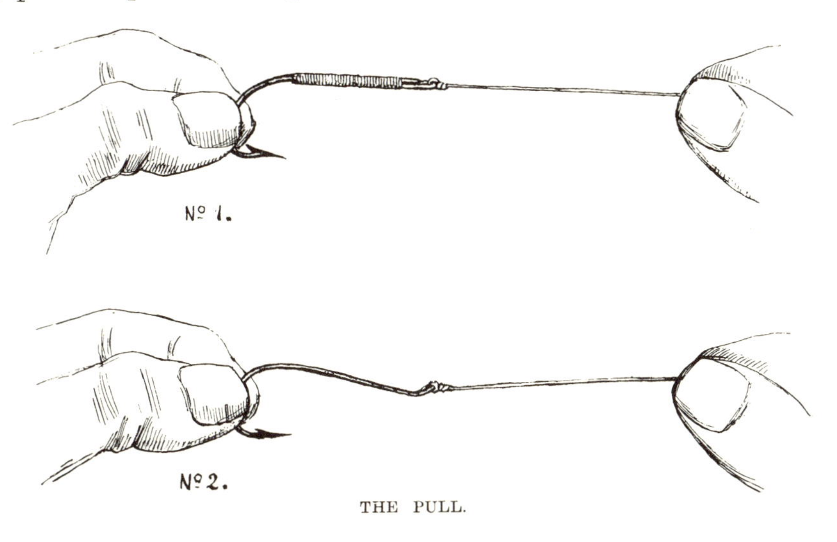

THE PULL.

in regard to "the pull" with those hooks having turned-up eyes. I need not make quotations, for the student who has followed the foregoing arguments will clearly perceive the awkward results of attaching the cast to a hook of that sort.

In the accompanying diagram No. 1 the reader will see an exact copy of one of my hooks with a piece of string attached for the purpose of demonstrating the *true* effect of "the pull"—*i.e.*, the string made fast in a line with the shank.

No. 2 indicates the *false* effect when the string (or the gut-line, it is immaterial which be used) is attached to a hook with an eye turned up.

Gut-loops administer to the result of "the pull"; metal loops (or eyes), besides having other faults, oppose it. Of course, much depends on the material as well as the make of gut-loops, a subject which I shall fully discuss later on.

I am not in favour of "eyed" hooks. The plain truth is that metal eyes are infinitely worse to fish with than gut-loops. Fix the line to a metal eye of any shape in whatever way you will, and the proverbial "hinge" soon comes in the gut close to the metal; and this causes the shank to hang in the water instead of keeping in a horizontal position.

The one solitary advantage in eyed hooks, which, curiously enough, their most ardent champions have overlooked, is that upon them flies can be dressed with extremely slender bodies. (It is quite a relief to find some redeeming quality.) In Ireland this is a decided advantage.

"Ah! yer honour, give me that!" the shrewd Irish gillie would exclaim; "it's a foine, sleek-bodied divil entoirely."

But as a set-off against this, the feather work requires careful and very unusual treatment, or the fly will quickly fall to pieces.

Perhaps I should not quit the subject of the hook's point without just mentioning that a man may start to fish with a hook whose point is bent absolutely sideways if he likes, but the chances of his coming home quite satisfied are not enhanced one atom; at least, I always found it so.

I shall not go so far as to say that *double hooks* are undoubtedly to be preferred to single. I think so myself; but I would rather disclose my reasons for so thinking than make a needlessly strong, imperative statement. First, they give a double chance of hooking a fish; and secondly, a double chance of holding it.

But, here again a great deal has been written (I must speak plainly) by men ready to pre-judge these hooks from their own unfortunate experience. Of these true Britons one has tried them by his own peculiar mode of striking; one by that of not striking at all, few by the right means, while some find fault without condescending to argument, and condemn them off-hand.

It has been said, and in places the statement has been generally believed, that "doubles" tear the flesh more than "singles"; also, that "during a fight one hook helps the other out." Doubtless these ideas originate, as I will show, from the old-fashioned principle of striking followed in using them.

In that admirable and instructive work, the *Badminton Library*, a gentleman of high angling ability—a Napoleon of the "Overhand" observes: "Long before the question as to the advantage of striking from the winch when using double hooks was discussed in the Sporting Press, I had given the double hook plan an extensive trial, but I lost so many fish with them that I gave them up." And in a letter to the "Fishing Gazette" the same authority goes on to remark: "All I said about double hooks (he was referring to a former letter) was that I had not been successful with them, and that, *perhaps*, this was in consequence of my not having adopted Mr. Kelson's plan of striking from the winch." I call attention to the word "perhaps" italicised here, as showing the care and judgment of the original writer on the subject.

But, on the other hand, Colonel Richardson throws an interesting side-light on the situation by a rather significant statement made in a letter to me to the effect "that the success of double hooks is in proportion as the means applied are adequate or inadequate. I never liked double hooks till I bought your winch at Farlow's, but I get a lot of fish with them now, and hardly ever miss one when I limit myself to size. A 2-0 hook is my largest."

Whilst endeavouring to remove the general stigma which these hooks have long borne, I shall hope not to offend the susceptibilities of any gentleman who does not concur in my opinion.

Now I am perfectly ready to admit that the value of certain fishing inventions—call them "novelties" if you will—can be very easily estimated; but anyone can see with half an eye that the questions touching on double hooks are not to be decided in a dining-room. Not even at the river-side can they be judged effectually without much experience in the matter of "presentation" as well as in the right and proper method of striking Salmon. Experience in the use of these hooks gained in a district where they are invariably used with perfection due to long habit, as on the Tweed, is more likely to prove valuable than merely a few temporary trials of an ordinary description.

After everything is said and done the fact seems to me indisputable, that in striking *from the winch* these hooks penetrate and remain fixed immovably in their place. And I maintain that the efficiency of the Lever Winch, which is fully explained in another chapter, has been abundantly proved by its successes. I have only to add here that double hooks are of great value to Anglers. They are generally used until fine tackle is indispensable; and on the Tweed there is an absolute unanimity of opinion in their favour, for not only amateurs—these the foremost amateurs—but people of all ranks use them up to a certain size, even in the lowest and brightest waters possible. It should, however, be borne in mind that people can be easily mistaken in regard to striking Salmon. Some think and say they never strike at all, though I must incidentally remark that I have never yet seen any Fisherman fail to put the hook into the fish by an *uplifting of the rod.* If that is *not* striking, I really do not know what is.

Gut-loops should always be made of the best gut twisted tightly, as explained in Chapter VIII., and provided always that they are stout enough and small enough, gut-loops, sufficiently twisted, will last longer than the flies themselves. In renewing a fly, I use mine again and again, doubling the gut at a different part.

The *Tag* is a valuable component in a fly. It plays a prominent part in the *tout ensemble* of mobility. The fly is usually seen by the fish from the rear, so that the "tag" is the point of the body nearest to him, and dominates the perspective of the whole. Remove the "tag," and the character of the fly, when viewed from that position, is often entirely changed.

Again, the "tag" is of importance in assisting the taper of the body, and in covering the part of the hook that must otherwise remain bare; for, as a rule, the body could not be extended to greater length to fill the place without disturbing the safe and proper proportions of the fly.

Furthermore, the tag is more or less a tribute to nature. Many flies, moths, and butterflies show marked alteration in colour at the extremity of the body. And so nature confirms what experience suggests.

It is interesting to trace the history of the "tag." Flies of a century ago were rarely, if ever, adorned with it. I can well remember that, in my earlier days, tags were invariably made with orange silk. Suddenly, however, Anglers on the Usk discovered that scarlet floss was an improvement, and in other places the fact was speedily confirmed. Indeed, I myself found that on other rivers Salmon decidedly prefer scarlet to orange. This lucky discovery led to my introducing into use several well-known standard flies—" Lady d'Eresby," with a blue tag; " Strathspey," with a violet one; " Nightshade," with pink; " Captain Walton," with cream; and many others.

In this new field of speculation I was soon followed by Wright, of Sprouston, who invented a "blue-tagged" fly that won for itself local honours and many admirers. Farlow, whose best is the "Baron," with a dark red-claret tag, and Bernard, of Church Passage, chimed in. The hint was soon taken by amateurs and the trade generally, and the tag has now won a distinguished place in the estimation of Anglers of varied experience.

Tags are usually made in two parts—first, gold or silver twist; next, floss silk. Directions for using these materials will be given in the next chapter.

Discussing the subject of tags one day by the river-side, a brother Angler asked me the following question: "Did you or any other man ever see a black and white dog having any white at all in its tail that didn't have it at the tip?"

The "*Tail*" of a fly comes next, and is of great service. It used to be the fashion to employ here nothing but golden "toppings"; but as the reader has heard enough of old fashions, his attention had better be drawn to forms new and approved. Besides "toppings," we use for "tails" tippet fibres and other parts of the Golden Pheasant; Toucan breast and under-tail; strips or sprigs of Teal and Canadian Duck, Macaw, Jungle-fowl, and feathers from the Chatterer, Indian Crow, Tanager, Blue Creeper, and others that are supple and showy, coloured and speckled.

In the more elaborate "tails" choice may be made of every thin-fibred wing-feather in our collection, so long as they are used in moderation.

Spreading tails, sometimes flat, sometimes in set-sail fashion, resembling closed butterflies' wings, are effective and telling. Tails may be "built" like wings, but with the fibres pointing upward. As a formal example, portions of yellow Macaw, Canadian Duck, Peacock wing, and powdered blue Macaw, all curving in one direction, with a similar set to back them, taken, of course, from the other side of feathers, make a grand mixture. But when this mixture is brought into requisition, the flies should be *butted* for, hold the scissors in cutting off the stumps in whatever manner you choose, a taper is formed which points the wrong way. The "butt" of Ostrich (the herl itself tapering well to a point) comes to the rescue, and brings matters right by covering the stumps remaining. If the fly is to be of the type known as "shovel-tailed," a similar mischievous tapering arises, and should be treated in the same way by the Ostrich herl. These matters will be better understood after perusal of the next chapter.

"*Body*." Of the three materials, Pig's wool, mohair, and Seal's fur, the last named (being the last introduced into use) is superior to either of the others for general purposes, as it is more tractable than Pig's wool, and more brilliant and alluring than mohair. It is to be observed, however, that where *bulk* of colour is a desideratum, as in the "Beaconsfield," mohair is still occasionally employed. On the other hand, the more sombre Berlin wool is sometimes preferred, as on Speyside.

In selecting Seal's fur, see that it is even in texture, rather hairy than woolly in character, and even in colour. Inferior samples are dull, lumpy, short, and downy.

Owing to its comparative coarseness and length, Pig's wool, now-a-days, is rarely employed except in large flies, for which use it has manifest advantages. Being the most brilliant of all dyed materials, except, perhaps, Goat's beard, it is unrivalled. To secure with it an evenly-tapered body careful treatment is required. The "wool" (for that is the usual name given to it) should first be rolled between the fingers, so that it forms a tapered length to spin on to the tying silk. Other furs are sometimes used for special patterns. The Silver Monkey is particularly valuable. Berlin wools are occasionally called for, but rarely by myself, as I prefer Seal's fur. When coils are wanted, as in Sun-flies, Berlin wool comes in handy for the purpose.

Mohair can be passed over, as I have said all that is needful.

As body-*material,* silks are of less equal value than furs if the stock of flies is to be a catholic one. The main care in procuring silk should be to get really fast colours, and, therefore, in purchasing, a first-class tackle shop is to be preferred to a Berlin *depot.* These floss silks are best stored in glazed paper, and laid straight in the length in which they are usually sold. The best silk in the market, I repeat, is "Pearsalls French Floss," dyed with his special unfading Eastern dyes.

Bodies are also made in part or wholly of chenille, in various colours. The "Black Creeper," well known on the Earn and Usk, is a most useful variety of Grub. It kills on some Scotch rivers in bright weather, and throughout Wales in dull.

Tinselled chenilles are also popular—the "Glowworm" (copper) to wit; and there are also bodies of silver and of gold tinsel, as everyone knows.

The materials named are those in commonest use, but, of course, there is a wider field for the adaptive inventiveness of the artist. Mr. Basil Field, for example, has successfully used a change on the silver body—a fly known as the "Kendle" is made by him of white floss silk, covered with gold beater's skin. Again, a body may be covered with small feathers, as in the "Chatterer."

Ribbings are chiefly of silver or gold tinsel (flat or oval), or lace, used singly or in combination with each other, and sometimes with floss silk, as in "Black Dog." There is a great difference of quality in these materials. Only the best should be used. Especially does this caution apply to oval tinsel, which is now-a-days so much in request. It has the merit over flat tinsel that it is not liable to become wholly severed by one rake of the Salmon's tooth, and so unwinding to the utter disablement of the fly.

To prevent confusion, the names of the several kinds are here given according to the system in general use among amateur fly-dressers. The manufacturers have unfortunately lately started a new series of names;

these are given in brackets as employed by Kenning, the wholesale maker of all the varieties here mentioned.

Thread. Solid round gold or silver wire.

Twist (thread). Is a white floss silk entirely covered with windings of fine silver wire; it is round, and used principally for "tags."

Lace (Twist). Is compound "twist"—*i.e.*, three lengths twisted together.

Tinsel (Plate) is either flat or oval. "Flat tinsel" is a ribbon of gold or silver made by flattening solid metal wire. "Oval tinsel" (Flat-worm) is made on the same principle as "twist," but is much stouter, and, in section, oval instead of round. The encircling silver or gold thread may be severed, but the silk core, with which this sort is provided, holds on, and, by its tightness, prevents the thread from unwinding. It is altogether better than flat tinsel and easier handled in work, but is not as yet made sufficiently broad for very large patterns.

Embossed Tinsel is also made in silver and gold, and lends the pretty effect of subdued brilliance to a body, as seen in the "Dusty Miller" and in the "Dunkeld," but it must be handled gently, as being of a very brittle nature.

With regard to the *colour* of twists and tinsels, silver is generally preferred for the Spring fishing, gold for the Autumn. Where, however, there is a preponderance of yellow tones on the body, I prefer silver early in the day, the rays of the gold being signally eclipsed by the materials it embraces; and gold in the afternoon.

For brightening tinsels of all sorts other than tinselled chenilles, Steven's "Silicon tablet" should be used. It is sold by Mr. Thomas, Chemist, Talbot Road, W. The little cardboard box contains a brush and a piece of wash-leather. The former is useful for polishing old silver bodies; the latter for twists and tinsels before being employed in fly-work. Silicon is used sparingly for gold. In polishing with the leather the tweezers are applied to those tinsels having a silk core, a small portion of which is exposed by nipping off the metal covering. The length for use is pulled with them through the wash-leather, not to the end, but near thereto; then the length is reversed and pulled through in the contrary direction.

Hackles. For a body-hackle, *shape* is a quality of importance, as, when wound on, the fibres ought to increase in length from the tail end of the body up to the throat. In some flies of mine, the "Penpergwm Pet" for instance, the fibres reach from the throat to the hook-point, or even beyond. In the case of the throat-hackle, this taper is not so requisite.

Experience will soon bring skill in choosing the right size of hackle for any definite pattern. The number of usual coils of a body-hackle is one less than the ribs, which are formed of gold or silver tinsel. The ribs number five generally, and overlap the point of the hackle at the beginning of the second coil. About three coils of the butt end of the hackle should, however, be reserved to form, or help to form, the throat. But much latitude is allowed as to the total amount of hackle to be displayed at the throat. A separate hackle is often put on in addition.

In all hackles, save and except those of the Eagle and Spey-cock tribe, get rid of all fluff at the root. In ordinary Cock's hackles, undyed, select those which are transparent, shiny, deepest in colour, and proportionately good in that respect underneath. A red "furnace," for instance, should not be of a very light appearance on the wrong side. These ordinary fowl's hackles must never carry a "cheesy" list—*i.e.*, a dull, opaque centre list tapering towards the point of the feather. The best Irish hackles are free from this blemish, which, however, must not be mistaken for the useful black list, as in "coch-a-bonddus." True "Eagle's" hackles are, so to speak, all fluff. They are wanted for certain purposes in fishing, but are expensive, and will probably increase in price. When pure white, perhaps no feathers dye so well. For my own use, especially as regards smallish flies, I have long since put up with samples after the form and character of the original; and no doubt dressers will be glad to know of them. They are taken from the thigh of a light-coloured hen Pheasant, are of a dirty white appearance, and have a broad mouse-coloured list from the middle part to the butt. These hackles are less in size and are not so fluffy as Eagle's. But for the Spey and other rivers (if there are any), where it is the practice to work the hackles on the hook from the butt of the feather, I prefer to use the breast of the common Bittern. These require to be dyed, otherwise nearly all of them are useless. They, moreover, need careful handling, but are strong enough when made up, and, by being longer at the point than at the butt, want no reversing to meet the object in view.

Comparing natural (ordinary) hackles with the dyed, we claim for the former that they fade but little, do not change their tone in water, and do not tarnish tinsel by contact, as some dyed feathers are liable to do. Good ones are difficult to get.

For dyed hackles we must claim, on the other hand, that they can be fairly well shifted from a "hospital" fly to a new one. (N.B.—Always keep a hospital for broken down flies, they frequently serve as materials if not wanted as specimens.) This shifting is chiefly owing to the fact that less material is used to produce a desired effect. Dyed hackles are easily obtained at any tackle shop.

Doubtless the art of dyeing is much improved, and will continue to improve; but hitherto it is far from perfect, particularly with regard to the blues. The best blue I know of, No. 3099, and the best yellow, called "Best Yellow," are easily obtained with Woolley's dye (Market Street, Manchester).

However well hackles may be dyed, with the exception of fiery browns, they never look so well, even when fresh, or are so effective in the water as natural ones. Take, for instance, the hackles of a Golden Bird of Paradise, the best dyed orange hackle in creation would be simply nowhere in competition with it. Where, again, is there a dyed blue hackle to compete favourably with the Jay, or, when no great amount of colour is needed, with the Vulturine Guinea fowl? This condition of depth of tone being conceded, mention also must be made of both the orange and red hackles of the Golden Pheasant.

I know of no dye or method of dyeing that will hit off to our liking that metallic lustrous sheen, which is a conspicuous feature on some of our best natural feathers, such as those on the back of the wild Turkey. The apparent resemblance produced by chemical combinations is a complete failure for practical purposes. When Seal's fur became more fashionable than Pig's wool, I accidentally produced this lambent sheen, and made a large stock of flies with various wing materials; but I soon found them to be utterly useless, except in discoloured waters.

As to *black hackles* it is well generally to use natural, and not dyed feathers. In discoloured water, however, the dyed shows surprisingly more; in fact, under such condition one never thinks of using a "natural," except on an emergency. They are not necessarily black before being dyed, and when originally white, they are even more conspicuous to the fish in the state of water just mentioned. This is not because white dyes a better black than anything else, but because the white hackles we dye are of a different consistency. Natural blacks, as a rule, are out and out the best in clear water; not only that, they are more mobile and last twice as long. Further observations as to their special use are made in another chapter. The chief feature to avoid in selecting natural blacks is the "cheesy list," previously mentioned; and our special object should be to seek a really deep black with a shiny surface.

The hackles most commonly used are the following:

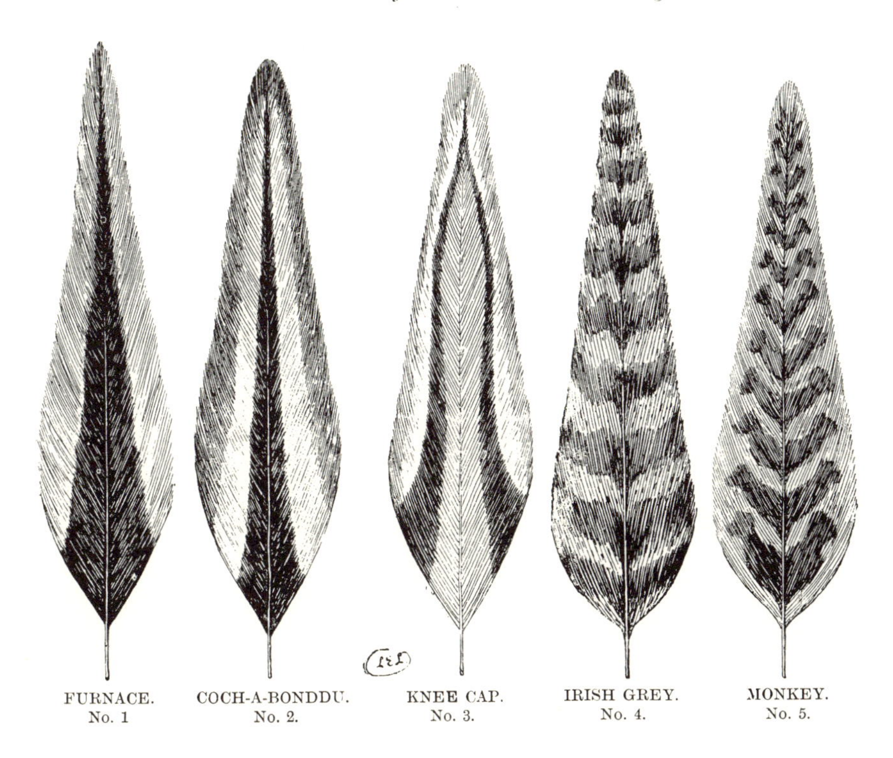

FURNACE. No. 1 — COCH-A-BONDDU. No. 2. — KNEE CAP. No. 3. — IRISH GREY. No. 4. — MONKEY. No. 5.

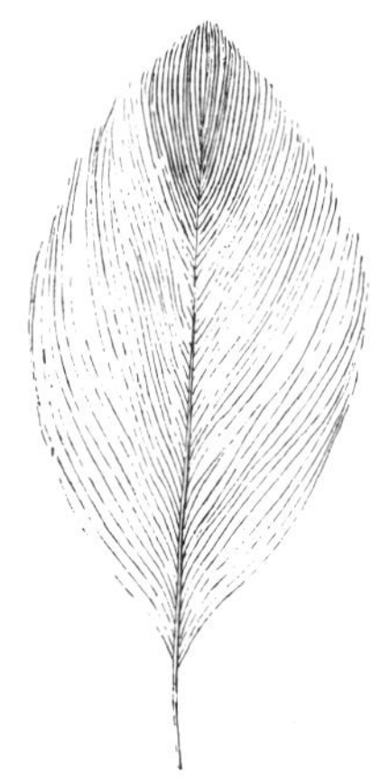

GOLDEN BIRD OF PARADISE.

SMALL VULTURINE GUINEA FOWL.

Cocks' hackles. The best, both in shape and degree of firmness, come from the neck; but feathers from the back are used on pressing necessity, or for Grubs.

The special varieties of these are :

1.—*Furnace hackles.* A red Cock's hackle with a tapered black list running up the centre; *White furnace* are white with a black list; *Blue*, with a blue list.

The distinction between "furnace" and "coch-a-bonddu" is of very old date. I have specimens of each collected in Wales by my Father in 1836, and carefully labelled by him with their different names. "Coch-a-bonddu," a Welsh word, signifies "red, with a black band." The advantage of giving the two names, "furnace" and "coch-a-bonddu," is so obvious, and the benefit derived from extending the signification to other feathers of their nature so apparent, that I make no apology for the nomenclature which I have given above.

2. *Coch-a-bonddu hackles.* A furnace hackle with black points. But the colour between the list and points of blue "coch-a-bonddus" varies. It may be of a reddish tinge, grizzly-grey, honey, or golden. Dipped in Bismarck-brown aniline dye (Woolley & Co., Manchester), this is one of the best of all hackles for general use in dead low water. White "coch-a-bonddus" may be dyed any colour. These are great favourites,

and I always "disgrace" "Childers" by dressing him with one dyed yellow—the black points being far more effective than those of the furnace-hackle.

3. *Knee-cap hackles* (a cross between Malay and Polish fowls). A red Cock's hackle with a slightly irregular black streak tapering, and running through the centre of red fibres on each side of the quill. The colours are much the same as in the "coch-a-bonddu," only that they are placed differently, as shown in the picture. They are very scarce.

4. *Irish-grey hackles.* A transparent, silver hackle, spotted and scored with dark pencillings. For Standard flies, Nondescripts and Grubs, the value of these feathers can scarcely be over estimated. They look well, and pay well, when put along the body of any sort or colour, and I have invariably found them useful in bright water, let the river be what it may. With the "Purple Emperor," dressed without the hen Pheasant at throat, I killed fourteen fish at Knockando in May, 1892, before changing the fly.

5. *Monkey hackles.* A transparent grey hackle having a series of curiously-shaped dark blotches on each side of the quill resembling a cat in a sitting posture. For Grubs these are invaluable. With the "Ringlet," at the time it was introduced at Usk, I killed, in one week, thirteen Salmon (averaging nearly 16 lbs.), when the water was low and winged flies played out.

Of *Heron's hackles,* I have a few words to say. Most of us know the ordinary grey Heron hackle is effective on many rivers. But on many other rivers it is underrated, for I often use the feather with success where Herons are unfashionable. Anglers are apt to fancy that because the hackle is twice as long as the hook the fly is thereby made twice as large. This is a mistake. The *size* of a fly is estimated by the length of its body rather than by the length of the hackle it carries. For some flies, as, for instance, the "Rough Grouse," the grey Heron is altogether surpassed by the "Crown Pigeon" hackle. The cinnamon Herons, of which there are several species, are not all of equal value. Of these, the Nankeen Night Heron (*Nycticorax calidonicus*), of New South Wales, provides a large number of exquisite hackles and wing feathers, and so does the one known as *Nycticorax Manillensis.* The *Demigretta gulans* is the best of the black species.

Among other natural hackles we have Bustard; the Lineated Bittern (*Tigrisoma lineatum*) from South America, which is superior to that from British Guiana, and of great value for its numerous cinnamon-brown mottled hackles of all sizes; Grouse, Partridge, Guinea fowl, Teal, Pintail, Widgeon, &c.

Yellow hackles are the easiest to get dyed and the most difficult to get undyed. *Toucan's*, however, are very useful, and scarcely fade in work. They are small and very fine in texture, so three times the usual amount is required for a fly. *Yellow Macaws*, on the contrary, are coarse and more opaque. These are used sparingly. But by far the best orange hackle, as yet discovered, comes from the neck of the *Golden Bird of Paradise* (*Xanthomelus aureus*), a native of New Guinea. This bird is about the size and shape of our missel thrush, and carries hundreds of magnificent hackles around its neck (see illustrated hackles). For "throats" or for Grubs, even for wings, these deadly feathers are perfect. They play exquisitely in the water, never fade, and, though fine in fibre, do not break or wear at the points.

Speckled Yellow is got from dyed Gallina (a feather we prize highly and dye many colours), Teal, and Widgeon.

Blue hackles. The best natural blues are taken from Jays, Vulturine, Guinea fowls, and from the Pitta (bertæ) from Borneo.

Jay's are scored with black bars; the two latter birds are of a pale blue, though the "Tocate" is of superlative brilliance. In mobility, Vulturine's are best, and as long in fibre as a medium Guinea-fowl hackle. *Blue Macaw* hackles, deep in tone, are no favourites of mine. A good blue—in fact, the best I have ever obtained—is easily secured by using as much of the powder as would thinly cover a threepenny piece of the blue dye just mentioned, No. 3099 (sold by Woolley & Co., of Manchester) in one pint of water. The plan is to first boil the dye in a saucepan, and, when removed from the fire, to immerse the hackles for a few minutes. They should be tied in dozens to the end of a stick, and well worked about in the dye. Choose the whitest looking feathers. On taking them out rub them on both sides, from roots to points, with a piece of transparent glycerine soap; wash, and dry. Turnbull of Edinburgh, Holland of Winchester, and Malloch of Perth have supplied me with some useful specimens. The Jay, however, for all-round work is the general favourite; but the feather must be split, as one side is useless. For dressing, choose feathers coloured on the right side of the quill, or they will have to be wound on the hook the reverse way, much to the annoyance of young dressers.

The easiest method of splitting the Jay is that of Major Traherne.

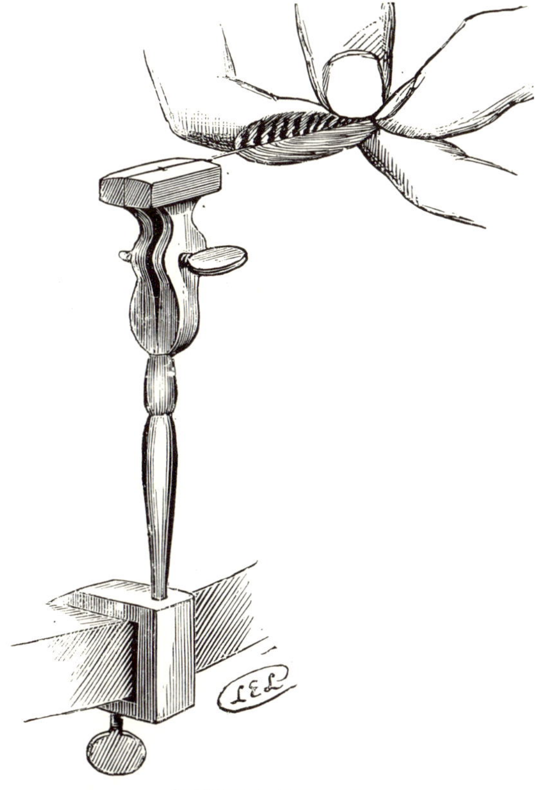

SPLITTING THE JAY.

The butt end of the feather is fastened in a fly-maker's vice, as shown, the best side uppermost. Seize the right and left fibres at the very point of the feather with the fore-finger and thumb of both hands, their backs facing outwards and slightly towards the ground. Keep the feather taut and pull gently *yet towards you*, when the quill will begin to split. Continue pulling steadily in this way till the feat is accomplished. Take care not to pull harder on one side than on the other, especially at starting. Next place the side to be used on a smooth, hard surface, the point end towards you, the butt away from you. Press the fore-finger on the point, the second finger on the butt, and, with a fine, sharp-pointed penknife, scrape away any remaining pith until not a particle remains. This delicate operation must be done with a light hand, or the quill will be severed. If the feather does not split as you wish, cut off with quite the point of the knife, say, half the quill by one stroke of the blade from end to end, and the feather is ready for use.

For myself, however, I never use a vice for any purpose. I find it easy enough in this case to seize the fibres in the way described above, and then place the butt of the feather between the teeth, and pull the coloured side away. Perhaps the vice may be used in making the bodies of all such patterns as "The Chatterer"; for when numberless small feathers constitute the body of a fly, the dresser *holds the hook, not by the bend, as usual, but by the shank*. Unless his fingers are in good fettle, the vice, under the circumstances, might be of some little service to him, especially in putting on Strip wings.

The old books on fly-dressing used to give directions for stripping off one side of a Cock's hackle, but this plan is a mistake. All hackles, equally coloured right and left of the quill, should be "doubled" before use. One hackle thus serves to take the place of two which were formerly used; the fly fishes better, and money is saved. Directions for "doubling" are given in Chapter III., in company with an Illustration of the process. But to meet the purpose needed, in some parts of Wales it is commonly supposed that these feathers can be "licked into shape," and that by "doubling," the fibres are bent and spoilt at their roots. This idea is an illusion, seeing that the minute portion of each fibre bent by the necessary pressure given is restored in the process of winding. The hackle being wound on its side, the stem "bites" the very portion supposed to be injured, with the result that the "spring" and "spread" of the lower fibres are, in all respects, equal to that of the upper ones.

Wings. Before detailing the kinds of feathers most commonly in use, it may be well to offer some remarks of a general nature upon them. To become an adept in the selection and manipulation of these materials, and for securing in the fly a permanent obedience to pattern, the student should make himself familiar with the characteristic qualities of the feathers, not only those which distinguish one bird from another, but those from different parts of the same bird. For example, he should learn that certain kinds of feathers are more easily induced to "marry" than others, and that those of a stiffer nature are best placed lowest in the wing in order to ensure the necessary quality of mobility; thus, in working with Mallard, Teal, and Golden Pheasant tail, the Mallard poses above, and the Teal in the centre. Also, that a leading tail feather of the Golden Pheasant, in point of tractability and ease of manipulation, is out of all comparison to be preferred to other tail feathers from the same bird.

It is hardly necessary to insist that feathers should be gathered at the right season of the year. The best season for almost all English bred birds is Christmas, at which time the new livery has neither been tarnished by wear, nor by the rays of a burning sun. But there are exceptions. Early in the autumn, for instance, the Golden Pheasant, reared in this country, struts about in its new outfit before other birds begin to cast off their seedy summer coats. Again, a good speckled Teal is rarely, if ever, met with till the end of the month of January. During summer and autumn the feathers of birds, as a rule, are faded and limp—a condition the fly-dresser always avoids. No necks change more in colour, or quality between winter and summer, than the well-known blue-duns.

Writers have very properly objected to the prevailing practice of stripping birds of their winter covering. The scissors should always be used; the operation then is painless, and with a little extra protection in the fowl-house at night, the birds never suffer. "Pulling necks" is injurious, for the next crop will team with lighter and weaker feathers, whereas the scissors tend to produce an opposite effect. Free feeding with hempseed in the moulting season, once every other day, makes a vast difference to feathers in fineness, transparency, sheen, pencillings, and depth of tone. The feathers of mature birds are better than those of young ones. This is very noticeable with Turkeys; the best "white tips" for "Jock Scott" are sometimes found under the tail of old male birds, and at the bottom of the back. Feathers should be obtained as fresh as possible. "Peacocks" tails, especially, soon become brittle and lose their virtue. I preserve my collection in tin boxes, and sprinkle among them crystals of naphthaline, which is the best means of preventing insect intrusion. This crystal, extracted by distillation from coal tar, has a strong aromatic smell, but the sprinking must be renewed about three times in one year. *Albo carbon* is cheaper and also answers the purpose.

The best way to keep large "toppings" is to cap one exactly over the other in bundles of four. Held at both ends by one person, they should then be well whipped at the butt with unwaxed tying silk, by another, and put on their sides—some bundles on their right, and as many on their left—in a partition of the fly box just wide enough to hold them without interrupting their natural bend.

The process of "marrying" strips of feathers for wings will be explained in the next chapter.

All the commonly-used feathers of the Duck tribe are pre-eminently "philogamists" (if I may coin a word)—Canadian Duck, Teal, Pintail, and more especially Widgeon. Turkey, Peacock wing, and Bustard are not difficult to marry either. All the Pheasant tails are somewhat coy; whilst red Macaw is simply exasperating to a "match-making" fly-dresser. A little patient practice will reveal the cases in which lasting unions are easiest effected, and give point to our doctrines on the qualities in feathers, some to be secured by careful choice, others to be dealt with by skilful management.

Before grouping feathers and making further comments upon them, it is as well to remind the reader that wing-feathers, such as dyed Swan, are liable to curl up and get out of shape. Into this, an occasional examination is prudent and advisable. Many of these feathers can be smoothed into shape with clean, cool fingers, and repacked carefully as before; but other special directions will be given in Chapter VIII. Jungle-fowl (*Gallus sonnerati*), as a wing decoration, is not included; it stands by itself; there is nothing to group with it. Hackles are best tied up in bundles. Full descriptions of feather boxes will also be found in Chapter VIII.

The following are the kinds of feathers in general use. They are grouped according to their affinities and to the relative place in the wing they are best qualified to occupy, from the top downwards.

Group I. Mallard, Canadian (or Summer) Duck, Teal, Widgeon, Pintail, Grey Mallard, Gallina.

From Canadian Duck onwards, not including Gallina, these are given in the order of their value in markings. Teal is strongly defined, and lends great character, whether as wing-element or as hackle. Canadian Duck is more telling in its way; it is especially showy as "sides" or in tails. Pintail—not quite such a favourite of mine as Widgeon—is an advance on Grey Mallard in distinctness of pencilling.

By "*Mallard*," we always understand the rich, brown-mottled feathers, few in number, found on each side of the back of the wild Mallard or the tame species, just in a line with the shoulder, but as far back as the flank. In some districts—the west of England particularly—the brown tinge extends deeper down the fibres, thus taking the place of the objectionable ash-coloured blurr, which is a terrible eyesore in wings for other rivers than the Spey. These feathers vary considerably in pencilling and depth of tone. The decoy Mallard often gives us a useful reddish, un-mottled, white-tipped feather—one less valuable than that of the *two* Mandarin Drake gems, which are taken from the back, whence they protrude. The latter kind are highly prized on the Earn. (A few years ago when shooting I got a singular specimen of the leading tail feather of an ordinary cock Pheasant. It is of a clear cinnamon-brown colour throughout, and without the sign of a mark in the fibres. For single strip-winged flies none of its kith and kin equal it, either in colour or character. There would be an insatiable demand for them if Nature displayed her freaks in this direction more frequently. The cross between the Gold, or the Painted, and the Common Pheasant often results in a feather somewhat similar, but inferior in quality.)

Grey Mallard requires a little explanation. It is easily obtained, owing to the great stock which most Ducks produce. But, although the term "grey mallard" is commonly given in fly-description, the feather itself is hardly ever used in fly making! It is too flimsy and too little marked. Our best "grey mallard"—I would rather not change the term—is taken from the Widgeon and Pintail. The feathers are found on the flank of the bird, and can always be recognised by their irregular darkish lines, running crossways, and increasing in depth of tone towards the end of the feather, which is far less pointed than in any of their kindred. In short, numerous Drakes supply us with "grey mallard," but the term practically extends no further than to Pintail and Widgeon.

Teal is thus written in description. Its value is often under-estimated. Any amount of it can be obtained at the Game shops in the month of February. Canadian Duck is to be had only of tackle makers. Some tiers call this Summer Duck, others Wood Duck. Owing to its increasing scarceness, it is necessarily expensive to purchase.

My favourite feather of the *Gallina* (or guinea fowl) is the double-speckled sort from the back. The "eyed" feathers from under the wings are reserved for dyeing. But, to my mind, the best black and white *speckled* hackle is taken from a Rail (*hypotœnidia torquata*). which is a native of the Philippine Islands; and the best black and wnite *barred* hackle from the Banded Cymnogene (*polyboroides typicus*), found in Africa and Madagascar.

Group II. Turkey, Bustard, Florican, Peacock-wing, Golden and Amherst Pheasant tails.

The domesticated Turkey affords greater variety in colour marking, size, and texture than any other single class of birds, wild or tame. It is most useful to the Fly-dresser. The feathers which are most difficult to get are of a rich cinnamon tone, and should be taken from the tail. Turkeys ought to attain their third year before the scissors are used. On no account should these feathers be "pulled," as the crop coming after not only falls short in richness of colour, but also in the element of mobility, of which quality the Turkey has none too much. The "double-white"—a white feather having a black bar near the point—is also rare. I have only once seen a double-white having a good ginger bar; but I made good use of it while it lasted.

When "white-tips" are employed, as in "Jock Scott," the points should be white, not creamy. The latter are used mostly in "modifications." But the Great American Cock — a wild Turkey — (*Meleagris gallopavo*) is a great favourite. It has a superb cinnamon-brown mottled tail, and its thighs are covered with magnificent scarlet hackles having a black bar.

In *Bustard*, those of the Indian and African species are the best. Bustard, both light and dark, is an effective decoration. The various degrees of clearness of marking give considerable scope of choice for effect. The hackles neither dye so well, nor wear so well, as those of the Gallina. The best bird I ever saw was shot by Mr. Mobray M. Farquhar, in Matabeleland, early in the season of '95. Being brittle, fibres of Golden Pheasant tail should be mingled with those of all Bustards *when employed for mixed wings.* The male bird is the more valuable. He has about twenty tail feathers; he is larger than his mate, and differs from her in one interesting feature, to which I may be permitted to allude. The male Bustard has a kind of bag or pouch situated in the forepart of the neck, and capable of containing two quarts. The entrance to it is immediately under the tongue. They are generally supposed only to run like an Ostrich aided by the wings, but when once in the air they can fly several miles without resting. The South African (*Otis Ludwigi*) is the largest and best of the dark species. The European species (*Otis tarda*) is sometimes used, but the bird is less valued. It is commonly known as the Great Bustard, and, instead of mottled feathers, this sort has dark bars across the ferruginous groundwork.

The feathers from the little Bustard are sometimes used in small patterns.

The Asiatic Florican provides us with much brighter feathers and hackles darker in the bars, and lighter in the ferruginous ground of the feather. It is scarcely so brittle as Bustard, and, although a strip for extended "cheeks" is often telling, we generally use it for small strip-winged patterns, such as are fashionable on the Ness and Locky.

The Peacock, as they say, has "a plumage of an angel, the voice of a devil, and the stomach of a thief"; but for all that, he is a useful friend to the dresser. The herls from the tail and sword feathers are sometimes used for "butts" and "bodies," but more frequently for "wings." No feathers deteriorate more rapidly, unless placed at once in an air-tight compartment. The hackles are occasionally wanted, as for instance, on the Towy. The creamy, transversely-speckled feathers found in the wings brighten up a fly, and heighten the effect of Mixed wings. Some years ago I had a quantity of them sent me from India. These contained brilliant shades of blue, yellow, red, and green; but alas! they were soon swallowed up in fly-making, and I have never been able to replenish my store.

The Golden Pheasant is subordinate to none. It has attained the highest pitch of popularity among Fly-makers, mainly by virtue of its crest. Not only has it enjoyed a rare continuance of public favour, in this, as in other repects—for "all the bird" is valued, but it will always be in fashion, if only for the tippet feathers, which are wanted in numberless Standard patterns. It is needless to remind the reader that the *leading* feather in the tail is incomparably the best of the bunch.

The *Amherst Pheasant* is also invaluable. Some years since, Mr. George Horne, of Hereford (a well-known Salmon Angler), seeing the merits of the tail feathers, devoted his attention to breeding and crossing these birds with others of their species. The tail of the three-quarter-bred Amherst with the Golden Pheasant is particularly fine. By this means, the black bars in the former feathers become numerous black spots, which are most effective on the whitish ground. A dash of Amherst blood improves the tail of the Gold, and richly enhances the colour of the toppings. Mr. Horne keeps a fine stock of all the best birds, and sometimes disposes of their feathers. I have one, the fibres of which measure nearly five inches in length; but a little in a fly goes a very long way.

Group III. Scarlet Ibis (though I much prefer the wing of the Tourocou for tails); dyed Swan and dyed Turkey; tail feathers of the Macaw; Golden Pheasant tippet; Peacock herl and sword feather.

This group comprises chiefly colour and ornament. *Ibis* should be used almost exclusively for tails and wings. As a hackle it is poor and lifeless in the water, and has acquired a wholly justifiable measure of dislike. *Swan* is exquisitely suitable for our work, and far better than *dyed Turkey*. *Tippets* vary much in size, shape, and purity of colour. On each side of the neck the feathers of a good bird assume a natural curve; these are paired off and reserved for use in winging such flies as the "Ranger" tribe. It will not bear much manipulation in the strip, and obstinately refuses all overtures for "marriage." As a hackle for winged flies, the tippet is not popular; but for grubs—the "Tippet Grub," for instance (the feathers are used as hackles)—it is grand; and, in point of contrast, when so used, few feathers equal it. *Herls* and *sword-feathers* have already been mentioned. For making a whole wing of the former, strands should be selected from each side of the feather, and packed together on their backs, in separate bundles for each wing, the top part of the wing taking the longest fibres. The sword feather is also used in wings, as in "Jock Scott."

If the beautiful and useful be incompatible, the beautiful must give way; even the old "Cock o' the Rock," the celebrity I have known as being endowed with some malady, is altogether neglected on account of constitutional debility. It is here, as Shakespeare would have it, that expectation failed most. The colour which led us to expect great results was more than counterbalanced by the weakness and limpness of the fibres. There is, however one species—*Rupicola sanguinolenta*—from Andes of Ecuador, that is exceedingly useful. The bird is similar in shape, but in colour, character of fibre, and style of feather, it differs materially. The feathers are not orange, but almost scarlet; they are not soft, but sufficiently firm, and make good hackles, which almost shine either in the water or out. The Kingfisher changes colour, and has yielded to the Blue Chatterer from Vera Paz. This latter is now well known; but the Banded Chatterer is uncommon. The former (*Cotinza amabilis*) is light blue; the Banded (*Cotingacincta*) from Cayenne is dark.

The common accompaniment, by the bye, of all good feathers in all good boxes is—consumption. Believe me, I speak it deliberately and with full conviction, the only method of preserving our bulk of material is to keep adding to it. Amongst that portion of our present stock, for which I am held responsible, we have the Banded Chatterer, the Great American Cock (wild turkey), the Nankeen Night Heron, the South American Bittern, and the Cock o' the Rock from Ecuador. But the greatest find that has fallen to my lot is the Golden Bird of Paradise.

May this luck be your luck, brother Fishermen, as it has been mine! It will only cost you £10!

For enumerating these feathers for wings, I have mentioned those in general use; but so far from seeking to limit the area of choice, I would rather urge and stimulate the student to seize on, and trim up and try those unproclaimed materials that may fall to his hand, and by their appearance, promise to be of service to him. In this respect, the amateur fly-tier is apt to ignore the fact that he does not do as much as he ought to do for the advancement of experimental research. He surely has the power and means to push further and further onward into that ocean of knowledge, of which we have, as yet, but gathered a few shells upon the margin. The principles to guide him in exploration and selection are readily furnished by a thorough acquaintance with those materials which have already won their way into public appreciation and minister to that pride in honest fly-work, which, at the present period, is certainly one characteristic of the British Craftsman.

CHAPTER III.

SALMON FLIES: HOW TO "DRESS" THEM.

"Bad workmen find fault with their tools, but no workman can finish for use a good fly with bad materials."

ANON.

WORKING APPLIANCES AND PRELIMINARY REQUIREMENTS.

THE working appliances which I consider necessary are the following:—

1.—A SHARP PAIR OF SCISSORS WITH FINE UPWARD-CURVED POINTS, which may be obtained at Fisher's in the Strand. These are specially adapted by their shape to reach and cut close off at the hook certain waste ends of silk and feather, as also to cut fibre stumps at an angle so as to get a taper, as in forming the head of a fly; both operations are only awkwardly and inefficiently managed with straight-pointed scissors. I use the smallest kind which have plenty of finger room in their rings.

2.—SPRING PLIERS ("tweezers"), preferably of brass, and procurable, for a trifle, at any tackle-shop. These should be pliant. Care should be taken that, whilst the inward edges of the points are not sharp enough to sever a herl or the shaft of a delicate hackle, the points themselves meet accurately, not only at the extremities, but also along the whole length of the jaws. In other words, the jaws must neither overlap, nor bite at the extremities only. Those pliers are to be preferred, which, at the handle end, are formed into a ring for the finger.

3.—The stiletto, which has uses unsuggested by its simplicity, should be of the best-tempered steel, and without any sort of handle fitted to it. Besides being a treasure alike to the fly-dresser and the Fisherman, it can be used to pick up small feathers, etc., by placing its point under the object, on which the tip of the fore-finger is then pressed in conjunction. Some persons, however, use for this and similar purposes a pair of spring forceps, such as are commonly supplied with microscopes. A stiletto of admirable quality and shape may be bought for fourpence at Messrs. Wilcox & Gibbs, Sewing Machinists. The one I use in fishing is punctured at the end to hold a thin piece of elastic, and fits in an outside socket-pocket in my jacket.

4.—A box of Stevens' silicon and a small bottle of varnish, together with cobblers' wax will complete the list.

I never use varnish made of shellac and spirits of wine (which, however, can be improved by the addition of a small piece of "Venice turpentine," about half the size of a nut to a 2-oz. phial), seeing that Turnbull, of Edinburgh, has introduced a far better sort that dries as quickly, does not change its black tone in the water, and lasts considerably longer. For flies, not intended for immediate use, copal varnish should be used with the shellac. The two will not mix in any ordinary way. Dip the stiletto point into copal, and put the small drop adhering to it on the back of a saucer; then take a similar dip into the other, and mix the two drops quickly with the instrument, and apply to the fly-head immediately. A head thus treated never requires varnish again; but it takes about a week to get dry enough for use.

5.—Cobblers' wax must be fresh made. I form mine into small pills, and keep them in a stoppered bottle filled with water.

It should be specially noted by those who dress flies at night that the misleading influence of the yellow rays from an ordinary artificial flame may be counteracted, and, what is much more important, a full light concentrated upon the work, by the use of what is known as the "Engraver's Glass." Since writing this sentence, my friend, "Detached Badger," has contributed an article to the *Field* on dressing flies by artificial light. So full and explicit are the instructions given that I make the following quotations from them, with that gratitude which is due to an author to whom Anglers are indebted for much useful and trustworthy information.

"In the earliest attempts I used a gas lamp, but this was soon discarded in favour of a paraffin lamp, and this in turn gave way to a colza lamp, as giving a much softer light and far less heat. With either of these illuminants I used an ordinary engraver's bottle or globe, to direct the light on to the fly in the jaws of the vice. The engraver's globe was filled with a solution of sulphate of copper, with a small quantity of liquid ammonia, and the blue fluid, acting as an absorbent of some of the coloured rays, tempered the light so as to render it less trying than when taken through a colourless medium. Since then, as the outcome of numerous microscopial experiments directed to producing at moderate cost and without complicated apparatus, a light which is practically monochromatic, it was discovered that this result could be obtained by filtering the light of an ordinary lamp through a solution consisting of 160 grammes pure dry nitrate of copper, 14 grammes of chromic acid, and water added to make up to 250 c.c. This liquid is held in a flat bottle, of which the parallel sides are half-inch apart. This solution, reduced by the addition of water in proportion to the increased thickness of the medium in the engraver's globe, will be found preferable to the old solution of sulphate of copper and liquid ammonia. With this form of apparatus the illumination with diffused light directed on to the object was fairly well attained, and there was nothing in the way of the fingers. The system, however, had the grave fault of subjecting the eyes to too much glare. After trying various forms of shades worn over the eyes, all of which were more or less uncomfortable and inconvenient, I eventually made a large opaque brown pasteboard screen, with a round hole through it to admit only sufficient light to illuminate the object. This arrangement was moderately successful, but it had the great disadvantage of leaving the greater part of the working table in darkness, so that it was not easy to find the wax, feathers, scissors, pliers, &c., when required for use, and after a time the idea of dressing flies at night was temporarily abandoned.

"Later, however, when removing to another house, I fitted up a room in accordance with my own design, providing amongst other things, a convenient working-table, fixed in a bay window, facing nearly due west, so that, as far as daylight was concerned, there was practically all that could be desired. Having adopted electric lighting throughout the house, I had the wires carried to an ordinary concentric wall plug just above the level of the table, and resolved at leisure to try and work out the problem under these conditions.

"After exhaustive consultations on the subject, a good friend, an engineer by profession, with a first-rate knowledge of optics, designed a lamp, which having successfully stood the test of nearly a year's use, may, I think, be deemed fairly perfect for the purpose. It is entirely of bronze and consists of a heavy foot, on which is raised a hexagonal pillar, 18 inches in height. The fitting to hold the lamp and reflector slides up and down on the pillar, and is secured at the desired height by a thumbscrew. The carrier of the lamp and reflector is attached to this fitting by a knuckle joint, so that it can be inclined to the angle required for directing the light on the object. Another thumbscrew tightens and fixes this joint when the angle is once adjusted. The wire from the fitting of the wall plug is carried to the lamp in the ordinary way, and is of sufficient length to enable the stand to be moved on the table as required. The source of light is an ordinary eight-candle incandescent ground glass lamp, and for convenience of lighting or extinguishing without connecting to or disconnecting from the wall plug, has an independent switch fixed to the carrier. The reflector, also of bronze, with the interior or reflecting surface heavily plated and polished, has a true parabolic figure. The eight-candle lamp is placed in the carrier, so that as near as possible the source of light is at the focal point of the paraboloid. Scientifically, a light thus placed is reflected in parallel rays of equal intensity in the direction of the axis of the paraboloid, but this would only be possible if the source of light was a geometrical point, and any increase of the area of the light produces bundles of rays originating at various angles, and hence diverging and converging. This is mentioned to prevent confusion, as it is impossible for an apparatus of this description to be made so that all the rays are parallel, and the disc of light of equal intensity throughout.

"This arrangement carries out all the requirements laid down in the earlier portions of this article. The light is sufficient to illuminate, and yet modified by the ground glass of the bulb so as to be pleasant. By raising or lowering and inclining to the requisite angle, the light can be directed on to the object with the reflector at such a distance from the vice as to be quite out of the way. If all is properly adjusted, the light itself is invisible to the worker, and none of the rays are reflected into his eyes. The area of the table illuminated is also sufficient to enable him to find any materials or implements he may require for his work. The heat given off by electric light is much less than by any other illuminant known, and is certainly not enough to cause any serious inconvenience to the operator. Some readers may pertinently inquire what substitute can be suggested where the modern improvement of electric light is not available. The answer is that a paraffin or colza lamp, or an ordinary candle, can be fitted in a very similar manner, but the distance of the lamp from the vice must be accurately determined, and the angle at which the axis of the paraboloid should be inclined from the perpendicular calculated, and the reflector fixed accordingly. It would not do to fit the reflector on a knuckle joint, as when the inclination was varied the lamp or candle would not be perpendicular, and hence would not burn satisfactorily. If the light from the lamp or candle should be too intense, it could be modified by the interposition of ground or coloured glass, or a bottle containing the monochromatic fluid described above between the reflector and the object."

To resume our subject, the first essential preliminaries to the operations of fly-dressing are (1) Hands as clean and free from natural grease as possible, for the sake of the more delicate materials, and of the wax on the tying-silk, which any grease is apt to spoil or remove. (2) The thumb-nails and finger-nails fairly long and even, a hint the learner will soon appreciate. (3) The requirement by practice of the proper manner of holding the hook, and an expert familiarity with the four frequently-used operations that form the A B C of all manipulations in fly-dressing, namely—

"The Stop."
"The Catch."
"Making Off."
"Setting In."

In entering upon an explanation of these, it cannot be too strongly impressed upon the learner, that a correct manipulation is of the first importance; and that he should practise so thoroughly and precisely the minute directions here given as to the exact position of the fingers, etc., and the several ways of grasping and holding, that the modes may become habitual to him. That training over, he will find awkwardness and failure in dressing Salmon-flies to be virtually for him among the things of the past.

In taking the small amount of pains needed for the mastery of this system, it is encouraging to remind ourselves that we start not from the point where our fathers started, but where they left off. We may pluck the fruit of an accumulated experience, learning to adapt the best method known, in each particular detail. These details are, it is true, insisted upon with somewhat tedious particularity; but then let it not be forgotten that each detail is a dearly bought link in the chain of instruction. All these little improvements have probably cost, in the aggregate, months of thought, endless bird skins, and furs enough to stuff and cover Chancellors' Woolsacks for a century, to say nothing of friendly discussions and of controversies heated up to the full blaze of the *odium piscatorium*.

To the non-military eye the soldiers' little red drill-book does not disclose the generations of thought expended on its mechanical instructions, all so accurately calculated to answer the rigid (one might say mathematically rigid) demand of orderly movement. Nor in our present instruction on fly-dressing is the amount of previously expended ingenuity any more manifest at first sight. Experience, however, will show that here, too, in each mechanical direction a distinct purpose is kept in view; and the learner may set to work with the assurance that the chief excellences in a Salmon fly—strength, neatness, proportion, and working symmetry—can be combined only by a correct manipulation, an exact adjustment of parts, and a carefully calculated-distribution of material.

To wax Tying-Silk. Cut from an old glove an oval piece of kid, say two inches in diameter. Hold a pointed piece of cobblers' wax for a moment near the fire, and, when soft, "dab" it (not daub it) on the inner side of the kid, not quite in the middle. Now double the kid over quickly, and, with warm fingers, press the equal halves together. Partially open them again, and, if not laid on too quickly, the wax will be seen to cover a considerable part of the kid with a thin layer. The kid is to protect the fingers from mess, and the tying-silk from getting too much wax. In the operation itself only the edge of the layer of wax is exposed for use—the less, in reason, the better. To avoid breaking the silk, observe that "union is strength," so do not try to wax only one length at a time.

Take in your left hand the reel of "Pearsall's Gossamer Silk," which is much the best for your purpose. Break off any loose end, as the portion will have become weakened by the twist having in part gone out of it. Place the reel, that it may revolve, between the left forefinger and thumb, and hold it loosely. With the right hand take hold of the end close up to the reel, keep the right hand stationary, and draw from the reel, by moving away the left hand, about twenty-eight inches of the silk. Pass the withdrawn portion once round a small hook (or your stiletto stuck upright in your fly-table, if you please), and back over your left little finger, which now holds taut from the hook or stiletto, a pair of reins, as it were, each fourteen inches in length. You now want just as much more silk withdrawn; so with the right hand pulling and receding from the hook, the left hand barely sustaining between its fingers the reel, and advancing the while towards the hook, continue gently to withdraw the amount required by pulling the hands thus, alternately working them backwards and forwards. (The hook or stiletto must be smooth for the silk to have free play, as the looped end has round the little finger. No mischief follows this sawing motion of the hands when the silk is allowed to work loosely behind the hook.) Place, as before, the second portion round the hook, thus giving another pair of reins into the grasp of the left hand. Break off the silk close to the reel, but do not relax your left grip, or the ends will untwist. As the lengths lie close, side by side, first wax the part nearest to your fingers to prevent any further danger from untwisting, then wax the rest from the other end, and snip the lengths across at each end with the scissors.

Simple as the operation of waxing is, the pressure put on the pad, together with a light, quick, lifting motion to prevent adhesion fore and aft, cannot be assured until the novice has had a little practice. This is worth learning, if only to secure the strength of the silk. Besides, you will have four lengths ready for use.

HOW TO HOLD THE HOOK PROPERLY. Take in the left thumb and forefinger a hook, No. 1½ "Redditch" scale, which, as a convenient size, we may adopt for a standard throughout the course of instruction. The illustration of "THE STOP" will convey a fair idea of the general position of the fore-finger and thumb in grasping the hook. (The middle finger need only be advanced in making THE STOP; in merely grasping the hook, it will fall back naturally in reserve.) Attention, however, is called to the particular parts of the fore-finger and thumb, in immediate contact with which the hook is held fixed—viz., *the top of the ball of the thumb* against *the edge of the ball of the forefinger.*

This position secures a firm grip of the hook, and, at the same time, gives ready access to that intervention of the middle finger-tip (or, rather, *the edge* of that tip), which is called "putting on THE STOP."

HOW TO "SET IN" A LENGTH OF TYING-SILK.

Maintaining with the left hand the grasp of the hook, as shown in the picture of "THE STOP," lay one end of the silk between the ball of the fore-finger and thumb of the same hand. With the right forefinger and thumb take the tying-silk four inches from the shank, and proceed to make two or three open coils round the shank headwards. Now bind the open coils tailwards with two turns; when the first-named end of the silk will have been fixed, and may be set free to be cut off.

If the setting-in has to be done at the "head" end of the hook, it will be seen that a slight difference must be made in the method for convenience sake; the end of the silk, in that case, must be held between the left third and little fingers, which are to be extended towards the head end of the hook for the purpose.

Proficiency in this being attained, we may pass on to "The Stop." Set in a length of tying-silk, waxed, and take a few turns round the shank headwards. Still keeping the original grasp of the hook, and holding the tying-silk gently taut with right fore-finger and thumb, place the right, or near, edge of the ball of the left middle finger firmly against

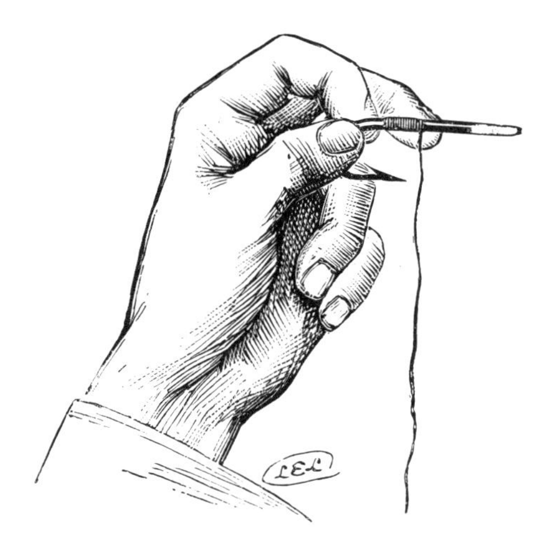

THE STOP.

the hook and silk at the place whence the latter, as held taut, issues forth from behind the shank. Let the silk go free from the right grasp, and you have "The Stop." This is a most useful expedient to prevent, temporarily, turns of silk, coils of tinsel, etc., from unwinding or loosening from the hook-shank, or even to set the right hand at liberty.

"THE CATCH" is another plan adopted at any time during the operation of fly-dressing, to set the right hand free for any purpose. It is made thus:—Supposing we have just put on "THE STOP"; resume the tying-silk in right fore-finger and thumb, keep it taut, and remove THE

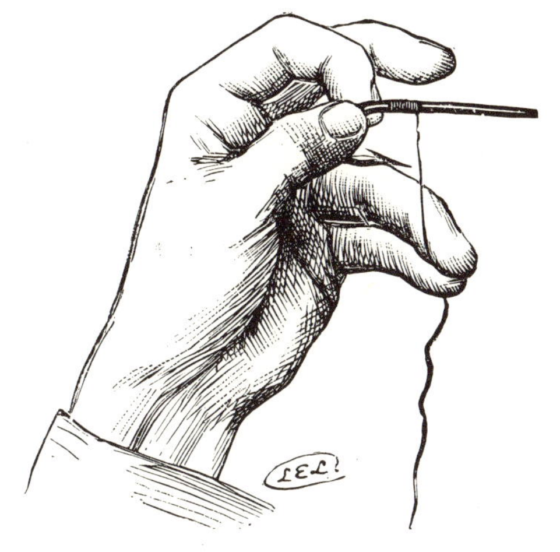

THE CATCH.

STOP finger of the left hand. Now pass the silk in between the ball of the left third and finger nail of the little finger and grip it with them, keeping taut all the time, so as not to allow the last-made coils to slacken, and you have "THE CATCH."

MAKING OFF the tying-silk (as shown in Operation II.) is a plan by which knots are dispensed with, and so any clumsiness is avoided. It is accomplished at any stage in the work by simply running a few temporary, hasty turns headward round the shank (more thickly together at the head), and then fixing the tying-silk (held taut) in the cleft between the end of the shank and the gut-loop.

TO TIE ON THE GUT-LOOP. After the "SETTING IN," the close turns of silk are begun at a sufficient distance from the extremity of the shank to leave room for the foundation of the wings. That is how this convenient little cleft comes into existence.

These four operations are the foundation of facility and certainty in manipulation, and a constant and patient practice of them will soon bring its own reward.

* * * *

With a piece of white card-board, say twelve inches by six inches, lying immediately in front of you on the table, to serve as a back-ground in aid of the eyesight, proceed to practise the following chief operations of fly-dressing; noting, in passing, that the back of your card-board may be utilised as a medium on which to record for ready reference, scales of hooks, lengths of gut for loops, and other measures of proportion. (These remarks, I need hardly say, are intended solely for beginners.)

INSTRUCTION FLY No. 1.

For instruction in general, and also specially to illustrate the making of a silk and fur body, and a "Built" wing.

OPERATION I.

Tying on the Gut-loop. The length of the proposed body being $1\frac{1}{16}$ inch, a suitable length of twisted gut, extra stout, for the loop will be $1\frac{3}{4}$ inches. Soak this length thoroughly in soft water (or for making a single fly, you may put the gut in your mouth for eight or ten minutes), and bend it so that one side shall be a little longer than the other. The *single* ends, also of the twisted gut, should vary in length, and their points pared. Cut the *inside* strands when binding down, in order that the foundation for the body may taper evenly and truly towards the tail.

Take waxed silk (doubled to about 16 inches), and make four or five open turns headwards, tight enough to cause the waxed silk to adhere to the hook-shank. Begin three parts of the way down the shank, and leave off at just $\frac{1}{8}$ inch from its extremity. In doing this it is best to hold the hook barb upwards.

These foundation-turns not only afford a hold to the gut, but also help to keep it from drawing when the fly is in use. After putting the tying-silk into "catch," take the gut-loop by its loop, and, holding it horizontally, flatten with the front teeth a considerable portion of the gut-ends. Apply these ends in their full length to the underside (now uppermost) of the shank, with a due allowance for the eye of the loop projecting clear of the shank end (the amount may be judged from the illustrations, but the smaller it is, in reason, the better), and holding hook and gut firmly (gripping the sides, not top and bottom), whip the gut on with regular, close turns of the silk tailwards, holding and working the silk at the distance just now mentioned. In "whipping," employ all the power you can without breaking the silk, and make use of the "CATCH" two or three times, in order, as the work proceeds, to be able with the right nails to press both sides of the gut into straightness with the hook shank. Be careful in starting the turns to leave a full $\frac{1}{8}$ inch of the shank end for the purpose explained. When the gut is covered with these turns, tie off with one half hitch, and cut off the silk. The point upon the shank to which the silk binding should come will be seen from the Analytical Diagram in Chapter II. The arrangement of the ends of the gut "twist" should always be made so as to secure this relative proportion in all sizes of hooks. In the size of hook we have selected for instruction, this point on the shank is about $\frac{1}{8}$ inch short of a straight line drawn through the hook-point, and cutting the shank at right angles.

Without delay, whilst the gut is still soft, *nip the loop*. Holding the hook now barb *downwards*, push the stiletto through the loop from underneath, far enough to form an eye of the required size; then with the *nails* of

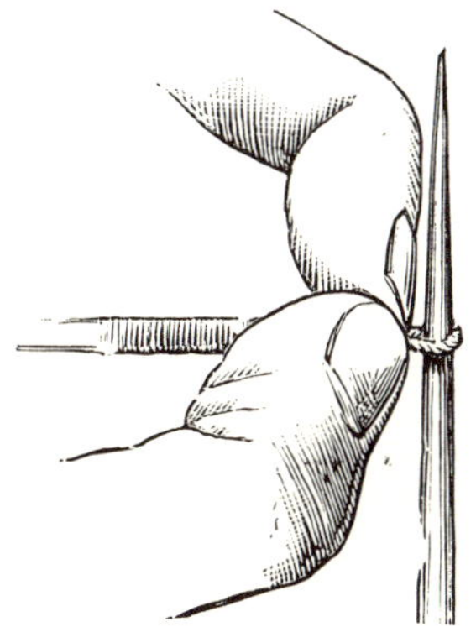

NIPPING THE LOOP.

the left hand "STOP" finger and thumb, *nip* the loop together at the neck. If the gut does not readily yield to the correct shape, the pressure should be maintained whilst the loop is moved to and fro by the stiletto within it.

The object here is that the loop sides shall lie parallel to each other in their entire lengths quite up to the point where, in the completed fly, they leave the shank, and expand immediately into the eye of the loop.

Of course, the $\frac{1}{8}$ inch next the eye is not fixed in place until the turns of tying-silk for the foundation of the wings cover and bind it—a later process. When the fly is in use, the "nipping" has the effect of helping to maintain the correct direction of strain upon the gut at the head, and so of preventing that general loosening and consequent loss of feather, caused by the part usually forked, working itself straight. This defect is present at the heads of un-nipped flies, and so the part of the gut-loop under the wings is left V shaped.

OPERATION II.

TYING ON THE TAG, TAIL, AND BUTT. It may be well to recall to mind here that the fly we now propose to tie is one intended solely as a convenient starting point for instruction, and the several operations involved in it will be described consecutively, up to its final completion. Afterwards, the modifications requisite for tying various types of flies will be sufficiently explained in their order.

Section I.—Select the following materials:—two inches of silver twist, three inches of floss silk, a Golden Pheasant topping an inch in length, and an Ostrich herl.

Section II.—Prepare the silver twist by stripping off from one end enough ot the silver wire to leave bare about $\frac{3}{16}$ of an inch of the silk core. This is done by pressing the silver twist at the proper point with the sharp edge of the left thumb nail down on the ball of the left fore-finger, and simultaneously uncoiling the wire with a tug of the right hand and snapping it off quickly. Cut off half the thickness of the core with the scissors, and then strip the other end of the silver twist, and manage it in the same way. The coils of the twist are now driven closer together, and brightened up by the aid of a small piece of chamois leather, on which a little Steven's silicon has been rubbed.

Either end of the core is held between the left fore-finger and thumb, whilst the chamois leather is gently drawn in a direction away from the point held and down over the silver twist, but not so far as to loosen the coils at the other end. These in their turn are tightened and brightened up by a like operation from their own end of the core.

Now take the hook, point *downwards*, and "set in" tying-silk at the place on the shank shown by the diagram, and cut off the waste end.

Apply the twist with the right fingers to the hook-shank by laying the trimmed core end along its upper side, and then hold it there in the left hand; the last coil of the silver coating (*i.e.*, the point where this core end issues from its silver casing) being located just a little to the left of the last turn of the newly "set in" tying-silk, so that after binding it

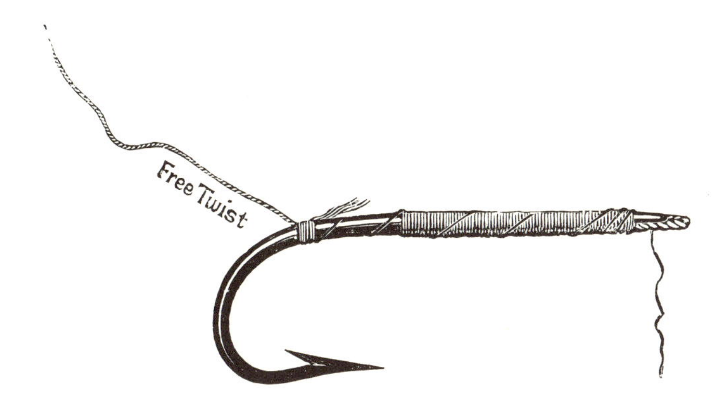

down the first coil of the twist, when wound on, rests exactly above the *middle* of the barb (see diagram). The first coil of the twist lies on the bare hook, and the next on the last of the few turns of the tying-silk which, having bound the core to the shank, form the foundation for the tag, as shown.

The last turn of silk, made close to the silver, will have pressed or carried the twist over to the far side, out of sight, as it were, thus helping us "to keep the best side to town."

Pass the tying-silk round the former work in wide open turns headwards, and "make off." Cut off the waste core at right.

The silver twist is now wound on *from* you, the first coil being laid on the naked hook. (No material should be tied down upon the bare shank, or rest upon it, except in this one instance.) It is desirable, however, before beginning this, to tug the twist gently upwards and against the last made turn of the tying-silk, in order to dispose the first coil of twist to start in a direct line. Proceed to place it upon the silk foundation in four close, neat coils headwards. (I use the "STOP" on the coils to prevent them unwinding, but recommend the beginner to use the tweezers throughout the process.) Release the tying-silk, bring it to the twist close to the last coil, give one turn over the twist, and put it in "CATCH"; pull twist so as to tighten the coils; and, after releasing from the "CATCH," give another turn, or perhaps two, over the twist and "make off," but do not allow the silk on its way to bind the waste of twist.

Compress the coils of silver twist together, evenly all round, with the nails of the thumb and middle finger of each hand, working each pair of nails against the other pair. Cut the twist, leaving about a quarter of an inch, from which the silver wire is now removed, and bind it down with say ten close turns of tying silk.

Section III.—Prepare the floss next, thus:—(Here I would remark that, in smoothing floss silk by stroking it between the right fore-finger and thumb, care should have been previously taken to make *sure* of the way to smooth it, whether to hold it at this end or that. That way is the right way, which, on trial—cut a small piece off to try—puts up in the stroking fewer loose ends of fibre than the other.) Take, then, to begin with, one end of it in the left fore-finger and thumb, stroke it with the right forefinger and thumb "the right way," and put it down as ready for use.

(The student will now understand that, in constructing both tags and bodies with floss silk, the "stroking" business is carried on during each and every turn made with it, so that, in putting it down as ready for use, he must remember which end is for tying on. I find it handy to take it from the left hand, with the right catching hold at the end which is held by the left, and with a sweeping motion towards the right, I drop the floss on to the piece of card-board. In taking it up to tie on the shank, I catch hold of it at the same place as before, and, with a yet quicker sweep to the left, bring it steadily back again, and let it drop into its place, the hook being held in readiness, of course, by the other hand.)

Lay the length of floss upon the left hand, which is now holding the hook, and draw it gently along to its position for tying on—*i.e.*, $\frac{1}{8}$ of an inch from the compressed coils of silver twist. Open the left fore-finger and thumb just enough to grip the part of the floss nearest them. Release the tying-silk, and bind the floss with three even, close turns headwards to form some more of the foundation for the silk part of the tag. Put tying-silk in "CATCH," and cut off wastes of floss and twist core. Make off.

Put the floss in "CATCH" between the left *middle and third* fingers, which are to be extended as far as possible, to secure a good length of floss between them and the hook. Untwist the length, catching hold of the extreme end while you momentarily release "CATCH," and with the fore-finger *over* it and thumb *under* it, stroke the length from the point of tie between the finger and thumb, passing each stroke through the "CATCH" to the very end of the floss until it is rendered straight and glossy. (By passing *through* the "CATCH" is meant opening the "CATCH" fingers and allowing the stroking fingers to pass through, and closing them again whilst the right hand fingers have hold of the end of the floss.)

On the last stroke given, whilst the fingers hold the end, pass the floss under the hook-shank, and put it in "CATCH" *there*. Now with the fore-finger, placed this time *under* the floss and the thumb *over* it, stroke and smooth once and wind the floss tailwards, reaching the twist in two turns. In completing the tag headwards over the former work use "CATCH" fingers at each turn in the manner just described. The reader should bear in mind that this is the way silk-bodied flies are constructed, so far as the actual winding of the floss is concerned; and that, virtually speaking, the taper of the whole body work begins from the twist in the tag.

Four, or perhaps five, coils of floss are enough, and, rightly laid on in increasing closeness, should form an even taper. Put "STOP" on floss, and fix with the tying-silk much in the same way as with the silver twist, save that after setting free the tying-silk, which has been *made off*, the floss end should be passed into "CATCH," the "CATCH" fingers being brought well under the shank, and the floss held taut by them. It is best that the first turn of tying-silk be firmly made, not at the very edge of the last floss coil, but a little in upon it. Continue binding with two more turns *tailwards*, and so form a level foundation for the tail. Make off, and cut off waste floss.

Section IV.—Prepare the topping by stripping off the dull, short, downy filaments at its root. Fix it in place by the following method, which will obviate all difficulty. (Of course, a topping which has been carefully kept and has retained its proper shape is more manageable than one which has been allowed to get warped or twisted.) Holding the hook as before—*i.e.*, by the bend—take the topping, curve upwards, by its bare quill between the right fore-finger and thumb, so that with them it may be laid in its place upon the top of the shank, and then held in the same left grasp. The feather will be in its place when the lowest point from which its fibres spring is laid coincident with the upper (or headward) end of the completed tag, so that when the topping has been bound on no fibres will be bound down, and no quill left uncovered tailwards. Now, the right hand grasping the root firmly together with the hook-shank, pass the left fore-finger and thumb with a coaxing, smoothing action down over the topping tailwards, gently pressing it down upon and conforming it to the bend of the hook; and, finally, hold it fixed in that down-curved position. Let go the right fingers from the quill, which will then spring up a little, but which, as the main part of the topping is held firm in the grasp, will not refuse to be easily and correctly bound down upon the foundation prepared for it. Bind it down. To do so, begin with a long diagonal turn of the tying-silk tailwards, then give an encircling turn close to the tag headwards, and also another. Put the silk in "CATCH" and let the topping go free to see whether it sits correctly. This scrutiny is only for the tyro—practice will soon bring instinctive certainty. Bind on two more turns headward. Make off.

Section V.—Proceed now to form the butt. Take the Ostrich herl, root to the left, flock downwards, and lay its point diagonally on the near side of the shank at the place where the tail is tied on; release tying-silk and unwind carefully two turns of the former work.

These turns were made to strengthen the work temporarily in its progress; and we remove them to lessen the bulk and obtain neatness—

a practice that should be observed wherever possible, consistently with proper strength.

Take, as was done in tying on the tail, a diagonal turn of the silk tailwards, and bind the herl on with five close turns headwards. Make off.

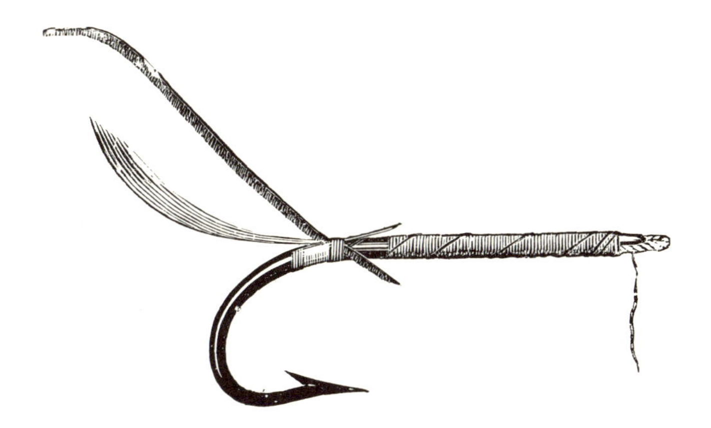

The stage now arrived at is illustrated in the diagram. The bare interval of hook shown between the binding of the gut-loop and that of the herl is purposely left in order to give room for exactness in adjustment of the various constituents at this point, and is filled up partly by tying in such position of the waste ends of tail and butt as may be required, and partly with the ends of the floss, tinsel, or other materials set in subsequently to form the body.

Wind on the herl, giving the first coil such a bias that its flock is turned tailward. The herl being easily damaged, it is best not to use the tweezers to begin with. Rather use the "STOP" at the first turn in the way specified in winding on the floss. Now adjust tweezers for making the final coils. The tweezers are kept from twirling round at the far side by steadying them with the "CATCH" fingers.

When the tying-silk is released up to last coil of the herl, bind the herl down with three turns headwards, and make off.

The waste ends have a further use, and are not to be cut off yet.

OPERATION III.

Forming the Body. Section I.—For a silk and fur body in equal proportions (see diagram p. 82), head half hackled, select these materials :—

Three inches narrow tinsel, oval ; three inches broader tinsel, flat ; seven inches floss ; some black Seal's fur ; a natural black hackle and a Gallina hackle.

Section II.—Prepare the oval tinsel in the same way as the twist for the tag, using the silicon, which preserves lustre besides producing it. Lay the tinsel in between the left fore-finger and thumb (which are now holding the hook), so that while the core-end lies along the far side of the shank, the termination of the silver coincides with the finishing roll of the herl of the butt. Release the tying-silk, unwind it so carefully as to leave only one turn fixing the herl, and bind this core-end with two or three turns headwards ; then put the silk in "catch." A *mere suspicion* of the core should now be visible between the first turn of tying-silk and the silver as a sort of flexible hinge in starting to lay down the ribs.

Now, with the stiletto-point evenly distribute round about the shank the waste ends of the tail, butt, and core of tinsel ; cut them to such a length, and so bind them that they may exactly fill up the before-mentioned interval of bare hook left for adjustment. Make off.

Section III.—Prepare the floss as for the tag. Release tying-silk, unwind two turns of it, and put it in "catch." Lay the proper end of the floss in the place of the unwound turns. Release tying-silk and, in making the two turns again, bind over floss. Make off. Now, with the right fore-finger and thumb take hold of the floss beyond the shank, and smoothing all twist out of it as before, pass it into left "catch." Put the right fingers under the shank, take hold of the floss, and begin winding diagonally tailwards; pass floss after each diagonal coil into left "catch," and stroke and wind alternately in increasingly wider coils up to the butt; then continue headwards, as already described for the tag, taking yet more care to stroke and smooth whilst winding on coils in decreasing closeness. These are not diagonal coils ; the silk is to be worked as nearly as possible straight over the shank.

In thus proceeding headwards, allow the coils to so decrease in closeness that a gradual taper is maintained by them. On covering the whole of the former layer of floss, put "STOP" on the last coil. Release tying-silk, gently unwind the two turns given to the floss at first, and tie down with two firm turns in the same manner as with the floss of the tag; put tying-silk in "CATCH" while you cut off waste floss; give one more turn with tying-silk, and make off.

To obtain a perfectly level, glossy taper, arrange with the right thumb nail any unevenesses, pressing headwards or tailwards, as may be requisite; and afterwards "iron" the floss—*i.e.*, press the whole of the section lightly between the fleshy balls of the fore-finger and thumb of the right hand, whilst you turn the hook round and round by the bend with those of the left.

Section IV.—To form the "ribs" for this, the lower section of the body, take the oval tinsel in the right fore-finger and thumb and wind it over the floss in three open coils (see illustration) at regular distances apart, using the "STOP" at each coil. Arriving at the end of the section and having attached tweezers to the end of tinsel, release the tying-silk and bind down the last coil of tinsel at the far side of the shank. Do this with two turns, and *not tight*, as, on now putting the silk into "catch,"

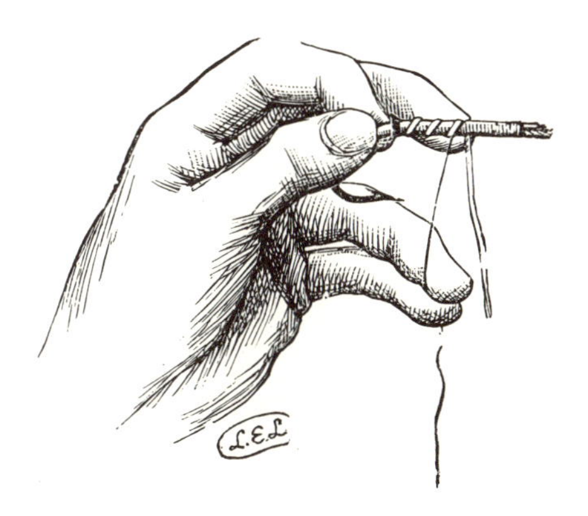

the tinsel coils are to be tightened by pulling the waste end towards you with right fore-finger and thumb, using the nail of the right middle finger against the hook as a fulcrum. Make off. See diagram given simply to show position of fingers; "CATCH" and "STOP" being used simultaneously. Now cut off waste end of tinsel, not too close, unwind or pull away the silver covering up to last turn of tying-silk, and bind down the core with three turns headward. Make off.

Section V.—The hackle is next prepared by being "*doubled*" in the following manner:—

Take the hackle by its point between the left fore-finger and thumb; remove all fluffy fibres from the root of the quill, and then cut the bare quill so as to leave about half an inch of it.

Put the end of the quill between the jaws of the tweezers (in a straight line, and not an angle with them), and let the pliers thus attached hang loosely in the palm of the right hand, so that the quill of the feather lies just within the edge of the ball of the right fore-finger, the bright side of the fibres being *downwards*. Now bend the quill of the hackle over the edge of the right fore-finger ball by sinking and turning from you the left

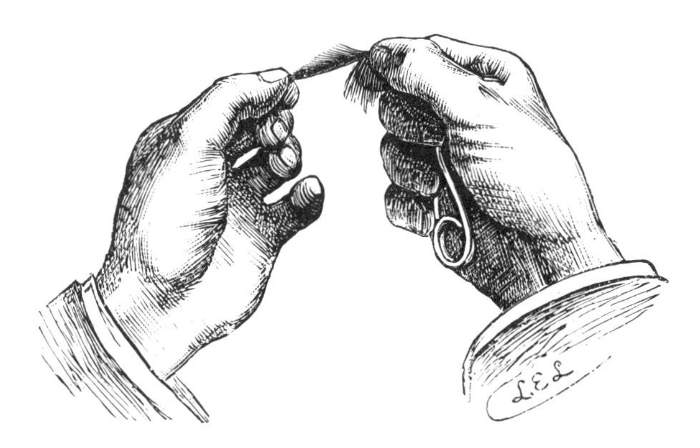

DOUBLING THE HACKLE.

hand, in which the point of the hackle is being held, to a slightly lower level than the right hand. Moisten the outer edge of the point of the right thumb, and, pressing this part of the thumb over the bent part of the quill of the hackle, and against the fore-finger underneath, urge, with one movement, the far side fibres towards and over to their near side companions, first, by a decided rub of the thumb *along* the quill towards you, and then by stroking both sides of fibres between the thumb and finger to their points slightly from you.

Repeat the rubbing and stroking in the manner described until the far side fibres are brought over towards the others and remain "doubled."

Continue this over the whole of the feather, taking half an inch at a time, thus finally bringing the fingers of the right hand close to those of the left. The tweezers are allowed to drop lower and lower in the right hand as the work proceeds. All the fibres will then be found to retain their position on the correct side of the quill. *Great care must be taken, during the rubbing, not to twist or warp the quill in any degree.* Moisten and coax to a peak the end of the hackle from the point of tying on, and pull the doubled fibres with the others from that point well back out of the way of future work.

Prepare also the flat tinsel, brightening it with silicon, and cutting it diagonally at one end to a long point.

Section VI.—First set in the point of the hackle (its root to the left and fibres downwards) on the far side of the shank, close up to the end of the section. For this, undo two turns of tying-silk, make a turn over the hackle-point to steady it, and hold all the work in position, putting the tying-silk taut in "CATCH." Now set in the pointed end of the tinsel close to the hackle (letting the main part rest over the left hand) also on the far side of the shank, in continuation of the former ribbing, with its cut edge tailwards. After unwinding tying-silk, put two or three turns of silk over it headwards, and make off.

Section VII.—Take a pinch of Seal's fur large enough when rolled on to well cover the lower half of the shank. Judgment in the exact amount of material will soon come with experience. Rub this pinch to and fro between the right fingers and thumb so as to form a cone. Let it drop on the table, choose the best tapered end, and proceed thus:—

Taking the hook firmly in the left hand, close up to the latest work, holding the hackle-fibres and tinsel well away, release the silk and put it in "CATCH." Lay the chosen end of the Seal's fur cone against the far side of the shank immediately on the tying-silk, and put "STOP" on both fur-end and tying-silk. Then, transferring tying-silk to the right fore-finger and thumb, but keeping it in the same line of direction in front of the fur, pass the left third and fourth fingers behind the fur and against it into such a position that, whilst the fur is being spun on the tying-silk, they shall serve for the combined fur and tying-silk, as the bridge of a violin does for its strings, and prevent the spin given from untwisting. Spin the fur on the tying-silk by laying it in its entire length along the latter, and holding both together fairly taut between the right fore-finger and thumb; and then, with that finger and thumb, twirl the fur upon the silk. Twirl from right to left, and at each completion of a full passage of the thumb across the fore-finger place the fur and silk in the left "CATCH," and thereupon stroke the tying-silk lightly down with the right fore-finger and thumb, in order to pass the twist in it on throughout its whole length beyond the "CATCH," and away; otherwise the spun part will liberate itself from the twist imposed on it, and silk and fur will part company again. The failure to do this accounts for much imperfect amateur "dubbing" in all kinds of flies. Remember to maintain the left "STOP" all the while; and observe that the violin bridge arrangement gives facility for a proper distribution of the fur.

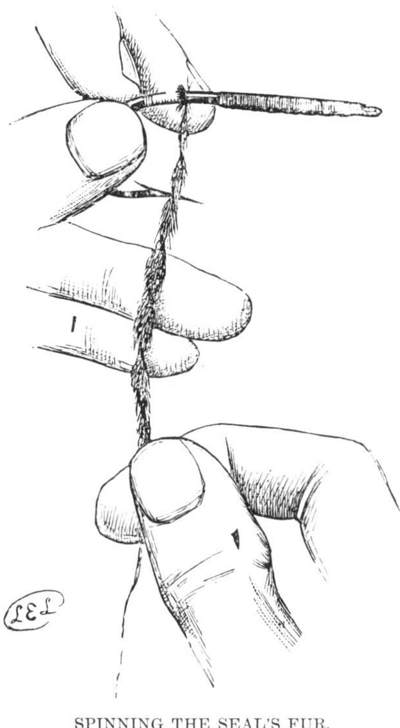
SPINNING THE SEAL'S FUR.

The fur being well spun on the silk, wind it round the shank in close coils headward, but not so far as to encroach upon the space intended for the wings. On arriving at that point put silk in "CATCH," strip all superfluous fur off the end of it; and with the right fore-finger and thumb

Plate 2

Thunder & Lightning

The Harlequin

The Lion

John Ferguson

The Baron

The Silver Doctor

press tailward, and away from the head-end of the fly, all the bristling ends of Seal's fur; move up the left fore-finger and thumb to hold these ends neatly down, and tie two turns of silk, tailwards, over the extreme end of the fur. Make off.

All the lumps in the fur are now dispersed, and the taper-shape of the body assisted by inserting the stiletto-point lightly into the fur at the head-end, and teasing the fur, by a kind of combing action, tailwards and outwards. In doing this, hold the stiletto almost but not quite parallel to the hook-shank.

Section VIII.—Make three open equi-distant ribs with the flat tinsel, use "STOP" on last coil, as before, and tie down with two turns headwards. Tighten the tinsel by pulling, as in the case of oval tinsel, give another turn of silk, and make off.

Cut off the waste tinsel at an angle, and turn the tiny point back over the tie, for security, *under the hook*.

Section IX.—Next, keeping the hackle on its side edge and the fibres downwards, wind it tightly as close as possible to the tinsel ribbing on the *tail* side, at each coil letting go with the right and using "STOP" with the left. Use the tweezers only after the first coil of hackle. After sufficient coils are made, use "STOP," let tweezers hang, insert the point of the stiletto, and strip the superfluous hackle fibres off. Then, with tweezers on, tie the shaft under the shank with, say, two turns; pull the stump of it, and give two more turns to fix the hackle firmly. Make off.

Press all the fibres so as to compel them to incline towards the tail. It is safer *not* to cut off the hackle waste yet.

Double the "Gallina" hackle for the throat.

Section X.—At this stage we shall probably have exhausted our length of tying-silk, and must "set in" a new one, doing so with two turns, close up to the hackle, before putting it in "CATCH." After cutting off the waste end of new silk, tie in the point of the Gallina, or throat hackle, on the near side of the hook, with three turns of silk, holding the doubled fibres neatly in left grip (which also holds the hook), and then put the silk in "CATCH." Release from *make off* the end of *old* tying-silk and cut it off, together with the waste of both hackles (but not too short). Make off.

Section XI.—Now attach tweezers, and make two or three close coils of the Gallina hackle. Let tweezers hang. Press with the finger-nails the coils close up together, release silk and fasten root with two turns of it. Catch silk again; pull hackle tight, cautiously, and bind the stump end of hackle-quill alongside the other under the shank with six even, close turns, thus fixing it out of the way of the wings, and making a little more than half of the foundation for them. Make off. At this particular

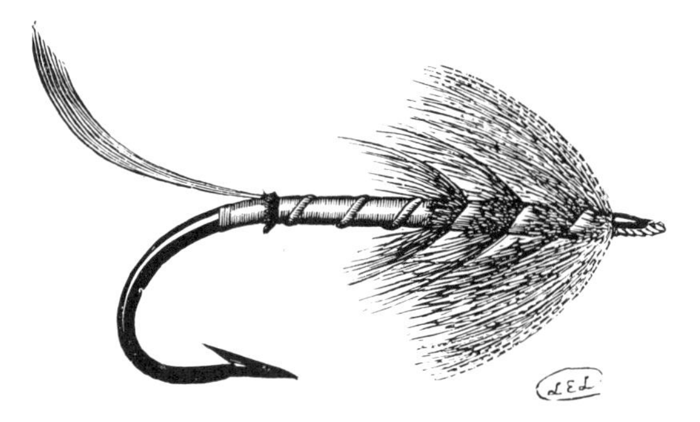

part of the fly the very utmost neatness is essential to the final correct set of the wings, and the smallest unevenness in the foundation work for them will defeat all subsequent attempts to compact and fix a wing which shall preserve its natural and proper shape.

I say "*preserve*," because it is possible, by a certain amount of dexterous manipulation to get the feathers of the wing to sit temporarily in position; but on the wing being handled, or put to the test of use, it soon drops its company manners and betrays its real character. Its strands or strips refuse to curve together, part company, and stick out in all directions, like a badly-used birchbroom. With such a fly, there is no guarantee that the wing is not top-sided, or otherwise so wanting in balance of material or balance of action, that in the water it is productive of wobbling, or some other irregularity of conduct not conducive to good sport.

OPERATION IV.

(*Built wings, with under-wing.*)

Putting on the Wings.—We adopt a type of wing here, not as being the easiest to learn to tie—like the mixed wings—but as most instructive to the learner.

Section I. Take right and left strips of, say white-tipped Turkey (as used in "Jock Scott") about eight strands broad of the feather, as described for that fly. Lay these together, dull sides inwards, that is to say, "back to back."

The turns of silk which tie the throat hackle should have occupied about half the space intended as foundation for the wings; the other half, for the time being, is bare.

With the right fore-finger and thumb take the strips (which should lie close alongside each other, and accurately coincide along their edges and at their points) and coax them with the left fore-finger and thumb into proper curve. Hold their stumps in the right hand during the process, so as to allow the upper strands to be increased in length if necessary. (By this means only can these wing-feathers be so shaped as to form a fairly regular line at their extremities, as shown in the Analytical Diagram, Chapter II.) Then, holding the hook in the left fore-finger and thumb by its bend, place the arranged strips in their proper position upon the foundation intended for them, with their lower points measured to extend just beyond the extremity of the "tag." The right fore-finger and thumb (which are then to grasp the strips *from above*) will seize, in the same grasp with them, the head-end of the hook-shank also, and hold them upon it. The left fore-finger and thumb grasp loosely (*also from above* and right up to the hackle tie) both the strips and the body of the fly. Then, working from *the wrist*, draw the left fore-finger and thumb, with a curving movement over the wing, so as to conform it to the bend of the hook. Having done this, hold the strips close down upon the top of the body-work in the left grip.

If these strips of feather in hand are at all intractable, I guide them (after they are grasped and the left fore-finger and thumb are well extended for tying down, the left hand being so level as to permit a tumbler resting on it) down to envelope the hook bend, each on its own side of the shank. This should not crumple them; and when liberated they should easily assume their proper position before being finally fixed.

Release the right hand from its grip, and proceed to tie down the wing thus:—A turn of silk is passed lightly over the wing, close to the hackle, and put into CATCH. In this case, the CATCH fingers are brought up somewhat near to the shank beforehand so as to allow room for them to pull.

Then, with these CATCH fingers draw the silk gently taut downwards, while the right fore-finger and thumb grasp the strips at the point of tie, so that the wings shall not be bent over to one side or the other, but sit regularly on edge when completed. This regularity is secured on the one hand by the grasping, and on the other, by keeping the other end of the strips strictly in position by a well-sustained pressure of the left fore-finger and thumb, while the tying-silk is pulled taut. CATCH silk.

Maintain the left pressure, and before putting further turns of silk headwards, lift up the waste ends *on to the top of the hook*. This lifting serves a double purpose. In the first place, it so affects the strips that they " sit down " close along the body-work, leaving little space between them and the butt; and secondly, it helps to keep them in the desired position when the fly is finished. The waste ends are taken in one grasp, and somewhat forcibly made to rest *on* the shank, instead of posing by the side of it. Give further turns; make off, and inspect work.

The under-wings should now be easily stroked with the right fingers into their correct position (as shown in the Analytical fly), unbroken in fibre, and each presenting a similar appearance, especially at the point of tying on. Were it not for the *lifting*, the strips would " sit up " much above the body work, and so be almost obscured by the materials worked on afterwards. But it is not expected that the student will be pleased or satisfied with his effort at the onset. Success in this detail cannot be reached without practice, and the endeavour to attain it. If, however, he chooses, he can resort to the far more simple method of fixing mixed wings, which I will explain presently. By such method he can master Turkey strips in an hour; and Mallard strips, or even those of Teal, in a day.

It will assist the learner at this point to remind him that the single strands of wing-feathers are *not round*, but more or less knife shaped, and that all strips or strands must be so tied to the hook, when tied on either side, that the knife edges shall incline *upwards*.

To recognize this fact means getting at the root of the problem of correct winging. By taking a good big strand of feather, one, for example, from the tail of the blue Macaw, the knife shape is distinctly visible. Observe narrowly the edge of the strand, and then, for practice, tie it on to the side of a hook shank with a couple of turns of silk. If tied sharp edge *down*, the strand will not curve properly in the water, however well it may appear to do so out of it. Tied sharp edge *up*, and the curve can be made at the desired angle by stroking with the right hand, not too late, in fixing, and remain unalterably so. I would add, that in taking off strips of feather from the quill itself, the point of the stiletto can be used for dividing the portion wanted, which is afterwards grasped by the right fore-finger and thumb, and stripped off rapidly by those fingers, whilst the left hand holds the upper part of the feather. This, in my opinion, is the best plan for a beginner; and, with such elaborate directions, practice should ensure expertness in the operation of fixing under-wings, provided always that the grip of the left be correctly made and firmly sustained, until the strips have been regulated as aforesaid, and tied down. By "correct" is meant that the tips of the fore-finger and thumb first make their grip of the under-wings *from above*, at that part of the body from which the fibres of the throat-hackle spring; the fingers, still gripping, then proceed to draw all the fibres a little back out of the way of the work, and do not become relaxed in their hold.

Section II.—The inspection being over, and foregoing hints digested, pass the silk from Make off into "CATCH"; and with point of scissors laid level with the direction of the shank (the point of the scissors turn up, remember, at an angle of about 30°). If straight-pointed scissors be used, they must be laid at an angle of about 30° as best they can; cut away the waste fibres, so forming a taper headward, and make off again.

Section III.—Next take from, say, a Bustard feather, right and left strips, each of about five strands in breadth, and similar strips from right and left Mallard feathers. Marry these two sorts, right with right, and left with left, and lay them on the table.

By "marrying," is meant, so joining two or more strips of feather to each other by their adjacent edges as to form one strip, equivalent in size to the several breadths added together. In the present instance, take the right strip of Bustard and of Mallard (strongly inclined to marriage are these), and place them alongside each other (the Bustard below) that the points of the upper strip extend a little. Hold them, so applied together, at the points by the left fore-finger and thumb; and, with the right fore-finger and thumb, gently press and hold the roots together (which may not be the same in length), and let the points free. To form the union, stroke and coax with the left fore-finger and thumb the two strips, so held, *from* the roots along their whole length, when it will be soon found that their edges cohere naturally and firmly by the interlocking of the tiny, fluffy filaments at those edges.

Put silk in CATCH. Take in the right fore-finger and thumb the married strips intended for the far side wing, and lay them, bright side out, with their root ends against the shank at the tying point, and at such an angle to the shank that, not only the lower edges of the married strips may conform themselves to the upper curve of the under-wing, but also that the tips shall extend in gradation beyond its extreme point.

The shape of wing desired is illustrated in the Analytical-fly, Chapter II.

Section IV.—At this stage we arrive at what is undeniably the *crux* of fly dressing; the above-described operation, however, being mastered, the student will easily tackle any kind of wing. He will give the wing that compactness, that graceful curve, and will exhibit in its destined place each constituent fibre or strip of feather that is so pleasing to the veteran Fisher's eye and so fatal to the fish.

The correct curve is obtained by laying, or offering, the wing-strips at their destined angle, *at first only temporarily*, for the purpose of ensuring their proper length by measurement. Then, without disturbing their natural coherence in the least degree, the married strips are gently brought up into a nearly erect position—*i.e.*, at nearly right angles to the shank. Hold them so to the shank with the right fore-finger and thumb, which grip both strips and hook-shank; seize with left fore-finger and thumb the main part of the strips, and, by a curving stroke, press them down tailwards, and hold them, with the underwing, *well down nearly upon the hook*. This position is such that a slight hump, like a cat's arched back, is created in the strips, close to the grip of the right fore-finger and thumb. Gradually relax the right grip, and at the same time apply the left STOP, to preserve the "hump." Release the silk, and tie on these strips. Easily said, no doubt, but not quite so easily done, unless one knows how. Thus then :—

Using the STOP to keep the fibres in their regular, natural order, and not lapping over each other, pass the silk round them, *but not as if you were running cord round a parcel.* The silk must be passed round *loosely*, the STOP finger must then press down *from above* against it, and be kept firm whilst the silk is drawn fairly taut. Partially remove the STOP finger while you place silk again over to far side, give another turn, tighter still, whilst the STOP finger presses as before. Make off. Be very careful to kéep all fibres in position.

Section V.—This done, move left fore-finger and thumb up close to the tying point, and hold that part together with the work behind it in a firm grip ; release silk and put it in CATCH, and with right fore-finger and thumb lift up the waste ends of the strips of wing upon the top of the shank. If they are too short to catch hold, push the waste ends up with point of stiletto, which should be held in a vertical position.

The wing-strips should, hereupon, present an orderly appearance, both in their "marrying" and in their springing neatly and well together from the same point, like a half-shut fan.

They will not yet, however, sit down close upon the under-wing; that union will be effected by subsequent work.

Section VI.—The near wing-strips are similarly laid on and treated. In their case, however, a different principle is adopted. The very binding and pressure of STOP finger of the far side strips compels the sharp edges to assume their correct position, whilst on the near side of the wing, the tying-silk has an opposite effect. It is, therefore, necessary after placing the strips in position (the silk being in CATCH) to make the left thumb serve the same purpose as the STOP finger in the former instance—that is to say, the thumb presses the part of the strips that is to be tied down *from above.* Without relaxing the pressure so given, the thumb is then slightly drawn back out of the way temporarily, in order that the tying-silk may be placed over, and the work continued. Some dressers prefer to tie down the near wing by hitching the silk under the point of the hook-shank, and then winding it towards them; but the plan is not one to be recommended in this book. Before making off, do not forget to lift up the waste ends, as in the former instance; and do not be discouraged if the wings are not yet accurately in their final position. To put the finishing touches on, much is done by further manipulation. After lifting up the ends, transfer silk to CATCH, give another turn of it, then cut roots taperingly, and make off.

Section VII.—Select further materials for each wing—say, strips, three strands broad, of Swan dyed red, of ditto blue, of ditto yellow; and two broader strips of Teal. Marry them all together, Teal lowest, for the separate wings, as before. By the grips of right and left fore-fingers and thumbs (already described) reproduce the "hump," lay into place the new instalments of wing, previously measured as to length, and tie down as previously directed, catching, lifting up, and making off. Select head herl.

Section VIII.—Prepare a topping of suitable length by stripping it as before of any dull, short, downy fibres at the base, and making a furrow transversely in its shaft to receive the tying-silk. To make the furrow, lay the shaft along over the ball of the right thumb, the main curve of the feather projecting out beyond and in a perpendicular plane, the point turning downwards and neither to right nor to left. With nail of right middle finger indent gently at the required spot, keeping your eye all the while fixed on the feather to see that it does not turn sideways out of the straight plane, which, however, the direction of the pressure might regulate.

Now touch thinly with varnish the top of the head of the fly where the topping is to lie.

Release silk and put it in CATCH.

Section IX.—Take the topping in right fore-finger and thumb, by its root, and lay it in position. Then with the left fore-finger and thumb seize the main part of the feather together with the whole wing close down to the work. Pass the silk once over it, and into CATCH. If not already in a straight line with the shank, and quite on the top of it, the root of the topping should now be put into that position. Bind on with six tight turns loopwards. Put silk in CATCH. Cut off all wastes. Then, with the stiletto point, work a little varnish thoroughly in among the stump ends and round them; tie loopwards, almost to the end of the shank, and then about three more turns, backwards towards the tail, and put silk in CATCH.

Section X.—Next, with its root end to right, tie in on near side the point of the head-herl, *with its flocky edge downwards.* To do this, hold the point of the herl by the left thumb, which raise slightly from its grip of the hook to receive it—and, allowing half an inch of herl for waste, closely wind the silk tailwards up to the wings. CATCH the silk once more. Ascertain, by gentle pull over and turn over, if necessary, whether the herl will lie rightly, that is, *flock loopwards* ; attach tweezers and wind four coils of herl tailwards, reaching close up to the wing. Let tweezers hang. Transferring silk from CATCH into right fore-finger and thumb, extend the three unengaged left fingers straight out from you and pass the silk taut under the hook (as if unwinding) into CATCH of left middle and third fingers so extended. Varnish the taut silk for about half an inch, beginning from the fly, outwards; loop the unvarnished part immediately beyond the part varnished, and pass the loop, when made to form a half-hitch, over the whole head, so that it may come to rest between the wings and the herl head. Hold it there with STOP finger, and pull taut with right fore-finger and thumb. This will form a single varnished knot, and will be perfectly secure (as well as neat) when the varnish is quite dry.

Section XI.—In extended CATCH-grip seize tweezers and waste of silk, now both hanging down ; turn the left hand over towards you, and,

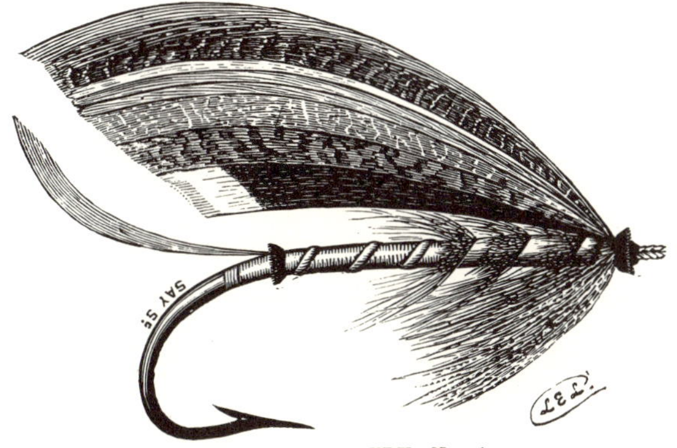

INSTRUCTION FLY No. 1

with the point of the scissors, cut the waste of herl and tying-silk neatly off, and then the waste point of herl.

Finally, trim the fur and hackles with the stiletto-point, laying the fly against the balls of the STOP and the adjacent fingers whilst combing the various hackle-fibres and inclining them tailwards. The different portion of the wing will readily conform themselves to their respective positions by a little coaxing and stroking between the right finger and thumb.

INSTRUCTION FLY No. II.

(Silver Doctor variation.)

TO ILLUSTRATE MAKING THE BEST SORT OF METAL BODY AND THE MIXED WING. Materials :—hook, twist, and floss (dark yellow) as in Fly No. 1. A topping :—1½ inches scarlet Berlin wool ; 8 inches broadish silver tinsel ; 3½ inches oval silver tinsel ; 8 inches white floss ; Blue hackle, and Gallina hackle. Strips (⅛ inch broad) from right and left of Peacock-wing, Bustard, Golden Pheasant tail, light mottled Turkey, black Turkey white tipped. Amherst Pheasant tail, Gallina, three strands of right and of left Swan dyed red, yellow, and blue. A topping for the wings.

Proceed with loop, tag, and tail as in No. 1 Fly. Next prepare scarlet wool for butt. Take a small length of Berlin wool and shred it. This is easily done. Hold at one end the piece in the left hand ; and, with the thumb-nail of the right hand, press the point of the other end on the ball of the right fore-finger and snip away shreds. Continue this, and when sufficient stock is collected, put it all together, lengthwise, and gently roll it between the fingers, so as to form a cone. Spin the cone on to the tying-silk after the fashion of spinning on Seal's fur, but ensure more smoothness by giving extra spins. The cone for butt or head is one inch and a quarter in length, and is tapered at each end to a very fine point. Form the butt with close consecutive coils headwards. Make off.

The butt will assume at once a level, even form, more oval in section than round, but a little manipulation is yet required. Press it towards tag with nails of right thumb and middle finger, giving support with the corresponding nails of the left hand in front of the coils.

Bevel one end of the flat broad tinsel by cutting it with the scissors at an angle, a good ¼ of an inch in length. Do not forget the silicon. Prepare oval tinsel as before.

Now bind down stump of topping, so that the whole space left bare between the butt and binding of gut-loop is nearly levelled up. Put tying-silk in CATCH. Lay the oval tinsel on the far side of shank, take tying-silk, and bind the core of tinsel with two turns.

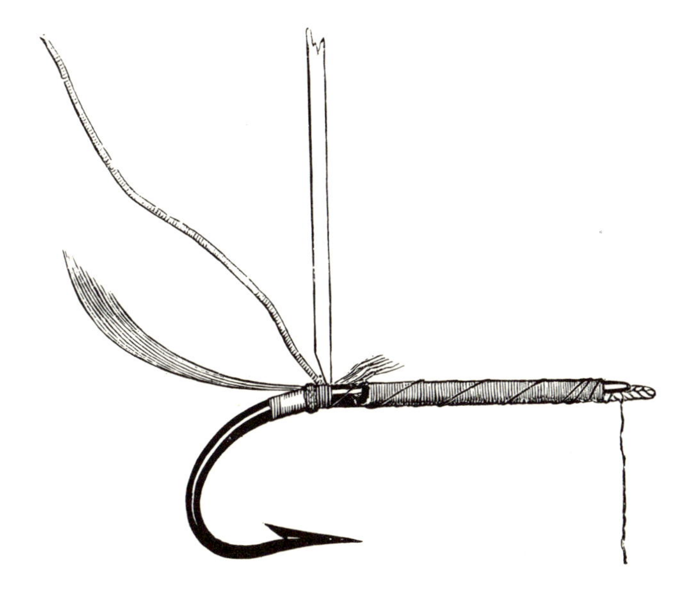

(Note that the third or next turn of tying-silk constitutes the first turn which binds the broad tinsel.) Remember that a mere suspicion of the core should now be visible between the turns of tying-silk and the silver. Put silk in CATCH. Lay on broad tinsel next the oval, with the bevel facing tailwards. With two turns tie it, but not tightly, at about one-quarter way up the bevel; raise the tinsel into an upright position and pull the turns taut. The subsequent turns bind down waste and core upon former foundation. Tie them down. With the final two turns of this binding, tie in on the near side the white floss, which is employed only in first-class work to secure absolute neatness of body tinsel. It is tied at that part of the floss so as to leave two-thirds of the length tailwards, one-third headwards. Make off. Wind headwards the right portion of floss towards you, placing the coils gradually closer together to form the taper. On arriving at the head pass two turns of tying-silk round the floss just *upon* the end of the gut binding. Put silk in CATCH; cut off floss waste; make off.

With the point of a needle gently tease the floss coils, and then by the process of "ironing" them (as explained) the foundation, so far, should be smooth and fairly tapered.

Wind on left portion of floss from you, tailwards and back over all, headwards. At each coil put floss in CATCH and smooth it. As you proceed with the coils watch the progress of the taper. In finishing at the head, place the floss in CATCH, undo the former two turns of tying-silk, and tie the completed foundation down *in their place*. Make off.

(Some Amateurs fasten the floss at the head end of the hook and coil it, in one length, first tailwards and then headwards—a method I recommend only for silk-bodied flies after weeks of practice.)

Wind on flat tinsel in *close* coils; these are not diagonal coils, the tinsel is worked as nearly as possible straight over the shank. In coiling it you will observe that the point of tie on the bevel was so cut or bevelled that the edge of the first coil shall lie close alongside the butt. On completing this first coil put tinsel in CATCH, and flatten with right middle finger nail the part where it first bends over, the left thumb being placed under shank in support. Continue these coils, which must not overlap, but lie *close* alongside each other, so that in the end they resemble the desired appearance of a piece of piping.

Put STOP on last coil while you apply tweezers, and pass two turns of tying-silk over it, not too tightly. Examine latest coils; press them together tailwards with the finger nails, pull last coil taut; tighten tying-silk and put it in CATCH.

The tinsel is now partially secured under the shank.

Bend last coil of tinsel back, and press it close down *upon* the two turns of tying-silk which hold it fixed. Flatten the bend with the finger nail by turning the back of left hand towards you to facilitate matters. It is obvious that this "bending back" gives extra holding power and makes the work secure. When the first few of the next turns of tying-silk (tailwards) have passed half way over the part bent back, put silk in CATCH, cut off the waste tinsel close there, and after binding down with two more turns tailwards, the foundation for the head-hackles will have been thus formed. Make off.

Now proceed with the ribs, and do not fail to give this tinsel a final pull before completely fixing it.

Next prepare and put on the two hackles, by the method as laid down in No 1, Sections 4, 5, 10, and 11. Mark here that, in this instance, these two hackles are intended for the throat, and that, in consequence, a trifle more room must be allowed as bedding for their coils, than in those cases where one of them is used for a body-hackle. When these are fixed on by the directions previously explained, put the fly down and prepare the wings.

At this stage I would remark that the wings selected for this type of fly I call "Mixed Wings." As the pioneer of this system, perhaps I may

say without egotism that, amidst the many changes which have occurred of late years, not only in the formation, but in the method of making certain flies, "mixed wings," with the exception of "Grubs," have met with the greatest share of approval and success. I personally worked out this original style of winging, and made it generally known among my immediate friends on finding how well it answered in actual use. Many years afterwards, in 1883 or 1884, I described the method of forming these wings in the *Fishing Gazette*, and it is gratifying to note that mixed wings are advocated by the authors of recent treatises on the subject. But the way of formation was considerably improved by me in 1888, and the method of fixing has since been entirely converted. Not only was the dresser formerly limited to the size of the hook, but, in the absence of long practical experience, was heavily handicapped by the method of mounting as then practised. I am, however, glad to say that I have satisfactorily overcome these disadvantages, and have, in fact, reduced the whole business well within the management of *a beginner at fly work.* Nor is this all; for I have had a few years to give the latter system a right and proper test, and have no hesitation in endeavouring now to explain it.

Mixed wings are now formed by mixing together fibres of different lengths of feathers.

Select first, say, four fibres from the shorter and finer feathers, such as Teal, Ibis, Gallina, tippet, powdered blue Macaw, and Summer Duck (all of them if you please) for part of one wing, and corresponding feathers for part of the other wing. Place them in consecutive working order on the right and left side of your table, and proceed to make up three bundles of *single* strands from one of these two sets at a time. These bundles will eventually form what is now termed the " skin " of the wings on their respective sides—fibres taken from the left side of the quill or shaft for the far wing, and from the right side of the quill for the near one. It is not necessary for these fibres to be of equal length in the made up bundles.

Take, for example, a single fibre from each of the three feathers in rotation (using, say, the left set first), and place them one by one upon the ball of the left fore-finger alongside each other, holding them all curving down, and gently pressing them with the thumb, the point of which is partially raised each time, for the purpose of putting others there.

Having taken, say, your half dozen strands (two of each feather), and having put them in this way, carefully place the thumb and fore-finger of the right hand *across* the roots to hold them while the left finger and thumb, pressing on the fibres, are drawn thence out, towards, and beyond the points. This will induce the sides of the fibres to adhere to one another, and so form a " skin " in one apparent strip. Two more of these strips or slips, so made up, and of the same materials, will constitute the whole of one skin.

In placing and joining the three side by side extend the middle strip beyond the lower and the upper strip beyond the middle one. When they are all together, a little manipulation of the hands and fingers will regulate the "step-like" outline of their points. Make up the right set in a similar fashion.

Select next, feathers, say, from Peacock wing, Golden Pheasant tail, Turkey, Bustard and Swan dyed red, yellow, and blue. Arrange their order and continue the work as before. After manipulating their points so that they shall gradually increase in length towards the top part of the wing, put each of these two new made-up sets on the inner side of the two skins, taking care that, in so doing, their points extend beyond the others to the length of wing desired.

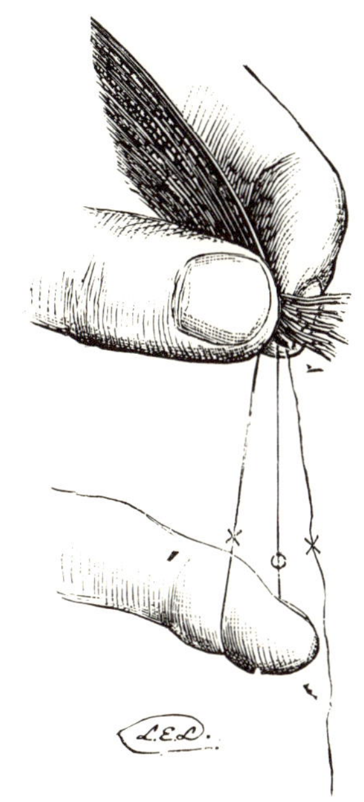

NEW METHOD OF FIXING MIXED WINGS.

The right and left wing, so composed, that is to say, enveloping the "two new made-up sets," are now put together (back to back) and tied on the hook by the following method, which, in theory, is just as commendable, as in practice the result is, or should be, inevitable, and in fishing effectual.

Having touched with varnish the coils of tying-silk forming the foundation, seize the whole wing by the roots with the right hand, and measure the proper length of the wings by offering them to the hook. Now hold the wings and the hook in the left hand, the fingers being straight with the shank. The fingers and hook-shank being now in a horizontal position (see diagram), release tying-silk and pass it first round the left little finger point from O towards you to X, then up, under the left thumb, over the wings and under fore-finger grip. Now pull X—X *together* until the wings are gently and symmetrically brought straight down upon the hook and into place, *maintaining the grip of the left hand upon them throughout.* Remove little finger from its engagement, but not the left grip, and pull the slack over and taut, catching hold of the end of the tying-silk for the purpose. Bind with three more turns in the *usual* way, headwards, using STOP. Make off.

In binding down such wings as these by the ordinary method, the unpractised artist sees a strong tendency, throughout the early process, for them to tilt over the far side. This always creates difficulties for him; whereas, by pulling X and X together, with due care, all tilting is obviated, and the wings are drawn evenly down into their permanent position on to the *top* of the shank. The first turn of the tying-silk should rest *close* against the throat-hackle and go straight up, over the wings. It must not pass beyond that turn (tailwards) in subsequent fixing. In making the "three more turns," put silk in CATCH after every one, in order to press back the roots of the fibres over towards you with the nail of the right middle finger, that they shall finally rest exactly upon the top of the shank. Make off.

INSTRUCTION FLY No. 2.

At this stage, the wings, although fairly firm, will not decline to yield to the pressure given in "humping"—our next procedure.

"Humping" is a scheme by which a superb shape of wing is secured —a good curve given to the upper fibres, whilst the lower ones run almost parallel with the shank of the hook and close to it. The "hump" is produced by holding the wings with a good grip of the fore-fingers and thumbs—those of the left hand gripping just on the head side of the middle part of the feathers; those of the right close to their tying point. The wrists, at first elevated to the top of the dotted curve in the diagram, are now slowly depressed, and the fore-fingers and thumbs of the respective hands, at first touching each other at the side edges of their nails, draw wider and wider from each other, *as if hinged at their extreme points.*

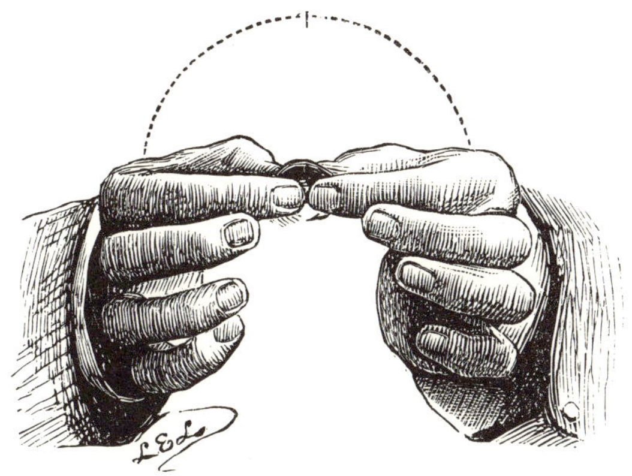

HUMPING THE WINGS.

The peculiar pressure necessary is given harder at the top of the wings with the right hand than below them, whilst the lower part of the wings in the left hand is held firmer than the upper part. Accordingly the roots covered by the tying-silk slightly yield to the pressure, with the result that the fibres now poise from the head in a more upright line of direction. See if it is necessary to repeat the process; but if all has gone well, permanently tie the wings down in the following manner:—

Release from "Make off"; hold silk taut, carefully unwind the three last turns, and bind down in the ordinary way with four fresh turns, headwards; at each turn use STOP against both the tying-silk and the fibres to prevent them shifting as you pull. Put silk in CATCH. Cut off roots of fibres, pointing scissors tailwards, as before explained, to form taper; touch with varnish, release silk; finish by binding on in close turns headwards, and then back. Put silk in CATCH on reaching the last turn but one tailwards, varnish silk as usual, and tie with a half-hitch (see

Instruction Fly No. 2, Chapter II.). The practical advantages of this modern plan have been mentioned, and no one reading the particulars in their entirety, be he amateur or professional, will fail to mentally realise the result of the method—a method which will at least materially simplify matters for untrained hands.

We have now completed a first-class metal-bodied, mixed-winged fly, and the head, when dry, should receive another coat of varnish. (For ordinary fishing purposes, the floss silk foundation is omitted by expert dressers.) But sometimes it is desired to crown the wings with a strip of Mallard on each side. Such a "cap." steadies them in the water. Sometimes a topping is used to finish; whilst a narrow strip of Teal added to each side gives great effect and life. And "horns" and "cheeks," "sides," and a "head" may be fancied and wanted. In any of these cases, the additional material is tied upon the former work, after the waste ends have been cut off, and before varnishing.

Such are the secrets of fly making to be generally followed; but let us look now to certain other particulars.

1.—Silk-bodied flies.
2.—Oval tinsel-bodied flies.
3.—Sides.
4.—Cheeks.
5.—Whole Feather winged flies.
6.—Strip winged flies, and Spey type.
7.—Topping winged flies.
8.—Chenille bodies, etc.

In forming a silk body (No. 1 of these particulars), the point I would make clear brings to light a distinction which is rarely observed. Thus, instead of fixing floss at the tailward end of the gut loop, as before explained, it is tied in at the head-end of the fly, and the whole length coiled first tailwards and then headwards. During the process it is "stroked," "smoothed," and "ironed," as explained in Operation 2, Instruction Fly No. 1. On reaching the butt, it is held taut in CATCH, whilst the foundation coils made are so regulated as to form an even surface to finish off upon. Any little lump in them is pressed level with the thumb nails, whilst any little dip is frayed up with the point of a needle before the final ironing takes place. It is only necessary to add that the final layer of floss itself binds the point of the hackle at the place desired.

(As most floss silks change colour in use, the dresser can acquaint himself with their appearance by applying paraffin with a camel's hair brush to any of them. But I much prefer dyed quill to the best of floss silk, and I get it from Courtney, at Killarney. It is easily cut into narrow strips, and far easier than silk to put on the hook. Quill is doubly useful. It lasts longer than silk, *and you know where you are in keeping accounts of, and making deductions from, the circumstances and conditions attending the rises and captures of fish.* Consequently, you are less likely in future to fall into error, and be mistaken in choosing a particular coloured fly for similar occasions and conditions. Once you make a "Jock Scott" with good yellow quill, and you will not hurriedly return to floss silk.)

No. 2.—Oval tinsel bodies may be briefly dismissed.

Prepare the oval tinsel by exposing the core to tie on, and by brightening with silicon. In coiling it headward, press each coil with right thumb and middle finger nails, tailwards, whilst the length of tinsel is held taut in CATCH. This tinsel ties in the body-hackle.

No. 3.—Sides: Generally of one Jungle feather put on each side of the wing in the centre, and extending from the head to the middle of the wing. Strip stump of Jungle, and partially fix with two turns of tying-silk, tailwards; inspect work by raising left thumb on near side, and fore-finger on far side. Provided the feather lies close all along the wing, carefully replace thumb and finger, and tie down headward. But if, on inspection, either feather turns outwards or upwards, twist it by catching hold of root to the position desired before tying down.

No. 4.—Cheeks are one third the length of sides, and are generally of Chatterer.

Follow directions given for Sides.

No. 5.—Whole feather winged flies.

Measure length; strip end; indent for tying-silk.

No. 6.—Strip winged flies. Here I would first recommend for beginners the method of fixing given in the illustrated instructions for "mixed wings." By following it the fibres are *made* to sit on their side edges, back to back, like the *underwing*-strips as formerly explained. The majority of strip wings, as many Anglers know, lie flat and spread out from the head of the fly. These are the most popular and, in places, seem to be ever present. Proof of this, proof that in the Spring months they have comparatively no rest in the North, is furnished by familiar experience on several rivers, notably the Dee, where, in truth, there are two occasions on which they are used—when fish are taking and when they are not. However, the key to practical success lies in adjusting the strips so as to keep them intact. The fibres should not split, and this can only be prevented by drawing them together tightly and regularly just at the point of tie. Of the two best methods for the business some details are necessary. One method is by the aid of the vice, the other without it. Peter Milne, at Garden's establishment, Aberdeen, is an adept with the vice. After fixing the bend of the hook in it, he selects both strips of such length that the point of tie comes close to the quill. Having prepared them, so that no more than a mere suspicion of quill remains to keep the fibres from separating, he holds the far side strip alongside the hook, by placing the left thumb above and the forefinger below, and then throws the tying silk over it close to the part so held. With the right hand put under the fly, he catches hold of the silk and brings it up gently to the near side of the work; and before pulling it towards him, looks to see that the coil is in its proper place, *i.e.*, *close to the left fingers, and in a straight line over the work.* The silk is now pulled steadily, during which operation any shifting of the fibres is easily detected. If the fibres are not coming one upon the other, evenly towards each other, so that finally they shall represent a closed fan, the beginner should stop pulling at once and try again. Two subsequent turns of silk are now given and the waste of the strip cut off. The near side strip is put on by a similar process, but the left finger in this instance is placed above it and the thumb below, in an exactly reversed position.

George Blacklaws (Kincardine O'Neil) works by a method of my own. It is recommended here because I have given up using the vice, and believe the student will earlier succeed in getting strength and neatness. However this may be, working without the vice calls for far more skill in manipulation. Select, as in the former method, a feather suitable for the size of hook. The fibres must be of such a length that when the strip is severed from the feather (by means of cutting it along the centre of the quill) the part tied shall be, as I have said, *close to the quill.* The quill is trimmed in like manner as before, particularly the portion underneath. The silk is then set in, if necessary, and when the foundation is made—binding first loopwards and back to the throat hackle—take the far side strip, *the longest fibres being outwards,* in the left hand and squeeze the fibres together at their roots by pinching the strip crossways with the right hand thumb and finger nails at the quill end. The strip is then taken at the pinched root, placed and held at the desired angle against the upper part of the side of the hook, and with the left hand one turn of tying silk is given *from* you and drawn tight, in order that the fibres shall come as close to each other as possible. This is simple enough to do, but when done, the chief thing is to keep the silk taut while seizing it with the right hand. Now place the left thumb above and fore-finger below the strip, *close to the tie,* give two more turns with the right hand in the usual way and cut off waste. Make off. By the same process prepare the near strip. Apply it to the hook, noting that on this occasion the strip is placed somewhat flatter to the side of the shank than the former one (the outer side of which was slightly elevated) as the tying silk will draw up the lower fibres into their proper position. With the left hand give one turn from you, holding the silk taut as before, and then seize it with the right hand. Now grip the wings sideways with the left hand, allowing the fingers to point a little downwards, and give three turns with the right hand. Cut off waste and finish.

But the Spey style of fly calls for more minute details. Take the "Gold Riach" for an example. One side of the Spey-cock hackle (which is wound from its root along the body) is stripped of its fibres, leaving the better side for use. If the tinsels are wound from you (a matter decided according to which side the hackle is stripped), the hackle is brought *over* them towards you, and *vice versa.* Along with the tinsels is fixed a length of tying-silk for binding the hackle at intervals of, say, $\frac{3}{16}$ of an inch. This is done simply to protect the hackle from uncoiling if cut by the tooth of a fish. Of necessity, the silk is worked in between the fibres which are separated with the stiletto. But it is in respect of the wings that some knowledge and much practice is needed. Take two strips, say, of Mallard, both from *the same side of the feather;* place one over and upon the other, so as to form one strip. Hold the fly in the left fingers by its loop. Place the strips so arranged on their backs, that their roots reach the throat hackle, with their points extending beyond the loop. Bind them down, *headwards*, from the throat hackle to half way along the space left for the wings. Now turn the fly round, and holding it in the usual way, bend the strips back over the work and body, pass the silk to the end of the shank, and with it make close coils, tailwards, up to and just on upon the bent part of the wings. The object is to make the wings "sit up" in use. Put silk in CATCH; divide the strips into two equal parts, and work the silk first between them, and then round, in and out, in a figure of eight fashion, and finish off with a double half-hitch *on the body side of them.* Varnish.

No. 7.—Topping winged flies (six toppings). Put on these feathers in the following way.

Take two of equal length, indent, and tie them down together on the far side with two turns of silk. Take two more of similar length, and after unwinding one of the former turns, fix them in like manner on the near side. Put on the final two feathers singly, one at the top of the work on the far side, the other likewise on the near side. Give four turns; put silk in CATCH, now pull and coax with the left fingers into order all the toppings together, while gently holding them *close to the head* between the right thumb and fore-finger; release silk; shift left thumb and fore-finger towards head, so as to hold the feathers close to it. Unwind one or two turns of silk, and finally tie down and varnish.

No. 8 brings me to the final items in the count—namely, chenille, etc.

But before entering into details, I would remind novices at this work that it is easier for an entirely uninstructed man to acquire a correct method, than a misinstructed one, who has to shed bad habits and unlearn. Perseverance is required, too, in order to quite master the subordinate branches of fly making—"doubling hackles," "getting the fingers under control," "marrying strips of feathers," etc. The student should not over-burden his mind with "too much at once"; he should learn to think, not what others think, but to think for himself. For whilst the memory is loaded, the understanding remains unexercised, or exercised in such trammels as constrain its motions and direct its pace.

The wisest course in fly making is not to dawdle in premature attempts with silk bodies, bodies of Seal's fur, or of silver tinsel; or even with "built," "mixed," or other forms of wings. The business is far more comprehensible and memorable *when the entire attention is devoted to Grubs*, until the student at least perfects himself in hackling, in "tags" and "tails," and in the manipulation of chenilles, together with their accompaniments as, for instance, Jungle for cheeks of Grubs.

My object in not mentioning this matter before is obvious, and is vindicated by the fact of not having to travel twice over the same ground of instruction. The student is, for example, familiar with the working of hackles, tags, and tails; but of chenille, I have a few words to say.

Suppose, then, we have lying before us a "Jungle Hornet" fly (in course of preparation), showing the tying-silk made off after the butt hackle has been so tied down that the "interval" on the shank of the hook is partially filled in; how is the fly to be completed?

Select first, three pair of Jungle. Choose for "cheeking" the butt hackle the two smallest, and prepare them by stripping the fibres on each side of the stem up to the black and white spots. Fix them. This is best done by holding the hook in the right hand, whilst the left fingers encompass and draw the fibres of the hackle over and beyond the tag, where they are held with the hook, out of the way of the work.

Take the Jungle feather by the root, place it in the desired position on the near side; raise the left thumb so as to grasp the feather whilst one turn of the tying-silk is given, which is now put in CATCH. Fix the far side cheek in a similar manner, and cut off the waste ends at a point that they fit the "interval" on the shank of the hook. Release silk, give two more temporary turns of it, and make off.

Having cut off two six-inch lengths of yellow and black chenille for the body, remove the fluff at one end of each for, say, one quarter of an inch to expose the core, by snipping off small portions with the right finger nails. Release silk, and put it in CATCH after carefully unwinding the two temporary turns. Put the exposed core of the yellow chenille on the far side, and give two turns of tying-silk over it. The next turn of the tying-silk binds down the black length alongside the yellow. CATCH silk again, cut off the waste ends of chenille, so as to fit interval, and tie all down permanently in close turns. Make off. The levelling of the "interval" is now complete. Coil chenilles alternately, and give two turns of each one at a time. To do this, take first the yellow piece in the right hand, whilst the left fore-finger and thumb grasp, as before, the fibres (and cheeks) out of the way; put it once over the shank, and into CATCH. Repeat this. Put STOP on second coil, but pass CATCH fingers behind black chenille, and urge it with the little finger into the background, tailwards. Maintain STOP; seize black chenille on the left side of the yellow, and pass it over the shank (binding down yellow with this first coil), and into CATCH. Make second coil. Holding black in CATCH, work yellow again, using CATCH and STOP, as before.

By this process, continue forming the body until the place on the shank is reached for the second or centre hackle of the Grub.

Release tying-silk from Make off, and while using STOP on both chenilles, tie them down with two turns, and put silk in CATCH. Tie in centre hackle, binding ends of chenilles as you proceed; coil it, fix it, and add cheeks as before. The number of coils from first to last depend upon the amount of hackle wanted, either for a light or a heavy Grub; but one coil more is given to the second hackle, and two or three more to the one at the head, which is longest in fibre.

In preparing the hackles, do not take off too many fibres at the butt end, for these are easily removed after sufficient coils are made. For the purpose of removal, fix tweezers to the butt end of the hackle, and put them into CATCH. With the point of the stiletto pushed in between the fibres from the far side, urge a small number of them down with it on to the ball of the right thumb, and while squeezing them there with the stiletto, a gentle but sudden down-stroke of the hand will snip off superfluous material.

In binding down cheeks and head hackle loopwards, cut off all waste ends when four turns have been given; and, on reaching end of shank work the tying silk back over the former turns firmly and closely, and finally tie with a half-hitch. To make a half-hitch extend the left third finger, and form the required loop by putting the tying-silk under and round it; the loop itself is then taken, passed over head and pulled towards you into position. When there, the half-hitch is made by using STOP while the silk is tightened. Varnish head. I have only to add that in fly making, as in any art, we frequently see that a novelty in system or in practice is too much for the student, and cannot be duly appreciated till time has sobered the enthusiasm of its advocates. But is not success sooner reached, in any undertaking, by practising that system which, intelligently followed, never brings for the student the necessity to unlearn? Increasing practice will assuredly result, not only in increasing respect for our system, but also that measure of excellence, which, at least, will suffice for all practical purposes. Obedience, then — a virtue to be caressed in acquiring skill in fly making—is good and indispensable here. The student will soon engage himself upon Instruction Fly No. 1, and make it again and again, until, being disciplined by experience, as in the case of Grubs, he becomes so familiar with every detail that, without reference to these particulars, he proceeds precisely in the manner described.

CHAPTER IV.

A LIST OF ABOUT 300 STANDARD FLIES WITH THEIR DRESSINGS

(ALPHABETICALLY ARRANGED).

EXORDIUM.

SILK.—Is intended for floss silk unless otherwise stated.
HERL.—For Ostrich herl unless otherwise stated.
WOOL.—For Berlin wool.
MALLARD.—For the brown mottled feather unless otherwise stated; and when mentioned at the end of the list in company with, or in the absence of, a topping, a right and left strip form the cap of the wing. As a general rule, materials for the wing come upon the hook in the same order as set forth in these descriptions. But married strips of dyed feathers as, for instance, yellow, red, and blue Swan, are sometimes built *in* the wing and sometimes *on* the wing; whilst similar strips of natural feathers as, say, Ibis, Teal, and powdered blue Macaw, invariably serve as "sides," in which case they are put *on* the wing immediately before "cheeks," toppings, and horns.
TIPPET.—Is from the neck of the Golden Pheasant unless otherwise stated.
TOPPING.—Is the crest feather of the Golden Pheasant.
PARROT.—Is green unless otherwise stated.

TINSEL.—Is flat silver or gold tinsel unless otherwise stated.
G. S.—General Standard.
S. S.—Special Standard.

THE ABINGER. G.S.

(KELSON.)

TAG.—Silver twist and yellow silk.
TAIL.—A topping and Teal.
BODY.—Yellow, light claret, blue and black Seal's fur respectively, in equal parts.
RIBS.—Silver tinsel (oval).
HACKLE.—Natural black hackle, from claret fur.
THROAT.—Jay.
WINGS.—Tippet and Gallina in strands, Teal, Mallard, and a topping.
HORNS.—Amherst Pheasant.

This old "standard" was the late Lord Abinger's favourite pattern on the Lochy.

AKROYD. G.S.

(GEORGE BLACKLAWS.)

TAG.—Gold twist.
TAIL.—A topping and tippet strands.
BODY.—The first half of yellow Seal's fur, having a yellow hackle along it; followed by black Seal's fur, and a black hackle along it.
RIBS.—Gold tinsel.
THROAT.—Black Heron.
WINGS.—Two strips of cinnamon Turkey showing light points.
SIDES.—Jungle (short and drooping).

An excellent Dee pattern. For early fishing in snow water this fly is often dressed with double white wings; the first pair (strips) at centre of body, the others at head. This variation has proved of much service on many rivers, and was introduced some years since by Garden, of Aberdeen.

ALLAN'S FANCY. G.S.

(MAJOR "GLEN"-GRANT.)

TAG.—Gold twist and yellow silk.

TAIL.—A topping.

BODY.—Three turns dark yellow silk, followed by majenta silk (short).

RIBS.—Gold tinsel (double, oval).

HACKLE.—A natural red Cock's hackle from majenta silk.

THROAT.—Jay.

WINGS.—Tippet strands, light mottled Turkey, Golden Pheasant tail, Mallard, and a topping.

HEAD.—Black herl.

THE AUTUMN CREEPER G.S.

(Grub.) (KELSON.)

TAG.—Gold tinsel and yellow silk.

BUTT.—(Or No. 1 Hackle) Red Macaw hackle, cheeked on each side with Chatterer.

BODY.—Black chenille.

CENTRE HACKLE.—Yellow Macaw, cheeked with Chatterer.

HEAD HACKLE.—Vulturine Guineafowl (a natural blue) and black Heron, cheeked as before.

A successful Grub in September and October.

THE BADGER. G.S.

(W. GARDEN.)

TAG.—Silver twist.

TAIL.—A topping and tippet strands.

BODY.—Crimson Seal's fur.
RIBS.—Silver tinsel (oval).
THROAT.—A natural silver furnace hackle.
WINGS.—Two strips of light, mottled Turkey.

This summer pattern, used on the Dee, is dressed on very small double hooks.

THE BAKER.

G.S.
(JEWHURST.)

TAG.—Gold twist and light blue silk.
TAIL.—A topping and Gallina.
BUTT.—Black herl.
BODY.—Yellow silk, light orange, blue and dark claret Seal's fur, equally divided.
RIBS.—Gold tinsel.
HACKLE.—Dark claret from second turn.
THROAT.—Gallina and light blue hackle.
WINGS.—Two tippets (back to back) veiled with Golden Pheasant tail, light Bustard, Grey Mallard, Peacock wing, Swan dyed light blue, yellow, and dark claret; and Mallard above.
HORNS.—Blue Macaw.

One of the oldest standards, and a favourite on most rivers.

BALMORAL.

G.S.
(GARDEN.)

TAG.—Silver twist.
TAIL.—A topping and tippet strands.
BUTT.—Black herl.
BODY.—Green and dark blue Seal's fur, equally divided.
RIBS.—Silver lace and silver tinsel.
HACKLE.—Black Heron from green fur.

THROAT.—Widgeon.
WINGS.—Two strips of plain cinnamon Turkey.
SIDES.—Jungle (short and drooping).

A favourite Dee fly.

THE BARKWORTH.

G.S.
(W. T. BARKWORTH.)

TAG.—Gold twist and dark orange silk.
TAIL.—A topping. Summer Duck, and Toucan from under-tail.
BUTT.—Black herl.
BODY.—In two equal sections: No. 1, straw-coloured silk, ribbed with gold tinsel (oval, fine); butted with Toucan (orange) above and below, and black herl: No. 2, dark orange silk, having a dark orange hackle along it, and ribbed with gold tinsel.
THROAT.—Gallina, dyed blue. (Jay for small patterns.)
WINGS.—Two tippets (back to back) light mottled Turkey, dyed dark orange, two strips of blue Macaw, Swan dyed straw-colour, Golden Pheasant tail and two toppings.
SIDES.—Jungle.
CHEEKS.—Chatterer.
HEAD.—Black herl.

"Use this fly in dark coloured water," writes a friend of mine, "and you will not regret it. The inventor himself succeeds with it on the Wye when the water is positively muddy."

THE BARON.

G.S.
(FARLOW.)

TAG.—Silver twist and dark red-claret silk.
TAIL.—Topping.
BUTT.—Black herl.
BODY.—In two sections. The first half with silver tinsel (flat) ribbed

with silver tinsel (oval) and butted with Indian Crow (extending to tag) and black herl. The second half with black silk, ribs of silver tinsel (oval), having a dark red-claret hackle along it.

THROAT.—Jay.

WINGS.—Tippet strands, Swan, dyed yellow, Summer Duck, blue and red Macaw, Golden Pheasant tail, Peacock wing, Mallard above and a topping.

SIDES.—Jungle.

CHEEKS.—Chatterer.

HORNS.—Blue Macaw.

HEAD.—Black herl.

An excellent fly in Norway as well as on the Shannon, Blackwater, Earn, Test, and Usk. The Baron is a fly I am very fond of and, with it, Sir Hyde Parker killed his memorable 60 lbs. Salmon.

BEACONSFIELD. G.S.

(GEORGE BLACKLAWS.)

TAG.—Silver twist and yellow silk.

TAIL.—A topping, Teal, and Ibis.

BUTT.—Black herl, followed by two turns silver tinsel.

BODY.—In three equal sections ; the first two, doubly butted ; thus No. 1 of yellow silk with a yellow mane (mohair), black herl, and two turns of silver tinsel. No. 2, red-orange silk ; a red-orange mane (mohair), black herl and two turns of silver tinsel. No. 3, claret silk.

THROAT.—Light blue hackle.

WINGS.—Two tippets (back to back) veiled with Golden Pheasant tail, light and dark mottled Turkey, Bustard, Teal, Swan dyed yellow, red, and light blue ; Mallard and a topping.

HORNS.—Blue Macaw.

HEAD.—Black herl.

A very useful, showy fly, well known on the Test ; but it seems to have been forgotten on the Dee.

BENCHILL.

G.S.
(MALLOCH.)

TAG.—Silver tinsel and red-claret silk.
TAIL.—A topping and scarlet Ibis.
BUTT.—Black herl.
BODY.—Dark yellow, light orange, red-claret, and light blue Seal's fur in equal portions.
RIBS.—Silver tinsel.
HACKLE.—Light blue, from red-claret fur.
WINGS.—Two tippets (back to back) extending only to end of dark yellow fur, veiled with light mottled Turkey, Swan dyed yellow and red, Bustard, Golden Pheasant tail, Teal, Mallard and a topping.
HORNS.—Blue Macaw.

This is a special favourite of mine; and I consider it as the best pattern on the Earn. I have also used it with much success on the Tweed, Spey, Lochy and Blackwater, Co. Cork. When dressed thin in body and wings, Benchill used in Summer is an excellent Dee pattern.

BERESFORD'S FANCY.

G.S.
(R. H. BERESFORD.)

TAG.—Silver twist and claret-majenta silk.
TAIL.—A topping.
BODY.—Blue and orange silks, in equal divisions.
RIBS.—Silver tinsel (oval, fine).
HACKLE.—A natural black hackle from second turn.
THROAT.—Claret-majenta hackle and Jay.
WINGS.—Tippet (strands) Bustard, Swan dyed claret-majenta, blue and orange; and Mallard.
HORNS.—Blue Macaw.
HEAD.—Black herl.

According to an account given by the inventor, this is one of the best spring flies on the Lenam; it is known also by the name of "The half blue-and-orange."

BERRINGTON'S FAVOURITE. G.S.

(A. D. BERRINGTON.)

TAG.—Silver twist and scarlet silk.

TAIL.—Ibis, and point of Jungle.

BODY.—Two turns of scarlet Seal's fur, followed by dark orange Seal's fur.

RIBS.—Silver tinsel (oval).

THROAT.—A dark coch-a-bonddu.

WINGS.—Two strips of dark mottled Turkey over an underwing of light mottled Turkey.

HORNS.—Blue Macaw.

A general favourite on the Usk.

THE BLACK AND GOLD. G.S.

(O'FEE.)

TAG.—Silver twist Gold floss.

TAIL.—A topping and Indian Crow.

BUTT.—Black herl.

BODY.—In two equal sections: No. 1, Gold tinsel, ribbed with silver tinsel (oval) having Indian Crow above and below and butted with black herl. No. 2, Black silk, ribbed with silver tinsel, and a gold hackle from second turn.

THROAT.—A claret hackle and Jay.

WINGS.—Dark Turkey having white points, Bustard, Red Macaw, light mottled Turkey, Mallard, Swan dyed red and blue, and two toppings.

SIDES.—Jungle.

HORNS.—Blue Macaw.

CHEEKS.—Chatterer.

HEAD.—Black wool.

BLACK AND ORANGE. G.S.

(ENRIGHT.)

TAG.—Silver twist and violet silk.

TAIL.—Toucan and Indian Crow.

Body.—Orange and black silk, in equal divisions.
Ribs.—Silver tinsel.
Hackle.—Jay, from centre.
Wings.—Light and dark Bustard, Gallina, yellow and blue Macaw, Ibis, Parrot, and a topping.
Cheeks.—Indian Crow.
Head.—Black herl.

THE BLACK CREEPER. G.S.
(Grub.) (Kelson.)

Tag.—Silver twist and light blue silk.
Tail.—Ibis, and powdered blue Macaw mixed in strands.
Butt.—No. 1 hackle natural black; cheeked with Chatterer.
Body.—Black chenille,
No. 2 hackle, in centre of body and cheeked as before,
No. 3 hackle, a still larger natural black, and cheeked as before.

Earn and Usk, and upper waters of the Beauly.

THE BLACK DOCTOR. G.S.
(Wright.)

Tag.—Silver twist and yellow silk.
Tail.—A topping and Chatterer.
Butt.—Scarlet Berlin wool.
Body.—Black silk.
Ribs.—Silver tinsel (oval).
Hackle.—Blue hackle from second turn.
Throat.—Jay.
Wings.—Tippet in strands; Pintail, dark mottled Turkey, Swan dyed blue and yellow, Red Macaw, Gallina, Golden Pheasant tail, Mallard and a topping.
Horns.—Blue Macaw.

CHEEKS.—Chatterer.
HEAD.—Scarlet Berlin wool.

An old and general favourite.

THE BLACK DOG. G.S.
(G. KELSON.)

TAG.—Silver twist and canary silk.
TAIL.—A topping and Ibis.
BUTT.—Black herl.
BODY.—Black silk.
RIBS.—Yellow silk, and silver tinsel (oval) running on each side of it.
HACKLE.—Black Heron from third yellow rib.
WINGS.—Two red-orange hackles (back to back) enveloped by two Jungle; unbarred Summer Duck, light Bustard, Amherst Pheasant, Swan dyed scarlet and yellow and two toppings.

An old standard of my Father's, and a useful high water fly—very good on the Spey, Wye, etc.

BLACK DOSE. G.S.
(G. KELSON.)

TAG.—Silver twist and light orange silk.
TAIL.—A topping, Teal and Ibis.
BODY.—Three turns light blue Seal's fur, followed by black Seal's fur.
RIBS.—Silver tinsel.
HACKLE.—Natural black, from blue Seal's fur.
THROAT.—Light plum-claret hackle.
WINGS.—Two tippets (back to back) veiled with Teal, light mottled Turkey, Golden Pheasant tail, unbarred Summer Duck, Peacock herl, Ibis, green Parrot, and Mallard.
HORNS.—Blue Macaw.
HEAD.—Black herl.

One of the original standards invented and introduced into use by Bernard for my Father.

THE BLACK GOLDFINCH.

G.S.
(ENRIGHT.)

TAG.—Silver twist and red-orange silk.
TAIL.—Toucan and Indian Crow.
BODY.—Black silk.
RIBS.—Silver tinsel (oval).
HACKLE.—Jay, from centre.
WINGS.—Two Indian Crow (back to back) and three toppings.
HORNS.—Blue Macaw.
CHEEKS.—Chatterer.
HEAD.—Black herl.

A well-known Irish pattern.

THE BLACK JAY.

G.S.
(KELSON.)

TAG.—Silver twist and dark yellow silk.
TAIL.—A topping.
BUTT.—Black herl.
BODY.—Two turns black silk, followed by black Seal's fur.
RIBS.—Silver tinsel, and silver lace (large sizes).
HACKLE.—Natural black, from silk.
THROAT.—Jay.
WINGS.—Tippet, Ibis and Gallina in strands; Bustard, Golden Pheasant tail, Teal, black Cockatoo's tail, Swan dyed green and dark yellow; and Mallard.
HORNS.—Blue Macaw.
HEAD.—Black herl.

Introduced for me by Farlow many years since.

THE BLACK KING.

G.S.

BODY.—Orange Berlin wool (three turns) followed by black wool (short).

RIBS.—From far side gold tinsel (narrow), from near side silver tinsel (same size) both wound the reverse way, an equal distance apart.
HACKLE.—From end of body, a black Spey-cock hackle, but wound from the root instead of from the point, in the usual direction, thus crossing over the ribs at each turn given.
THROAT.—Teal, one turn only.
WINGS.—Two strips of light brown mottled Mallard.

SPECIAL NOTE.—This is one of the old standard flies on the Spey. For full particulars see the "Green King."

THE BLACK PRINCE.

S.S.
(TRAHERNE.)

TAG.—Silver twist and dark yellow silk.
TAIL.—A topping.
BUTT.—Black herl.
BODY.—Three equal sections of silver tinsel (flat) butted above and below, with two black feathers (back to back) from the nape of the Indian Crow, and black herl.
WINGS.—Five or six toppings.
HORNS.—Blue Macaw.
HEAD.—Black herl.

This is generally used as an "Exaggeration."

THE BLACK RANGER.

G.S
(WRIGHT.)

TAG.—Silver twist and yellow silk.
TAIL.—Topping and Indian Crow.
BUTT.—Black herl.
BODY.—Black silk.
RIBS.—Silver tinsel (oval).

HACKLE.—Natural black, from second turn of tinsel.
THROAT.—Light blue hackle.
WINGS.—Four tippets, partly overlapping and enveloping two projecting Jungle (back to back) and a topping.
CHEEKS.—Chatterer.
HORNS.—Blue Macaw.
HEAD.—Black wool.

This fly is well known throughout the United Kingdom.

THE BLUE BARON.

TAG.—Silver twist and claret silk.
TAIL.—A topping and Chatterer.
BUTT.—Black herl.
BODY—In two sections—(1) Oval Tinsel, butted with Toucan above and below, and black herl; (2) blue silk having a blue hackle along it.
THROAT—Teal.
WINGS—Golden Pheasant tippet and tail in strands, Swan dyed blue and claret, Mallard and a topping.
SIDES—Jungle.

BLUEBELL.

S.S.
(TRAHERNE.)

TAG.—Silver twist and dark orange silk.
TAIL.—Topping.
BUTT.—Black herl
BODY.—Blue silk.
RIBS.—Silver tinsel and silver lace.
HACKLE.—Powdered blue Macaw (one side stripped).
THROAT.—Yellow Macaw.
WINGS.—Red Macaw in strands and two toppings.
SIDES.—Jungle.

HORNS.—Blue Macaw.
HEAD.—Black herl.

Fishing in 1886 at Stanley-on-Tweed, the author of Bluebell wrote :—
" For the last three days the fish would look at nothing, but I tried a Bluebell last night and have had rare fun with it to-day, killing three fish in one pool, the largest 28 lbs. . . ."

THE BLUE BOYNE.

G.S.
(TRAHERNE.)

TAG.—Silver twist.
TAIL.—Two Indian Crow (back to back).
BUTT.—Black herl.
BODY.—Silver tinsel (oval, the finest), intersected by four sets of Chatterer above and below at equal distances apart. 1st set at one-fourth of space between butt and head : 3rd set forming throat.
WINGS.—Two strips of yellow Macaw and two toppings.
HEAD.—Black herl.

One of the best low water flies in summer. The hook should be no more than $\frac{3}{4}$ inch in length ; smaller patterns are also very effective.

THE BLUE CHARM.

G.S.
(W. BROWN.)

TAG.—Silver twist.
TAIL.—A topping.
BODY.—Claret silk.
RIBS.—Silver tinsel (oval).
THROAT.—Blue hackle.
WINGS.—Broad strips of Mallard, two narrow strips of Teal above and a topping.
HEAD.—Black wool.

A good summer fly used chiefly on the Dee, and dressed on small double hooks.

THE BLUE DOCTOR.

G.S.
(WRIGHT.)

TAG.—Silver twist and yellow silk.
TAIL.—A topping and Chatterer.
BUTT.—Scarlet Berlin wool.
BODY.—Light blue silk.
RIBS.—Silver tinsel (oval).
HACKLE.—Light blue hackle from second turn.
THROAT.—Jay.
WINGS.—Tippet in strands, Gallina, Golden Pheasant tail, light mottled Turkey, Pintail, Swan dyed yellow and light blue, Ibis, Mallard, and a topping.
HORNS.—Blue Macaw.
CHEEKS.—Chatterer.
HEAD.—Scarlet Berlin wool.

One of the early fancy patterns on the Tweed and well known on all rivers.

THE BLUE GOLDFINCH.

G.S.
(ENRIGHT.)

TAG.—Silver twist and red-orange silk.
TAIL.—Toucan and Indian Crow.
BODY.—Light blue silk.
RIBS.—Silver tinsel.
HACKLE.—Jay from centre.
WINGS.—Two Indian Crow (back to back, long) and four toppings.
HORNS.—Powdered blue Macaw.
CHEEKS.—Indian Crow.
HEAD.—Black herl.

THE BLUE-OVER-BLACK.

G.S.
(Colonel KELSON.)

TAG.—Silver twist and pink silk.
TAIL.—Red Toucan (from undertail), yellow Macaw, powdered blue Macaw, and Gallina, in strands.

Body.—Two turns scarlet silk and black Seal's fur.
Ribs.—Silver tinsel and silver lace.
Hackle.—A white coch-a-bonddu dyed dark blue, from second turn.
Wings.—Two strips Turkey showing white tips, Golden Pheasant tail and Peacock herl mixed together in strands, and Mallard.
Sides.—Teal.

This fly, now known by the above name, was invented in the "forties" for the Usk. It is a capital fly in dirty water, and was originally called "William Bass" after a bass singer and chimney sweeper residing then at Sevenoaks.

THE BLUE PALMER. G.S.

(Hardy Bros.)

Tag.—Silver twist and dark blue silk.
Tail.—A topping.
Butt.—Black herl.
Body.—Dark blue silk.
Ribs.—Silver tinsel (oval).
Hackle.—Light red-claret from second turn.
Throat.—Jay.
Wings.—Tippet strands, dark Turkey, Bustard, Golden Pheasant tail; married strips of Swan dyed yellow, red, and blue; and two strips of Mallard above.
Head.—Black herl.

An excellent Irish pattern; and, when lightly dressed and used in summer, kills well on the Dee.

THE BLUE WASP. G.S.

Tail.—A topping, Summer Duck, and Ibis.
Body.—Equal divisions of yellow and blue Seal's fur.

RIBS.—Silver tinsel (oval, fine) over yellow, and silver tinsel (flat and larger) over blue.

HACKLE.—A blue hackle along blue fur.

THROAT.—Jay.

WINGS.—Two strips of cinnamon Turkey having white points, and a topping.

SIDES.—Summer Duck.

HEAD.—Black wool.

One of the most popular patterns on the Earn.

BO PEEP.

S.S.
(KELSON.)

TAG.—Silver twist (plenty).

TAIL.—Toucan (three) and two small Chatterer (back to back).

BUTT.—Black herl.

BODY.—In three equal sections of silver tinsel (oval, the finest): No. 1, butted with Toucan above and below, followed by black herl. No. 2, butted with Indian Crow above and below, followed by black herl.

THROAT (or No. 3 section)—Double Chatterer feathers (back to back) on off and on near side.

WINGS.—Ibis and red Macaw in fibres, and three toppings.

HORNS.—Amherst Pheasant.

HEAD.—Black herl.

A very good fly in hot weather when the fish are sulky and settled down in small streamy Catches. It should be dressed thinly and very small.

BONNE BOUCHE.

G.S.
(KELSON.)

TAG.—Gold twist and yellow silk.

TAIL.—A topping and Gallina.

Butt.—Red wool.
Body.—One third yellow Seal's fur then claret Seal's fur.
Ribs.—Gold tinsel and silver lace.
Hackle.—Claret hackle from yellow fur.
Throat.—Gallina.
Wings.—Tippet, Teal, and Peacock wing for underwing; Amherst Pheasant, Golden Pheasant tail, Bustard, Swan dyed yellow and claret; and Mallard.
Sides.—Married strips of Teal and Ibis.
Horns.—Blue Macaw.
Head.—Red wood.

A good fly on the Earn, Usk, and many Irish waters; also from the middle of May, on the Spey.

BRITANNIA.

G.S.
(Bernard.)

Tag.—Gold twist (plenty).
Tail.—A topping.
Butt.—Black herl.
Body.—Red-orange Seal's fur.
Ribs.—Gold tinsel.
Wings.—Shovel duck and a topping.
Sides.—Jungle.
Cheeks.—Chatterer.
Horns.—Blue Macaw.
Head.—Dark blue hackle.

Excellent Wye pattern and an old standard on the Thurso.

THE BROWN DOG.

G.S.
(D. Watson.)

Tag.—Gold twist and gold silk.
Tail.—A topping and Indian Crow.

BUTT.—Black herl.
BODY.—Dirty orange and brown Seal's fur, in equal divisions.
RIBS.—Gold tinsel (oval).
THROAT.—Grouse.
WINGS.—Golden Pheasant tippet in strands; Teal, Swan dyed yellow, red, and light blue; and a topping.
SIDES.—Jungle.
HEAD.—Black wool.

One of the best flies on the Ness. To be had of the inventor, 19, Inglis Street, Inverness.

THE BRUCE.

G.S.
(Colonel BRUCE.)

TAG.—Silver twist (plenty).
TAIL.—A topping.
BUTT.—Black herl.
BODY.—Silver tinsel.
RIBS.—Silver tinsel (oval).
HACKLE.—Claret hackle, from second turn.
THROAT.—Gallina.
WINGS.—Silver mottled Turkey, and Golden Pheasant Tail.
HORNS.—Blue Macaw.
HEAD.—Black wool.

The Bruce kills well on the Test.

BUMBEE.

G.S.
(W. GARDEN.)

TAG.—Silver twist.
TAIL.—A tuft of orange wool (short).
BODY.—One-third orange wool, followed by black Seal's fur.

RIBS.—Silver tinsel (oval).
THROAT.—A coch-a-bonddu hackle.
WINGS.—Mallard.

A good fly in summer on the Dee; it is usually dressed on small double hooks.

THE BUTCHER.

G.S.
(JEWHURST.)

TAG.—Silver twist and yellow silk.
TAIL.—Topping, Teal, and powdered blue Macaw.
BUTT.—Black herl.
BODY.—In four equal divisions of Seal's fur, viz.: light red-claret and light blue, dark red-claret and dark blue respectively.
RIBS.—Silver tinsel (preceded on large hooks by silver lace).
HACKLE.—A natural black, from light red-claret Seal's fur.
THROAT.—A yellow hackle and Gallina.
WINGS.—A tippet, and breast feather of the Golden Pheasant (back to back) veiled with Teal, Golden Pheasant tail, Gallina, Bustard, and Peacock wing; strands of Parrot and Swan dyed yellow; and Mallard.
HORNS.—Blue Macaw.
CHEEKS.—Chatterer.
HEAD.—Black herl.

This old standard is used everywhere. For my own work I always add a topping to the wing.

BUTTERSCOTCH.

S.S.
(KELSON.)

TAG.—Silver twist and violet silk.
(Gold twist and gold ribs in Autumn).
TAIL.—A topping.

BUTT.—Scarlet wool.
BODY.—Black silk.
RIBS.—Silver tinsel (oval).
HACKLE.—Black hackle from second turn.
THROAT.—Jay.
WINGS.—Two strips of plain cinnamon Turkey.

A useful bright-water pattern for rivers that are fished with dark flies in bright weather.

THE BYREL.

G.S.
(WRIGHT.)

TAG.—Silver twist and yellow silk.
TAIL.—A topping, Ibis, and powdered blue Macaw.
BUTT.—Black herl.
BODY.—Silver tinsel.
RIBS.—Silver tinsel (oval).
HACKLE.—Light blue hackle from second turn.
THROAT.—Light orange hackle and Widgeon.
WINGS.—Two extended Jungle (back to back) veiled with Widgeon, Gallina, Bustard, Peacock herl (fine, small quantity), Ibis, Parrot, Mallard, and a topping.
HORNS.—Blue Macaw.
CHEEKS.—Chatterer.

In many places this fly has a better reputation than either the "Silver Doctor" or the "Lion."

CAMPBELL.

G.S.
(DAVID MURRAY.)

TAG.—Silver twist and yellow silk.
TAIL.—A topping and Chatterer.
BUTT.—Black herl.

BODY.—In two equal sections: No. 1, Silver tinsel, ribbed with silver tinsel (oval, fine) and butted with black herl. No. 2, light claret Seal's fur, ribbed with silver tinsel (oval).

HACKLE.—A yellow hackle from centre.

WINGS.—Two strips of cinnamon Turkey (plain), narrow strips of Swan dyed red, yellow, and light blue, married ; Bustard, Golden Pheasant tail, Teal, and a topping.

SIDES.—Jungle.

One of the best patterns on the South Esk.

THE CANDLESTICK MAKER. G.S.

(HOLBROW.)

TAG.—Silver tinsel (oval, fine).

TAIL.—Ibis and Summer duck.

BODY.—Three turns of black silk followed by black Seal's fur.

RIBS.—Silver tinsel.

HACKLE.—A dark fiery-brown, from Seal's fur.

WINGS.—Double Jungle and two toppings.

HEAD.—Black wool.

THE CAPTAIN. G.S.

(KELSON.)

TAG.—Silver twist and light blue silk.

TAIL.—A topping and Chatterer.

BODY.—The first half formed of two turns of light orange silk. Two turns of dark orange Seal's fur, two turns of dark red-claret Seal's fur ; followed by dark blue Seal's fur.

RIBS.—Silver tinsel (oval).

HACKLE.—A white coch-a-bonddu, dyed light red-claret, from orange silk.

THROAT.—A blue hackle and Gallina.

WINGS.—Teal, Pintail, Gallina, Peacock wing, Amherst and Golden Pheasant tail, in strands; Swan dyed light and dark orange, claret, and dark blue. Mallard and a topping.

SIDES.—Jungle.

HORNS.—Blue Macaw.

HEAD.—Black herl.

Originally introduced into Scotland by Bernard, where it is erroneously called the Poynder.

CAPTAIN WALTON.

G.S.
(KELSON.)

TAG.—Silver twist, cream silk, and crimson silk.

TAIL.—Ibis, powdered blue Macaw, tippet, and Peacock wing, in strands; with two (shorter) narrow strips of Summer Duck.

BUTT.—Black herl.

BODY.—Claret silk (two turns), dark blue Seal's fur, and black Seal's fur, in equal divisions.

HACKLE.—Black Heron from blue Seal's fur.

THROAT.—Gallina.

RIBS.—Silver tinsel and silver twist.

WINGS.—Peacock wing dyed claret, powdered blue Macaw, red Macaw, and Teal, in strands; Golden Pheasant Tail, Gallina, Mallard, and a topping.

SIDES.—Jungle.

CHEEKS.—Indian Crow.

HEAD.—Black herl.

Used with success on the Dee, Spey, Lochy, Garry, Blackwater, and Beauly.

CARNEGIE.

G.S.
(DAVID MURRAY.)

TAG. Silver twist and scarlet silk.

TAIL.—A topping and Summer Duck.

Plate 3

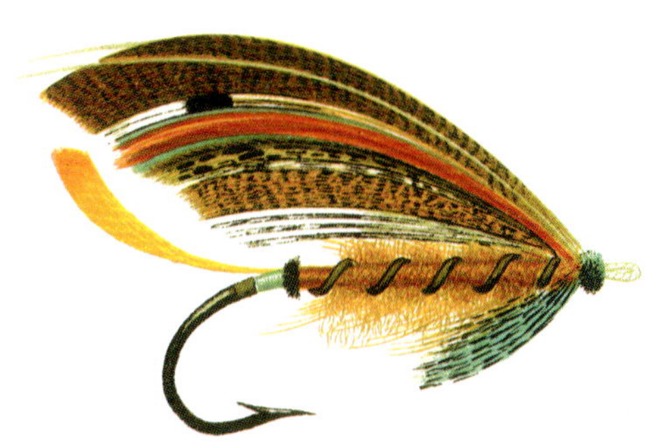
The Dirty Orange

Benchill

The Dawson

Taite's Fancy

The Durham Ranger

The Wilson

BUTT.—Black herl.

BODY.—In two equal sections: No. 1, yellow silk, ribbed with silver tinsel, butted with Indian Crow above and below, and black herl. No. 2, light blue silk, ribbed with silver tinsel (oval).

HACKLE.—A yellow hackle from centre.

WINGS.—Tippet fibres, Swan dyed yellow and red, Golden Pheasant tail, powdered blue Macaw, Summer Duck, and a topping.

SIDES.—Jungle.

HEAD.—Scarlet wool.

A popular fly on South Esk. For personal use I make the butt with scarlet wool.

THE CARRON FLY. G.S.

BODY.—Orange Berlin wool (short).

RIBS.—Silver tinsel (ordinary method).

HACKLE.—Black Heron from end of body (ordinary method).

WINGS.—Mallard showing brown points and light roots.

An old standard Spey fly.

THE CHALMERS. G.S.

(DAVID MURRAY.)

TAG.—Silver twist and yellow silk.

TAIL.—A topping.

BUTT.—Black herl.

BODY.—Majenta silk.

RIBS.—Silver tinsel, sufficient turns to ensure an equal width of silver and body silk alternately.

THROAT.—Majenta hackle.

WINGS.—Two strips of dark mottled Turkey showing white tips, and a topping.

SIDES.—Jungle.
HEAD.—Two turns of majenta hackle.

A favourite pattern on North Esk.

THE CHAMPION.

G.S.
(KELSON.)

TAG.—Silver twist and light yellow silk.
TAIL.—Topping, unbarred Summer Duck; Swan dyed light crimson and light blue.
BUTT.—Black herl.
BODY.—Two turns of light blue silk, and equal quantities of dark yellow, crimson, dark blue, and black Seal's fur.
RIBS.—Silver lace and silver tinsel.
HACKLE.—Natural black from Seal's fur.
THROAT.—Jay.
WINGS.—Two Summer Duck strips (back to back) partially veiled at bottom with married strips of Amherst Pheasant and Golden Pheasant tail; blue Macaw, Swan dyed crimson, Teal, unbarred Summer Duck, Swan dyed dark yellow, Peacock wing, Mallard, and a topping.
SIDES.—Jungle.
HORNS.—Blue Macaw.
CHEEKS.—Chatterer.
HEAD.—Black herl.

NOTE.—Use Pig's wool for large Spring patterns.

CHARLIE.

G.S.
(Captain DUNDAS.)

TAG.—Silver twist and light blue silk.
TAIL.—A topping.

BODY.—Yellow and black Seal's fur equally divided.
RIBS.—Silver tinsel (oval).
HACKLE.—Black hackle from yellow fur
THROAT.—Jay ; but for larger patterns Gallina dyed blue.
WINGS.—Tippet fibres, Golden Pheasant tail, and Teal for underwing; dark mottled Turkey, Bustard, Widgeon, Peacock wing, Swan dyed yellow, red, and light blue ; and Mallard.
HORNS.—Blue Macaw.
CHEEKS.—Chatterer (formerly Kingfisher).

THE CHATTERER.

S.S.
(TRAHERNE)

TAG.—Silver twist and light orange silk.
TAIL.—Two toppings.
BUTT.—Black herl.
* BODY.—Two turns of light violet silk making headway for numberless small Chatterer feathers, closely packed round the rest of the body.
THROAT.—Gallina.
WINGS.—Four Indian Crow feathers, in pairs (back to back), first pair longer than the second, having the point of a Jay feather on each side two-thirds of the length of the Crow feathers ; with five or six toppings above.
CHEEKS.—Chatterer.
HORNS.—Blue Macaw.
HEAD.—Black herl.

* These feathers are best put on by working headwards, holding the hook not by the bend in the usual way, but by the shank.

RIVERS.—All " Blue rivers." An excellent fly on the Tweed when dressed with built or mixed wings.

CHILDERS.

G.S.

(Colonel CHILDERS.)

TAG.—Silver twist and light blue silk.

TAIL.—A topping; strands of red, and powdered blue Macaw, and Pintail.

BUTT.—Black herl.

BODY.—Two turns of light yellow silk, followed by light yellow Seal's fur, and three turns red Seal's fur at throat.

RIBS.—Silver lace and silver tinsel (oval).

HACKLE.—White furnace hackle, dyed light yellow.

THROAT.—A red hackle and Widgeon.

WINGS.—Strands of tippet, and tail of the Golden Pheasant; brown mottled Turkey, Amherst Pheasant, Pintail, Bustard, Summer Duck, Parrot, powdered blue and red Macaw, Gallina; Mallard and a topping.

HORNS.—Blue Macaw.

CHEEKS.—Chatterer.

HEAD.—Black herl.

One of the best old standard patterns.

THE CLARET-BROWN.

G.S.

(KELSON.)

TAIL.—A few fibres of yellow Macaw.

BODY.—Three turns of orange Pig's wool, followed by claret-brown Pig's wool.

RIBS.—Silver tinsel.

HACKLE.—Crown Pigeon from centre.

THROAT.—Gallina.

WINGS.—Two strips of Glen Tana Gled and a topping.

HORNS.—Red Macaw.

THE CLARET JAY.

G.S.

(KELSON.)

TAG.—Silver twist and light yellow silk.

TAIL.—A topping, Ibis and Gallina.

Body.—Two turns of light red-claret silk, followed by claret Seal's fur.
Butt.—Black herl.
Ribs.—Silver tinsel (oval).
Hackle.—Claret hackle, from second turn.
Throat.—Jay.
Wings.—Strands of Teal, Tippet and Toucan; Parrot, light mottled Turkey, Golden Pheasant tail, Gallina, dark Bustard, Swan dyed yellow, light blue, and claret; and Mallard.
Sides.—Ibis and yellow Macaw (married).
Horns.—Blue Macaw.
Head.—Black herl.

Introduced for me by Farlow many years since.

THE CLARET PALMER.

G.S.
(Hardy Bros.)

Tag.—Silver twist and dark blue silk.
Tail.—A topping and Indian Crow.
Butt.—Black herl.
Body.—Light red-claret silk.
Ribs.—Silver tinsel (oval).
Hackle.—Blue, from second turn.
Throat.—Jay.
Wings.—Same as "Blue Palmer."
Head.—Black herl.

This fly is as popular in Ireland as the "Blue Palmer."

THE CLARET WASP.

G.S.
(Malloch.)

Tag.—Silver twist and yellow silk.
Tail.—A topping, Widgeon and Ibis.

BODY.—Equal parts of yellow and claret Seal's fur.
RIBS.—Silver tinsel (oval, fine) over yellow half, and silver tinsel.
HACKLE.– A claret hackle along claret Seal's fur.
THROAT.—Gallina.
WINGS.—Two strips of cinnamon Turkey.

A real favourite on the Earn and popular on many other Scotch rivers.

THE CLARK.

G.S.
(W. GARDEN.)

TAG.—Silver twist.
TAIL.—A topping.
BUTT.—Black herl.
BODY.—Dark blue silk.
RIBS.—Silver tinsel (oval).
THROAT.—Gallina and Teal.
WINGS.—Tippet fibres; Mallard and two narrow strips of Summer Duck above.

A summer pattern on the Dee. This fly is well known in many parts of Ireland, and also kills well on the Lochy and Ness. It is well dressed at Aberdeen by the inventor.

THE CLUNY.

G.S.
(W. GARDEN.)

TAG.—Silver twist.
TAIL.—A topping and Scarlet Ibis.
BODY.—Black silk.
RIBS.—Silver tinsel (oval).
THROAT.—Gallina.
WINGS.—Teal.

This favourite summer pattern on the Dee is dressed on very small double hooks.

COCK ROBIN.

G.S.
(G. KELSON.)

TAG.—Silver twist and yellow silk.
TAIL.—A topping and Ibis.
BUTT.—Black herl.
BODY.—Black silk, with two turns at throat of red-orange Seal's fur.
RIBS.—Silver tinsel (oval).
HACKLE.—Black hackle, from second turn.
THROAT.—Red-orange hackle.
WINGS.—Two tippets (back to back) veiled with Gallina, light mottled Turkey, Golden Pheasant tail, dark mottled Turkey, Swan dyed light yellow and red-orange ; and Mallard.
HORNS.—Blue Macaw.
HEAD.—Black herl.

A well known old standard pattern of my Father's.

THE COLONEL.

(Modern.)

G.S.
(FARLOW.)

TAG.—Gold twist and yellow silk.
TAIL.—A topping.
BODY.—Two turns of yellow silk, followed by yellow Seal's fur.
RIBS.—Black purse silk, gold lace, and silver tinsel (together).
HACKLE.—A yellow hackle, from yellow silk.
THROAT.—Light Bustard.
WINGS.—Strips of dark mottled Turkey, Golden Pheasant tail, and Bustard ; Swan dyed yellow, red, and blue ; and a topping.
HORNS.—Blue Macaw.
HEAD.—Black wool.

Thurso, Don, and very good on the Wye.

THE COMET.

G.S.
(KELSON.)

TAG.—Silver twist and yellow silk.
TAIL.—Toucan ; and tippet fibres varying in length.

BUTT.—Black herl.
BODY.—Copper tinselled chenille.
HACKLE.—Light fiery brown (two thirds of body).
THROAT.—Jay.
WINGS.—Two strips of tippet, veiled with Golden Pheasant tail, Teal, and Gallina; Mallard and a topping.
SIDES.—A married strip of yellow and powdered blue Macaw, and Ibis.
HORNS.—Blue Macaw.

An excellent fly on the Usk.

CROMARTY.

G.S.
(HOLBROW.)

TAG.—Silver twist and yellow silk.
TAIL.—Toucan.
BUTT.—Black herl.
BODY.—Black silk.
RIBS.—Silver tinsel.
HACKLE.—Black from second turn.
THROAT.—Gallina dyed blue.
WINGS.—Two tippets (back to back) veiled with light Bustard, Mallard, and a topping.
SIDES.—Swan dyed yellow and blue.
HEAD.—Black wool.

THE DALHOUSIE.

G.S.
(DAVID MURRAY.)

TAG.—Silver twist.
TAIL.—A topping.
BUTT.—Black herl.
BODY.—Gold embossed tinsel, first half, followed by black silk.
RIBS.—Silver tinsel (oval).

HACKLE.—Orange hackle, from centre.

WINGS.—Two strips of tippet, Golden Pheasant tail, Pintail, and a topping.

SIDES.—Jungle.

A good killer on North Esk.

THE DALLAS FLY.

G.S.

(JOHN DALLAS.)

BODY.—Three turns of yellow Berlin wool, followed by black wool.

RIBS.—Silver tinsel, gold tinsel (oval, narrow), red thread and blue thread, all running an equal distance apart.

HACKLE.—A black Spey Cock's hackle from end of body, but wound the reverse way, and so crossing *over* the ribs.

THROAT.—A red hackle from the Golden Pheasant.

WINGS.—Two strips of plain cinnamon Turkey.

HEAD.—Orange wool, picked out.

This capital fly on the Spey was christened by Mr. Little Gilmore. Like other local patterns, the body is short and begins a full $\frac{1}{8}$ of an inch in front of the point of the hook. The description given is from a pattern forwarded by Mr. C. M. Burn's Fisherman at Pitcroy; and proved to be correct by one being sent to me by Dallas himself.

THE DANDY.

S.S.

(WRIGHT.)

TAG.—Silver twist and yellow silk.

TAIL.—Topping, strands of Summer Duck and Chatterer.

BUTT.—Black herl.

BODY.—Silver tinsel, nearly $\frac{2}{3}$, and finish with light blue silk.

RIBS.—Silver tinsel (oval).

THROAT.—A light blue hackle and Gallina.

WINGS.—Two tippets (back to back) enveloping two projecting Jungle (back to back).

SIDES.—Summer Duck, covering lower part of tippet.
CHEEKS.—Chatterer.
HORNS.—Blue Macaw.
HEAD.—Black Berlin Wool.

RIVERS: Tweed, etc.

(NOTE.—This fly occasionally kills under general conditions of weather and water, but is frequently found useful as a special standard for moving sulky fish.)

THE DAVIDSON. G.S.

(W. J. DAVIDSON.)

(Pattern and particulars given to me by Mr. Davidson himself when fishing together on the Tay at Aberfeldy.)

TAG.—Gold twist and yellow silk.
TAIL.—A topping and Peacock wing.
BUTT.—Black herl.
BODY.—In two sections: 1st half of gold tinsel, ribbed with gold tinsel (oval) and butted with a Jay hackle: 2nd half, blue silk ribbed with gold tinsel (oval).
THROAT.—A tippet (hackle-wise).
WINGS.—Three toppings, the one in the centre is put on its back; the other two at the sides, projecting outwards.
HEAD.—Black herl.

The inventor, who introduced Frank Buckland to his first fish, used this pattern on all occasions when he found Salmon in a sulky humour.

THE DAWSON. G.S.

(KENNET DAWSON.)

TAG.—Silver twist and yellow silk.
TAIL.—A topping and Chatterer.

BUTT.—Black herl.

BODY.—In two equal sections of silver tinsel, butted at centre with Indian Crow and black herl.

RIBS.—Silver tinsel (oval).

THROAT.—Indian Crow, repeated as above, and light blue hackle.

WINGS.—Light mottled Turkey, yellow Macaw, Golden Pheasant tail, Teal, powdered blue Macaw, Ibis, dark mottled Turkey, grey Mallard; Mallard and a topping.

HORNS.—Blue Macaw.

HEAD.—Black herl.

This is a splendid pattern. I always take it with me. On some rivers it is known as "Baron Dawson."

THE DENISON.

G.S.
(DENISON.)

TAG.—Silver twist, claret and yellow silk.

TAIL.—A topping and Summer Duck.

BUTT.—Black herl.

BODY.—Silver tinsel (oval, fine, to centre) followed by light blue silk.

RIBS.—Silver tinsel (oval).

HACKLE.—A light blue hackle, from centre.

THROAT.—Jay.

WINGS.—Two tippets (back to back) enveloping two extended Jungle, veiled with yellow rump of Golden Pheasant on each side, Teal, and a topping.

HORNS.—Blue Macaw.

HEAD.—Black herl.

An old standard on the Ness.

THE DEWDROP.

G.S.
(KELSON.)

TAG.—Gold twist and yellow silk.

TAIL.—A topping and Jungle (point).

BUTT.—Black herl, followed by six turns of the gold twist used for tag.

BODY.—In two sections; No. 1, yellow silk to centre, ribbed with gold oval tinsel (fine) put on each side of a rib of black silk; butted with Toucan above and below, and black herl; No. 2, Black silk, ribbed with gold oval tinsel (fine) put on each side of a rib of yellow silk.

THROAT.—Light blue hackle and Jay.

WINGS.—One tippet, backed with red breast feather of Golden Pheasant; veiled with Teal, light and dark Bustard, Peacock wing, Gallina; Mallard and a topping.

SIDES.—Jungle.

CHEEKS.—Indian Crow and Chatterer.

HORNS.—Blue Macaw.

A successful fly on most rivers.

THE DIRTY ORANGE. G.S.

(KELSON.)

TAG.—Gold twist and light blue silk.

TAIL.—A topping and strands of tippet.

BUTT.—Black herl.

BODY.—Two turns of light orange silk, followed by light dirty-orange Seal's fur.

RIBS.—Gold tinsel (oval).

HACKLE.—Light dirty-orange from silk.

THROAT.—Jay.

WINGS.—Ginger Turkey (strips); Gallina, red breast of Golden Pheasant, in strands; Bustard, Peacock herl, Golden Pheasant tail, strands of black Turkey white tipped, red Macaw, Swan dyed dirty-orange and dark blue; and Mallard.

SIDES.—Summer Duck.
HORNS.—Blue Macaw.
HEAD.—Black herl.

Introduced for me by Farlow many years since.

DOCTOR LEONARD.

G.S.
(HI REGAN.)

TAG.—Silver twist and yellow silk.
TAIL.—A topping and blue mohair.
BUTT.—Black herl.
BODY.—Four close turns of silver twist. Two equal sections of black silk butted with four close turns (as before) of silver twist, each having a top mane of claret mohair (short).
THROAT.—Golden olive hackle and Jay.
WINGS.—Two strips of tippet; Golden Pheasant, trail Mallard and a topping.
HORNS.—Blue Macaw.

A favourite fly on the Moy (chiefly used above Ballina) and on the Owenmore.

THE DONKEY.

G.S.
(G. KELSON.)

TAG.—Silver twist and yellow silk.
TAIL.—A topping.
BUTT.—Black herl.
BODY.—Donkey's fur (now, Silver Monkey's fur).
RIBS.—Silver tinsel.
HACKLE.—A transparent natural blue-dun hackle, from second turn.
THROAT.—Jay.
WINGS.—Tippet, Teal, and Golden Pheasant tail, grey Mallard, dark mottled Turkey, Swan dyed yellow and red; and Mallard.

HORNS.—Blue Macaw.
HEAD.—Black herl.

This old standard of my Father's is a useful fly on the Lee and other Irish waters.

DR. DONALDSON.

G.S.
(MALLOCH.)

TAG.—Silver twist and yellow silk.
TAIL.—A topping, a few strands of tippet and points of Toucan.
BUTT.—Black herl.
BODY.—(After Jock Scott type) First section, blue silk, ribbed with silver tinsel (fine, oval) butted with blue Chatterer fibres above and below, and black herl: Second section, dark claret silk, ribbed with silver lace and silver tinsel, and a claret hackle along it.
THROAT.—Orange hackle and Widgeon.
WINGS.—Two extended Jungle slightly tinged in Bismarck brown; Golden Pheasant tail, light and dark Bustard, Swan dyed red, and yellow; and a topping.
SIDES.—Jungle (not dyed
HORNS.—Blue Macaw.

THE DUCHESS.

G.S.
(TURNBULL.)

TAG.—Silver twist and light yellow silk.
TAIL.—Two toppings, Indian Crow and blue Chatterer.
BUTT.—Peacock herl.
BODY.—Black silk.
RIBS.—Silver lace and silver tinsel.
HACKLE.—Black, from second turn.
THROAT.—Jay.
WINGS.—Six toppings.

SIDES.—Summer Duck.
CHEEKS.—Indian Crow and Chatterer.
HORNS.—Red, and blue Macaw; and light green Parrot.
HEAD.—Black herl.

The Master of the Dumfriesshire Otter hounds, using this fly on the Annan, recently caught ten Salmon varying from 17 to 26 lbs. in weight.

THE DUKE. G.S.
(KELSON.)

TAG.—Silver twist and yellow silk.
TAIL.—A topping.
BODY.—Light red fiery brown Seal's fur.
RIBS.—Silver tinsel.
THROAT.—Widgeon and Jay.
WINGS.—Strands of tippet; grey Mallard, a little Summer Duck, Mallard, and a topping.
SIDES.—Jungle.
HEAD.—Black herl.

A modern Spey pattern.

DUNKELD. G.S.

TAG.—Gold twist and orange silk.
TAIL.—A topping, and point of Jungle.
BUTT.—Black herl.
BODY.—Gold tinsel.
RIBS.—Gold tinsel (oval).
HACKLE.—Orange hackle, from second turn.
THROAT.—Jay.
WINGS.—Two strips of Peacock wing, Mallard, and a topping.

HORNS.—Blue and red Macaw.
CHEEKS.—Chatterer.

This old standard pattern has undergone considerable change of "toilette," and is now universally dressed as above. Formerly the body was made with gold embossed tinsel, which I prefer. I believe it was invented by W. J. Davidson.

THE DUNT. G.S.
(W. MURDOCH.)

TAG.—Silver twist and light blue silk.
TAIL.—A topping and Teal.
BODY.—Yellow, orange, red-claret Seal's fur, in equal sections.
RIBS.—Silver lace and silver tinsel.
HACKLE.—Black Heron, from claret fur.
THROAT.—Teal.
WINGS.—Two strips of plain brown Turkey with black bars and white tips.
SIDES.—Jungle, short and drooping over Throat hackle.

In the spring of 1893 this pattern accounted for seven Salmon out of the nine caught in the Birnam water on the Tay.

Mr. Murdoch writes:—"There is not a better all-round fly of the plain sort than the Dunt put upon the Dee in Spring or Autumn."

THE DURHAM RANGER. G.S.
(WRIGHT.)

TAG.—Silver twist and yellow silk.
TAIL.—Topping and Indian Crow.
BUTT.—Black herl.
BODY.—Two turns of orange silk, two turns of dark orange Seal's fur; the rest, which is about half, of black Seal's fur.

Ribs.—Silver lace and silver tinsel.
Hackle.—A white coch-a-bonddu dyed orange, running along the furs.
Throat.—Light blue hackle.
Wings.—Four tippets overlapping (two on each side) and enveloping two projecting Jungle (back to back), and a topping.
Cheeks.—Chatterer.
Horns.—Blue Macaw.
Head.—Black Berlin wool.

Rivers :—Tweed, Spey, Lochy, Tay, Don, Earn, etc., etc.

THE DUSTY MILLER.

G.S.
(Jewhurst.)

Tag.—Silver twist and yellow silk.
Tail.—A topping and Indian Crow.
Butt.—Black herl.
Body.—Silver tinsel embossed, two thirds; followed by orange silk.
Ribs.—Silver tinsel (oval).
Throat.—Gallina.
Wings.—Two strips of black Turkey white tipped, Golden Pheasant tail, Bustard, Pintail, Gallina, Mallard, and one topping put inside out on each side of wings.
Sides.—Jungle.
Horns.—Blue Macaw.

One of the oldest standard patterns.

ELSIE.

S.S.
(Kelson.)

Tag.—Silver twist (plenty).
Tail.—A topping and Summer Duck.
Butt.—Black herl.

BODY.—One third light blue silk, ribbed with silver twist and butted with fibres of Grande Breve Tocate above and below, and black herl; followed by claret silk having a dark claret hackle along it, and ribbed with silver tinsel (oval).
THROAT.—Jay.
WINGS.—Tippet fibres (plenty) veiled with Mallard; and a topping.
SIDES.—Jungle (*extra size*) and a short strip of large Summer Duck.
CHEEKS.—Grande Breve Tocate (*extra size*).

A special pattern for fish lying behind upright rocks and large boulders.

ETHEL.

G.S.
(TURNBULL.)

TAG.—Gold twist and light yellow silk.
TAIL.—Summer Duck.
BUTT.—Black herl.
BODY.—In two sections: No. 1, light yellow silk, ribbed with fine silver tinsel, and butted with Toucan (above and below), and black herl; No. 2, red silk, ribbed with gold tinsel.
THROAT.—Black Heron.
WINGS.—Two Snipe (back to back) for underwing, veiled with Peacock herl.
HORNS.—Blue Macaw.
HEAD.—Black herl.

An excellent fly on the Usk.

EXCELSIOR.

G.S.
(KELSON.)

TAG.—Silver twist and red silk.
TAIL.—A topping.
BUTT.—Black herl.

BODY.—In two sections: No. 1, Parrot green silk, ribbed with silver tinsel (oval, fine), butted with Indian Crow above and below, and black herl. No. 2, Black Seal's fur ribbed with silver tinsel (oval), and a natural black hackle along it.

THROAT.—Jay.

WINGS.—Golden Pheasant tippet and tail, and Gallina in strands; grey Mallard, Summer Duck; Mallard, and a topping.

SIDES.—Ibis and yellow Macaw (married).

HORNS.—Blue Macaw.

An old standard—useful on most rivers.

THE FAIRY.

G.S.
(FARLOW.)

TAG.—Silver twist.

TAIL.—A topping.

BODY.—One third yellow Seal's fur, followed by black Seal's fur.

RIBS.—Silver tinsel (oval).

HACKLE.—Black hackle, from yellow fur.

WINGS.—Mallard.

HORNS.—Blue Macaw.

For Canadian waters and a useful low water fly.

THE FAIRY KING.

G.S.
(KELSON.)

TAG.—Gold twist and scarlet silk.

TAIL.—Toucan and Jungle (point) dyed scarlet.

BODY.—Black Seal's fur.

RIBS.—Gold tinsel (oval).

THROAT.—Light blue hackle (long), and Gallina dyed orange.

WINGS.—Peacock's herl; Swan dyed yellow and scarlet; Summer Duck, capped with two strips of black Turkey, white tipped.

SIDES.—Jungle dyed scarlet.

HEAD.—Black herl.

An old standard on the Usk, and a great favourite of personal friends.

THE FAIRY QUEEN.

G.S.
(Kelson.)

Tag.—Gold twist and scarlet silk.

Tail.—Toucan, one small Jungle dyed scarlet, with two extending strands of Peacock wing.

Butt.—Black herl.

Body.—Two turns of black silk, followed by black Seal's fur.

Ribs.—Gold tinsel (oval).

Throat.—Medium blue hackle and Gallina dyed light orange (the same in colour as the Toucan).

Wings.—Gallina and tippet strands in different lengths for underwing, Peacock herl, Swan dyed light orange, scarlet, and blue; two thin strips of Summer Duck, capped with two strips of the black sheeny Turkey, white tipped, taken from the undertail of an old bird, and a topping.

Sides.—Jungle fowl dyed scarlet.

Horns.—Red Macaw.

Head.—Black herl.

A useful fly on the Usk and other "Red" rivers, when a thorough change is desirable.

THE FENIAN.

G.S.
(Kelson.)

Tag.—Silver twist and gold twist, respectively.

Tail.—A topping, powdered blue Macaw, and Teal.

Butt.—Black herl.

Body.—Orange Seal's fur, violet silk and black silk, in equal divisions.

Ribs.—Silver tinsel and gold lace.

Hackle.—From violet silk; one side of a red-claret and one side of a light blue hackle, forming one.

Throat.—Jay.

Wings.—Golden Pheasant tail and tippet strands; Teal, Mallard, and a topping.

Sides.—Ibis and powdered blue Macaw (married).
Horns.—Blue Macaw.

A good fly on most rivers used in sizes up to 2/0.

THE FIERY BROWN.

G.S.
(Rogan.)

Tag.—Gold twist and light orange silk.
Tail.—A topping.
Body.—Fiery brown Seal's fur.
Ribs.—Gold tinsel.
Hackle.—Fiery brown hackle, from second turn.
Wings.—Tippet strands, and broad strips of Mallard.
Horns.—Blue Macaw.
Head.—Black herl.

I would strongly recommend dressers to apply to Michael Rogan, Ballyshannon, for all shades of fiery brown.

FLOODTIDE.

G.S.
(Kelson.)

Tag.—Silver tinsel (fine, oval) and crimson silk.
Tail.—A topping and Summer Duck.
Butt.—Black herl.
Body.—Canary, yellow, dark orange, and crimson Seal's fur.
Ribs.—Silver tinsel and silver lace.
Hackle.—Yellow Eagle, from dark orange.
Throat.—Gallina (two turns) dyed crimson.
Wings.—Two Golden Pheasant sword (back to back) enveloping two extended Jungle (back to back); Bustard, Amherst Pheasant tail, Swan dyed yellow and crimson; and a topping.
Sides.—Jungle.
Cheeks.—Jungle (points).

One of the best standards for use "on the top of a flood." For Spring fishing I dress the body of Pig's wool; and for clear water and small sizes, a hen Pheasant dyed yellow instead of Eagle.

FRA DIAVOLO.

G.S.
(TRAHERNE.)

TAG.—Silver twist and light yellow silk.
TAIL.—Topping.
BUTT.—Black herl.
BODY.—One third red-orange silk, ribbed with fine silver tinsel (oval) having two Indian Crow feathers above and below, and butted as before; followed by light blue silk, ribbed with broad silver lace, having a light blue hackle along it.
THROAT.--Yellow Macaw.
WINGS.—Two strips black Turkey having white points, Amherst Pheasant tail, red Macaw, Swan dyed green Macaw, and two toppings.
SIDES.—Summer Duck and Jungle above.
HORNS.—Blue Macaw.
CHEEKS.—Chatterer.

RIVERS:—Tay, etc.

(With this pattern the inventor himself once caught thirteen fresh-run fish at Stanley in fifteen days.)

GALLANTINE.
(Grub.)

G.S.
(KELSON.)

TAG.—Silver twist and yellow silk.
TAIL.—Two starling dyed light red-claret (back to back).
BUTT.—(Or No. 1 hackle) A white furnace dyed light red-claret.
BODY.—Claret chenille. No. 2 (or centre) hackle, a white furnace dyed dark claret.

HEAD.—(Or No. 3 hackle) A large black hackle, and two turns of Gallina dyed dark blue.
CHEEKS.—Chatterer (small, taken from head).

An excellent standard Grub on the Usk. At the latter end of August, 1882, the water being very low, I killed fifteen Salmon in one week, varying from 13 lbs. to 22½ lbs. in weight with this fly dressed on a No. 1 hook.

THE GALLINIPPER. G.S.

(KELSON.)

TAG.—Silver twist and scarlet silk.
TAIL.—Toucan (half orange, half red from undertail) Amherst Pheasant tail strands, and point of Jungle.
BUTT.—Orange herl.
BODY.—Dirty orange, Mouse, and black Seal's fur equally divided.
RIBS.—Silver tinsel (oval).
THROAT.—Scarlet hackle and a natural blue-dun.
WINGS.—Two strips of Peacock wing, and Golden Pheasant tail in strands.
SIDES.—Teal and Ibis (married).
CHEEKS.—Indian Crow.
HORNS.—Red Macaw.

An old standard on the Usk, and a useful fly in Scotland.

THE GARDENER. G.S.

(W. GARDEN.)

TAG.—Gold twist and crimson silk.
TAIL.—A topping, and tippet strands.
BODY.—Yellow, green, and dark blue Seal's fur in equal divisions.
RIBS.—Silver tinsel.
HACKLE.—A topping (as hackle) from yellow fur.

Throat.—Black Heron.
Wings.—Two strips, plain cinnamon Turkey.
Sides.—Jungle (short and drooping).

One of Garden's best Dee patterns.

GENERAL SUMMER.

G.S. (Summer.)

Tag.—Gold twist and gold silk.
Tail.—A topping.
Body.—Claret Seal's fur.
Ribs.—Gold tinsel (oval).
Hackle.—Claret, from second turn.
Throat.—Jay.
Wings.—Mallard.
Horns.—Blue Macaw.

Invariably used on the Erne and most other Irish rivers. Also a good fly on the Usk.

THE GHOST.

S.S.

Tag.—Silver twist.
Tail.—Jay (points, back to back).
Butt.—Black herl.
Body.—In two equal sections: No. 1, Black silk (thin) butted with two turns of silver tinsel and two golden toppings above and below. No. 2, Black Ostrich herl.
Hackle.—Natural black hackle, from centre.
Wings.—Two strips of Shovel Duck.
Horns.—Blue Macaw.

This is an old standard and bears the reputation of killing fish on those occasions when pools have been over-thrashed with ordinary patterns.

GLEN GRANT.

G.S.
(Major GRANT.)

TAIL.—Golden Pheasant yellow rump (point).
BODY.—Yellow wool three turns, and black wool.
RIBS.—Silver lace and silver tinsel (usual way).
HACKLE.—A black Spey Cock hackle from end of body, but wound from root the reverse way crossing over ribs.
THROAT.—Teal.
WINGS.—Two long Jungle (back to back) two reaching half way, and two still shorter, and Teal.
HEAD.—Yellow wool.

An old standard on the Spey.

GLEN GRANT'S FANCY.

G.S.
(Major GRANT.)

TAG.—Silver twist and red-claret silk.
TAIL.—A topping.
BUTT.—Black herl.
BODY.—Light olive-green Seal's fur.
RIBS.—Silver tinsel.
THROAT.—Jay and Teal.
WINGS.—Tippet strands, Gallina, light mottled Turkey, Golden Pheasant tail, Mallard, and a topping.
HEAD.—Black herl.

A modern standard on the Spey.

GLENTANA.

G.S.
(GARDEN.)

TAG.—Silver twist.
TAIL.—Red breast feather of Golden Pheasant.
BODY.—One-third light orange Seal's fur; and light claret Seal's fur.

RIBS.—Silver lace and silver tinsel.
HACKLE.—Black Heron, from orange fur.
THROAT.—Widgeon.
WINGS.—Two strips of plain cinnamon Turkey showing light points.

An old Dee fly.

THE GLOW-WORM. S.S.
(Grub.) (KELSON.)

TAG.—Silver twist, and yellow Seal's fur well picked out.
TAIL.—Ibis.
BODY.—Copper tinselled chenille having three coch-a-bonddu hackles (1) at Butt: (2) at centre of Body: (3) at Head.

An old standard on the Usk, and a general favourite on other hard fished waters.

THE GOLDEN BUTTERFLY. S.S.
(TRAHERNE.)

TAG.—Silver twist and light blue silk.
TAIL.—A topping.
BUTT.—Black herl.
BODY.—Light yellow silk. The body is divided into five sections, butted at each with two tippet feathers (back to back) above and below, slightly increasing in size, as well as with black herl.
RIBS.—Three in each section of fine silver twist.
WINGS.—Six toppings.
HORNS.—Blue Macaw.
HEAD.—Black herl.

(NOTE.—Our best "Exaggeration," for special use in bright weather and water.)

RIVERS:—Where it has actually killed the Tweed, Wye, harling on the Tay, and in Norway.

THE GOLDEN CANARY.

G.S.
(Hi Regan.)

Tag.—Gold twist and dark yellow silk.
Tail.—A topping and light (barred) Bustard
Body.—Golden-yellow Seal's fur.
Ribs.—Gold tinsel (oval).
Throat.—A light Bustard hackle.
Wings.—Light and dark Bustard (strips), and two toppings.
Horns.—Blue Macaw.

A successful old standard in Norway, used in discoloured (glacier) water.

GOLDEN DROP.

G.S.
(Kelson.)

Tag.—Gold twist and cream silk.
Tail.—A topping and Jungle point.
Butt.—Black herl.
Body.—In two sections; No. 1, gold tinsel and silver ribs, butted with Toucan and black herl; No. 2, black silk and gold ribs.
Hackle.—Orange, from centre.
Throat.—Jay.
Wings.—Light mottled Turkey, Golden Pheasant tail, Swan dyed orange, light green, and Scarlet; Gallina, Mallard and a topping.
Sides.—Jungle.
Horns.—Blue Macaw.

A general favourite.

THE GOLDEN EAGLE.

G.S.
(*Partridge.)

Tag.—Gold twist and gold silk.
Tail.—Tippet in strands.

* "Golden Perch," Oxford Street, London.

BODY.—Gold and fiery brown Pig's wool, equally divided.
RIBS.—Gold tinsel.
HACKLE.—Eagle hackle dyed gold over one-third of body.
THROAT.—Teal.
WINGS.—Two strips of silver mottled Turkey.

An old standard at Ringwood.

THE GOLDFINCH.

G.S.
(BERNARD.)

TAG.—Gold twist and gold silk.
TAIL.—A topping.
BODY.—Gold silk.
RIBS.—Gold tinsel.
HACKLE.—A yellow hackle from second turn.
THROAT.—Jay.
WINGS.—Six toppings.
HORNS.—Red Macaw.
HEAD.—Black herl.

A very old standard.

THE GOLD JUDGE.

G.S.
(TURNBULL.)

TAG.—Gold twist and yellow silk.
TAIL.—A topping and blue Chatterer.
BUTT.—Peacock herl.
BODY.—Gold tinsel.
RIBS.—Gold tinsel (oval).
HACKLE.—Olive green, from second turn.
THROAT.—Fiery brown and Jay.
WINGS.—Cinnamon Turkey, Pintail, Swan dyed yellow and red; Summer Duck, and two toppings.
HORNS.—Blue Macaw.
HEAD.—Black herl.

THE GOLD RIACH.

G.S.
(RIACH.)

BODY.—Orange Berlin wool three turns, followed by black wool.

RIBS.—From different starting points, of gold tinsel (narrow), gold twist, and silver twist, not wound as usual, but in the reverse way (towards head) and placed an equal distance apart.

HACKLE.—A red Spey Cock, from end of body, wound from the root of feather instead of from the point of it, and crossing *over* the ribs the whole way.

THROAT.—Teal, two turns.

WINGS.—Two short strips of Mallard with brown mottled points and grey mottled roots.

(See page 101, for particulars of dressing.)

Most of our flies are better at one time of year than at another, and some are used only on special occasions. The "Golden Riach," like "Jock Scott," etc., kills best in Spring and Autumn. The "Purple King," unlike the "Green King," kills well on the Spey throughout the season. The records kept at Wester Elchies of fish caught in the district during five years from 1st August to 15th October give the following results :—

1.—Gold Riach 51 Salmon.
2.—Purple King 47 ,,
3.—Jock Scott 36 ,,
4.—Miss Jackson 35 ,,
5.—Lady Caroline 35 ,,
6.—The Carron Fly 34 ,,
7.—Glentana 19 ,,
8.—Thunder and Lightning 11 Salmon.
9.—Blue Doctor 11 ,,
10.—Green King 10 ,,
11.—Black King 8 ,,
12.—Dunkeld 8 ,,

This list is considerably curtailed; many other patterns met with some success. The "Green King" sinks into insignificance from the fact that it is rarely used except in its own short season when the natural insect is flying about.

THE GORDON.

The taste for varying this pattern has doubtless arisen from the fact that there are Fishermen who, like myself, are not always satisfied with any of the standards. We tone them down or brighten them up as circumstances in fishing direct.

"But," writes a friend who knew the inventor, "the swift impress that a truthfully dressed 'Gordon' makes on the mind of a Dee Fisherman is one it needs no special studio training to enjoy."

As most people know, this fly is simply "lionised" on the Dee; not even "Jock Scott" can boast so many friends and supporters in any one district. But what the "Gordon" *was* and what it *is* are two widely different things. No two dressers of to-day make the fly alike.

Mr. Cosmo Gordon, the inventor, used to be particular about the colour and amount of hackle, frequently using two feathers together. He also had Jay at the throat instead of the dyed hackle as used now. He, moreover, had the tippet in strands, and objected to the whole feather in the wings.

"At one time," says William Brown, "Jay was employed as a throat hackle."

Mr. Gordon was not only a good Salmon-angler, but also a good judge of flies, an experience not picked up at home, by any means, for the Dee was, and is still, early in the season, little more than a four-fly river in his day. It is reported that he fished with other people's flies; but I, who knew he bought them, stoutly maintain that they were his own. Of the many doubtful but conscientious representations of the "Gordon" I have decided to give the two following dressings as practised at present in Aberdeen.

THE GORDON. G.S.

(Cosmo Gordon.)

(By William Brown, George Street, Aberdeen.)

Tag.—Silver twist and yellow silk.
Tail.—A topping.
Butt.—Black herl.
Body.—One third yellow silk, and claret silk.
Ribs.—Silver lace and silver tinsel (flat).
Hackle.—Claret hackle, from yellow silk.
Throat.—Blue hackle.
Wings.—One tippet backed with a sword feather of Golden Pheasant; Peacock herl, Bustard, Swan dyed light blue, light green, and red-claret; Amherst Pheasant tail and a topping.
Sides.—Jungle.
Head.—Black wool.

THE GORDON. G.S.

(Cosmo Gordon.

(By William Garden, Union Street, Aberdeen.)

Tag.—Silver twist and yellow silk.
Tail.—A topping and tippet strands.
Butt.—Black herl.
Body.—One-third dark yellow silk, and claret silk.
Ribs.—Silver lace and silver tinsel (flat).
Hackle.—Claret hackle, from dark yellow silk.
Throat.—Blue hackle.
Wings.—Two light red-claret hackles (back to back) veiled with Peacock herl, light (grey) mottled Turkey, dark mottled Turkey, Golden Pheasant tail, Bustard, Swan dyed yellow and blue; light mottled Turkey dyed claret, and a topping.
Sides.—Jungle.
Horns.—Blue Macaw.
Head.—Black wool.

GORDON CUMMING. G.S.

(A. P. Gordon-Cumming.)

Tag.—Silver twist and red silk.
Tail.—Two toppings.
Butt.—Black herl.
Body.—Yellow silk.
Ribs.—Silver lace and silver tinsel (oval).
Hackle.—A light blue hackle, from second turn.
Throat.—Jay..
Wings.—A tippet backed with red breast of Golden Pheasant, veiled with Teal, light mottled Turkey; Mallard and two toppings.
Sides.—Swan dyed, yellow, red, and blue (married).
Horns.—Blue Macaw.

Sir Alexander was one of the best if not the finest amateur dresser in his day. He had, besides this one, several other patterns of his own, all of which were in constant demand on the Findhorn five-and-twenty years ago. One of them had a butt of red herl, a second one in the centre of the body, and a third at the head; but I am unable to give the correct dressing of the fly. I have described the above from a faded pattern which was given to me by the inventor himself; and in order to get at the true colours as near as one could, I pulled the fly to pieces for the purpose. The inventor hardly ever used the standard patterns without varying them more or less. "Jock Scott" for instance, he made with a blue silk head section, instead of the usual black one; and perhaps this was the origin of the "blue-Jock-Scott."

THE GREEN HIGHLANDER. G.S.

(Grant.)

Tag.—Silver twist and canary silk.
Tail.—A topping and Teal.
Butt.—Black herl.
Body.—Two turns of yellow silk and green Seal's fur.
Ribs.—Silver tinsel.

HACKLE.—Green from yellow silk.

THROAT.—A yellow hackle.

WINGS.—Two tippets (back to back) veiled with light and dark Bustard, Golden Pheasant tail, dark mottled Turkey, Swan dyed green, Mallard and a topping.

HORNS.—Blue Macaw.

THE GREEN KING. S.S.

BODY.—A dull shade of green, composed of a mixture of light and dark green, brown, and a little yellow Berlin wools.

RIBS.—From separate starting points of gold tinsel (narrow), silver tinsel (narrow) and light olive-green sewing thread. These are all wound the reverse way an equal distance apart, but the sewing thread is left until the hackle is put on. The two metal ribs run *under* the hackle, the sewing thread is put *over* it, between the fibres.

HACKLE.—From end of body, a red Spey-Cock hackle, but wound from the root instead of from the point, in the usual direction, thus crossing *over* the metal ribs.

THROAT.—Teal, two turns only.

WINGS.—Two strips of Mallard, having brown mottled points and grey mottled roots.

The old standard Spey flies, like this one, are dressed upon long shanked hooks. The bodies start from a point as much *before* the direct line of the point of the hook as the work in ordinary standard flies starts *behind* it ; that is equal to saying the bodies are comparatively very short. The wings are also very short, in fact, no longer than the bodies, if so long.

In preparing a Spey-Cock's hackle, do not remove *all* the fluffy fibres at the root, but leave about three on each side of the quill. "The Green King" is dressed after the local fly of that name. It appears in enormous numbers about the end of April, and is an exceedingly large insect, twice the size of a hornet or even larger. I have seen them emerge from the chrysalis and float down-stream before the wings expand. When left alone by the Salmon they soon rise from the surface and fly at a great pace up and down the river. On these occasions the counterfeit fly, like the March-brown on the Dee, is very deadly. There are several of these curious old standards on the Spey. Amongst others, the "Secretary" and the "Green Riach" find some supporters; but they resemble other flies so closely that I have thought it unnecessary to add them to the present list.

N.B.—These old Spey standards were specially dressed for this work by Charles Stuart, Fisherman, Aberlour, under the supervision of John Cruikshank. Better authorities do not exist.

GREEN MIXTURE.

G.S.
(Enright.)

Tag.—Gold twist and dark orange silk.
Tail.—Toucan and Indian Crow.
Body.—Light pea-green silk.
Ribs.—Silver tinsel.
Hackle.—Jay, from centre.
Wings.—Golden Pheasant yellow rump, Gallina, powdered blue and red Macaw, Indian Crow, Bustard, Mallard and a topping.
Head.—Black herl.

A useful Irish pattern.

THE GREEN PARROT.

G.S.
(Enright.)

Tag.—Silver twist and yellow silk.
Tail.—A topping and tippet strands.
Body.—Violet silk.
Ribs.—Silver tinsel.
Throat.—Parrot hackle (light green).

WINGS.—Golden Pheasant tippet and yellow rump feather (point), Parrot, Gallina, Ibis, yellow Macaw, and Mallard.
CHEEKS.—Indian Crow.
HEAD.—Black herl.

THE GREEN PEACOCK.

G.S.
(W. MURDOCH.)

TAG.—Silver twist and yellow silk.
TAIL.—A topping.
BODY.—Light blue silk.
RIBS.—Oval tinsel.
THROAT.—Light blue hackle.
WINGS.—Peacock herl, sword feather.

Writing from Aberdeen, Mr. Murdoch states :—" On blazing, bright, hot days, during June and July, there is no fly so fatal on the Dee, taking the river all over, as the Green Peacock dressed on Nos. 7, 8, and 9 *double hooks*. Brown of George Street and Garden of Union Street always dress it true to pattern."

THE GREEN QUEEN.

G.S.
(KELSON.)

TAG.—Gold tinsel (narrow).
TAIL.—Yellow rump, Golden Pheasant (point).
BODY.—Same mixture of Berlin wools as for the " Green King."
RIBS.—Gold tinsel.
HACKLE.—Crown Pigeon or Grey Heron—one side of a feather stripped—from second turn.
THROAT.—Bittern dyed yellow—the white speckled feather.
WINGS.—Dark cinnamon Turkey with lightish points; or, better still, the " Gled."

As a general pattern in bright weather and water I prefer this to the " Green King," which, however, is one of the best on the Spey when the fly itself is " up," say, from the third week in May to the second week in July. The " Queen " is also a capital fly on many other rivers.

GREENWELL.

G.S.
(Wright.)

Tag.—Silver twist and light orange silk.
Tail.—Topping and Jungle.
Butt.—Black herl.
Body.—Light blue silk.
Ribs.—Silver lace and silver tinsel (flat).
Hackle.—Light blue, from second turn.
Throat.—Widgeon.
Wings.—Two strips of black Turkey, white tipped ; Golden Pheasant tail, light and dark Bustard, Gallina, Swan dyed green and scarlet ; grey Mallard, Mallard, and a topping.
Sides.—Jungle.
Horns.—Blue Macaw.
Head.—Black wool.

Rivers :—Tweed, Shannon, Erne, Tay, etc.

GREY EAGLE.

G.S.
(Jewhurst.)

Tag.—Silver twist.
Tail.—Red breast feather of the Golden Pheasant.
Body.—Yellow, light blue, and scarlet Seal's fur.
Ribs.—Silver lace and silver tinsel.
Hackle.—Grey Eagle, from blue fur.
Throat.—Widgeon (Teal for large patterns).
Wings.—Two strips of brown mottled Turkey, with black bars and white points.

A well-known dark water fly on the Dee.

THE HARGREAVES.

G.S.
(Colonel HARGREAVES.)

TAG.—Silver twist.
TAIL.—A topping.
BODY.—Two turns of canary silk and black silk.
RIBS.—Silver tinsel.
HACKLE.—Black hackle, from canary silk.
THROAT.—Jay.
WINGS.—Peacock's herl (sword feather) veiled with two broad strips of Summer Duck.
HORNS.—Blue Macaw.

THE HARLEQUIN.

G.S.
(BERNARD.

TAG.—Gold twist and olive-green silk.
TAIL.—A topping.
BUTT.—Black herl.
BODY.—In three equal divisions of orange, light blue, and pink silk.
RIBS.—Gold embossed tinsel (ordinary method) and silver tinsel (reversed) passing over the gold.
THROAT.—Orange and light blue hackles respectively.
WINGS.—Two tippets capped with light and dark Bustard; Golden Pheasant tail, and a topping.
HORNS.—Blue and red Macaw.
SIDES.—Jungle.
HEAD.—Gold twist.

THE HELMSDALE.

G.S.
(RADCLIFFE.)

TAG.—Silver twist and orange silk.
TAIL.—A topping.
BUTT.—Black herl.
BODY.—Two turns of light yellow silk and yellow Seal's fur.

RIBS.—Silver tinsel, and fine oval tinsel.
HACKLE.—Yellow hackle along fur.
THROAT.—Light blue hackle.
WINGS.—Brown mottled Turkey slightly white tipped.

A very old favourite on the Helmsdale.

THE HEATHER DOG. S.S.
(Grub.) (KELSON.)

TAG.—Silver twist (plenty).
TAIL.—Yellow Macaw.
BUTT.—Small furnace hackle dyed red (coiled), and cheeked with points of Jungle on each side.
BODY.—Alternate coils of red and black chenille.
CENTRE HACKLE.—Red undertail of Toucan, cheeked, as before, with Jungle.
HEAD HACKLE.—Two turns of Teal dyed yellow, and a black Heron hackle, cheeked with Jungle.

Salmon feed voraciously on a caterpillar (found on the hills in the North) when brought down by heavy rains. On those occasions, and for some days after, general standards fail, while this pattern, which somewhat represents the living red and black striped insect itself is often effective.

HEMPSEED. G.S.
(KELSON.)

TAG.—Silver twist and yellow silk.
TAIL.—A topping, Parrot; and Jungle (point).
BUTT.—Black herl.
BODY.—Four turns of yellow Seal's fur, four turns claret ditto (halfway), and light blue Seal's fur.
RIBS.—Silver lace and gold tinsel.

HACKLE.—An Irish-grey hackle, from yellow fur.

THROAT.—A claret hackle and Widgeon.

WINGS.—Two extended Jungle (back to back) Teal, Amherst Pheasant, and Golden Pheasant tail, Mallard and a topping.

SIDES.—Swan dyed yellow, claret, and light blue (married).

HORNS.—Blue Macaw.

CHEEKS.—Chatterer.

An old Tweed pattern.

THE HEMPSEED GRUB.

G.S.
(KELSON.)

TAG.—Silver twist.

TAIL.—Ibis and yellow Macaw (mixed).

BUTT.—No. 1 hackle a natural red Irish-grey, cheeked with Jungle points.

BODY.—Yellow and claret Seal's fur (half-way) ribbed with silver tinsel (fine, oval). No. 2 hackle, a similar one and cheeked as before, followed by blue Seal's fur and ribs.

HEAD.—No. 3 hackle as before, and Widgeon, cheeked again with Jungle.

THE HIGHLAND GEM.

G.S.
(KELSON.)

TAG.—Silver twist and yellow silk.

TAIL.—A topping, Ibis, and Summer Duck.

BUTT.—Black herl.

BODY.—In two equal sections: No. 1, of yellow silk, ribbed with narrow (oval) silver tinsel, and butted with Golden bird of Paradise or Toucan above and below, and black herl: No. 2, blue silk ribbed as before alongside broad silver tinsel (flat).

HACKLE.—Black Heron, from centre of blue silk.

THROAT.—Gallina.

WINGS.—Amherst Pheasant strips and three toppings.
HORNS.—Black Cockatoo (tail).

An excellent spring pattern on the Spey and Shannon.

HOLLAND'S FANCY.

G.S.
(G. HOLLAND.)

TAG.—Gold twist and gold silk.
TAIL.—Ibis, yellow Macaw, and unbarred Summer Duck, in strands.
BUTT.—Blue Chatterer, used as a hackle.
BODY.—In two equal sections of gold silk, butted with blue Chatterer hackle; and violet silk.
RIBS.—Gold tinsel (oval).
THROAT.—Black Heron and unbarred Summer Duck.
WINGS.—Swan dyed gold and violet, single married strips of each. Amherst Pheasant and two toppings.
HORNS.—Blue Macaw.

THE HOP DOG.
(Grub.)

G.S.
(KELSON.)

TAG.—Silver twist (plenty).
TAIL.—Indian Crow.
BUTT.—Toucan (as hackle), cheeked on each side with Chatterer.
BODY.—Alternate coils (wasp-like, not spiral) black, and red-orange chenilles; in centre, Toucan and Chatterer as before.
HEAD.—Toucan, and Gallina dyed red-orange forming third hackle, and Chatterer repeated.

This Grub comes into use earlier than all others except the "Spring Grub."

IKE DEAN.

G.S.
(G. KELSON.)

TAG. Silver twist and pink silk.
TAIL.—A topping.

Butt.—Blue Chatterer, as hackle.
Body.—In two equal sections: (1) Silver tinsel (oval), butted with Golden bird of Paradise: (2) Black silk, ribbed with silver lace.
Hackle.—Black Heron, from centre of black silk.
Wings.—Grey Mallard, Golden Pheasant tail, Swan dyed blue and yellow, with two strips of cinnamon Turkey, and a topping.

"Ich Dien," the original name of this excellent pattern, was introduced on the Lochy by my Father. It was one of the first of the fancy flies and became very popular a few years before the advent of the "Butcher." The singular success attained on the upper pools of this river by our servant named Ike Dean, led to the general use of the pattern on other rivers in Scotland, where the fly is known only by the name given with the description.

THE IMPROVED HELMSDALE.

G.S.
(Nicol McNicol.)

Tag.—Silver twist and yellow silk.
Tail.—A topping and Indian Crow.
Butt.—Black herl.
Body.—Silver tinsel.
Ribs.—Silver tinsel (oval).
Hackle.—Light green hackle (half-way).
Wings.—Golden Pheasant strands, Peacock herl, Swan dyed red and yellow, and a topping.
Sides.—Indian Crow (large).
Cheeks.—Indian Crow (small).
Horns.—Blue Macaw.
Head.—Black wool.

One of the best Helmsdale patterns and a great favourite in the North. To be had of Nicol McNicol, Reay, Thurso.

THE INFALLIBLE.

G.S.
(Farlow.)

Tag.—Silver twist and light blue silk.
Tail.—A topping.
Butt.—Black herl.
Body.—Four turns of claret silk, followed by dark yellow silk.
Ribs.—Silver tinsel (broad).
Hackle.—Claret hackle, from claret silk.
Throat.—Jay.
Wings.—Two tippets (back to back) capped with Golden Pheasant tail, Bustard, Peacock wing; red, and blue Macaw, and a topping.
Sides.—A narrow strip of Summer Duck.
Horns.—Blue Macaw.
Head.—Black herl.

A well-known old standard. Kills well on the Bundrowes and Blackwater; an excellent low-water fly on the Shannon and a general favourite throughout Scotland and Wales.

THE INVER GREEN.

G.S.
(C. Austen-Leigh.)

Tag.—Gold twist.
Tail.—A topping.
Butt.—Black herl.
Body.—Light olive-green silk.
Ribs.—Gold embossed tinsel.
Hackle.—Light olive-green, from second turn.
Wings.—Two strips of tippet; Bustard, Pintail, Swan dyed crimson, Golden Pheasant tail, and Mallard.
Horns.—Blue Macaw.
Head.—Black herl.

An excellent fly on the Inver.

THE JEANNIE.

G.S.
(W. BROWN.)

TAG.—Silver twist.
TAIL.—A topping.
BODY.—One-third yellow silk, followed by black silk.
RIBS.—Silver tinsel.
THROAT.—A natural black hackle.
WINGS.—Mallard.
SIDES.—Jungle.

A great favourite in summer on the Dee. It is dressed on small double hooks.

THE JOCKIE.

G.S.
(W. BROWN.)

TAG.—Silver twist.
TAIL.—A topping.
BODY.—One-third yellow silk, followed by dark claret silk.
RIBS.—Silver tinsel (oval).
THROAT.—A coch-a-bonddu hackle.
WINGS.—Mallard.
SIDES.—Jungle.

A useful fly in summer on the Dee. It is dressed on small double hooks.

JOCK SCOTT.

G.S.
(JOHN SCOTT.)

TAG.—Silver twist and yellow silk.
TAIL.—A topping and Indian Crow.
BUTT.—Black herl.
BODY.—In two equal sections: No. 1, of yellow silk (butter-cup colour) ribbed with narrow silver tinsel, and butted with Toucan above and below, and black herl: No. 2, black silk, ribbed with broad silver tinsel.

HACKLE.—A natural black hackle, from centre.
THROAT.—Gallina.
WINGS.—Two strips of black Turkey with white tips, Golden Pheasant tail, Bustard, grey Mallard, Peacock (sword feather) Swan dyed blue and yellow, red Macaw, Mallard, and a topping.
SIDES.—Jungle.
CHEEKS.—Chatterer.
HORNS.—Blue Macaw.
HEAD.—Black herl.

"Jock"—for the inventor of this renowned fly was hardly known as John Scott—was born at Branxholme early in February 1817. When thirteen years of age he began his Salmon-angling career under the directions of Robert Kerss, head keeper to the (then) Marquis of Lothian. In two or three years, on leaving his situation, he entered the service of that Prince of sportsmen, the late Lord John Scott, with whom he remained, as Fisherman, for full five-and-twenty years of his life. Afterwards "Jock" spent a year or two at the fly-table, and lived honourably by the constant practice of that art which he was born to enrich. He then became keeper to the present Earl of Haddington M.F.H. in whose service the poor old fellow died, 24th January, 1893. "Jock" was no giant, but had a big heart and a constitution of iron. Second to none at other sports and pastimes in the North, his soul was chiefly in fishing and most of his time was spent in the water without waders.

Admired by many, respected by all, trustworthy to a degree, good at fishing, excellent at fly-making, he distinguished himself for his inventive genius in connection with this particular pattern. Not long before his death (he had been my attendant when young) he gave me a specimen of his own make, and said that he set about the original in 1850.

"When you are too old, Sir," he added, "send to Kelso for them Neither Forrest nor Redpath* ever have that nasty dark coloured silk in front (meaning in the order of construction) and know how to keep yellow silk a good colour when put there by themselves."

* Redpath and Co. are wholesale people well known in the trade for their beautiful flies, etc., etc.

It is hardly necessary to say that the utmost triumph of two essential qualities, namely, harmony and proportion, is admirably illustrated in this—one of the most popular fancy patterns ever designed by man.

It is only just possible to find a river or a catch, be it in pools, streams, rapids, or flats, shaded or exposed to the light of day, in which a "Jock Scott," when dressed properly, has not made for itself a splendid reputation. Remembering what has been urged in these pages with regard to judging at the riverside which kind of fly is best for the time being, we shall find that no pattern illustrates my theories so perfectly and so satisfactorily as this one.

But it should be borne in mind that orange silk (too often used instead of yellow) even closely coiled on the hook, once saturated, always turns a dirty brown shade, intensified in many cases by the roughly waxed tying-silk underneath. That colour is not only objectionable, but undesirable, the material features of the fly in this instance being altogether robbed of both beauty and effect while doing duty in clear water and bright weather.

The only correct account of the life and exploits of the inventor appeared in the *Field* 18th February, 1893, over the signature of "Punt Gun," a gentleman who knew "Jock" intimately as a Fisherman on the Tweed. "Every word," says the writer of it in a recent letter to me, "was taken from his own life, or the writings of his son and family. I was very fond of him; and it was a labour of love to me to write all I knew of the poor old fellow."

The interesting biography concluded with these words: "With 'Jock's' death has passed away another link with old days, when to be a sportsman was, at any rate, to be a man. . . May he rest in peace."

JOHN CAMPBELL.

G.S.
(Wright.)

Tag.—Silver twist and orange silk.
Tail.—A topping.
Butt.—Black herl.

BODY.—Black silk.
RIBS.—Silver lace and silver tinsel.
HACKLE.—Natural black, from centre.
THROAT.—An orange hackle.
WINGS.—Tippet strands; Pintail, Florican, light and dark Bustard, Golden Pheasant tail, Swan dyed yellow, Mallard, and a topping.
HORNS.—Blue Macaw.
CHEEKS.—Chatterer.
HEAD.—Black herl.

A good fly on the Usk, Tweed, and Dee, and said to be an old standard on many other rivers.

---

*JOHN FERGUSON.

G.S.
(WRIGHT.)

TAG.—Silver twist and dark yellow silk.
TAIL.—A topping.
BUTT.—Black herl.
BODY.—Blue silk and salmon coloured silk, equally divided.
RIBS.—Silver lace and silver tinsel.
HACKLE.—Orange hackle, from blue silk.
THROAT.—Gallina.
WINGS.—Pintail, Golden Pheasant tail, Bustard, Parrot, red Macaw, black Cockatoo's tail, Gallina, Mallard, and a topping.
SIDES.—Jungle.
HORNS.—Blue Macaw.
HEAD.—Black herl.

An old standard on most Scotch rivers.

* Named after an Edinburgh gentleman who, in former days, was one of the best Anglers on the Tweed.

THE JONAH.

G.S.
(Kelson.)

Tag.—Silver twist and golden-yellow silk.
Tail.—A topping and Chatterer.
Butt.—Scarlet wool.
Body.—Silver tinsel (flat).
Ribs.—Silver tinsel (oval).
Throat.—Light blue hackle and Gallina.
Wings.—Fine Peacock's herl (plenty), from extremity of eyed feather, and two narrow strips of Ibis above.
Horns.—Blue Macaw.
Head.—Scarlet wool.

A favourite Autumn fly.

THE JUNGLE HORNET.
(Grub.)

G.S.
(Kelson.)

Tag.—Gold twist (plenty).
Tail.—Ibis (two strips).
Butt.—No. 1 hackle, a coch-a-bonddu, slightly tinged in Bismarck brown, cheeked with Jungle.
Body.—Twelve alternate coils of yellow and black chenille. No. 2, hackle in centre, and No. 3, at head, as before, cheeked.

This Grub (illustrated), a vast improvement on "Ajax," is far more successful for general purposes than any of its kind. It is easily varied for all rivers. The tail may be composed of yellow Macaw, with or without Summer Duck. The body, instead of yellow, may have either blue or red chenille. Taking the last five seasons, this fly has killed for me twenty-seven Salmon. One day in the year 1882 while fishing the Bryn stream above the town of Usk, I caught two Salmon with it averaging 28 lbs. in weight. The fly may be dressed either large or small; and is very useful when the water is slightly coloured.

KATE.

G.S.

(Mrs. Courtney.)

Tag.—Silver twist and light yellow silk.
Tail.—A topping.
Butt.—Black herl.
Body.—Two turns of crimson silk, and crimson Seal's fur.
Ribs.—Silver tinsel (oval).
Hackle.—Crimson, from second turn.
Throat.—Light yellow hackle.
Wings.—(Thin) Grey Mallard, and tippet strands, Bustard, Golden Pheasant tail, Swan dyed light yellow, crimson, and light blue; Mallard and a topping.
Sides.—Jungle.
Horns.—Blue Macaw.

One of the best flies on the Tyne.

THE KENDLE.

G.S.

(Basil Field.)

Tag.—Silver twist.
Tail.—Two toppings and Chatterer.
Body.—White silk, bound closely with a thin strip of gold-beater skin about the width of the broadest tinsel, each join being covered with fine gold tinsel (about eight turns in one inch).
Throat.—Yellow hackle (or yellow Macaw for large hooks) and a blue hackle over it (or Gallina dyed blue for large hooks).
Wings.—Swan dyed blue and yellow, Bustard, Golden Pheasant tail, with an upper and lower strip of Teal.
Horns.—Blue Macaw.
Head.—Black herl.

One of Mr. Field's best patterns. It is an old favourite on the Test, and is often useful on many other rivers. On the upper part of the Wye I once had five Salmon with this fly, fishing between the hours of five and seven in the evening.

Plate 4

Bluebell

The Captain

The Chatterer

Greenwell

The Dandy

Beaconsfield

THE KILLARNEY PET.

G.S.
(Mrs. Courtney.)

Tag.—Gold twist and crimson silk.
Tail.—A topping, Summer Duck, and tippet strands.
Butt.—Black herl.
Body.—Light yellow silk, and light orange silk, equally divided.
Ribs.—Gold tinsel (oval).
Hackle.—Jay, from second turn.
Throat.—Light orange hackle.
Wings.—Tippet (strands), Golden Pheasant tail, Bustard, Summer Duck, Swan dyed crimson, yellow, blue and orange; red Macaw, and Mallard.
Horns.—Blue Macaw.
Head.—Black herl.

One of the best patterns for the Suir.

KING ALFRED.

S.S.
(Kelson.)

Tag.—Silver twist and blue silk.
Tail.—Toucan, tippet strands, and Teal.
Butt.—Black herl.
Body.—Two turns of silver tinsel, three turns of red-claret silk, four turns of gold tinsel, five turns of dark blue silk (or in such proportions).
Ribs.—Silver tinsel (fine, oval).
Hackle.—Blue, from gold tinsel.
Throat.—Jay.
Wings.—Underwing (long) Amherst Pheasant tail, and Golden Pheasant tippet strands; two long Jungle, and two shorter (understood as "double Jungle") and three toppings.
Horns.—Blue Macaw.

The special use of this pattern is referred to on page 244.

KITTY.

G.S. (Kelson.)

Tag.—Silver twist.
Tail.—Toucan and Teal.
Butt.—Black herl.
Body.—Two turns of red silk, followed by red Seal's fur.
Ribs.—Silver tinsel (oval).
Hackle.—Red hackle, from centre.
Throat.—Two turns of Gallina.
Wings.—Teal and Peacock wing in strands; Mallard, and a topping.
Horns.—Amherst Pheasant, and red Macaw.

Lochy, Spean, and Ness.

LADY BELL.

S.S. (Kelson.)

Tag.—Gold twist and gold silk.
Tail.—A topping and Indian Crow.
Butt.—Black herl.
Body.—In two sections: No. 1, gold embossed tinsel, ribbed with silver tinsel (oval, fine), butted with two small toppings above and below, and black herl; No. 2, gold silk, ribbed with black purse silk (fine) and gold tinsel (oval) alongside it.
Throat.—Red and yellow Macaw.
Wings.—Two strips of Swan dyed gold, and three toppings.
Cheeks.—Indian Crow.
Horns.—Blue and red Macaw.

On those rivers where dark flies are used on bright days and fail, I have many times witnessed the success of this pattern.

LADY BLANCHE.

G.S. (Bernard.)

Tag.—Gold twist and yellow silk.
Tail.—A topping.

Body.—Blue silk.
Ribs.—Gold tinsel (oval).
Hackle.—Jay, from third turn.
Wings.—Tippet strands, Teal, Summer Duck, Mallard, and a topping.
Horns.—Blue Macaw.
Head.—Black herl.

A very old standard pattern.

LADY CAROLINE. G.S.

Tail.—Golden Pheasant red-breast, a few strands only.
Body.—Brown and olive-green Berlin wool mixed together in proportion of one part olive-green, two parts brown.
Ribs.—From separate starting points, of gold tinsel (narrow), gold twist, and silver twist, wound the usual way, an equal distance apart.
Hackle.—Grey Heron, from tail (tied in at the point as usual) wound alongside gold tinsel.
Throat.—Golden Pheasant red-breast, two turns.
Wings.—Two strips of Mallard showing brown points and light roots.

An old standard Spey fly. See the "Green King."

LADY D'ERESBY. G.S.

(Kelson.)

Tag.—Silver twist and light blue silk.
Tail.—Toucan and Amherst Pheasant.
Butt.—Black herl.
Body.—Yellow silk, red-orange, and black Seal's fur all in equal parts.
Ribs.—Silver tinsel (oval).
Hackle.—Light blue, from black Seal's fur.
Throat.—Jay.

WINGS.—Golden Pheasant tippet and tail in strands, Amherst Pheasant, Bustard, grey Mallard, Widgeon, two strips of brown Mallard above and a topping.
HORNS.—Blue Macaw.

LADY GRACE.

G.S.
(GARDEN.)

TAG.—Silver twist.
TAIL.—Red-breast feather of Golden Pheasant (point).
BODY.—Light orange, red-orange, claret and blue Seal's furs.
RIBS.—Silver tinsel.
HACKLE.—Gallina dyed yellow, from claret fur.
THROAT.—Light orange hackle.
WINGS.—Two strips of Swan dyed yellow.

A famous low water fly on the Dee.

THE LEE BLUE.

G.S.
(HAYNES.)

TAG.—Silver twist and yellow wool.
TAIL.—A topping.
BUTT.—Black herl.
BODY.—Blue Seal's fur.
RIBS.—Silver tinsel (oval, fine).
HACKLE.—A blue hackle, from second turn.
THROAT.—A yellow hackle.
WINGS.—Tippet (strands), Golden Pheasant tail, dark mottled Turkey, Swan dyed yellow and blue; and Mallard above.
HORNS.—Blue Macaw.
HEAD.—Black herl.

A very old standard on the Lee.

LEE BLUE AND GREY.

G.S.
(Haynes.)

Tag.—Silver twist and yellow wool.
Tail.—A topping and Indian Crow.
Butt.—Black herl.
Body.—In two equal divisions of blue Seal's fur with a blue hackle along it, and silver Monkey with an Irish-grey hackle.
Ribs.—Silver tinsel.
Throat.—A yellow hackle.
Wings.—Tippet (strands), Bustard, Golden Pheasant tail, Summer Duck, Swan dyed yellow, red, and blue ; Mallard, and two toppings.
Cheeks.—Chatterer.
Horns.—Amherst Pheasant.
Head.—Black herl.

One of the oldest standards on the Lee.

THE LEMON GREY.

G.S.
(Jewhurst.)

Tag.—Silver twist and yellow silk.
Tail.—A topping.
Butt.—Black herl.
Body.—Silver Monkey (modern), Rabbit fur (ancient).
Ribs.—Silver tinsel (oval).
Hackle.—An Irish-grey hackle (modern), a natural blue-dun (ancient), from second turn.
Throat.—A yellow hackle (modern), a lemon hackle (ancient).
Wings.—Tippet in strands, Teal, Gallina, Mallard, and a topping.

According to my Father's notes dated 1833, this fly was dressed in Ireland with a claret hackle under the lemon throat, and with horns of blue Macaw. It is one of the best flies on the Shannon and Lee and a great favourite on most rivers, especially in Ireland.

LEIGH'S SUN FLY. S.S.

(C. AUSTEN-LEIGH.)

TAG.—Silver twist and pink silk.
TAIL.—A topping.
BUTT.—Black herl.
BODY.—Evenly divided coils (wasp fashion) of yellow, majenta, light blue, plum-claret and dark blue Berlin wools.
RIBS.—Silver lace.
THROAT.—Light blue hackle and Jay.
WINGS.—Four toppings.
HORNS.—Blue Macaw.
HEAD.—Black herl.

An excellent fly in very bright weather on the Inver, Usk, Tweed, Spey, Blackwater, Boyne, Test, and Wye, etc.

THE LION. G.S.

(WRIGHT.)

TAG.—Silver twist and yellow silk.
TAIL.—Topping.
BUTT.—Black herl.
BODY.—Silver tinsel (flat), one fifth part at the throat being reserved for scarlet Seal's fur.
RIBS.—Silver tinsel (oval).
HACKLE.—Natural black, from second turn.
THROAT.—Gallina.
WINGS.—Tippet, sword feather of Golden Pheasant, and Peacock herl, in strands. Yellow Macaw, red Macaw, Bustard, Golden Pheasant tail, Teal, Gallina, Mallard, and a topping.
SIDES.—Jungle.
HORNS.—Blue Macaw.
HEAD.—Black wool.

RIVERS: Tay, Tweed, Lyon, Spey, Lochy, with bright Jungle; Usk, Findhorn, and Erne with dull Jungle.

THE LITTLE KELLY.

G.S.
(Kelson.)

Tag.—Gold twist.
Tail.—A topping and Ibis.
Body.—Dirty yellow Seal's fur.
Ribs.—Silver tinsel (the original pattern which I introduced myself on the Usk, years since, in company with "Harry Giles," was made with gold ribs).
Throat.—A coch-a-bonddu hackle.
Wings.—Peacock herl.
Horns.—Blue Macaw (originally red Macaw).

This fly holds a high reputation on the Tweed for Summer use, and is an old standard on the Usk.

THE LIZZIE.

G.S.
(W. Garden.)

Tag.—Silver twist.
Tail.—A topping.
Body.—Green, yellow, violet, and crimson Seal's fur, equally divided.
Ribs.—Silver tinsel (oval).
Hackle.—Blue hackle, from yellow fur.
Wings.—Tippet strands; Gallina, Swan dyed light blue, yellow, and crimson, Mallard, and a topping.
Horns.—Blue Macaw.

A good bright water fly in Summer on the Dee. It is also a great favourite on the Lochy when dressed on small double hooks.

THE LOGIE.

G.S.
(W. Brown.)

Tag.—Silver twist.
Tail.—A topping.

Body.—Dark claret silk.
Ribs.—Silver tinsel (oval).
Throat.—Light blue hackle.
Wings.—Two strips of Swan dyed yellow, veiled with broad strips of Mallard.
Sides.—Jungle.

An excellent Summer pattern in dull weather on the Dee. It is dressed on small double hooks.

LORD HENRY. G.S.

(Kelson.)

Tag.—Silver twist and light red-claret Seal's fur.
Tail.—Topping and Ibis.
Butt.—Black herl.
Body.—The first half, equal proportions of canary, orange, and fiery brown Seal's fur respectively; the rest, blue Seal's fur with a blue hackle along it.
Throat.—Jay.
Ribs.—Silver tinsel.
Wings.—Two tippets (back to back) strips of silver speckled Turkey, married strips of Teal and Swan dyed orange and red-claret; and a topping.
Horns.—Blue Macaw.
Head.—Black herl.

Rivers: Earn, Lee (Macroom district), Spey, and, when dressed small, a useful fly in summer on the Usk.

LORNE. G.S.

(Bernard.)

Tag.—Gold twist and orange silk.
Tail.—A topping.

BUTT.—Black herl.
BODY.—In three equal sections of "Green Macaw" silk, ribbed with fine gold tinsel; each section butted above and below with fibres of Parrot, followed by black herl.
THROAT.—Parrot hackle.
WINGS.—Golden Pheasant tail, Gallina, Summer Duck, and a topping.
HORNS.—Red as well as blue Macaw.
HEAD.—Black herl.

It is remarkable that the only Salmon ever known to have been taken in the river Trent fell victim to a green body. In a letter I received from Gainsborough a few years since the Rev. H. Caferata says:—"The evidence you gave at the House of Lords the other day (*re* the Trent Navigation Bill) in regard to our Salmon exactly coincided with my own opinions. There is no doubt whatever that several reaches of our river could be rendered suitable to meet the exigencies of fly-fishing. The Trent being void of many natural catches is the very reason why artificial ones should be established; and then, after a year or two, we should soon teach the fish to rise to and take flies. I have made every enquiry in connection with the opinion you ventured to offer, and I find that a Salmon *has* been taken not far from this town with a fly. . . But is it not curious that, considering there are so few rivers where green flies pay, that the only Trent Salmon known to have been caught with a fly, should have been taken with one of them?"

LOUISE.

G.S.
(BERNARD.)

TAG.—Silver twist and pink silk.
TAIL.—A topping.
BUTT.—Black herl.
BODY.—In three sections butted with black herl: No. 1, light lilac silk; No. 2, dark lilac or slate coloured silk; No. 3, pink silk.
RIBS.—Silver tinsel (fine).
HACKLE.—From third butt, a natural straw coloured coch-a-bonddu.

WINGS.—Gallina, Summer Duck, Swan dyed red-claret and yellow, Golden Pheasant tail and tippet, and a topping.
SIDES.—Jungle.
HORNS.—Blue Macaw.
HEAD.—Black herl.

A favourite in Ireland and a general fly on the Hampshire Avon.

THE LOVAT FLY. G.S.

(LORD LOVAT.)

TAG.—Silver twist.
TAIL.—Point of the red-breast of Golden Pheasant.
BODY.—Two turns of yellow Berlin wool, followed by blue Berlin wool.
RIBS.—Silver tinsel (broad).
HACKLE.—Black hackle, from yellow fur.
WINGS.—Bronze Peacock's herl.
HEAD.—Yellow mohair, picked out.

One of the best spring patterns on the Beauly.

THE MAJOR. G.S.

(Rev. A. WILLIAMS.)

TAG.—Gold twist and scarlet silk.
TAIL.—A topping, Teal, and Ibis.
BODY.—Light blue, yellow, claret, and dark blue Seal's fur, equally divided.
RIBS.—Silver tinsel and gold lace.
HACKLE.—Claret hackle, from claret fur.
THROAT.—Scarlet hackle and Gallina.
WINGS.—One tippet, backed with a claret hackle veiled with a Snipe feather on each side, Bustard, Ibis, Swan dyed yellow, and a topping.
HORNS.—Blue Macaw.

The first fancy fly used on the Usk and a universal favourite of to-day.

THE MANDARIN DRAKE. G.S.

(KELSON.)

TAG.—Gold twist and yellow silk.

TAIL.—A topping and tippet strands.

BUTT.—Black herl.

BODY.—In two equal sections: No. 1, yellow Seal's fur, ribbed with gold tinsel, and with a small yellow hackle from second turn; having two strips of Mandarin Drake (white tipped) to form one set of body wings: No. 2, dark blue Seal's fur, ribbed with broad gold tinsel, and with a light blue hackle from second turn.

THROAT.—Jay.

WINGS.—Two strips (a trifle longer than the others) of Mandarin Drake (white tipped).

This double strip-winged fly is a superb pattern on the Earn. It takes after the style introduced on the Dee by Garden of Aberdeen.

MARCH BROWN. G.S.

TAG.—Gold twist.

TAIL.—A topping.

BODY.—Silver Monkey's fur and a little dirty-orange Seal's fur, mixed together.

RIBS.—Gold tinsel (oval).

THROAT.—Partridge hackle.

WINGS.—Hen Pheasant tail.

An old standard fly on the Dee, Usk, etc. It is dressed on small double hooks.

MAR LODGE. G.S.

(JOHN LAMON T.

TAG.—Silver tinsel.

TAIL.—A topping, and points of two small Jungle above, back to back.

BUTT.—Black herl.

Body.—In three equal sections: No. 1 and No. 3 of silver tinsel; centre of black silk.

Throat.—Gallina.

Wings.—Underwing of married strips of Swan dyed yellow, red, and blue; strips of Peacock wing, Summer Duck, grey Mallard, dark mottled Turkey, Golden Pheasant tail, and a topping.

Sides.—Jungle.

Horns.—Blue Macaw.

Head.—Black wool.

A favourite Dee pattern. The inventor writes:—"1893, Her Royal Highness the Duchess of Fife has been most successful with the 'Mar Lodge' fly. Apply to Garden, Aberdeen."

THE McMILLAN. G.S.

(Nicol McNicol.)

Tag.—Silver twist and yellow silk.

Tail.—A topping and Indian Crow.

Butt.—Black herl.

Body.—In two equal sections: No. 1, Silver tinsel, butted with Parrot above and below and black herl: No. 2, gold tinsel with a gold hackle from centre butt.

Throat.—A green hackle (matching Parrot in tone).

Ribs.—Gold tinsel (oval) from centre.

Rivers: Thurso, Forss, Halladale, Helmsdale and Naver.

THE MEMBER. G.S.

(David Murray.)

Tag.—Silver twist and yellow silk.

Tail.—A topping.

Butt.—Black herl.

Body.—Chocolate silk.

RIBS.—Silver tinsel.
HACKLE.—Light orange hackle (one-fourth of body).
WINGS.—Tippet, Golden Pheasant tail, Pintail and a topping.
SIDES.—Jungle.
HEAD.—Two turns of hackle same as before.

A useful North Esk pattern.

MISS GRANT. G.S.

(JOHN SHANKS.)

TAG.—Silver twist.
TAIL.—Teal, in strands.
BODY.—Two turns of orange silk followed by olive green Berlin wool.
RIBS.—Silver tinsel.
HACKLE.—Grey Heron, from second turn.
WINGS.—Two strips of Golden Pheasant tail.

A modern Spey pattern.

MORAY DOONE. G.S.

(KELSON.)

TAG.—Silver twist and pink silk.
TAIL.—A topping, Peacock wing and Summer Duck.
BUTT.—Black herl.
BODY.—Quill dyed yellow, with four turns of red-orange Seal's fur at throat.
RIBS.—Silver tinsel (oval, narrow) and silver tinsel (flat, broad).
HACKLE.—A silver coch-a-bonddu from second turn; hen Pheasant hackle dyed yellow from Seal's fur.
THROAT.—Widgeon.
WINGS.—Two tippets (back to back), two extending Jungle (one on each side), Swan dyed yellow and red-orange, and two toppings.
SIDES.—Jungle.

HORNS.—Blue Macaw.
HEAD.—Black herl.

A good early fly on the Dee, Spey, etc.

MRS. GRANT.

G.S.
(Major GRANT.)

TAG.—Silver twist and yellow silk.
TAIL.—A topping and Indian Crow.
BUTT.—Black herl.
BODY.—Copper tinselled chenille.
HACKLE.—A red Spey-cock hackle, from centre.
THROAT.—Jay.
WINGS.—Tippet strands, Bustard, Golden Pheasant tail, light mottled Turkey, grey Mallard, and a topping.
HORNS.—Red Macaw.
HEAD.—Black herl.

A modern standard on the Spey.

MY QUEEN.

G.S.
(KELSON.)

TAG.—Gold twist and light blue silk.
TAIL.—A topping and Chatterer.
BUTT.—Red Pig's wool, well picked out.
BODY.—Gold embossed tinsel.
RIBS.—Gold tinsel (oval).
HACKLE.—A natural black hackle, from second turn.
THROAT.—Jay.
WINGS.—Six toppings.
HORNS.—Blue Macaw.
HEAD.—Red Pig's wool, well picked out.

A useful pattern on bright days for still deep sheltered pools.

THE MYSTERY.

G.S.
(Michael Maher.)

Tag.—Silver twist and gold silk.
Tail.—A topping.
Butt.—Black herl.
Body.—Gold silk.
Ribs.—Silver tinsel (oval).
Hackle.—Natural blue-dun, from second turn.
Throat.—A claret hackle.
Wings.—Two strips Swan dyed yellow and a topping.
Horns.—Red Macaw.
Cheeks.—Chatterer.

With this pattern the inventor killed his memorable Salmon weighing 57 lbs. in the Suir. The fly is very popular in the neighbourhood of Cashel.

THE NAMSEN.

G.S.
(Kate Daly.)

Tag.—Silver twist and yellow Seal's fur.
Tail.—A topping and Indian Crow.
Butt.—Black herl.
Body.—Red-orange, dark blue, and claret Seal's fur, equally divided.
Ribs.—Silver tinsel (oval).
Hackle.—Dark blue on dark blue Seal's fur, and dark claret on the claret.
Throat.—Gallina.
Wings.—An extended red breast Golden Pheasant (best side down); Golden Pheasant tail (in strands principally); light Bustard and Gallina.
Horns.—Blue Macaw.
Head.—Black wool.

An old standard high water fly on the Sundal dressed from No. 3/0 to 7/0 (Courtney, Killarney).

NAPOLEON.

G.S.
(Courtney.)

Tag.—Silver twist and red wool.

Tail.—A topping and Indian Crow.

Butt.—Black herl.

Body.—In two sections: No. 1, of blue silk, forming one-third, ribbed with fine silver tinsel and butted with a claret hackle. No. 2, silver Monkey, ribbed with gold tinsel.

Hackle.—An Irish-grey hackle, from blue silk.

Throat.—A yellow, a claret, and a light blue hackle.

Wings.—Tippet (strands) Golden Pheasant tail; Swan dyed blue, yellow, and claret, Bustard, Mallard, and a topping.

Horns.—Blue Macaw.

Cheeks.—Indian Crow.

Head.—Black herl.

One of the old Lee patterns, and in general use in the Spring of 1893. The "Blue-grey-and-brown" is a variation of this fly.

NIAGARA.

G.S.
(Turnbull.)

Tag.—Gold twist and black silk.

Tail.—Two strands of Amherst Pheasant (long).

Butt.—Black herl.

Body.—In four equal sections of silk: No. 1, yellow, butted with yellow hackle; No. 2, pea-green, butted with pea-green hackle; No. 3, red, butted with red hackle; No. 4, dark blue.

Ribs.—First three sections gold tinsel (oval, fine); silver tinsel (oval, fine) over dark blue.

Throat.—Dark orange hackle and black Heron.

Wings.—Two natural black, shiny, saddle hackles (back to back) veiled with Teal, Bustard, tail of Golden Turkey (North America), Mallard, and two toppings.

Sides.—Summer Duck.

Horns.—Red Macaw.

Head.—Red wool (small).

NICOL'S FAVOURITE. G.S.

(Nicol Mc Nicol.)

Tag.—Silver twist and yellow silk.
Tail.—A topping and blue Chatterer.
Butt.—Black herl.
Body.—Silver tinsel.
Ribs.—Silver tinsel (oval).
Hackle.—Yellow, from mid-way.
Throat.—Unbarred Summer Duck.
Wings.—Yellow mohair and a topping.
Sides.—Large Chatterer and Jungle over.
Horns.—Blue Macaw.

A killing fly in peat or porter coloured water in all rivers North of the Grampians.

NIGHTSHADE. G.S.

(Kelson.)

Tag.—Silver twist and pink silk.
Tail.—Orange Toucan and red Toucan.
Butt.—Black herl.
Body.—Light red-orange and dark red-orange Pig's wool.
Ribs.—Silver tinsel (oval).
Hackle.—From dark red-orange wool (half-way) a Vulture hackle (or a small Eagle or hen Pheasant hackle), dyed dark red-orange.
Throat.—Black Partridge (grey speckled).
Wings.—Two strips of black and white mottled Turkey.

A good late evening pattern.

THE ORANGE GUINEA HEN. G.S.

Enright.)

Tag.—Silver twist and dark blue silk.
Tail.—Toucan and Indian Crow.

BUTT.—Black herl.
BODY.—Orange silk.
RIBS.—Silver tinsel.
THROAT.—Gallina.
WINGS.—Tippet strands, Gallina, Ibis, powdered blue and yellow Macaw, and Mallard.
HEAD.—Black herl.

THE PEACOCK FLY.

G.S.
(WRIGHT.)

TAG.—Silver twist.
TAIL.—A topping.
BODY.—Yellow and black silk in equal divisions.
RIBS.—Silver tinsel (oval).
HACKLE.—Natural black, from centre.
THROAT.—Jay.
WINGS.—Tippet; Peacock, sword feather; Gallina, Teal, and Summer Duck.

An old standard on the Lochy and Spean.

THE PEARL.

G.S.
(KELSON.)

TAG.—Gold twist.
TAIL.—Toucan, Teal, and Chatterer (small).
BUTT.—Black herl.
BODY.—In two sections: No. 1, silver embossed tinsel, butted with Indian Crow above and below, and black herl; No. 2, black silk, ribbed with gold oval tinsel, and a natural black hackle along it.
THROAT.—Jay.
WINGS.—Tippet, Teal, and Peacock wing in strands; Golden Pheasant tail, Amherst Pheasant, dark Bustard, Swan dyed blue, yellow, and red; Mallard and a topping.
CHEEKS.—Chatterer.
HORNS.—Blue Macaw.

PENPERGWM PET.

G.S.
(Kelson.)

Tag.—Silver twist and yellow Seal's fur.

Tail.—Summer Duck, strands, varying in length, of Ibis; and Indian Crow.

Butt.—Black herl.

Body.—Yellow, crimson-majenta, Mouse, and plum-claret Seal's fur, in equal divisions.

Ribs.—Silver twist.

Hackle.—A coch-a-bonddu slightly tinged in Bismarck brown, from second turn.

Wings.—Double white Turkey, ginger speckled Turkey, Bustard, Mallard, black Cockatoo's tail, red Macaw, powdered blue Macaw, Parrot, and Teal, all in double strands. Two strips of rich brown Turkey above, having black bars and white points.

Cheeks.—Chatterer.

Head.—Black herl.

This is one of the most successful flies on the Usk.

PITCROY FANCY.

G.S.
(Turnbull.)

Tag.—Silver twist.

Tail.—A topping and strands of tippet.

Butt.—Scarlet wool.

Body.—Silver tinsel.

Ribs.—Silver tinsel (oval).

Hackle.—Grey Heron, from centre.

Throat.—Gallina.

Wings.—Tippet (large strips), light mottled Turkey, Pintail, Mallard, and a topping.

Sides.—Jungle.

Head.—Scarlet wool.

A modern Spey standard.

THE POPHAM.

G.S.
(F. L. Popham.)

Tag.—Gold twist (plenty).
Tail.—A topping and Indian Crow.
Butt.—Black herl.
Body.—In three equal sections: No. 1, dark red-orange silk, ribbed with gold tinsel (fine), butted with Indian Crow above and below, and black herl; No. 2, yellow silk, ribbed and butted as before; No. 3, light blue silk, ribbed with silver tinsel (oval), and Indian Crow above and below.
Throat.—Jay.
Wings.—Golden Pheasant tippet and tail, Gallina, Parrot, light brown mottled Turkey, red Macaw, Bustard, Mallard, and a topping.
Cheeks.—Chatterer.
Horns.—Blue Macaw.
Head.—Black herl.

A very useful old Standard pattern.

POWELL'S FANCY.

G.S.
(Powell.

Tag.—Gold twist and dark blue silk.
Tail.—A topping.
Body.—Red-orange Seal's fur.
Ribs.—Gold tinsel (oval).
Hackle.—Red-orange, from second turn.
Throat.—Jay.
Wings.—Tippet strands, Swan dyed yellow, red-orange and dark blue Peacock wing, Bustard; dark mottled Turkey, Gallina and Mallard.
Horns.—Blue Macaw.
Head.—Black wool.

PRINCE'S MIXTURE.

G.S.
(Kelson.)

Tag.—Silver twist and yellow silk.

Tail.—A topping, two strands blue Macaw, and a small blue Chatterer.

Butt.—Black herl.

Body.—Silver tinsel (flat) in two equal sections, the first butted with Toucan under Indian Crow, followed by black herl ; at the throat repeat Toucan and Indian Crow, and add a Jay hackle.

Wings.—Amherst Pheasant, Golden Pheasant tail, and black Cockatoo tail in strands. Swan dyed blue and scarlet, Teal, Bustard, two strips of Mallard and a topping.

Horns.—Blue Macaw.

Head.—Black herl.

THE PURPLE EMPEROR.

G.S.
(Kelson.)

Tag.—Silver twist and yellow silk.

Tail.—Tourocou, strands of Summer Duck and powdered blue Macaw.

Butt.—Black herl.

Body.—Silver tinsel (oval, fine) with four turns of violet Seal's fur at throat.

Ribs.—Gold tinsel (oval).

Hackle.—A silver coch-a-bonddu from butt.

Throat.—A hen Pheasant dyed yellow.

Wings.—Two Jungle (back to back), Widgeon, Swan dyed yellow, Golden Pheasant tail, Tourocou, grey Mallard and a topping.

This is a capital fly on the Spey early in the year. At Wester Elchies, in May, 1891, I was fortunate in getting "the fish of the river" with it for the season ; and, on the water above, at Knockando in 1892, followed up this success with a Salmon of 33 lbs. in weight. In bright weather and water the throat is better of Teal.

THE PURPLE KING. G.S.

BODY.—Blue and red Berlin wool mixed together—proportion, one part blue, two parts red.

RIBS.—From far side, gold; from near side silver tinsel (narrow) wound the reverse way an equal distance apart.

HACKLE.—A red Spey-cock hackle, from end of body, but wound in the usual way from the root of the feather instead of from the point, thus crossing *over* the ribs at each turn given.

THROAT.—Teal, one turn only.

WINGS.—Two strips of Mallard showing brown points and light roots.

SPECIAL NOTE.—An old standard Spey fly which, for *general work* is the best of the "Kings." . . . See the "Green King."

QUEEN OF SPRING. G.S. (KELSON.)

TAG.—Silver twist and canary silk.

TAIL.—A topping and Summer Duck.

BUTT.—Black herl.

BODY.—Silver tinsel and black silk equally divided.

RIBS.—Gold lace and silver tinsel.

HACKLE.—Black, from silver tinsel.

THROAT.—Jay.

WINGS.—Tippet, Amherst Pheasant and Golden Pheasant tail, grey Mallard, Swan dyed canary, red and light blue; Mallard and two toppings.

HORNS.—Blue Macaw.

SIDES.—Jungle.

CHEEKS.—Chatterer.

In the Autumn this fly is dressed with gold twist and gold tinsel (body) and is known as the "Queen of Autumn." It is a favourite of mine on most rivers, and a very old pattern.

THE QUILLED EAGLE.

G.S.
(Kelson.)

Tag.—Silver twist and quill dyed yellow.

Tail.—A topping, and two strands of Peacock herl (sword feather) of Bustard and Ibis.

Butt.—Black herl.

Body.—Quill dyed yellow, leaving space for four turns of orange Seal's fur at the throat.

Ribs.—Silver tinsel (oval).

Hackle.—A grey Eagle hackle, from centre.

Throat.—Gallina (spotted feather).

Wings.—Two tippets (back to back) veiled with extending Jungle, a strip of Ibis and Bustard, and a topping.

Sides.—Jungle (to centre of former pair).

I rarely use any other "Eagle" but this, though I sometimes dress it with a yellow instead of a grey hackle.

RAY MEAD.

G.S.
(Kelson.)

Tag.—Silver twist and light blue silk.

Tail.—A topping, Ibis and Summer Duck.

Butt.—Black herl.

Body.—One-fourth of yellow silk, followed by silver tinsel (oval).

Ribs.—Gold tinsel (oval).

Hackle.—Large Irish-grey from oval tinsel.

Throat.—Teal, three turns.

Wings.—Alternate narrow strips of Swan dyed yellow and black, married; Summer Duck and a topping.

Sides.—Jungle.

Cheeks.—Chatterer.

Horns.—Blue Macaw.

One of my oldest and most successful patterns at the present time.

THE RED DRAKE.

G.S.
(KELSON.)

TAG.—Gold twist and light blue silk.

TAIL.—Toucan, Ibis, and Amherst Pheasant.

BUTT.—Black herl.

BODY.—One third of buttercup silk and black silk, having a red-orange hackle down it.

THROAT.—Jay.

RIBS.—Gold tinsel (oval).

WINGS.—Two spreading strips of the Mandarin Drake, white tipped (a fair imitation is occasionally found on the domestic Mallard) and a topping.

HORNS.—Blue Macaw.

HEAD.—Black herl.

Used on the Earn, Aberdeenshire Dee, Teviot, Blackwater (Mallow district), Usk and Wye.

THE RED KING.

G.S.

BODY.—Red Berlin wool (brick colour).

RIBS.—Gold from far side, silver tinsel (narrow) from near side, wound the reverse way an equal distance apart.

HACKLE.—A red Spey-cock hackle from end of body, but wound in the usual direction from the root instead of from the point, thus crossing *over* the ribs at each turn given.

THROAT.—Teal, one turn only.

WINGS.—Two strips of Mallard, showing brown points and light roots.

An old standard Spey fly. See the "Green King."

THE RED ROVER.

G.S.
(DAVIE MURRAY.)

TAG.—Silver twist and yellow silk.

TAIL.—A topping.

BUTT.—Black herl.
BODY.—Majenta Berlin wool.
RIBS.—Silver tinsel (oval).
HACKLE.—Yellow hackle, from second turn.
THROAT.—A red hackle.
WINGS.—Tippet, Peacock wing, Bustard, Swan dyed red, Golden Pheasant tail, and a topping.
SIDES.—Jungle.

An old standard on the North-east coast of Scotland.

THE RED SANDY. G.S.

(NICOL MC NICOL.)

TAG.—Silver twist.
TAIL.—A topping and Indian Crow.
BUTT.—Scarlet wool.
BODY.—In two sections of silver tinsel (oval), No. 1 butted with Indian Crow and scarlet wool.
HACKLE.—Scarlet, along No. 2 section.
WINGS.—Indian Crow—four double feathers overlapping each other and enveloping extended Jungle (back to back), and two toppings.
HORNS.—Red Macaw.
HEAD.—Scarlet wool.

A good fly on the Halladale; and highly prized in Iceland.

THE RINGLET. S.S.

(Grub.) (KELSON.)

TAG.—Gold twist (eight turns).
BODY.—Amber coloured chenille.
HACKLES.—Five monkey hackles in equal divisions increasing in size an bulk. No. 1 forms the butt, and No. 5 the Head.

RIVERS: Wherever Grubs are fashionable (best size 1/0 hook).

THE RIVAL.

S.S.
(Kelson.)

Tag.—Silver twist and light blue silk
Tail.—Topping, and two strands of unbarred Summer Duck.
Butt.—Blue herl.
Body.—Silver tinsel.
Ribs.—Silver tinsel (oval).
Hackle.—Natural black along body.
Throat.—Jay.
Wings.—Tippet, Peacock wing, and Gallina strands; Mallard strips and a topping.
Cheeks.—Chatterer.
Horns.—Blue Macaw.
Head.—Blue herl.

A useful pattern on all rivers in reflected light. It is dressed on small double hooks.

ROCKE'S FANCY.

G.S.
(Colonel Rocke.)

Tag.—Silver twist and blue silk.
Tail.—Golden Pheasant sword (point).
Butt.—Black herl.
Body.—Yellow silk.
Ribs.—Silver tinsel (oval).
Hackle.—Yellow hackle, from third turn.
Throat.—Red Macaw.
Wings.—Two broad strips of yellow Macaw, and a topping.
Cheeks.—Chatterer.

An old standard on the Usk and kills well in the Wye.

THE ROUGH GROUSE. G.S.

(Cruikshank's Variety.)

Tail.—A few fibres of yellow Macaw's hackle.
Body.—Black Berlin wool (short).
Ribs.—Silver tinsel.
Hackle.—Grey Heron from third turn.
Throat.—Black and white speckled Turkey.
Wings.—Black and white speckled Turkey (strips).

A splendid fly on the Spey in dull wet weather. The pattern can be varied for other rivers, when it may have either "mixed" or "built wings," and an ordinary Cock's hackle where Heron's do not serve faithfully; but the speckly characteristics in both parts of the fly must be maintained. I have done better with this fly when using the Crown Pigeon instead of Grey Heron.

ROY NEAL. G.S.

(Kelson.)

Tag.—Gold twist and mouse-coloured Seal's fur.
Tail.—Tippet, Ibis and Summer Duck in strands, and two points of Jungle (back to back).
Butt.—Black herl.
Body.—Gold tinsel (oval) three parts, followed by red Seal's fur.
Ribs.—Silver tinsel (oval).
Hackle.—A natural blue-dun, from second turn; and a hen Pheasant dyed red, from Seal's fur.
Wings.—Two long Jungle (back to back), Swan dyed red and yellow, Bustard, Golden Pheasant tail, and two toppings.
Sides.—Summer Duck.

This is one of the best patterns in dirty water. I invariably use it on the Earn, Tweed, Usk, Spey; and in very high water on the Lochy.

THE SAILOR.

G.S.
(W. Brown.)

Tag.—Silver twist.
Tail.—A topping.
Body.—Yellow Seal's fur and blue Seal's fur, equally divided.
Ribs.—Silver tinsel (oval).
Hackle.—Blue, from yellow fur.
Wings.—Two strips of Teal and a topping.
Cheeks.—Chatterer.
Head.—Blue wool.

An excellent fly on the Dee in summer. It is dressed on small double hooks.

SHERBROOK.

G.S.
(W. Garden.)

Tag.—Silver twist and dark yellow silk.
Tail.—A topping.
Butt.—Black herl.
Body.—One-third dark yellow silk, followed by light blue silk.
Ribs.—Silver tinsel fine (oval), and silver tinsel (flat).
Hackle.—Light blue hackle, from yellow silk.
Throat.—Widgeon.
Wings.—Bustard, dark mottled Turkey, Golden Pheasant tail, and a topping.
Horns.—Scarlet Ibis.

A general standard in summer on the Dee, and a great favourite at Braemar.

THE SHOCKER.

G.S.
(Rev. G. H. Nall.)

Tag.—Silver twist and crimson silk.
Tail.—A topping and Chatterer.

BUTT.—Black herl.

BODY.—In two equal sections of dark blue and crimson silk respectively. The blue silk is butted with a small dark blue hackle.

THROAT.—A coch-a-bonddu tinged in Bismarck brown.

RIBS.—Silver tinsel (oval).

WINGS.—Strands of scarlet Ibis, red Macaw and powdered blue Macaw, veiled and capped with brown Mallard, and a topping.

SIDES.—Small Jungle.

HORNS.—Blue Macaw.

RIVERS : Ogne and Birkrem.

THE SILVER ARDEA.

G.S.
(KELSON.)

TAG.—Silver twist and yellow silk.

TAIL.—Golden Bird of Paradise (3).

BODY.—Silver tinsel.

RIBS.—Silver tinsel (oval).

HACKLE.—Bright red-claret (a white coch-a-bonddu dyed in "*Cardinal," 2288, Woolley & Co., Manchester).

THROAT.—White Heron, dyed light blue.

WINGS.—(Mixed) Peacock wing, Bustard, Golden Pheasant tail, Amherst Pheasant tail, black and white mottled Turkey, Red Macaw, Swan dyed yellow and blue and a topping.

SIDES.—Jungle.

HEAD.—Black herl.

This is the only standard fly having extra long hackles over a silver body.

The "Black Ardea" is simply a variation, the only difference being that the body is made of black silk instead of silver tinsel.

* If there is any difficulty in using the dye with water, add a little methylated spirits of wine.

THE SILVER BLUE.

G.S.
(W. Brown.)

Tag.—Silver twist.
Tail.—A topping.
Body.—Silver tinsel.
Ribs.—Silver tinsel (oval).
Throat.—Blue hackle.
Wings.—Two broad (double strips) of Teal.
Head.—Blue wool.

A capital summer fly in bright sunshine on the Dee. It is dressed on small double hooks.

THE SILVER DOCTOR.

G.S.
(Wright.)

Tag.—Silver twist and yellow silk.
Tail.—A topping (the inventor sometimes adds Chatterer).
Butt.—Scarlet wool.
Body.—Silver tinsel.
Ribs.—Silver tinsel (oval).
Throat.—A blue hackle and Gallina.
Wings.—Strands of tippet, Summer Duck, Pintail, Gold Pheasant tail, Swan dyed light yellow and light blue, Bustard, Mallard and a topping.
Horns.—Blue Macaw.
Head.—Scarlet Wool.

A great fly throughout the United Kingdom, to say nothing of its popularity on Norwegian and Canadian rivers.

THE SILVER GREY.

G.S.
(Wright.)

Tag.—Silver twist and yellow silk.
Tail.—Topping, two strands blue Macaw, and unbarred Summer Duck.

Butt.—Black herl.
Body.—Silver tinsel (flat).
Ribs.—Silver tinsel (oval).
Hackle.—A silver coch-a-bonddu hackle along the body.
Throat.—Widgeon.
Wings.—Golden Pheasant tippet and tail in strands, Bustard, Swan dyed yellow, Amherst Pheasant, Gallina, powdered blue Macaw, Mallard, grey Mallard, and a topping.
Horns.—Blue Macaw.
Sides.—Jungle.
Head.—Black Berlin wool.

This fly is used with success on all rivers.

THE SILVER SPECTRE.

S.S.
(Kelson.)

Tag.—Silver tinsel (oval, fine).
Tail.—Red Macaw (hackle strips) enveloped in two strips of Summer Duck.
Body.—Silver tinsel (flat).
Ribs.—Silver tinsel (oval).
Hackles.—Three in number, at the butt; (No. 1) Jay and black herl at the centre; (No. 2) red Macaw butted with black herl at throat; (No. 3) black (dyed).
Wings.—Copper coloured Peacock's herl.
Cheeks.—Blue Chatterer.
Horns.—Black Cockatoo's tail.
Head.—Black herl.

My favourite fly for flaked water.

THE SILVER TEST.

G.S.
(Basil Field.)

Tag.—Silver twist.
Tail.—A topping, and a dark topping from the Impeyan Pheasant.

BUTT.—Black herl.
BODY.—Silver tinsel.
RIBS.—Gold lace (fine).
THROAT.—Red Toucan (undertail) and Gallina dyed blue.
WINGS.—Two strips of Tippet, two strips of Golden Pheasant tail, Teal, Mallard, and a topping.
CHEEKS.—Chatterer.
HEAD.—Black herl.

One of the best flies on the Test, and well-known in the north.

SIR HERBERT. G.S.

(Sir H. MAXWELL.)

TAG.—Silver twist and yellow silk.
TAIL.—A topping and Indian Crow.
BUTT.—Green Peacock herl.
BODY.—Gold tinsel (flat) to near the throat, having ribs of gold tinsel (oval), and a dark yellow hackle along it; then two or three turns of scarlet Seal's fur.
THROAT.—Crimson hackle.
WINGS.—Two tippets (closed) at top, spreading slightly over the body at bottom; Bustard, Swan dyed light blue and rose, Turkey strands (white tipped), Peacock's herl, and a topping.
SIDES.—Jungle or Summer Duck.
HORNS.—Red Macaw.
HEAD.—Peacock herl.

RIVERS: Tweed, Usk, Blackwater.

SIR PERCY. G.S.

(Sir PERCY DYKE.)

TAG.—Gold twist and gold silk.
TAIL.—A topping and Chatterer.

Butt.—Black herl.
Body.—Two turns of claret silk, two turns of claret Seal's fur, followed by black Seal's fur.
Ribs.—Gold tinsel (oval).
Hackle.—Natural black, from claret fur.
Throat.—Jay.
Wings.—Tippet strands, two strips of Mallard, and a topping.
Sides.—Jungle.
Head.—Black herl.

An old standard fly on the Deveron.

SIR RICHARD.

G.S.
(Rycroft.)

Tag.—Silver twist and orange silk.
Tail.—A topping and Indian Crow.
Butt.—Black herl.
Body.—Black silk.
Ribs.—Silver tinsel, and oval tinsel (fine).
Throat.—Gallina and Jay.
Wings.—Dark mottled Turkey, Golden Pheasant tail, Peacock wing, Parrot, Ibis, Mallard, and a topping.
Horns.—Blue Macaw.
Cheeks.—Chatterer.
Head.—Black wool.

A useful standard on any river.

THE SKIRMISHER.

G.S.
(Kelson.)

Tag.—Silver twist and light yellow silk.
Tail.—Toucan, with two strips of Ibis.
Butt.—Black herl.

BODY.—Two turns of light dirty-orange silk, followed by dirty-orange Seal's fur, well picked out.
RIBS.—Silver tinsel (oval).
THROAT.—Coch-a-bonddu hackle tinged in Bismarck brown.
WINGS.—Golden Pheasant tail and Peacock herl mixed in strands.
SIDES.—Teal and Ibis (married).
HORNS.—Blue Macaw.
HEAD.—Black herl.

RIVERS: Tweed, Usk, Earn, and Don.

SKIRROW'S FANCY. G.S.

(Rev. W. SKIRROW.)

TAG.—Silver twist.
TAIL.—A topping and Indian Crow.
BUTT.—Black herl.
BODY.—Two turns of red Seal's fur, followed by blue Seal's fur.
RIBS.—Silver tinsel.
HACKLE.—Blue hackle, from second turn.
THROAT.—Jay.
WINGS.—Doubled strips of Teal.

An old Tweed pattern much sought after on the Dee when dressed small.

THE SMITH. G.S.

TAG.—Silver twist and yellow silk.
TAIL.—A topping and Indian Crow.
BUTT.—A yellow hackle.
BODY.—In three equal sections of silver tinsel (oval): No. 1, butted with a red hackle; No. 2, with a light blue hackle; No. 3 (or throat), Gallina. (Some dressers put silver tinsel and rib it with silver tinsel, oval.)

WINGS.—Two sword feathers of Golden Pheasant (back to back), grey mottled Turkey, Bustard, Golden Pheasant tail, Swan dyed blue, yellow, and red ; and a topping.
SIDES.—Jungle.*

One of the oldest patterns on the Tay, the original dressing is unknown.

* Turnbull's dressing.

THE SPRING GRUB.

G.S.
(KELSON.)

TAG.—Silver twist and light blue silk.
TAIL.—Ibis and blue Macaw (married).
BUTT (or No. 1 hackle).—A furnace hackle dyed orange.
BODY.—First half of yellow silk, ribbed with black chenille, No. 2 hackle a Vulturine Guinea fowl (natural blue) ; second half, black silk, ribbed with silver tinsel (oval) ; No. 3, or head hackles, a coch-a-bonddu and Gallina dyed dark orange.

A very old standard on all rivers where Grubs are known. I have used it successfully as early as the first week in May.

STEVENSON.

G.S.
(WRIGHT.)

TAG.—Silver twist and light blue silk.
TAIL.—Topping, and strands of tippet.
BUTT.—Black herl.
BODY.—Two turns of orange silk, followed by orange Seal's fur.
RIBS.—Silver lace and silver tinsel.
HACKLE.—Orange hackle, from orange silk.
THROAT.—Light blue hackle.
WINGS.—Four double tippets (back to back) enveloping two extended Jungle ; and a topping.

SIDES.—Jungle.
HORNS.—Blue Macaw.
HEAD.—Black wool.

RIVERS: Tweed, Tay, Spey, Don, Wye, Blackwater, and Lochy.

NOTE.—Veil wings with Teal for Wye and Lochy, and use in tail strands of Summer Duck instead of tippet.

STRATHSPEY.

G.S.
(KELSON.)

TAG.—Silver twist and violet silk.
TAIL.—Toucan (four feathers) and Teal.
BUTT.—Black herl.
BODY.—Three turns of yellow Seal's fur, followed by violet Seal's fur.
RIBS.—Silver tinsel; and fine silver lace running between each turn.
HACKLE.—A natural blue coch-a-bonddu (long), tinged in a Bismarck brown.
THROAT.—Teal.
WINGS.—Plain cinnamon Gled (strips) and the point of a small Teal feather tied (flat) in between them.
HORNS.—Blue Macaw.

For smooth water.

THE SUMMER DUCK.

G.S.
(KATE DALY.)

TAG.—Silver twist and yellow Seal's fur.
TAIL.—Two red-breasts of Golden Pheasant (back to back).
BUTT.—Black herl.
BODY.—Light and dark orange (half way) followed by dark claret Seal's fur.
RIBS.—Silver and gold tinsels (oval).

HACKLE.—A dark claret hackle, from centre.
THROAT.—Blue hackle.
WINGS.—Two red-breasts of Golden Pheasant (back to back) reaching tag, Peacock herl (principally), Golden Pheasant tail, red Macaw, and a topping: veiled, to centre of body, with a Summer Duck feather on each side.
HEAD.—Black wool.

Tied in sizes varying from No. 4/0 to 7/0, this is a favourite high water fly on the Sundal. (Courtney, Killarney).

THE SUNDAL BLACK. G.S.

(COURTNEY.)

TAG.—Gold twist and yellow silk.
TAIL.—Tippet (strands); Ibis, and Gallina.
BUTT.—Black herl.
BODY.—Black Seal's fur.
RIBS.—Gold tinsel (oval).
HACKLE.—A natural black hackle, from second turn.
THROAT.—A dark blue hackle.
WINGS.—Two strips of dark mottled Turkey, veiled with two strips of the Great Bustard.
HORNS.—Blue Macaw.
HEAD.—Black herl.

SWEETMEAT. G.S.

(KELSON.)

TAG.—Silver twist and pink silk.
TAIL.—Ibis, yellow Macaw and Teal.
BUTT.—Black herl.
BODY.—Two turns of red chenille, followed by yellow chenille.
RIBS.—Silver tinsel (oval).

HACKLE.—From red chenille, a white coch-a-bonddu dyed light Bismarck brown.
THROAT.—Gallina.
WINGS.—Two tippets, enveloping two extended red hackles; veiled with grey Mallard, black Cockatoo's tail, and Teal; Mallard and a topping.
CHEEKS.—Indian Crow and Tanager, respectively.
HORNS.—Red Macaw.

One of the original fancy flies on the Usk and a useful pattern at the present time on most rivers.

TAITE'S FANCY.

G.S.
(TAITE.)

TAG.—Silver twist and blue silk.
TAIL.—Topping and Toucan.
BUTT.—Black herl.
BODY.—Silver tinsel (flat).
RIBS.—Silver tinsel (oval).
HACKLE.—Claret, from second turn of ribs.
THROAT.—Blue hackle.
WINGS.—Hen Pheasant tail, Peacock wing, Swan dyed red-orange, Golden Pheasant tail, and two strips of Mallard above.
HORNS.—Blue Macaw.
HEAD.—Black herl.

RIVERS: Tweed, Usk.

NOTE.—One of our best silver bodied "modifications," often varied in tail, hackle, throat and wing.

THE LITTLE INKY-BOY.

G.S.
(KELSON.)

TAG.—Silver twist and one turn of crimson Berlin wool.
TAIL.—A topping.

BODY.—Fine Trout gut dyed black, closely coiled.

THROAT.—Three turns of silver coch-a-bonddu dyed yellow.

WINGS.—A few tippet strands, two narrow strips of unbarred Summer Duck and a topping.

Long experience decides this to be one of the best Summer flies for general use. Several nondescripts of mine take the character of The Little Inky-boy, the gut being dyed in different colours. These patterns are best made with thin bodies and light wings.

THE THISTLE.

G.S.
(TURNBULL.)

TAG.—Gold twist and light yellow silk.

TAIL.—Two toppings, with Indian Crow above and below.

BODY.—Light fiery-brown and black pigs wool in equal divisions.

RIBS.—Gold tinsel (flat).

HACKLE.—Black, from second turn.

WINGS.—Teal, dark Bustard, fibres of Golden Pheasant breast, and of Amherst Pheasant; Mallard and a topping.

SIDES.—Jungle.

HORNS.—Red, and blue Macaw.

HEAD.—Black herl.

THUNDER AND LIGHTNING.

G.S.
(WRIGHT.)

TAG.—Gold twist and yellow silk.

TAIL.—Topping.

BUTT.—Black herl.

BODY.—Black silk.

RIBS.—Gold tinsel (oval).

HACKLE.—Orange hackle, from second turn of tinsel.

THROAT.—Jay.

WINGS.—Mallard and a topping.

SIDES.—Jungle.
HORNS.—Blue Macaw.
HEAD.—Black wool.

This fly is exceedingly popular and has a well earned reputation for its destructive qualities at a time when rivers begin to rise after rain. General B—— has introduced an excellent variation of this old standard; he puts an underwing of tippet, and brown mottled Turkey strips. His dressers are Mitchie & Co., of Stirling, N.B.

THE TIPPET GRUB.

G.S.
(KELSON.)

TAG.—Silver twist and scarlet Seal's fur. No. 1, hackle (or butt) three turns of Tippet.
BODY.—Light green-olive chenille. No. 2, hackle (in centre) four turns of tippet one size larger.
No. 3, hackle (or head) five turns of tippet, still larger.

An old favourite for a "thorough change."

THE TORRISH.

G.S.
(RADCLIFFE.)

TAG.—Silver twist and yellow silk.
TAIL.—A topping and Ibis.
BUTT.—Black herl.
BODY.—In two equal sections of oval tinsel; the first butted with Indian Crow above and below, and black herl.
THROAT.—A red-orange hackle, in colour similar to the Crow.
WINGS.—Two strips of black Turkey white tipped, Bustard, Peacock wing, Gallina, Golden Pheasant tail; and two strands of Swan dyed red (white) and blue married; Mallard and a topping.
CHEEKS.—Indian Crow.
HEAD.—Black herl.

A great favourite on the Helmsdale.

THE TRI-COLOUR. G.S.

TAG.—Silver twist.
TAIL.—Red breast feather of the Golden Pheasant.
BODY.—Yellow, light blue, and scarlet Seal's fur.
RIBS.—Silver lace and silver tinsel.
HACKLE.—Natural grey Heron, from blue fur.
THROAT.—Widgeon (Teal, large patterns).
WINGS.—Two strips of plain, cinnamon Turkey.

A standard fly on the Dee, which, when dressed with a red breast hackle of the Golden Pheasant and with white (strips) wings, is known by the name of "The Killer."

THE TOPPY. G.S.

(Rev. A. WILLIAMS.)

TAG.—Silver twist.
TAIL.—Toucan and Ibis.
BUTT.—Claret herl.
BODY.—Three turns of red-claret silk, butted with a red-claret hackle; followed by black Seal's fur.
RIBS.—Silver tinsel.
HACKLE.—Black hackle, from claret butt.
WINGS.—Two strips of black Turkey white tipped, in single strips.

A general Usk pattern.

TURNBULL'S SIR RICHARD. G.S.

(TURNBULL.

TAG.—Silver twist and golden-yellow silk.
TAIL.—A topping, and Indian Crow above and below.
BUTT.—Peacock herl.
BODY.—Black silk.
RIBS.—Silver lace and silver tinsel (narrow).

HACKLE.—Gallina, one-third of body.
THROAT.—Jay, and one turn Gallina over it.
WINGS.—Two broad strips of Swan dyed scarlet, veiled with Bustard, Mallard, grey Mallard, Parrot, and a topping.
SIDES.—Summer Duck.
HORNS.—Blue Macaw.
HEAD.—Black herl.

This is the best of Turnbull's, and has long since become a general favourite.

UNA. G.S.

(KELSON.)

TAG.—Silver twist and gold twist.
TAIL.—A topping, two strands of powdered blue Macaw, four strands of Summer Duck, and Chatterer.
BUTT.—Black herl.
BODY.—In two equal sections; No. 1, of silver embossed tinsel, ribbed with gold tinsel (oval) and butted with black herl; No. 2, of gold embossed tinsel, and ribbed with silver tinsel (oval).
HACKLE.—One side of a blue, and one side of a claret hackle, from centre.
THROAT.—Two turns of orange hackle and Gallina.
WINGS.—Two strips of Peacock wing, veiled with Teal and Gallina (underwing); Golden Pheasant tail, Parrot, red Macaw, Summer Duck, Powdered blue Macaw, Mallard, and a topping.
HORNS.—Blue Macaw.
CHEEKS.—Indian Crow and Chatterer.
HEAD.—Black herl.

A bright water fly and is often of service in sizes up to No. 2/0. A minute description is given as Una is usually overdressed.

VANSITTART'S WASP.

G.S.
(VANSITTART.)

TAG.—Gold twist.
TAIL.—A topping.
BODY.—Yellow and black Seal's fur in equal divisions, with a topping above yellow fur.
RIBS.—Silver tinsel (oval).
HACKLE.—Black hackle, from yellow fur.
WINGS.—Tippet strands ; Gallina, Swan dyed yellow and red, Golden Pheasant tail, Bustard and Mallard.
HORNS.—Blue Macaw.
HEAD.—Orange herl.

Well known on the Grimmersta and on small rivers in Argyllshire.

THE VARIEGATED SUN FLY.

This pattern is fully described, as well as its variations, in Chapter V.

THE WASP GRUB.

S.S.
(KELSON.)

TAG.—Silver twist.
TAIL.—Point of red undertail of Toucan.
BODY.—Yellow and black chenille in close coils, not spirally but wasp-like.
HACKLE.—A natural blue coch-a-bonddu slightly tinged in Bismarck-brown, beginning at centre of body and ending with four or five coils at head.
HEAD.—Black herl.

A simple but effective low water pattern in certain localities during the wasp season. On the Usk, for instance, I have been singularly successful with it. The fly is useful on the Dee.

THE WHITE WING.

G.S.
(Wright.)

Tag.—Silver twist.
Tail.—A topping, and tippet strands.
Body.—The first half of yellow, and orange and claret Seal's fur, equally divided, followed by black Seal's fur.
Ribs.—Silver lace and silver tinsel.
Hackle.—A natural black hackle, from second turn.
Throat.—A blue hackle.
Wings.—Two strips of white Swan.

An old Tweed pattern.

THE WIDGEON.

G.S.
(Enright.)

Tag.—Silver twist and orange silk.
Tail.—Toucan and Indian Crow.
Body.—Mauve silk.
Ribs.—Silver tinsel.
Throat.—Widgeon.
Wings.—Tippet strands, Swan dyed yellow, Parrot, Ibis, Gallina, and Mallard.
Cheeks.—Indian Crow.
Head.—Orange herl.

A successful Irish pattern dressed on small double hooks.

WILKINSON.

G.S.
(G. Kelson.)

Tag.—Silver twist.
Tail.—Two toppings, tippet, and Indian Crow.
Butt.—Scarlet wool.
Body.—Silver tinsel.

RIBS.—Silver tinsel (oval).
THROAT.—Majenta and light blue hackle.
WINGS.—Tippet, Teal, Peacock wing, Golden Pheasant tail, Swan dyed red, yellow, and blue ; Mallard and a topping.
HORNS.—Blue Macaw.
SIDES.—Jungle.
HEAD.—Black herl.

This is one of my Father's earliest patterns and is patronised on most rivers.

THE WILSON.

G.S.
(TURNBULL.)

TAG.—Silver twist and cream silk.
TAIL.—Two strips of Summer Duck.
BUTT.—Black herl.
BODY.—Silver tinsel.
RIBS.—Gold tinsel (oval).
THROAT.—Vulturine Guinea fowl and black Heron.
WINGS.—Egyptian Goose, little Bustard, silver speckled Turkey, grey Mallard and a topping.
CHEEKS.—Indian Crow and Chatterer.

A superb killer on most rivers. The fly was named after Mr. Wilson of Moffat.

THE WYE GRUB.

G.S.
(KELSON.)

TAG.—Silver twist and red silk.
TAIL.—Yellow Macaw, and a few strands of Ibis.
BUTT.—No. 1, a white coch-a-bonddu dyed yellow, cheeked, after the "Jungle Hornet," with Jungle on each side.
BODY.—Yellow Seal's fur.

RIBS.—Silver tinsel, fine (oval). No. 2, or centre hackle, as before, cheeked. No. 3, or head, a larger hackle (same sort) and two turns of Gallina dyed orange, cheeked as before.

An old standard on the Wye and a great favourite at the present time.

YATES' FANCY.

G.S.
(F. YATES.)

TAG.—Silver twist and yellow silk.
TAIL.—Tippet, Summer Duck, and Gallina.
BUTT.—Black herl.
BODY.—Rose silk two turns, followed by claret, blue, and black Seal's fur equally divided.
RIBS.—Silver tinsel.
HACKLE.—White coch-a-bonddu dyed light Bismarck brown.
THROAT.—Jay.
WINGS.—Tippet, Teal, Gallina, Golden Pheasant tail, Bustard, Swan dyed yellow and green; Ibis, Mallard, and a topping.
CHEEKS.—Chatterer.
HORNS.—Blue Macaw.

An excellent general fly.

YELLOW EAGLE.

G.S.

TAG.—Silver twist.
TAIL.—Red breast feather of the Golden Pheasant.
BODY.—Yellow, scarlet, and light blue Seal's fur.
RIBS.—Silver lace and silver tinsel.
HACKLE.—Eagle dyed yellow, from scarlet fur.
THROAT.—Widgeon (Teal, large patterns).
WINGS.—Two strips of grey mottled Turkey having black bars and white points.

A well-known dark water fly on the Dee.

YELLOW LAHOBBER.

G.S.
(Enright.)

Tag.—Silver twist and dark orange silk.
Tail.—Toucan.
Body.—Black silk.
Ribs.—Silver tinsel.
Throat.—Yellow Macaw, and powdered blue Macaw.
Wings.—Golden Pheasant yellow rump, Parrot, Gallina, Bustard, red and powdered blue Macaw.
Sides.—Jungle.

YELLOW PARSON.

G.S.
(Rev. A. Williams.)

Tag.—Silver twist and violet silk.
Tail.—A topping and tippet strands.
Body.—Two turns of yellow silk, followed by yellow Seal's fur.
Ribs.—Silver tinsel (oval).
Hackle.—Yellow hackle from silk.
Throat.—Scarlet hackle, veiled with two small toppings.
Wings.—Two tippets (back to back), a strip of Summer Duck on each side, and two toppings.
Horns.—Blue Macaw.
Cheeks.—Chatterer.

An old Usk fly, used also on the Thurso, Wye, and Don.

Though the absence of a few old flies is to be regretted, I have, after investigating the matter to the best of my power and ability, determined to adopt the foregoing list. No end of old time standards have sunk into desuetude, disappeared from the scene, and vanished altogether. In some cases this is a pity; in many others a relief. Veterans, for instance, may deplore the loss of the "Rainbow," the "Quaker," or the "Assassin;" but few would look twice at "Mentor," Queen Mab," or even "Rob Roy," and the original "Ray Mead." The loss is due, in my opinion, to a kind of trade rivalry, and to a prevalent desire on the part of certain dressers to produce some sensational effect by inconsistently varying any fly they make while still using the old name. Let me not be misunderstood. To cleverly vary a fly, under certain principles, in order to meet some particular case or condition, is a feat often practised by first-class men; but there really is no such thing as "producing sensational effect" by the mere process of haphazard variation. A "bit of novelty" in most standards, though accidentally effective, soon wears off in general use, and is pretty sure to spoil the pattern for good and all.

On the other hand, it is true that some flies, as for instance "Bonnie Dundee," "Daily News," and the "Blue Charm" of old, are susceptible of vast improvement; but, as I say, some of the best have entirely lost their value by passing through phases of irresponsible treatment, and might well receive their congé from some reliable judicative source.

A good example of this sort of importunate treatment is manifest in a collection of old standards, which have been on my table for weeks and months. Most of them were sent to me for the purposes of this work, and have come from all parts of the United Kingdom. So inconsistent has been the changes made in bodies and wings generally, even in the different specimens of three such favourites as the "Assassin," "Ray Mead," and the "Quaker," the first and last of which, in the fulness of their celebrity, riveted themselves on my recollection, that it is almost impossible to identify them. For this reason they, like others, cannot be truly described. Among these patterns, nevertheless, I see a rather good looking variation of "Ray Mead." The wings take after a fly invented by my Father, and the body assumes the character of a silver and blue "Jock Scott." I have, however, seen patterns on the Bann, Owenmore, Waterville river, the Bush, Bundrowes, Shannon, and Blackwater, differing so much from their original dressing, that I am driven to overlook them in this collection. As an example take, say, "Tim's Moke," which, however, is eminently deserving of some sort of notice. This fairly useful fly is known on the West coast as the "Monkey Grey," whilst on the other side of Ireland it enjoys the appellation of "Red Tag." It takes somewhat after the "Lemon

Plate 5

Rocke's Fancy

The Butcher

The Silver Grey

Stevenson

The Popham

John Campbell

Grey," but has red silk at the tag, and a red hackle under Jay at the throat. What an endless and perhaps impossible work it would be to explain all these patterns in detail!

The Clarets on the Erne, and other Irish flies whipped up with a black hackle and plain Mallard wing still hold their own, like the Blues on the Lee, but the majority are hardly worth describing, as the local manufacturers dress them in a variety of ways merely to please the fancy of customers in their own particular district.

Scotland, like Ireland, but not to such an extent, has necessitated considerable enquiry. The "Gordon," one of the champions of the North, has cost more for postage stamps than the fly is worth in the South. But this, the best of all the Dee flies, is hardly ever dressed by two men alike. The fish *will* have it, in Spring and Autumn, and I am quite at a loss to decide which of the two foregoing descriptions is to be recommended. However, I use the sword feather of the Golden Pheasant only for the largest patterns. The "Blue Charm," among others to which prominence is given, has never been heard of in out of the way places. Even in England this fly is hardly known by sight or name; indeed, in districts not far south of Aberdeen many would like to class it with those of the Irish division for having changed its costume. But in its own neighbourhood, as made now, during the months of April, May and June the pattern has no rival nearer than "Jeannie," or "Logie," which little companion flies are still turned out in their original garb.

Among the Scotch flies, not included in this list, is the "Gledwing," (otherwise remembered as the "Glentana Gled,") from the fact that the hawk of the same name formerly supplied materials for the wing. But when the hawk died on Deeside the fly died too; or, in more staid language, the kite is now extinct in that neighbourhood, and, as far as regards any special distinction, so is the fly, for no imitation of its attractive wing-feather has proved of equal avail.

But what a number of instances I could bring forward as proof positive of the singular value and special effect of certain of the Standard patterns! Alas, for the class of Fishermen who fondly imagine they can hold their own anywhere at the present time with no more than three or four flies in their book! Their ideas must be accepted as affording remarkable evidence of the want of *varied* experience, particularly that experience which led me to my variations in fly-work, now with this object, now with that, and which brought to light so many practical advantages of the system. Perhaps I should say that, in the progress of my experiments, every failure was a step to success; every detection of what was bad and fruitless helped me to find what was really wanted.

In concluding these observations, it is a great privilege to be able to state that the descriptive particulars of all the above flies, save and except those referring to the "Butcher," "Gordon," "Gold Riach," a few introduced by Miss Daly (now Mrs. Courtney) and those of my own, have been read and approved by that one living authority, Colonel Richardson, on whom Salmon Anglers and dressers alike may place the utmost reliance for his wide experience and accurate knowledge of the whole subject.

Anglers can inspect all the Standard patterns at Farlows. The trade can be supplied wholesale by Redpath and Co., and they can rely on getting all shades of the dyed materials with scarcely a fault.

CHAPTER V.

THE CHOICE OF FLIES.

"Nature ever indicates the way to her best secrets without leading us thither by her own hand."

STUDENTS of angling history will probably agree with me that in days gone by all men "roughed" it. There were no sporting newspapers to encourage discussion on the choice of flies, nor other means of communicating experiences; and as for the publication of a work on the sport, that was a matter of serious cost, whilst the popularity of the author depended on his literary style, rather than on the skill with which he handled the subject. Consequently there was little intercourse among Fishermen of different rivers. All this is now changed. Modern facilities for travel, and the dispensation of knowledge, have ensured that the angling world will ever possess new lights and copious records. Art and science lend their aid to furnish the Angler with improved appointments that serve to instruct him in the habits of his prey; and, at a relatively small expense, he can avail himself of the experience of those men who, with larger opportunities for acquiring it, now command some fifteen yards in excess of the cast which our ancestors made with an old "hickory" and a line of "silk and hair!"

But notwithstanding these modern advantages, it seems to me that, apart from a certain happy class who want no instruction, much ill-digested information exists among Salmon-anglers on the great question of flies. To the class of Fishermen who, victimised by some haphazard success, profess to believe that the selection of a fly is immaterial, I do not address myself. To those who believe that in fishing, as in other arts, there is a right and a wrong method, and that the right method—the method best calculated to secure success—can only be acquired by a careful observation and comparison of facts, I venture to offer some assistance in reconciling apparently conflicting conclusions of late years. A considerable advance has been made towards the ideal in fly-manufacture. And not only does the expert fly-tier possess more varied dressing materials, and study with greater care their arrangement upon the hook with a view to harmony, but the expert fly-fisher proceeds with more system, and consequently with greater confidence in the choice of his lures for ordinary use as well as for "refreshing" contingencies. The progress of the Salmon-angler in these respects has been slow, but sure and satisfactory.

I have no wish to review the progress made with respect to rods and lines in this chapter. The old patterns had to be abolished, and have long since been replaced by new ones. But as soon as railways afforded facilities of access to rivers, Anglers increased enormously in number, with the result that "methods and principles" forced themselves upon fly-dressers in proportion as fish became more shy or more educated.

A man must have faith in his fly as well as in himself.

"Confidence in oneself," a great writer tells us, "is the chief nurse of magnanimity." But I shall never forget wandering home one evening in company with others intent on fly-lore, when suddenly a member of the party exclaimed, with the unaffected sincerity of one who is concerned to tell the truth, "For goodness' sake don't derange my mental equilibrium. I have killed more fish than any of you, and the evidence on the simpleness of Salmon-fishing is quite enough for me. I tell you they came like bulldogs at 'Jock Scott'—the first fly I picked out; so no sermons on flies for me!"

The touch of human nature which these impulsive remarks evinced will in no way diminish our satisfaction with knowing that sometimes Salmon seem bound to provide any amount of sport for the novice; but although early success may engender overweening confidence, the tyro should by no means presume upon his good fortune, as I shall endeavour to show forthwith.

It was my young friend's first effort, and he fished like a Trojan from morning till night. He knew nothing; he would listen to nothing; he was told nothing; and, though in the intoxication of a temporary success, he made earnest and repeated attempts to follow it up, the Salmon had settled down; the first fly in the book, and many a successor selected without discrimination, failed him; not another fin did he move. Little did he dream that the sport admits of endless diversity, affording an agreeable and useful exercise of one's judgment in the choice of flies, as well as in the use of them.

The explanation in this particular case is not far to seek.

Having entered upon the scene of action, keen and self-possessed, this young Angler had much in his favour—*e.g.*, the Spring of the year, when the fish are often as keen as the Fisherman; the best of rivers; prawns, worms, and other such injurious baits being prohibited; the water and weather in perfect condition after a spate—sky cloudy, wind westerly; and agreeably, to the best wishes of us all, he remained in possession of the "Field" casts, which held, by the way, two of our best pools, easily covered by an ordinary Trout rod.

Under such circumstances as these, a run of luck often attends the novice; but when it comes to a question of "presentation" and choice of flies, Fortune forsakes all but the initiated. Formerly, the Angler might rely upon three weeks of easy fishing after a flood with "the first fly picked out"; but in these days of drainage he cannot count upon such indulgence for one-fourth of the time; and then the waters fall and get vapid, fish settle down and get sulky, and the issue depends, not on merely walking over the course with "Jock Scott," but on a system founded throughout all its parts on certain well-ascertained principles, which have proved themselves by the results achieved. Then only is it that the novice realises the true position, and the necessity for him to learn, or, perhaps, even to unlearn.

How often have I seen the inexperienced man positively woo failure! For instance, in his over-eagerness and slap-dash style of approach and of using the tackle, he puts fish down prematurely, and then spoils his chance altogether by infringing the rule best calculated to bring him success—*i.e.*, not to persevere too long with the "very fly that really *ought* to kill." This is a fatal practice. But apart from all such transgression the fact still remains that, the best fly in one season falls into desuetude in another, the perfect pattern in the morning sometimes fails at noon, and destroys all chance of success in the evening.

In this relation, I have more than once known the right man "lower his waders"; walk home to dress a certain set of patterns for a special purpose; and use but *one* variation after all. And why? Because the surroundings at the Catch remained as they were.

Another matter not devoid of interest which I would deal with here alludes to the prevailing partiality shewn for certain standards. "Jock Scott" furnishes a grand example for consideration.

It is commonly said that fish see this fly oftener than others, that it reigns supreme because Anglers persist in using it wherever they go. But to ascribe the reputation of any fly to this bald fact is just one of those cock-and-bull stories which derive their origin partly from imagination and partly from hearsay. A man has no ghost of a chance if he is constantly led away by such a statement. No; the key to "Jock's" repute may be traced to the dexterous hand of the inventor. His construction is of a "decided" nature. He is exact in the observance of laws relating to harmony of colour, proportion, and symmetry; the possession of which qualities must, in the long run, secure for any pattern a vastly superior chance over its rivals. It may be taken for granted that the persistent employment of any one fly is absolutely certain to bring it into bad repute temporarily, as the fish are sure to get sick at the very sight of it. In "Jock Scott," perhaps, we find the nearest exception. It is the acknowledged King of built-wing flies, fit to reign over his own large circle of admirers. It is not an ordinary fly. Analyse this Scotch pattern under any reasonable test, and the fly is usually found to possess a singular excellence, though, on the authority of "Silver Grey" (Sept. 16th, 1893), *Land and Water* says;

"I know one stream in Ireland and another in Scotland, in which, though often tried, 'Jock Scott' has never done the trick yet."

Only those who rise superior to prejudice, and who pin their faith on the proper pattern for each particular occasion, can realise how absurd is the remark that "one fly is as good as any other at any time." Yet, even men of "light and leading" sometimes fall into the trap, and mount a favourite pattern, regardless whether it is, or is not, suited to the surrounding conditions. When difficulty arises, out comes the fly book, and "Hang those doctrines that tell of miracles worked in this or that light, so on goes the one that has rarely failed me, Hamish." Knowing the exact lie of the fish, the spot to an inch where to stand and how to cast—half the battle, all this—they occasionally succeed with it, because the very conditions that called for the use of the particular fly happened to exist. Not unfrequently they would experience dismal failure; but the keen observer is never slow in detecting the true reason.

A most important point to be considered in choosing a fly is the nature and condition of the pool in which it is to be used. Each pool has its own distinguishing features. Some are shallow, others deep; some are in the shade, others in the full sunshine; some have a pebbly bottom, affording little shelter to the fish, others abound with rocks and boulders. In some the current runs smooth and straight, in others the waters boil and twist themselves into eddies—all being more or less affected by the rise or fall of the river. It hardly requires to be stated that one identical fly cannot be equally attractive in all pools, or in every condition of the same pool; and that it is of the utmost importance to pay attention to the size of the hook, which the existing local conditions may demand. Almost any pattern of suitable size in straight running waters early in the season, would, at least, show that it was made of the right stuff, provided always that it be one of those specimens warranted never to "skirt" or "wobble." But the Spring of the year is soon over, and as the mild weather sets in, fish take to streams, and get more or less difficult to please as the water gets low and the days hot. Then is the time for observation and reflection; and for the use of "The Little Inky-boy" (p. 214). My Father used to say, "To fish without reflecting is like eating without digesting." I followed this aphorism of his, and with what advantages! But alas! reflect how I may, it is not within my power to bear in memory all the actual details of past adventures in such a manner that they can be brought vividly before the mind of the reader. Memory recalls most of them, at all events; and yet it would seem wiser for the Angler to take notes for himself (as I did at a later period) than to trust to after-thought. It was, for instance, only by comparing notes that I learned to understand the advantage of using natural coloured feathers in fly-work as the season wears on. By the same process I also arrived at the fact that marked effects can be produced by certain distinctions in flies, especially as regards sulky fish. But perhaps the most singular, if not, indeed, the most fortunate, discovery I thus made, and upon which the utmost reliance may be reposed, shows how the rule relating to *proportion* in a fly may be broken. Although the reader's attention is elsewhere drawn to it, I here take as an every day example, a rough *stream* in June, when, from lying close behind a boulder, or better still, an upright ledge of rock, a fish, game for rising, cannot get a glimpse of your fly till it goes well over him. At such a juncture observe the constant effect of using small patterns adorned with extra large "Jungle," or an unusually large strip of Summer Duck for sides! I am afraid to say how frequently I used to be called upon to demonstrate these principles, and how seldom success of some sort, even under the fevered stress of jostling competition, did not attend the trials. Oh, the happier dreams of restfulness and amusement and peace on private waters!

But, of course, it needs some little experience, as well as the power of reasoning by analogy, to determine which fly to mount, even at the best of times.

Pools, as I have said, are ever changing. They are affected by the height, and consequent strength, of the water; by objects washed into them; and by the constantly varying amount of light and shade thrown directly or indirectly over them. For these reasons alone no definite instructions can be offered for general acceptance. In fact, it would be as foolish for a young Fisherman to place faith in any given set of rules which exact undeviating adherence, as to anticipate constant results with a fly that may have carried all before it on a former occasion.

However, as far as I can do so, I intend giving examples of certain measures and methods which are approved by my own experience. Whether the information will be fruitful of result for the student must depend largely on himself. He must use judgment, and especially be on his guard against those well-meaning counsellors at the river-side, who, with evident sincerity, "know all about it," and who honestly believe themselves, like Hamlet, born to "set right" a "world out of joint." Who, with but trifling experience, will not agree that the governing (uncharitable folks call it meddling) faculty is extremely strong in some natures? "Your fly is a mile too big," "Try so and so; that's your only chance," etc., etc. That's the badge to know them by.

It is also only too true that a vast amount of mischief goes on outside the field of operations. One representative of a wider public protests in this wise:—

"Light and shade; the ways of the Salmon; the condition of the river—how can they have anything to do with the choice of flies? What learned nonsense, what scientific humbug!"

Much allowance must be made for opinions emanating from experience acquired in an easy-chair in a library. But it is to be regretted for the sake of novices that some writers wage bitter and unrelenting war against men who, in seeking the solution of fly problems, apply the same methods as have conduced to the establishment of principles in physical research.

Passing over vexatious criticism we must all freely acknowledge the liberal spirit with which our subject is occasionally treated. One amiable critic (Mr. E. T. S., now of the *Field*) says:—

"When we come to study the problem of flies and grasp the meaning of one particular theory, we begin to wonder how it is possible to catch fish under any other system (meaning my own). Seeing is believing, and all those who have seen have believed."

Only at a recent casual meeting of Salmon-anglers engaged in discussing flies, etc., I was myself astonished to see the interest taken in the subject. Twenty years ago, not a man would go a yard out of his way to discuss them. When I was asked to give my experience, I began by reading aloud portions of this book from the manuscript. Afterwards, I asked those present how far they agreed with the principles set forth.

"I don't believe in any principle at all," said one; "but the sombre fly business you recommend for dull days pays well enough on the Usk."

"Not so with us on the Lochy," another remarked. "We think it best there to use a good showy pattern in dull weather, like the 'Silver Doctor.'"

"Exactly so," I observed to the latter. "And by your universal practice you have unfortunately brought the fish round to your way of thinking."

Then in Highland tones I was asked—

"What system would be advantageous on the Dee?"

"None," I replied, "beyond that in connection with *contrast*. The legislator forms an estimate from the multitude of rivers, not from the select few. But do not forget the 'March brown' in its season."

"I know nothing about system," a well-known Spey-angler said; "at any rate, we use thin wings on cold days."

"At Macroom, we study 'colour' and 'character.' One day they come at blue bodies, another at grey ones; but we don't know till we try."

Elsewhere I was complimented by the observation that Wye men had but little faith in any system until I introduced the "Wye Grub" and the "Sun fly," which, by their frequent success under certain conditions, created quite a stir in some of the districts.

And so I went on until I obtained a fair amount of confirmation, which I fully expected, from one source or another.

Now I look upon it that the diversity of these opinions, and the very opinions themselves, go to support my view of the *value* of system, to illustrate which this book is chiefly written.

The question seems to be this: Should the inquiring Angler fall a victim to men whose ingenuity and skill extend no further than, say, from Loch Tay to Perth, where, for even twenty years, they have diligently trailed their half-dozen flies at the stern of a boat; or to others, whose means are neither more nor better than experience picked up on two, three, or may be four rivers? I must answer boldly. *No;* for I am fully of the opinion that the man who has fished as many as a dozen rivers, *unless they had been specially selected for the purpose*, cannot possibly have derived sufficient knowledge to deal in a satisfactory manner with a mean proportion of cases constantly cropping up. Put him at Macroom, for instance, and how would he tell whether to mount the blue or the grey fly?

So far as the foregoing examples of the "meddling faculty" are concerned, the student will, of course, arrive at some conclusion for himself, but I cannot help thinking that they take away some of the credit which the English race possess for common sense and intelligence. Meanwhile, we may do well to consider the two following common-place examples of practising the four-fly system—when one fly fails, another is tried. On what principle, then, should the Angler make his choice from the long list of Standards described in another chapter?

The reader must distinctly understand beforehand that obstinate fish, or, as some put it, "fish off the feed," *can* be induced to rise and take a fly of some sort. That very fly in most instances is to be found among the numerous standards given, though the absence of a few non-descripts or obscurities, sometimes useful on ordinary occasions, is, perhaps, to be regretted.

He should also understand that I am merely laying down the method of procedure which a good Angler would generally pursue; and that I am not here alluding to any special difficulty arising from a sudden change of temperature, a sudden fall of water, or even intervals of nausea, produced by pollution.

Now the tactics of Fishermen are governed by the circumstances that present themselves. Take, as the first of these examples, bright times, fish properly trained to the bright and dull fly system, and an ordinary Catch, in which a mixed wing fails to attract their notice. I should use a fly on, for instance, the Spey or Dee, of a particular class (say the "Gold Riach" on the former, the "Akroyd" on the latter). This selection would be equal, in respect of colouring, to that, say, of a "Jock Scott"—another class of fly which might be used on other rivers, on all, in fact, with perhaps half a dozen exceptions.

Then, a silver body; and be guided by the character of the river as to what sort—on the Wye, a "Silver Grey"; on the Usk, a "Wilkinson"; on the Lochy, a "Silver Doctor." In the fourth trial a "Grub," also suited to the river as regards *colour* of tail, body, and hackle.

For the second example, when a bright or a conspicuously-dressed fly fails (though, in the four-fly system, it would be considered as bad form to start operations with such showy feathers as Summer Duck in any pattern), I should give extra rest and try "Charlie," or some other black-looking fly; then a nondescript of this, that, or the other class, having still some marked characteristics prominently distributed; *e.g.*, extra long hackles, or tufts of short ones, plenty of the most favoured colour in the tail as well as in the body and wings; and finally mount a very large pattern.

I do not see any very "learned nonsense" or "scientific humbug" in all this, though possibly a few of the old school may feel slightly uncomfortable at the thought that the grand traditions of their unceremonious practice, imbued with no principle whatever, should be rudely interrupted by an outburst of formularities.

But Salmon-fishing, like anything else in the universe, must be governed by *laws, and can only best be followed by observing them at all points. I claim no complete knowledge of them, they are not immutable, but that is no reason why what I know of the subject should be valueless.

Judicious contrasts are as essential to Fishermen as to the well-appointed stage, and years of experiment suggest that one chief principle in Salmon-fishing is ever to use them.

Perhaps at this part of our inquiry it would not come amiss were I to relate a few of my earlier exploits, which resulted in finding the key to many intricate problems.

With twenty years or more of fishing experience, and with only misleading custom as a guide, I had a strong desire to investigate matters for myself. I therefore determined to devote attention at the riverside to the workings of Nature. As I began to decipher the more obscure passages in this great book, I became familiar step by step with numerous phenomena, in past days thought to be unconnected with angling, yet

* Our laws are not infallible, but what we may safely assert is, that the propriety of a rigid or elastic application of them depends upon the practice of fishing on each river. Care must be taken to estimate the effect of any practice. But if one finds that a district of thirty miles forms the boundary of a run of Salmon, and it takes one hundred men to "put them down" by improper flies or improper presentation, the Angler may decide for himself in what way, and to what extent, he is to apply our laws to do them justice.

now the subject of all our best Anglers' consideration. What I mean is, that I have frequently looked on "effect," and subsequently discovered the "agent" by which it was produced. This led me to study my work more diligently, and, with renewed effort, I was not only occasionally rewarded with that which I sought after, but also with something even more valuable. I learnt directly that useful knowledge must be superior to *chance*, though often indebted to it; that knowing the *why* and the *wherefore* are stalworth aids as to *how* to proceed; and that facts based on observation may (however good) mostly be best turned to use when helped by intuition. Once I rejoiced at being successful in a difficult situation for a second, or even for a third time, but at another time, on returning to the same pool, unconscious of its altered condition, I failed, owing to my having forgotten its peculiar requirements. I still persevered, and finally became convinced beyond all doubt that to the influence of local surroundings may be traced many important facts on which, to this day, I ponder before deciding what fly to use, and in what way to use it.

I am fully assured, too, that every conspicuous object by, or in, the water is eloquent with hints from which inferences may be drawn. Yet I am not one of those who believe that a little knowledge, which Pope pronounced a *dangerous* thing (though it did not, by the way, prevent him from translating Homer on a very slender proficiency of Greek)—even that little, in my estimation, is better for the Angler than total ignorance.

Compare, too, the pleasant issue attending one's labour under such tuition as I am now attempting—under training of the mind, eye, and hand—with that of men whose knowledge extends no farther than just to put up "Jock Scott" and "go a-fishing!"

Of course, circumstances crop up to upset one's most cherished convictions. The faith one has in the "bright fly" doctrine, for instance, that is to use gaudy patterns in clear waters on bright days, and to reverse the process under contrary conditions—see how easily this system can be upset. Supposing bright flies *have* previously failed in the hands of one who has been acquainted with the various Catches, say, for half a century, and upon whom you place the utmost reliance for his judgment in regard to size, and for his skill in regard to "presentation," you, fishing after him, would always adopt exactly the *opposite* practice. Nor would you follow his system on hard-fished rivers, though you had a district to yourself, unless it were respected and generally followed by others fishing below you. The bright fly will always be found to pay best on rivers where both fish and Fishermen have been properly educated. And this is not only because it is more natural, but because at such times fish see it farther from them. Salmon are always more determined to take a fly when rushing at it from a distance. The veteran did not happen to know that the Catch in question had been temporarily spoilt by a prolonged and injudicious employment of, perhaps, a dozen of the brightest flies in creation; but your knowledge of his failure is enough, and you proceed accordingly.

The only rule from which as yet I have never deviated refers to fishing in "flaked" water, and I shall now mention it.

For years I never had much heart in thrashing away under these trying conditions, which are of no uncommon occurrence on certain rivers.

"Flaked" water arises from thunderstorms pelting down after a spell of hot weather. When the hills with a Southerly aspect have for a time been exposed to the rays of a scorching sun, the higher precipices will be found covered with a more or less curly coat of thin, dry "draff." A heavy rainstorm racks off this skin in particles, which, by a gradual process of disintegration, afterwards rapidly thicken the water, till eventually the whole neighbouring pools become not exactly muddy, but "flaky." The discharge has only to be seen once to be remembered.

"Were it not for the flakes the water would be clear," I have heard it remarked. Yet the water may be clear though flaked.

Upon such occasions, I make it a standing rule to mount a "Silver Spectre," and to use it, not in confined stretches darkened by trees or overhanging rocks, but in open pools and places, where the whole light has free play.

In hazy weather I should use small dark flies.

In fishing a Catch over again from the other side, it is the usual practice to present a fly altogether differing in colour and character from what the fish have seen just before. It may also be smaller and brighter. The body, at any rate, should have extra attraction in the shape of colour, even amounting to gaudiness; and with "sides" and "cheeks," say, of Jungle and Chatterer respectively. Should the water be exceptionally bright, all these distinctions may prove advantageous.

On the first rise of water after rain—a time when Salmon take well if shewn the right thing—my favourite is the "Thunder and Lightning." But this fly is at its best when the body dressing measures no more than one inch and a quarter. (I have never killed a Salmon with a very large one.) It is, therefore, prudent sometimes to keep to the fly of which the fish have previously taken most notice; but it should be one size larger for pools, and two or three sizes for fast-running streams, when fished from the bank. As the waters rise, the fish in shelving pools fortunately shift across stream, or unfortunately work their way up river. The question of *size* on these occasions can be answered only by the local gillie. I have often gone in one bound from a No. 1 hook to a No. 3-0, and even to 4-0. On the Lochy, for instance, the water may rise as much as four feet without an atom of mud appearing to stay proceedings; but one has to be more careful there in the matter of size. The last time I visited the lower Beat, my friend J. C. H. captured five of these wanderers with a nondescript fly in one spot. It was dressed on a No. 3-0 hook, and had a body of crimson Seal's fur, with a natural furnace hackle along it, and Teal wings. Perhaps the river was five, or even six, feet higher than usual. I dressed the fly afterwards in different sizes, but never touched a fish with a single one of them, until the waters rose as before, when the same pattern again killed excellently. Local fly-dressers would do well to make a note of this. The pool was fairly open, the current not swirly, but straight running.

Close observation has proved that previous to a thunderstorm Salmon take badly—indeed, generally not at all. When the day is still and oppressive, denoting "electricity in the air," fish are "down," and refuse to rise at any fly. But when the grand crash comes the fun is sometimes fast and furious, no matter what fly is used. A few good peals of thunder, with its accompanying downpour of rain, speedily clear the atmosphere, and Salmon, in common with animals, and even human beings, are quickly influenced by the change.

On the top of a flood, before the water clears, an orange body, having a blue hackle over a black one at the throat, and a wing after the fashion of that of the "Black Dog," seems to prove best in the vast majority of cases. The "Jungle Hornet" is also a great favourite with me on small rivers. It is, however, varied according to circumstances, but on the top of a flood chiefly so in the materials used for the tail. For instance, on the Usk I should put a tail of scarlet Ibis, on the Wye one of yellow Macaw, and so on. Grubs with orange bodies, having cheeks of Jungle at each hackle, are also required when the water remains discoloured from mud or road washings.

In peat water (porter coloured) a blue-over-black or a grey Heron hackle also come into favour, as well as clarets and browns for the body; but the "Silver Doctor," "Silver Grey," and "Wilkinson" are sometimes preferred. These latter patterns kill best on many rivers in bright water and weather; but when silver bodies are constantly used on dark, cloudy days, as, for instance, on the Lochy they should never be left at home.

When the bottom of the river is dirty, and a green slimy growth on the stones sways to and fro, fish fast-running waters. Always reduce the size of your fly when a Salmon rises *after* your pattern has passed him.

In streams with plenty of uneven rocks temporarily or permanently located on the bed of the river, I do not often find a rival for "Elsie." Here again the dressing is varied; light colours being reserved for open situations, darker ones for those that are screened. This remark refers both to the body of the fly and the wings.

In the afternoon I usually dress flies with gold tinsel ribbing instead of silver, which answers best earlier in the day.

It may be taken as a general rule that one ought to mount comparatively large flies in cold weather, both for deep pools and level-bottomed streams. But if a sudden change of temperature takes place, the size must be immediately increased or decreased very considerably. Suppose the wind veers suddenly round to the east, and the thermometer falls much whilst the barometer rises, it is useless to persevere with any fly for more than an hour or so after the change sets in. But during that short period, although the fish will cease to show themselves, the Angler who works hard and mounts any of the more suitable patterns as large as those used in the early Spring may yet be rewarded for his pains. I have worked on this principle myself for many years, and recently succeeded in getting "the fish of the river" for the season with a fly as long as one's little finger, while only a few minutes previously an inch "dress" seemed ample for the occasion; in fact, my friend J. C. H. had been previously successful with even a still smaller pattern. On the occasion to which I allude, as on five out of six former instances recorded in my notes, the fish was taken *in the tail of the Catch*. I may say that I have heard of a somewhat similar experience, and that now I never waste time on these occasions at the head of any sort of pool.

For positive snow water—that is, when the snow itself is not dissolved and comes along thick enough to be felt striking the waders—flies, like the "Lovat Fly," composed entirely of Peacock's herl, but veiling a silver or gold tinsel body, and whose hackles *at the throat* are red, yellow, or blue, according to the favourite colour used on the river, should be selected; and, in my opinion, the Angler will find nothing to beat them. I have, however, met with unusual success on one occasion that presented itself, with a fly introduced to Dee-anglers by William Garden, of Aberdeen. It may be described as a double white-winged fly. Where white wings are fashionable the times to use them are (1) on dark days; (2) in dark water; (3) when the sun has nearly set, or when it has quite disappeared.

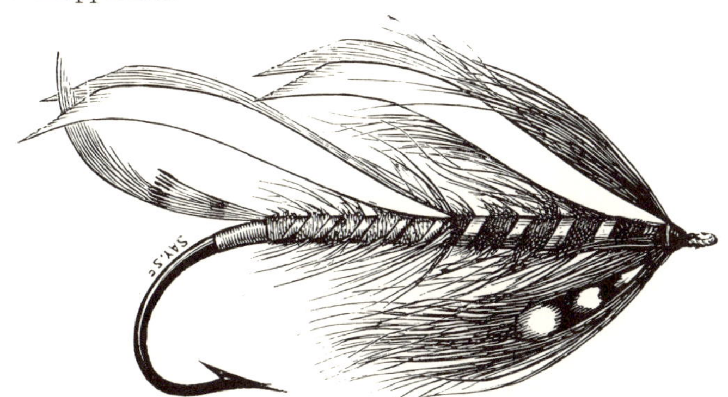

DOUBLE WHITE-WINGED AKROYD.

Dress the "Akroyd" in a similar fashion, and you have the pattern which you see in the engraving. Spey-anglers would do well to give it a trial, varying the wings with Mallard for ordinary occasions. Usk men would probably put black Turkey, having white points, for the sectional wings; whilst on the Earn four strips of Mandarin Drake* have already secured more than one "tight line."

But that sort of snow water which presents to the eye a milky appearance is extremely detrimental to sport. As soon as the milkiness passes away the rise of water caused by the melted snow is not so injurious as many people imagine; still it is nearly useless fishing with any fly until the water has fallen one inch outright, and become clearer.

In snow water, bright as gin, use transparent hackles, as, for example, the silver furnace, or silver coch-y-bonddu.

These observations apply rather to the northern than to the southern rivers. In fact, I have never done any good at all in the Test or Usk when snow water hangs about, but have had grand sport on the Spey when the milkiness disappears. But in all countries sport depends much upon the state of the river when the fish enter it. Running up in mild weather, and soon afterwards meeting with snow water, Salmon "go off" directly and will look at nothing in the shape of flies; but under reversed conditions they "come on" just as quickly. The presence of snow in fresh water does not always deter Salmon from leaving the sea; and when they *run* in it, the Angler may depend they will *take* in it. However, this subject is more fully dealt with in Chapter VII., for, like several other topics, for instance, rain, side reflection, etc., it cannot be condensed into paragraph form with only one or two specimen flies recommended for use.

Whatever state the water may be in, and at whatever station the Angler may be engaged, no matter whether the pattern selected is bright or sombre, the longer the hackle the less the fly should be played.

In choosing a long-hackled fly, select, from the sort you want, one with the feather having the most life in it. This holds good on all rivers, exclusive of the Spey, and I fancy the cheesy, inanimate "Spey-cock hackle," though worshipped locally, will soon be superseded by others which are more mobile and never "drone" or "droop." There is, for example, more life in a "Grey Heron" or a "Night Heron" (red) than in

* Vide the "Mandarin Drake" fly, Chapter IV.

a "Black Heron"; more life, in fact, in any hackle—those of the "Eagle" class excepted—than in the fluffy butt of a "Spey-hackle." But the question of colour, whether natural or artificial, must not be overlooked in any case.

On no account should the student select a gaudy fly to begin fishing with ; for, without considerable interval, it hardly ever pays to present a sombre one afterwards.

He should always mount a fly one size less than recommended rather than one size larger, unless exceptional circumstances occur. For instance, the very principle of attack may necessitate either a small or a large pattern ; that is to say, when wading you may use a one-inch "dress"—fishing the same water from the shore, a two-inch "dress." In the former case the fly dwells over the catches, whilst the large fly "fishes" quickly. Again, as a general rule, he should fix upon a fly having ribs of silver early in the year. In Summer, and particularly in Autumn, all patterns, even silver bodies, are more effectual when dressed with ribs of *gold* tinsel.

I would call the reader's special attention to the next paragraph.

When flies characterised (like Dee patterns) by thin wings and long hackles fail, and the pool or other fishing-place is long enough, rough enough, and spacious enough to bear the work of four or five such flies, one should first select patterns of dull decoration, and in choosing brighter sorts, should hasten the pace of the fly as it comes across the water. either by bringing the rod round faster, or standing farther out from the fish. (Jungle, for instance, unless good, has a brownish tint over the white spots—Turkey may have creamy points instead of pure white ones.) Afterwards you choose from patterns dressed with short hackles and heavy wings. But although badly-marked feathers of this description are not generally considered to decorate the dresser's cabinet, they minister to his wants by helping to tone down any pattern for the preliminary proceedings in this and similar instances.

Supposing the bed of the river to be of a slaty nature (recognised by the Trent term "skerry") and the day dull, dark blue, dark claret, or even dark orange, with black Seal's fur or silk at the throat, will form the best body materials. And where the fish will stand it, a few or more strands of Peacock's herl should be added to any built wing. Spey fish object to herl; Usk fish adore it.

But if the bed of the river be light in character, say, owing to bright gravel, or even chalk, crimson-majenta coming on the body before any kind of claret; bright yellow before any blue often produce good results; whilst heavy wings, short hackles, and Ibis "sides" give way to strip wings, long hackles, and "cheeks" of red Crow.

For a fish lying in a deep dip *in a pool* behind an upright rock mount a very bright-bodied fly (especially if the weather happens to clear) having two or three toppings over wings of double Jungle; should the sun shine, the pattern may carry four, or even five, toppings—"King Alfred" is my favourite at such a place under such conditions.

Where light is reflected from white or shiny cliffs, use bright colours throughout the combination with plenty of tinsel ribbing, and let the fly be rather small. Coming upon this condition in deep, somewhat discoloured water having a comparatively rough surface, a silver-bodied fly perhaps twice as large is necessary; the wing should be composed of herl. The "Silver Spectre" would meet the case.

For large flies in the Spring of the year Pig's-wool bodies are often more deadly than those of Seal's fur.

"Sides" and "cheeks" invariably adorn the pattern for *very* deep water; and for rapids select cheeks of the enamelled Thrush, Indian Crow, or Jungle, and not Summer Duck.

For dark, wet days, as a rule, nothing beats black and white speckled wings over a dark body having a long hackle, with a short one at the throat of a similar black and white speckle. This characteristic can be maintained in making up any type of fly, but is best shown when the wings are in strips. Take, for instance, the "Rough Grouse" on the Spey. It has a black body, grey Heron hackle, and a speckled Turkey throat and strip-wings from the same bird. Again, on a bright day, cinnamon wings over black are hard to beat. And when the water is very clear in Spring—though it be snow water—I like a long Irish grey hackle on almost any kind of fly.

To those who are unable to dress or "cobble up" their own flies, it may be urged with confidence that when a fish rises and refuses, one must lessen the effect of the pattern in use by taking from the wing part of the more conspicuous materials before allowing the fish to make a second inspection. Thus "Jock Scott" having risen a fish, the Angler cuts, *not pulls*, from the wing the "Jungle" sides, as well as the under, *not the upper*, half of the white-tipped Turkey underwing. He will resort to this practice only in the event of his being without a sombre-winged fly (such as "Charlie" or "Fairy") having a yellow and black body. The Angler, however, who is familiar with the practice is always prepared with various "modifications" of the general standard flies of the river he is fishing.

All modifications belong to the list of "nondescripts," but a few have become standards. The more intimately acquainted the Angler makes himself with the specific purpose of each one of these, the better for his season's record. The real purpose of any "nondescript"—I allude to those not as yet classed or described, but which are found in the book of an adept—is simply illustrated in the above case of the "yellow and black body"; in other words, some sort of companion fly has to be presented to the fish which rises and refuses. As another illustration, the "Lee Blue" would be followed by the "Lee Blue and Grey."

The really formidable consideration which will confront the learner is that connected with the Salmon's play hours and "half-holidays."

These intervals come as suddenly as they end. What I mean is, that fish, up and down the river, suddenly cease to take good hold of a fly, and rise only to tug at it. Yet even here Time is a reasoner too powerful to be overcome. Success, if attainable at all, is not denied in such a crisis to those who come at once down to small, sombre patterns, to "Elsie" and her class, which carry extra large and extra showy "sides" and "cheeks." But if these intervals arise from thunder or pollution, the Angler may rest for awhile. Grilse, however, do not so much mind a thunderstorm.

In my opinion, all flies should have their "Grub"; by this, I mean a wingless nondescript having three, four, or five sectional hackles on the body. But with all the foregoing examples, I have touched scarcely more as yet than the fringe of the subject! Perhaps I ought to come now to discuss the effects upon fish of a certain secret force latent in Nature, and then describe the flies which I have found to produce remarkable effects under certain collateral circumstances and conditions.

It is under circumstances, about to be mentioned, that experience teaches us clearly how much we have yet to learn before we can confidently rely upon any pattern as yet invented. Every Fisherman who knows his business is, however, aware of the facility with which we can both *choose* and *use* a fly for ordinary occasions. But the invention of flies, indeed, presents an almost inexhaustible field for the solution of doubts; and there are certain occasions when an Angler of the greatest skill as a wader and caster will scarcely secure a fish by aid of the best pattern.

If the cause of these things lie in obscurity, the fact remains. Accordingly, a note of warning is here sounded to this effect, that the mere knowledge of any secret trick does not always enable the person initiated to kill fish. Success largely depends, not only on covering every inch of the water with a special fly, but also on the position and manner the Fisherman assumes. In vain may he fish with an ordinary pattern from the wrong spot. But of his "manner" I have a word to say by way of preface to this deep subject.

How much cerebral power Salmon possess no one can determine; but we know for a fact that fish hear as well as see, or, at all events, are capable of receiving impressions of sound. We also know that the presence of an Angler need not necessarily alarm the fish which see him. It would seem, too, that the hearing power of a Salmon is of small portent so long as the conduct of the Fisherman does not excite suspicion. The Angler must disarm all apprehension. His gait and mien must be as unconcerned among Salmon as that of the plough boy "trolling his song of the soil" among rooks. His *unconscious* presence in (or out of) the water, on the occasions about to be mentioned, must be where he can bring the fly over the catches, not sideways, but so that it fishes straight on reaching the area of the hold itself.

Unknown Agencies at Work.—As soon as the waters settle down, success in Angling nowadays is mainly due to (1) the correct reading of Nature; (2) the understanding of certain technical matters. Sir John Lubbock, in *The Pleasures of Life*, tells us that technical works bear the same relation to science as dictionaries do to literature. And says, "that without a knowledge of botany we may admire flowers and trees, yet only as strangers—only as one may admire a great man or a beautiful woman in a crowd."

These remarks might easily apply to Salmon-angling, for only the adept gets a full measure of enjoyment from it. With Anglers, as with other people, there is no accounting for the idiosyncrasy which leads one to simply observe with interest the development of phenomena, and another to analyse their causes. Sometimes the tastes of a Fisherman lead him only in the direction of getting at the action of an ideal rod, so as to make himself master of the various methods of casting. The taste of another inclines him to study temperature, light, and shade, or geological formation as affecting the choice of flies; or even to try experiments in fly composition on occasions when the fish seem positively spellbound and refuse to be inveigled; and so on. But with regard to this particular mood of the fish, it would be wise for the Angler to dispel from his mind the old-fashioned belief that Salmon have their own especial feeding times. When a pool, nay, the whole district, is blank, not a movement seen, not a "rug" had anywhere by anyone, surely some mysterious influence must be at work. As a matter of fact, we know that under certain conditions, those, for instance, when a whole reach is literally alive with fish, and within a few moments not a splash, not a ring seen for hours, it is absolutely useless to persevere with ordinary flies. We believe the fish have become amenable to some secret agency, the effect of which has been made only too evident to the observer as the waters have become more and more contaminated by the ever growing and disgraceful pollutions. Nevertheless, by the inductive process of reasoning from accurate observation and comparison of notes, we have managed to formulate certain rules in fly composition, and constant perseverance under the above circumstances with special patterns has led to a solution of, at any rate, one of our most intricate problems. May I repeat, if the cause of these things lies in some obscurity, the fact of our occasionally mastering these fish remains.

Now we may safely lay it down as a sound principle from which to start this interesting subject that the *lingering doubt* evinced by Salmon on certain days is not due to caprice, but rather to agencies, which, though busily at work, are not open to vulgar gaze. It will be long, perhaps, before we become thoroughly acquainted with all their peculiarities; yet we have to deal with them as best we may. One thing we do know, and it is this—the influences at work last longer over some fish than over others; and equally certain is it that fresh-run fish are the least affected, they being the first to show themselves when the "depression" is passing away.

When limited to the form of disturbance, which I have termed "lingering doubt," the influence is invariably of a local character. But in respect of more serious obstinacy, Nature sometimes decrees that the area of the mischief is not local, but general; and then every fish in the river seems restrained from stirring to acknowledge any fly presented in any way. On these occasions our hopes of success are so thwarted as to induce us to throw up the game in despair and wait "for the next deal."

(At this point I would remind the novice that failure to attract the fish at any time may arise from the fault of the Fisherman—a failure of no uncommon occurrence to those who do not care to study the subject of presentation. On the other hand, even if the rod is used to perfection, the Angler may yet fail from want of knowledge in connection with flies. He presents, well, just the very one he should keep dry in his book. He is trying a tiny or a thin fly; a big or a bulky one; a blue, or a poor thing without much colour or marked characteristics—whether the water is deep, shallow, ruffled or smooth. When once he gets over these preliminaries he will be better able to cope with the more common contingencies in fishing. How, then, should he proceed to do so? This is not a question to be easily answered. The young Angler, like the young fly-dresser, is often driven to find out everything for himself; no wonder he as often falls short of the achievements of experienced men of the day. Very plausible is the argument that many of the errors and indiscretions that we all commit in choosing and using flies might have been avoided by a timely reference to some authoritative treatise, written in such a way as to somewhat clear the ground for the uninitiated. And yet no man who overcomes one trouble escapes walking into another; but he walks with his eyes open, and with a knowledge of many of the conveniences and inconveniences likely to be entailed upon him thereby.)

Brushing aside these considerations and coming direct to the questions at issue, I say plainly, that while the laws which govern the Salmon in his choice of the composition and presentation of the flies he sees are enveloped in mystery, the recurrence and operation of the respective conditions which have induced us to adapt certain principles are so easily perceived and detected that, to a great extent, we have become familiarised to their ever-varying nature. This of itself is enough to show that the true pleasures of angling consist first, in grasping natural facts; secondly, in so encountering these facts as to render them remunerative to the very utmost extent. The truth is that Science is only just now beginning to unfold her wonders. At some far off period, perhaps, all the present lines of inquiry will have been followed to their conclusion, and new ones, as yet undreamt of, opened up.

Be that as it may, I am fully of opinion that we possess ample evidence to justify us in reconciling ourselves to the statement that some secret force is apt to affect the fish's physical organisation; yet it would puzzle a world of scientists to say where this sympathy lies, and what is the connecting link between the fish's psychical inertia and its physical sensations.

It is not my intention to discuss the subject which I have associated with these inert fish at any great length; still, I am bound to direct the angling student to the best means for their capture. He will doubtless be interested to hear that certain flies have been tested for many years with highly satisfactory results. Two of the most remarkable patterns have to be more or less varied, and I will now take them in review seriatim.

When the fish suddenly cease to show themselves, and that condition of "lingering doubt" is noticed in bright weather, we use

A Variegated Sun Fly

or

A Black Fancy.

I pause here to explain the system to follow in constituting these lures, for they best serve our purpose when so varied as to accord with the characteristics of the river on which we happen to be engaged. My reason is this:—It is obvious to all interested in this advanced treatment that, to describe an individual fly for every pool, every stream, rapid and flat, in any one district, considerable space would be occupied ; and that the volume itself would be insufficient to hold descriptions for the whole river.

The only practical course open to me provides a general observance of the laws framed to meet the exigencies of *colour* and *character* individually, and this, with a few general principles affecting the variations as a whole, should, I take it, be enough for dressers of experience, or of sufficient experience to understand the meaning and construction of "decided" patterns. (Perhaps a knowledge of that matter is purchasable without much practical experience. An unenlightened man might forthwith avail himself of the wisdom and experience of any of his superiors who would kindly inform him that all "decided" patterns are established and recognised by the proper distribution of any one colour through their constituent parts. Any one colour added to the tag, tail, body, hackle and wings results in forming a *very* decided pattern.)

How, it may be asked, are these results accomplished? The answer, both as to theory and practice, is extremely simple.

To begin with, a blue or any other coloured fly, deadly on one river, is repulsive to the fish on another. For that reason—in a technical angling sense—we may say there are "Blue rivers," "Red rivers," "Yellow rivers," and "Grey rivers"—each one of which is pretty sure to differ in respect of character. For instance, long bodies, long hackles, and light wings may do well on one river, and be out of character on another. The Spey, for one example, is predisposed to long hackles and light wings ; whilst Tweed fish prefer short hackles and a liberal amount of "built" wing. Again, the Usk and several Scotch rivers require fairly thick bodies and heavy wings ; though on the Inver, Lochy, Ness, Helmsdale, Earn, Erne, and most Irish waters, thin bodies, short hackles, and light wings predominate.

From these premises a dresser would suppose that he has to vary these two flies in four different directions ; but I shall deal with them separately in a few moments. I have chosen this way of entering into details as the interests of the average Angler are at stake ; *character*, for example, denotable in all ordinary flies dressed on up-to-date principles, is a stylish hall-mark of infinite importance in everyday fishing.

In illustration of the quality of colour, the Tweed and Earn fish love blue; the Dee (N.B.) and Usk fish prefer red; the Spey and Don, yellow; the Lochy and Wye, grey. It need not be inferred that the combination of any of these flies (or of other decided patterns) is not to include *some* blue, or *some* red, yellow, or grey, or even two or more of these or of other colours. The dresser completes his fly *en règle*, so as to make a decided blue-river pattern, a decided red-river pattern, etc., *as the order from the Fisherman necessitates rather than directs.* The silk tag, in all cases, tallies with the colour of the river, except in the case of grey rivers, when instead of grey silk, the dresser uses silk of any colour which, in common, also pleases the fish. The Lochy and Wye, as I have said, are grey rivers, but I use a yellow tag for both.

In order to obviate misconception about grey rivers, I would explain that, in making up everyday patterns for them, we depend more upon the effect of grey feathers than upon silks, furs, and wools. A "dash" of mouse-grey Seal's fur in some part of the body of an ordinary fly is admissable and helpful; but here we look more to a judicious employment of Teal, Widgeon, grey Mallard, Summer Duck, Gallina, etc.; and to Irish-grey or Plymouth Rock body-hackles, whilst we use Amherst Pheasant for horns.

The dresser may now wish to know how to enlarge his method of dressing. For this purpose, I will deal first with the Variegated Sun Fly by itself.

The chief point of all to bear in mind is *size.* I have tried large specimens for years, and never once succeeded with one. They are not to be dressed larger than No. 1 Redditch scale; No. 4 being considered as the most useful all-round size—even smaller, if the surface of the water happens to be smooth, would pay better. This condition cannot be too strongly put; from it *there is no departure.*

The results of my experiments have also led me to the conclusion that a thick body is desirable. So thick have I made these flies that the bulky lump at the throat would, without the greatest care, cause them to "skirt" and "wobble." To overcome this defect, I decided to make the bodies spindle-shaped. They answer uncommonly well—so much so, that, in the brightest sun, these little gems retain, and will for long retain, their deadly significance.

In nearly all cases, a short black hackle is employed *at the throat;* but two, or even three, turns in excess of what is usual are to be allowed. Sometimes, however, I use only a Gallina throat, as, for instance, on the Wye and Spey.

The best natural black hackles for the purpose are termed "bastard hackles." These are often found on the back or in the neck of a common grey-speckled cock, and on an imperfect Plymouth Rock. They are best on account of their sheen and depth of tone. But as regards black hackles, should warm weather set in early, that is to say, earlier than in the middle of May, a hackle dyed black is recommended. On the other hand, after June a natural black hackle is nearly indispensable, and especially so when the current is somewhat fast.

Now suppose the dresser has an order for this fly from the Usk, he will adopt *red* characteristics; accordingly he works up scarlet silk and scarlet Ibis for the tag and tail. He puts only red, yellow, and black coils in the body; and uses red Macaw for horns.

After all that has been said, I think this one example is quite sufficient for the dresser to be almost sure of achievement with any of these variations. I can vouch for the hints enumerated being of service to Anglers on the Lochy, Spey, Tweed, Wye, Usk, Earn, Shannon, Towy, Cothi, Findhorn, Don, Test, Lee, and Blackwater (Cork), South Esk, Helmsdale, Brora, Beauly, Erne, Conway, Torridge, Annan, and Blackwater (N.B.). Thick bodies fail on the Dee. How far it is advisable to be so particular in varying the fly for other rivers I cannot decide from actual experience; but I doubt if many exceptions will be found. A certain amount of sport may be had with any one variety, but the best of sport can only be obtained by a rigid adherence to the principles in varying the dressing which I have now laid down.

What now of the "Black Fancy?"

As a rule, it is well to try this fly over a fish before the other, but, on that point, the expert had better be left to his own resources. The body of it is of ordinary shape, and is made thick or thin as occasions demand. It is always of black silk; and, excepting "blue rivers," when the throat hackle is blue, the hackle for the *body and throat is black*, taken from one's collection of the natural or the dyed sort, according to the time of year as previously specified.

The tag, tail, and wings carry their share of the different coloured materials in order to produce the effect desired. And so far as regards the size of the Black Fancy, there is no limit.

Particulars relating to minor details, such as size of tinsel, fineness of hook, etc., I leave to the judgment of the Angler, who should, at all events, clearly express himself thereon in his letter to the dresser.

Taking the majority of rivers as a guide, I give the blue characteristics to the two dressings appended:—

THE VARIEGATED SUN FLY (Blue).

Tag.—Silver twist and medium blue silk.
Tail.—A topping and powdered blue Macaw.
Body.—In coils (wasp fashion and spindle-shaped) of red, black, yellow, and blue Berlin wool.
Throat.—Black hackle (plenty).
Wings.—Six toppings.
Horns.—Blue Macaw.

THE BLACK FANCY (Blue).

Tag.—Silver twist and medium blue silk.
Tail.—A topping and Chatterer.
Butt.—Black herl.
Body.—Black silk.
Ribs.—Silver tinsel (oval).
Throat.—Black hackle and Jay.
Wings.—Two short tippets (back to back) veiled on each side with projecting Mallard and two toppings.
Cheeks.—In this variety only, Chatterer.

At this stage I desire to point out not only what Salmon mistake flies for, but why they take them at all; and also to offer what evidence I can as to why they sometimes prefer one pattern more than another.

Now, I just want those who entertain various opinions, perhaps more or less injurious to their own interests, to concentrate their attention for a brief while upon certain established particulars of the

Salmon's habit of feeding, all of which happen to be within my own knowledge, for there is really nothing so much talked of in our pastime, and so little understood, as either the artificial or the natural Salmon-fly.

The natural fly which a Salmon will take has received, as yet, far less than its due meed of consideration, and so a little scepticism, if not a great deal, is pardonable. The modest silence in which local Anglers continue their investigations and experiments has most probably caused the matter to be kept from the knowledge of all, except those immediately concerned. I, for one, however, have long since known from actual observation that the natural Salmon-fly varies with a vengeance in size, in character, and in general appearance. That it confines itself to its own particular river, etc., etc., as we shall see a little later on.

For the present, I content myself with treating of the artificial specimen, and shall bring to light some of the scientific (and unscientific) explanations which have been hazarded about it.

I wish to treat the questions at issue, not from an aggressive standpoint, and yet, whilst exposing what, to my thinking, are the erroneous ideas of others, to state fairly my own, and give ample proof of the benefit to be derived from them.

I would first remark that, in these utilitarian days and practical results, all classes occasionally unite to express their opinion on these questions in the columns of contemporary journals. In order to obtain new ideas, the best of all possible reasons, Editorial encouragement is frequently held out by such invitations as, "perhaps some of our correspondents can enlighten us," so that any novice may write, as if invested with the fullest authority. The results of this practice are peculiar, but, as an old hand, what odds, I would ask, is it whether the truth is brought out by hook or by crook—or by book? They occasionally answer some purpose in fishing. But when these Editorial measures, though full of purpose, happen to be concerned with a question so pregnant as "*What is a Salmon-fly?*" Fishermen naturally think twice before trusting to haphazard opinion. "What is a Salmon-fly?" is the very point for us to consider just now, and though the solution may appear difficult, it certainly is not impossible; yet truth lies at the bottom of a well.

On the supposition that all the elements of the problem lie before us, nothing can be more preposterous than to imagine that the *exact truth* can be found out in a hurry. We have no direct communication with the fish. Still, admitting this, it must be acknowledged that certain points are already thoroughly well known, although confined to individual localities.

I invite the reader to look closely into the following facts, and to bear in mind, while so doing, that speculation must invariably occupy the ground where proof is wanting.

To attempt, moreover, to analyse rightly the points at issue without discussing analogous matters freely would be to engage in a task at once unprofitable, if not impossible. And this means that, in my case at least, very close compression is impossible.

Many will say, "I refuse to believe that your 'Jock Scotts' represent flies, as I fail to fix upon Nature's equivalent to them. I can comprehend what one member of this royal family—the Trout, to wit—says for himself in taking the "Alder" for an alder, the "May fly" for a may fly; I can also understand that Trout distinguish between one fly and another, no matter whether the pattern be less, or very much more, picturesque than Nature dictates; so I don't go to anybody to explain to me *why* it is that a Trout is sometimes taken in by a showy leg or an unnatural bit of wing colouring, or body ornamentation. One thing seems certain, in my estimation, Trout mistake our flies for *natural* flies, but I am all at sea with his majestic relative, the Salmon, and there ends the matter."

The answer is, that instinct directs the choice of food in all fish and in every animal. Those of the lowest order possess this instinct by which they are enabled to distinguish the appearance and taste of edibles generally. Even the sea anemone contributes entertaining evidence in showing a sense by which it recognises its proper food. When a small piece of fish is brought carefully to the tentacles of one of these animals, whose mouth is widely open, the food is seized and surrounded by them, and the morsel disappears; I mean, that we actually see it swallowed. If we present the anemone with a film of wool or cotton, it is refused.

I would also remark that, in maiden rivers, Salmon are not first taught to take flies of iridescent loveliness blazing forth in dazzling colours of radiant beauty, such as, a century ago, would have frightened all of them back to sea. Far from it. Enterprising men, imbued with the "spirit of modernity," have gradually educated Salmon up to taking patterns which have been imposed upon us by Necessity—the nursing mother of fishing in its higher forms; and though, in choosing flies,

> "Fashion is a living law, whose sway
> Men, more than all the written laws, obey,"

this supreme dictatress of taste often decides for us that the inartistic finish of a plain "March Brown" (Salmon size) or a coch-a-bonddu hackle with a plain Turkey wing, once considered by Mr. Salmon a tasteful rig, is undeniably uninteresting to him in these days of fashion and—competition. But put two fibres of red Toucan in the tail of a March-Brown, and see how it answers!

As a link in the chain of evidence that takes us from the caprice of these affectedly modest patterns, I perfectly remember the initial effect of certain gaudy feathers upon, not one, but several rivers. In their progress towards general use, the greatest care and judgment of the fly-tier prevailed, and the mere suspicion of their presence was enough to begin with. Early in the "fifties," for instance, Spey fish first saw "Jungle." For a time—brief, I admit—the feathers there were simply branded with the stigma of public opprobrium. But the fiat had gone forth. Nature knew full well that Salmon, like herself, show a decided preference for finery. She knew full well, too, that under certain pressure, fashions may, without exaggeration of words, be said to change from day to day. The sombre "trimmings" and "cut" which was *de rigeur* on a fly forty-eight hours ago may be placed under the ban of Forrests or Wrights, Farlows or Turnbulls, Mallochs or Redpaths, and so on. The Spey does not stand alone in this respect, for, although the best Spey fly among the old hands is a plain, flimsy, ragged-tailed "Riach"; yet, among the students of the "progressive" School, some have at length discovered with languid surprise that not a few good Spey fish are often led to destruction by a liberal use of Jungle and Summer Duck, Golden and Amherst Pheasant feathers.

Thus far, however, the reader is only reminded in my arguments (to which I shall return) that the Salmon's motive in taking flies is a problem which has frequently been misunderstood; and that, in the case of Trout, all doubts have long since been set at rest.

Naturally enough, in fishing either for Salmon or Trout, one judges by what comes under one's own immediate notice. On the Wandle, for instance, as a humble spectator myself, I have seen Trout prefer the artificial to the natural insect—that is to say, an "Olive Dun," by Holland or by Hardy, floating down stream in company with several living flies of the same kind has been so singularly attractive and effectual as to force the fish to leave the others alone, and "go" for it. Then on several rivers, Salmon always, and for the most obvious reasons, hold in abeyance habits of existence, which, however, invariably assert themselves at the first opportune occasion; and then a fly, equally true to nature as regards colour of body, or exact in some other peculiarity, *is just as necessary to ensure good sport.*

Now, if I may venture to say so, no further evidence is wanted to satisfy me that, in the matter of like and dislike, and discrimination as to what they conceive good to eat, Salmon are exceedingly nice. In fact, I attribute my greatest angling successes to the conclusion that, not long after a flood, the impetuosity of the Salmon's nature is held in check by a downright "business faculty" of a highly efficient kind, and that his "enthusiasm" rarely impels him to lavish even as much as curiosity upon a fly *unless it be the right sort—i.e., a tasty bit put before him in the right way.* And yet we encounter narrow worshippers who simply burn for the heat of the fray, and publicly declare they can hold their own in competition with only three or four patterns! Their doctrine is contrary to reason, it has no meaning, except on the Dee in Spring, and it is impossible.

But to the world at large to see for certain what a Salmon does is a rare accomplishment. People for the most part are not gifted with the power of sight, or the power to employ their sight, to detect its habits when feeding in fresh water; and have never seen the explanation given in books, because the writers could not explain; some, *even officials,* going so far as to say, "They don't feed at all!"

Even if we had the necessary power of vision and the inclination of mind to make inspections, one has to travel far and wide and there wait for an opportunity. At first, with the unaided eye, I saw little or nothing, and not half as much as I wanted to until after years and years of practice, and then only by the aid of powerful field glasses. At last I had distinct ocular proof that Salmon feed on flies, moths, wasps, and caterpillars, as well as on their own species. But this is not all, for, after baiting clear places for the purpose, I have seen them pick up prawns and pass by worms—indeed, it would appear unnatural for them to come across worms except in discoloured water.

There is no necessity to dilate on individual gifts, on incomparable skill, or on the magic power of the human eye. What one man can see and record with precision, even only after years of practice, is a feat not hopelessly impossible to others.

(The peculiarities of Salmon amongst fish suggest to me a likeness to the pigeon, and this prompts me sometimes to call the Salmon "the pigeon of the river." The bird's and the fish's homing propensity is persistent and followed with a like miraculous accuracy. As regards the Salmon, here is a case in point. The late Frank Buckland managed to secure several fish from the west coast of Ireland, all of which he marked and succeeded in transporting to the east coast, where they were set at liberty. In the Autumn of the same year, if I remember rightly, many of these fish were *captured in the very same rivers from which they had been taken in the early Spring.*)

I once ventured upon writing to the Press on the subject before us. Laymen, *cum multis aliis*, had aired their views in sporting books and angling newspapers. With the latter gentlemen I have little present concern save to tell them of a fishing companion's remark when he and I discussed certain (as I thought impracticable) speculations.

"Oh, I know!" said he, "somebody is going to bring out a fly having scales, and fins, and gills, and fish's eyes stuck on; this is paving the way for a new bait that will do honour to the inhabitants of Arcadia."

My letter led to further discussion. One eminent authority in Trout fishing stated that the "Alexandra" fly is taken for a Minnow. Another averred that "Jock Scott" is to the Salmon a mere variegated wrasse;

that some of our standards are simply representations of the mackerel tribe, prawns, and so on. Into any other curious theories than these I hesitate to pursue this delicate subject. Who, however, can possibly believe what we are told in another place, that Salmon take our flies for sea weed! Who can dream of supposing—but no. The inquiry, as I have said, is too delicate, and I will not bring other opinions forward.

But where is the evidence in support of these statements? How can they be substantiated? I am bound to say that all such ideas are entirely upset by my own experience in Salmon-fly fishing. Were it not so, the whole of this book, the materials for which have taken a lifetime to collect, falls to pieces. No particle of evidence is forthcoming to show that those who are interested in fly problems need accept such opinions.

I need not dwell on the subject, though it forcibly recalls a Scotch Gillie's definition of metaphysics :—

"It's joost this—twa men arguing togither. He that's list'ning dis na ken what he that's speaking means, and he that's speaking dis na ken what he means his ain sel'—that's metapheesics."

But perhaps I should add that I applied to the Editor of the sporting journal in question for permission to ventilate those opinions in these pages. The prompt and sympathetic reception my proposal met with, attested the interest my opinions had excited, and I recur to it now with a pleasure which is enhanced by my more recent observations.

I have a little to add and nothing to alter in the letter published in the *Field* in 1892 under the title of *Facts and Fancies in Fly Fishing*. My signature was appended, as I never write to the Press expressing opinions on these matters under a *nom de plume*, nor without volunteering explanations when it seems necessary.

The letter runs on these lines :—

"In fishing, matters of fact are to the Angler's judgment the same thing as food to the body. On the due digestion of facts depends the wisdom and success of the one, just as vigour and health depend on the other. By common consent it is agreed that in Trout fishing we have long since arrived at the plain truth about flies, from which, at all events, we derive much practical benefit. That is to say, we have satisfied ourselves that Trout take, or rather mistake, artificial flies for living insects, and we work on certain principles accordingly. We have determined this from evidence set before our very eyes, and it is little use disputing the fact. Strange as it must appear, however, to the uninitiated (for people think differently and set up all kind of theories), we have, in the opinion of some judges, reasons for coming to the same conclusion as regards Salmon. In fact, had we worked on any other principle it would have involved signal defeat in a vast number of instances extending over a period of many years. We shall presently also see whether it is better to follow mere speculative fancies, hopelessly ineffectual, or a well-authenticated summary of interesting facts. Let me remark at the onset that I have never yet heard or seen in print any one single statement from a first-class Salmon-angler—one recognised as an authority by the experienced—calculated to support the prevailing idea that Salmon fancy our flies represent living things on which they feed and fatten in the sea. This mistaken notion emanates from men conscientious enough to doubt, but who jump at conclusions without ever having had an opportunity by the riverside to enlighten them on the subject. My object in writing is to endeavour, for the sake of beginners, to upset these speculative fancies, and to show how I myself have profited by a system which sooner or later will be respected by all.

"Of late years the education of Salmon and Trout has become a subject of more general care and attention. Assuming that we tried for Trout with a straw-bodied May fly where the natural insect is unknown to the fish, say on the Anton which runs in that famous river for May fly-fishing, the Test, what sport could we expect? Simply none. Dame Nature, for some beneficent reason of her own, fails to furnish a supply of these ephemera on the tributary, yet within a stone's throw the yield on the main stream is very heavy. No wonder the sport in the May-fly season is good in one place and worthless in another. The fact is, Trout, in the selection of food, follow predilections implanted by Nature. The flies which, as a rule, best allure them must therefore copy as closely as possible the natural flies which are their most appreciated food. In the case of Salmon this is not quite so evident, and so Fishermen have come to the conclusion that man, for better or worse, educates Salmon, whilst Nature, for the most part, educates Trout. At any rate, this is especially evidenced on Salmon rivers, both in the combination of the actual materials employed in flies, and in the good or bad all-round system of fishing—I mean not only as regards the character, style, and size of the flies used, but also in the method of attack that prevails. As an average example of this training by Fishermen I killed fish thirty years ago with a No. 4/0 hook—body and wings of the most showy materials, whilst on the self-same waters to-day men devote themselves to flies that betray no resemblance to old favourites, either in colour, character, or size. Their patterns now are no larger than natural March-browns, and many of them almost as sombre in appearance. But the Trout-fisher often has to depart from the rule touching actual imitation. He often uses, and uses successfully, flies dressed from imagination, as for instance, the 'Governor' and 'Holland's Fancy.'

"We will direct our attention for a moment towards our favourite 'Coch-a-bonddu.' The 'Marlow Buzz,' as it is termed, is far from being a truthful likeness of the lady-bird, for which it is said to serve as deputy. The question arises, is it the Peacock herl body or the hackle of this Welsh pattern that captivates the fish? We may leave the body entirely out of the question, and as to the hackle, it no more resembles the legs of a lady-bird than the legs of the cockroach. To say, however, that Trout take the fly for a minnow is just what I find by my experience they do *not* take it for. On the other hand, *sometimes* Trout take every precaution, and in one particular respect so do Salmon, and unless the fly for both is extremely well copied--say, on the Wandle for Trout, and on various rivers spoken of presently for Salmon—suspicion is aroused at once, and a general stampede takes place. This teaching of Nature and training of man applies equally to the *size* of the fly as regards both Trout and Salmon. On one river—say, the Darenth—we use a small Iron Blue, because the living insect in Kent is small; and on another river—say, the Usk—the pattern is 'put up' twice as big, because there the living insect is twice as large. But on such a river, say, as the Lochy, the Salmon have learnt to take the most diminutive flies, because the Fishermen have for years been gradually decreasing the size of their artificials.

"At this point I would ask the reader to turn a ready and confiding ear to what I am about to whisper. Have not our acknowledged unmistakeable fancy flies a far greater attraction *at times* for all rising Trout than those dressed so delicately and so truthfully as to be the fac-simile of Nature herself? Does not the 'Alexandra,' for example, kill anywhere and everywhere when our perfectly-dressed Duns, Midges, and Gnats fail ignominiously? And has not this notorious pattern of mine occasioned such havoc in places as to be positively prohibited? Often and often will Trout take the most fancy pattern ever introduced, whilst in certain seasons (the May-fly season, for instance) they decline to notice our book flies unless they are dressed true to Nature. *It is the very same thing with Salmon.*

"Before entering into details, I would remark (1) That it is not uncommon to kill Trout with all sorts of flies when March-browns and Alders are at their best. With Salmon this is not so, for when *their* fly is in season they never deign to notice anything else. (2) That all rising Trout are what all Salmon are not—persistently partial to natural flies throughout life. As regards this partiality, it is necessary to remember the respective habits of Trout and of Salmon—the one species closely packed, struggling for existence in shallows and stickles; the other disbanded, in screened lay-byes and deep pools, peacefully blessed with the fulness of satiety, and not amenable to the pangs of hunger. (3) That all the young of Salmon show a decided preference for any fly, either natural or artificial. They come more greedily at them than Trout, whether the fly in use is naturally or ever so fancifully dressed; and though in after years some come much more kindly to

Salmon flies than others, there is not one single breed—not even that peculiarly stubborn sort bred in the Trent—that entirely refuses them. I cannot say so much as this of Trout, for there are some that never take flies at all.

"Trout of other breeds make flies their special food, but to see the gratification of a similar propensity amongst Salmon—I do not mean samlets—we have to travel far and wide. Seen it I have often, though once a year only do these fortunate occasions present themselves. They are chiefly familiar to the eye of the observer, not by reason of a show of myriads of little insects, but of untold numbers of large insects, winged and otherwise, which the average Angler never notices as affecting his interests with regard to the Salmon. Were he fishing in the Highlands he would be quite blind to this fact, even in the presence of the extraordinary so called 'Green Kings," which are remarkable for their effect upon the fish, and for their uncommon appearance and enormous size.

"I particularly remember the year 1848. It was the year in which my Father first sought consolation under distressing circumstances in a 'Milo Cutty' and in the 'Alexandra fly,' which I introduced at that time—just four years after I had killed my first Salmon. To omit all trivial details as regards this fly, I may say that I used to dangle it before the noses of timid Trout, which one day fed on flies and another on gudgeon and minnows. Could *they* not tell the difference? The very idea must be blotted out of our minds.

"Anyone determined to see for himself what a fly looks like by inspecting it from the bed of the river (which I have frequently done myself) would soon distinguish, not only the natural 'play' of the legs and wings, but also the great attractions of the hairy filaments with which the body is covered. Put a fly whose body is made of Peacock's herl into a tumbler of water and you may see much the same sort of thing. It looks no more like a gudgeon or a minnow than a cabbage, if I may so boldly give an opinion.

"I remember imitating black beetles' legs with single herls fixed to a cork body, which had been varnished black for a particularly sheltered spot on the upper part of the Darenth, and getting the largest Trout with this make-believe. The fish would not look at the 'monster' before the season for black beetles commenced, when, of course, they took it for the natural insect, as all Trout-anglers must surely believe. The large fish had no doubt fed on these beetles for years.

"Can any individual imagine that the firmly-rooted, passionate fondness, which, in infancy, Salmon show for living flies, does not remain liable on some provocation (peculiar to the district) in after life again to spring up as strong as ever? I venture to submit evidence of this recurrence in a number of cases, not as regards the once-favoured Alders, March-browns, Midges, and Gnats, but more in direction of insects which are as showy and as conspicuous to the fish as 'Jock Scott' itself. Space prohibits me from giving many instances, but it is within the domain of possibility to be mistaken on the river Spey. See the care, see the precision of even the most famous of the local Fishermen in copying the exact colour of the Green-king, deadly as any fly on Speyside dressed in such able hands. Could it be possible after fifty years of close research and experiment with all sorts of ways and means of hitting off the features of this extraordinary Highland fly, and making its picture consistently faithful, that a celebrated judge yet remains in utter ignorance of a pursuit from which he annually derives practical benefit? In watching him one day, I remarked how very careful he was with his trimmings.

"'Ah, sir,' he answered, 'but it pays, and I find they won't have it overdone. Please to look at those long red prongs in the tail of that grub."

I pointed out that the pattern was a combination of the grub and fly together, and that he had matched the prongs with the red sword feather of the Golden Pheasant.

"'But a little of it goes a long way whatiffer,' he replied.

"And with his Berlin wools would 'Cruiky' select and mix two or three shades so as to get the exact colour of the body before he would rest and be satisfied. The reader will draw his own conclusions from the constant practice of one who is bent on supplying his employers with the most effectual patterns of the day.

"Let me next refer to an instance connected with the Grub mentioned in the Badminton Library. Well do I remember the invention and introduction of this favourite apterous pattern on the Usk. At the top of the 'Withe Bed,' two miles above the town of Usk, there was one hold that required a very long cast. The 'Spey' was the only method by which it could be covered, and often enough in those days the catch was undisturbed. William Acteson, the bailiff, being under orders to inform my family when the water was in ply, we were advised accordingly. On arriving, we found the river lower than we expected, and until we came to the spot, had seen no Salmon breaking the water. After my Father had neatly commanded the catch, he said the fish had, for some cause or other, 'struck work.' Then I took my turn, with the result that neither of us got the least recognition. We then left the fish (we had seen it rise) like a parcel, "to be called for later on." I would incidently remark that these fish strikes should be settled by competent arbitration. They do not occur by chance, but each is the result of some definite cause, which, if ever repeated under the same conditions, would produce the same results. It is the interesting business of the Angler to trace the conditions and proceed accordingly. Well, we tried other resorts along the Withe Bed and found them all untenanted. Making for shadier places below, paterfamilias, in advance of me, spotted several fish in "Garcoid" rising and sucking in caterpillars falling from overhanging trees. Acteson was sent for the Trout tackle. My Father never liked to go home without sport of some kind, and said, with one of those rapid changes of manner, from grave to gay, which was one of his peculiar charms :—

"Take the field glasses and just tell me what size these fish are."

"Once on the high ground over the pool, peeping through the trees, I saw, as everybody who is anybody on a Salmon river, and several who are not, would have seen, that the fish were *not* Trout.

"'Salmon,' I shouted; 'seven of them close to the slab.'

"A few minutes later and I was by my Father's side with two or three of the little green, hairy creatures in my hand.

"'Well,' said he, 'we have a chance now! Whip up a big imitation, and we'll have some of these fine fellows on the bank.'

"The feather work proceeded, and we discussed the mode of attack (for we could not cast) should we 'bob' or fish the fly by paying out the line? Our wingless lure was soon dressed on a No. 2 hook; the body of green chenille, veiled in four sections with real Irish-grey hackles, that would have made the mouth of a Manning water, with a silver tag and tail of Ibis. I shall never forget the commotion in the water which the sight of the Grub caused. Directly it reached its destination all the fish seemed to go for it after the fashion of Chub for cheese. We knew what was up in a moment, and in a comparatively short time five of these unwary Salmon lay lifeless by our side. This sounds well to the uninitiated, perhaps, but no note of admiration is put to make it appear remarkable, for success of this description does not strike me in any way as being remarkable.

"'Perhaps our old friend above (I mean the 'parcel') gorged himself with these caterpillars. If you'll try for him, I'll cross the ford below the 'Whebbs' and watch how the fish behaves when he sees our imitation of one.' This suggestion from me was enough for my Father, and on getting to the spot and settling myself under an old wall I soon observed: 'Let the Grub come further round, you recover the line too soon.'

"On the second trial the line was allowed to dwell, and the fly worked in sight. But I saw nothing, even by the aid of the binoculars, until I heard the whirr of the winch—the dash of the fish being so sudden and so quick. In due course the gaff was used, and the Salmon, fresh-run, was literally chock-full of mashed caterpillars! Here, then, was the sixth killed in one day with the selfsame hook, dressed after the living things themselves.

"Though I tried that fly again and again to within the last year or two, I never had another rise to it, or even a pull. And this, in my idea, is because I have never since met with the same conditions.

"Another example is afforded by the 'Red Underwing' on the Earn? This fly is tied after the gaudy Cinnabar moth (*Euchelia jacobeae*), and is a superb killer at the end of the month of September, when the moth itself is seen up and down the river flying about in thousands. I am aware that this fly has been described as representing the *Catocula nupta*; but this is immaterial, as the fish do not stop to classify. Salmon, unlike Trout, spend only a portion of their time in fresh water, during which period they travel from district to district. How, then, can we expect their knowledge of the insects upon which they are accustomed to feed to be so precise as that of Trout, which keep to one place, if not to one spot, from year's end to year's end? Be this, however, as it may, I will relate my first experiences with the 'Red Underwing.'

"I was staying with some friends at the same hotel in Crieff. Overnight we had arranged plans for the next day. Mr. F. M. Mackenzie, whose identity I am at liberty to mention, decided to come with me. After a couple of hours, neither of us being in luck, my companion made off in another direction and left me alone for a time. All of a sudden a voice from behind enquired:

"'Halloa! Out of the water. What *are* you up to?'

"'I have just completed a couple of flies, one for each of us; the day ought not to turn out blank with this opportunity. Take a glance in what direction you like; look at the hundreds of those lovely 'red wings' flying about, and you'll guess what I am up to,' I answered.

"'You don't mean to say,' he replied, 'that you have taken all that trouble for me!'

"I told him that I had often killed fish in trying this principle when other means failed. The 'Dolly Varden,' a pool which had been fished twice down by me and several times by others, was given up to my friend. He was soon engaged in a fair up and down fight, and, as the day was drawing to a close, I made for a little catch below, which I knew held one good 'tenant.' To my friend's delight, he weighed in no fewer than three good fish that evening. But this is not all. The duplicate fly was seized directly in the catch below, a struggle ensued, and we were the only two successful Anglers of the day on the whole beat, five miles in length.

"No one intimately acquainted with the river Lee, and the way in which fly fishing has been ruined by bait fishing, would be likely to accept the remark just made about Salmon waiting to 'classify.' On settling down, the water in this river becomes so bright that with the unaided eye a pin can be easily detected lying at six feet depth. After an interval of many long years I spent three months in the vicinity of Macroom (early in 1889), and was sorry to find how extremely shy and particular the fish had grown. In former days a body of Rabbit's fur, veiled with a grey speckled hackle, and having a light wing was enough to ensure good sport. You would never stir a fin now with a body of this description, which changes colour soon after use. The insect that haunts these Irish waters, seen in magical numbers, almost double the size of a bluebottle, but grey in colour, and with speckled body, wings, and legs, is in these days imitated with the finest Irish-grey hackles taken from fowls bred on purpose, and with fur from a silver Monkey, which together produce the very image of the natural fly itself.

"I could multiply instances in support of the conclusion which has been forced upon me by experience, but it is needless. Winged flies, as well as caterpillars, can be imitated and used in Salmon fishing with success. Believing this, let alone the other arguments, I cannot insist too emphatically that Salmon take artificial flies from precisely the same motive as Trout; indeed, by reason of a long and varied experience, wherein I have over and over again noticed the movements of Salmon when they patronise natural insects, I hold the foregoing theories not only as being indisputable and indispensable, but also as being of sufficient weight to justify the conclusion that Salmon mistake artificial flies for natural insects rather than for anything else."

In sport, as in science, it sometimes takes a lifetime's devotion to master even the rudiments of a single branch. The expert in Salmon-fishing, should be as carefully trained as a diplomatist.

Had it not been for binoculars, which, after fishing for years in ignorance of these matters, I took with me on all occasions, I might never have discovered that the art of Salmon-angling might be placed upon a new and sounder footing.

It is not intended to imply by these observations that at all times and on all rivers, fly-work is quite so easy as has just been mentioned. Sometimes it is convenient, nay imperative, to resort to the most fantastic specimens of artificial entomology extant. On those occasions we are driven to master fish by force of *contrast*, and mount flies which have not unwisely been termed "exaggerations."

And now a few words about these.

Exaggerations are employed only in extreme cases, when in summer and early autumn, long after a flood, fish take to and remain in one particular haunt for days and days, and, as though having nothing else to do, play "follow-my-leader" round and round their pool of water whether it be beside streams or sheltered flats.

Some years ago, I ventilated this matter in the columns of a weekly paper, and was flattered to learn that it had obtained the favourable notice of some of the most expert and best instructed Salmon-anglers of the day. I revive it now for one or two reasons. To begin with, on every Salmon river in the United Kingdom there are local Anglers whose *dicta* in flies are taken and always adopted with little suspicion by those who have seen or heard of their success. On every river, too, as I have before said, certain special schemes of colour, size, &c., are found to prevail to the practical exclusion of others, which, sometimes, would assuredly do better. Yet despite colour schemes, schemes in presentation, accomplished local Anglers, and all common devices, days come everywhere when futility prevails.

To triumph on such days, one must provide a practical novelty that may rouse the "tiresome Salmon" from that too volatile or too inert mood which prevents him paying the least attention to the politest Sir Oracle or his ordinarily quite attractive flies. According to my opinion, a special work of art in respect of flies is, so to speak, an image, not necessarily of any living thing represented, but of the impressions or, shall I say, "phantasy pictures" forced by an independent reality on the mind of the experienced hand. And yet due thought must in all cases be given to the idiosyncrasies of Salmon. These distinguish the fish of one river from the fish of another. What are improperly called "fish humours" commonly but not invariably, depend on light, shade, the nature of surroundings, and so on. A fine Angler gives all these things justifiable weight, and whilst never supposing that all the fish in *this* river have an exclusive natural love of blue and hatred of red, and that, contrariwise, all the fish in *that* river are disinclined to blue and enamoured of red, sets himself to devise something really ticklesome for their acceptance rather than follow common practices and submit to barren statements founded on "fish humours."

These statements violate all rational probabilities, and to embrace them would simply compel us to accept the ridiculous proposition that all the fish which prefer blue go to one river, those affecting red to another river, and so on through the colours of the rainbow.

The humour of the fish is to recognise that which excites his curiosity, appetite, a singular sort of cupidity, or whatever it may be; and different combinations and tactics are often required to stir him.

Writing on the subject of "Exaggerations," *Land and Water* says:— "For sometime past, Mr. George M. Kelson has been explaining the minutiæ of this higher branch of fly-fishing in the Press. In his articles, the reader has not only the experience of one who has from boyhood fished in every quarter of the kingdom, but who has also the transmitted knowledge of a Father equally skilled as the son, both in tying the fly and handling the rod. . . . Put into a few words what Mr. Kelson advocates in the case of lazy fish, is *to first rouse them by an 'exaggeration.'* When a fish is roused into a condition of expectancy, it is as good as half caught; all that is then wanted is a 'modification' deftly manipulated.

The nature of this combination will be determined by the colour of the water, light and shade thrown upon it, natural aspects of the river bed; banks, and other surroundings, as well as by the particular character of flies generally used in the district."

To this Editorial statement—a pressing request for me to treat it fully being appended—I recorded several instances of the success of exaggerations which had occurred to myself and others, who, commencing as thorough sceptics, had become the most faithful of converts. From these I select first the following case.

A few years ago I was fishing some private water, immediately above which there were a couple of miles of the best holding pools on the river. Owing to the long continued drought, the water fell lower than it had been for years. So low did it become that my own pools were worthless for Salmon—in fact, in was impossible for the fish to stay in them. Above and below it was rumoured that Anglers were giving up fishing altogether, owing to sheer absence of sport. A party consisting of three rods on the water below, had been fishing all they knew for three whole weeks unsuccessfully, during which time they had special permission to fish the best waters. At the end of their visit they returned to Town.

Overnight I obtained permission myself to try the same water on the morning of their departure—the pools still getting lower and lower. Knowing that a strong "exaggeration" would be required, I was up betimes and tied a few flies dressed in the following manner:—Tag: silver twist, but three times the usual amount. Tail: Ibis, two extended strips of Summer Duck, and the point of a Jungle. Butt: scarlet herl. The first half of the body was divided into two equal sections, butted as before, as well as having two bunches of Goat's beard above and below arching after the fashion of the golden toppings; the first set, dyed crimson-majenta; the second, or those merging from the middle of the body, dyed light blue and extending over the former to the butt of the fly. The first section of the body was made of yellow silk, ribbed with gold lace and silver tinsel. The second section, of crimson-majenta silk, ribbed in the same way, but with larger materials. The other half of the body had dark blue silk, ribbed with very large gold tinsel, leaving space at the throat for a couple of turns of crimson-majenta Seal's fur, which was well picked out. Throat: Goat's beard dyed dark blue, and spotted Gallina over it dyed likewise, only of a lighter shade. Wings: underwing, two strips of dark brown mottled Turkey with black bars and white tips, partly veiled on each side with strips of Summer Duck, above which came two small tippets (back to back) dyed crimson-majenta, extending only to the middle of the body, enveloping two full sized natural Jungle, projecting over the tail of the fly, and two toppings above all. Sides: Cock-of-the-rock to the lower bar of the tippet, and two bright blue feathers (one on each side) from the back of the Pitta (bertæ) from Borneo, covering half of the Cock-of-the-rock. Cheeks: Scarlet Tanager. Horns, blue Macaw, red Macaw, and Amherst Pheasant. Head, a small fiery brown hackle, coiled.

During the day's fishing, so far as could be seen with the opera-glass, I rose nine fish with one or another of these extravagant flies, with the result that *six took hold of the changed flies afterwards* and were all brought to bank.

The changed fly, which took the fish, was in each case a decidedly sombre "modification" of the former fly, *i.e.*, the exaggeration by which I had roused the Salmon's attention. . . .

When visiting a different part of the world, I was watching a gentleman casting over a heavy fish which had already risen to his fly. It came twice in my presence. The fly which rose it three times was an extraordinary specimen of an "exaggeration," having four Jungles in the wing (two dyed red) and other showy feathers such as Ibis, Chatterer and red Macaw all plentifully distributed.

On the Fisherman leaving the pool and speaking to me I discovered that we were old friends, and that I had myself made the very fly he had been using. Forgetting how further to proceed, he consulted my opinion. He had already fallen into error. Here, however, was a fish that had risen three times, what was to be done?

(I should state that I never before saw, nor have I ever seen since, a Salmon rise three times to an "exaggeration." He *must* have wanted it badly!)

With materials provided by my friend I made up on the spot the following simple fly which caught the fish the moment it was presented. Tag: Silver twist and yellow silk. Tail; Toucan: Butt, black herl. Body, dirty-orange Seal's fur ribbed with silver lace. Throat, Grouse hackle. Wings Golden Pheasant tail and a few fibres of fine Peacock's herl mixed together, dressed on a No. 3 hook which was half the size of the exaggeration. (Of this particular nondescript let Annan Anglers take special note.)

Colonel Richardson, the gentleman to whom I have just referred, had at the time no belief in my system, but remembering what I had vaguely said some few years previously, tried the experiment out of mere bravado. But he was not satisfied after all, and failure on a subsequent occasion caused him to invite me to meet him. Just at the time I received his letter, I was on the Usk and we discovered that we were fishing within a few miles of each other. Ultimately we determined to try a pool in the Duke of Beaufort's water (Monkswood fishery) running under a well-known beech tree at the head of the "Binding." The river ran dead low and the fish were sailing round and round in the shade.

Resuming the usual tactics we put the extravagant fly in sight of the fish. They ceased to roam at once—a fact which we easily detected from the wooded bank. In due course the "modification" was presented and the Colonel killed two fish with it, one of 15 lbs., the other 18 lbs., in my presence. The "school" itself mustered eight in number.

I am also permitted to state that Colonel Richardson has since been practising the method with unusual success, and that at one time he averaged about one fish for every six daily trials. He, however, is of opinion that "the exaggeration practice will never be very popular. First, it requires immense experience in fishing to carry it through, and unless a man is his own fly-tier his chance is very poor. Secondly, and mainly, because the fish are apt to detect the business and it makes them more shy than ever."

But I look back with the greatest pride and exultation of all to the time when I "landed" my old friend and, on this question, opponent, the late Frank Buckland, for no one more ridiculed the idea of stirring sulky fish when it first became known than the original Editor of *Land and Water*. He with his friend Mr. Clifford were fishing their private

Beat at Llangattoc, and although the famous Bryn stream held fish nothing seemed to excite them. Day in, day out passed and nothing could be done. Walking up the river one evening, I found Mr. Clifford seated in his bower-bush, as usual, watching the water with his rod in readiness. As soon as I made my appearance the chaff that I was subjected to by both gentlemen is utterly beyond description in these pages. But next day I tried my scheme in their presence. I begged them to try the reach down beforehand with what flies they liked, merely stipulating that the "catches" were not to be overthrashed. After the stream had been fished from end to end three times, and fished well, too, I, choosing the part that held most fish, made two casts, no more, with an "exaggeration." A swirl in the water told me what to expect. In due course I put on a similar fly to that which Mr. Clifford had been using in vain for days and with it caught two Salmon, one of which *had another fish in its mouth.*

Of other friends' successes I desire to notice a triumph Mr. Basil Field achieved on the Tay. The water had been well tried with large local flies of the most gaudy description. On Mr. Field making his appearance he was consulted as to further proceedings. Hearing that a fish had risen he determined to try quite a foreign fly and selected for his modification a "Glow-worm." It was remarked that "he might as well throw his rod in." *But the fish took the Grub directly it reached the catch.*

There is really no matter for surprise in this system of rousing sulky fish. The very fact of their "settling down" has puzzled many a thousand Fishermen. The reason most probably is due to the combined lowness and staleness of the water, which condition acts upon the fish much in the same way as the smoky and vitiated atmosphere of a manufacturing town acts upon the hearty constitution of a countryman. His appetite becomes jaded, and he requires the stimulus of some dainty dish to tempt him. It is precisely the same with a Salmon.

There is generally an exception to every rule, but in Salmon fishing there are more exceptions than our grandfathers would have deemed credible. I have known several instances of fish taking the exaggeration when the dressing is not too much overdone. Take an example.

I have many a time roused a Salmon with the "Blue-bell"; but some years since, fishing at Stanley on the Tay, Major Traherne wrote to me:—"For the last three days the fish would look at nothing, but I tried a 'Blue-bell' last night and have had rare fun with it to-day, getting three fish in one pool, the largest 28 lbs. 'Blue-bell' is not satisfied with anything under 20 lbs. I don't think it should be regarded as an 'exaggeration' any longer."

Many years ago I visited some noted water on the Test. Doctor Lewin accompanied me purposely to inspect the principle of "exaggerations." Upon arriving at the river-side we were escorted by the water-bailiff and a despondent Angler who remarked:—"The best advice I can give you is to go home; there is not the ghost of a chance. No one has risen a fish here for a fortnight. They are there, but the water is low and foul to a degree positively offensive to the olfactory nerves."

The excellent disciple of Æsculapius drew a long face.

"Now is the very time," said I.

However, on reaching the pool for which I had set out my friend said:—"I should like to see you fish the water down with the usual flies before trying any of your pet theories."

"Certainly," I replied, but after a time, having done no good, I urged that it was "mere waste of time to use such flies."

"Ah, it's just my luck!" observed the Doctor. "Give it up and come to Sonning with me, for you might just as well try for a Salmon in the Thames."

At that moment a voice from behind a hedge exclaimed, "There's a fish about 14 lbs. in front of you and it has seen every fly in my book this morning."

But there was nothing for it, I sat down beside the hedge and, after making friends and a little explanation, in an hour or so had two or three hundred small Chatterer feathers, forming the body, on a 6/0 hook: whilst the wing, composed of Jungle and toppings, was further decorated with double Amherst horns. I splashed the lure (I should not do so now) just once about two yards above the spot indicated and gently drew it away.

Nothing was seen—not a stir.

Plate 6

The Gordon

Childers

Traherne's Wonder

The Cockatoo

The Silver Ardea

Nankeen

"I'm off, good bye and good luck to you," the Doctor said.

"No, not yet; come here and do what I ask. Do you see that tall foxglove? Go out into the field and make your way to it inch by inch without shaking the ground, peep through the foliage and tell me exactly where *this* fly goes."

I had mounted a tiny "Blue Boyne" dressed with the more sombre Blue Rock.

"Shall I tell you from there or come back?"

"From there. You needn't shout, and don't move."

"Oh, I can see it as plainly as possible, and the Salmon, too—what a lovely fish! The fly is three yards in front of him."

"Capital; now look out, but don't move a muscle."

I then made a short but rather sharp snatch of the rod, and a tremendous splash and the winch "busy" told its own tale. Twenty minutes later—the weeds causing a slight delay—the Doctor on all fours had his chance, but "missed," for truth to tell, he drew the gaff as gently as a German waiter a fork under a tender sardine. But on the second venture, after a dose of eloquence for the "specific complaint," the eminent authority on pulses gaffed the fish through and through, and in one motion flung the lot on the bank some feet from the water.

"Ah," observed Doctor L—— "it may be said of flies as of ladies and gentlemen—'*contrasts* make more intimate unions.' But why have I not seen these things before?"

"Because *you* look at Salmon-fishing with the trained eye of a medical man, *we* with the trained eyes of Fishermen."

Only the other day, having an exceptional opportunity of seeing the movements of a fish under treatment, I reduced to demonstration the effect of one of these overdressed flies in the Wester Elchies water. My friend J. C. H.—I wish I dared tell of our many enjoyable outings together—wishing to see the experiment tried, asked me to put an "exaggeration" before a fish in sight. The Salmon darted towards the fly at once. So far the plan succeeded, but the current went so slowly that, as I predicted, to catch the fish would be an impossibility; in fact, fly No. 2 scarcely supporting itself in the water did not reach the place.

I could fill pages with incidents relating to this the most novel and the most difficult of all systems in the use of flies, but pretty well enough has been said on this part of our subject.

"Exaggeration" in fly dressing proceeds from a true insight into Salmon-angling affairs. It is known under several headings. In one sense "exaggeration" means the largest and most showy feathers shortened in their quills or roots of fibres to fit hooks which some people would set forth as absurdly large for any purpose whatever. In another it means the longest of the less marked feathers to extend far beyond the bend of hooks of the size in use. But the truest definition really is that there must be some excess or repetition of our most gaudy feathers and other materials tied separately upon the hook; as, for instance, in the case of the "Black Prince" and "Golden Butterfly."

When we are unable to *see* the effect these flies have over fish we take it for granted that the work is done. The assumption is sometimes justified by the result which the puny productions bring immediately afterwards. These were called "condensations," but as this utterance of olden times lends itself most inconveniently to misrepresentation, we now call them "*modifications*."

The term, however, is often misapplied. To ordinary flies of sombre appearance, or to patterns simply lacking lustre, the word has no legitimate bearing at all. To "modify" a wing composed of very showy strips is a practice in fly-dressing which would not trouble the patience of the veriest novice. Only a small portion of each strip is taken for mixing in fibres, by which means the effect is distributed and consequently reduced.

The excellence of "exaggeration" consists in the quality of startling attractiveness, and is not governed by any known law. One of the most important items to consider in "modifications" is size. It should always be remembered that, in ordinary pools where the bed of the river is rocky, the smallest patterns in reason should be used, and that such decided feathers as Jungle and Summer Duck of the duller shades must be employed with unerring regard to the size of the hook. The smaller the hook the smaller should be the markings. If the weather as well as the water be very bright, a little lustre, by the means of a couple of strands of Bustard, or even of Peacock wing, may be added with advantage.

But if the fishing be under trees, on dull days, the fly should be toned down with such feathers as dark mottled Turkey without the white tips. On cold, windy days the size of all "modifications" must be increased. In hot weather, without wind, the bed of the river being fairly level we use large tinsel for ribs and put the coils closer—allowing six upon a No. 1 hook. In coloured water we make the whole fly dark in tone and increase the length of hackle.

Although *size* is so important, other matters must be observed. Never do we use floss silk to form the whole body of a "modification," but Berlin wool for dull days, Seal's fur for bright, and Pig's wool if the water be exceptionally deep. But in the event of the "exaggeration" that roused the fish having been dressed after the fashion of the "Chatterer" we make the body of the fly, which is to finish the business, with the same kind of feathers taken from the Blue Rock (a darker Chatterer); choose very much smaller feathers, and instead of putting them in uninterrupted sequence, arrange them in three small sections, filling up the spaces between, in this case, with floss silk of exactly the same colour.

In treating of silver bodies which were made with flat tinsel, we soften the conversion by the adoption of oval or round tinsel, or perhaps by gold beaters skin (Mr. Field's plan) over a white floss silk body. For that purpose the skin is cut in an even strip the thickness of our broadest flat tinsel.

The art of using these patterns is easy to describe. Carefully get No. 1 fly in front of the catch *by paying out line*, and in one minute remove it as carefully. Then cast in the ordinary way *after five minutes interval* with Fly No. 2.

I feel compelled to state that I have not yet quite worked out to my own satisfaction the systems of "exaggerations." I have only once or twice succeeded in rapids, and never in still pools. Streams and Flats are the only places in which a beginner may expect to find it answer. One thing, however, it is absolutely necessary for the Angler to be stationed in front of the catch, so as to be able to let the "exaggeration" go down straight to the fish. Drawn across the water, these preliminary agents are more frequently productive of harm than good.

If after all these particulars the key to some difficulty in the technique of fly-selection be missing, the inquiring mind may yet find satisfaction among the "instances" and "examples" put forward in other chapters. Young Fishermen should, at all events, be sufficiently enlightened in this branch of the subject by now to foresee—as, indeed, all reformers do—the genuine forms of advantage derived from the study of light, shade, and other natural surroundings. But as I began by saying—although "Nature ever indicates the way to her best secrets," I have long since convinced myself that they be the best choosers which, being learned, habitually incline to the traditions of experience, or, being students, resolutely incline to the methods of learning.

CHAPTER VI.

THE ROD AND SPECIAL EQUIPMENTS.

(1) THE ROD. (2) LINE. (3) WINCH.

"TESTIMONY *is like an arrow shot from a long-bow; the force of it depends on the strength of the hand that draws it.* ARGUMENT *is like an arrow from a cross-bow, which has equal force though shot by a child.*"

BACON.

THE ROD.

WITH striking brevity the above extract sets forth the two methods I wish to adopt in support of my case, together with the peculiar value inherent in each of them. The case itself, occupying the chapter's first half, may be stated as an attempt to turn the cooling stream of reason and fact upon one of the burning questions of the day; for in the whole range of Salmon-angling topics, there is, perhaps, no one single subject so liable to produce a heated discussion as the simple question, "What style of rod is the best?"

These discussions usually derive their warmth from sweeping generalisations that have no more solid basis than individual taste acquired by mere tradition or pure chance. Fifty generations and more have confessed that argument about matters of taste is argument thrown away; how much greater, then, is the waste of time and energy to argue from taste on what is not really a matter of taste at all, but a matter of fact, in which, moreover, the facts are simple enough for a final, because a thoroughly practical, decision.

Fishermen not only *may* but actually *do* acquire a taste for an inferior style of rod; that is to say, they accustom themselves to a style of rod built on the lines of those used with supposed infallibility by their ancestors, and their confidence in it has not been shaken even by the periodically frequent fractures of tops, and the yet more frequent loss of favourite flies. They will continue stoutly to affirm the style is best, but fail to make good the affirmation by sound logic, or acceptable facts.

But it will not do roughly to over-ride prejudices of this description; for if we put ourselves in the owner's place it is easy to imagine with what outraged feelings the curt contempt of some superior critic for the "sacred heirloom" style of rod would be received. This same heirloom is of good hickory, light in hand, costly, and well finished. Enough line may be got out with it to kill *some* fish, and the owner is accustomed, nay attached, to it. Though beaten in his efforts to reach distant lay-byes, the sentiment of many years hangs about this companion of his in so many happy scenes and successful days. In the consciousness of all these, its virtues and deeds, is it reasonable to expect him to stand quietly in the shoes of stoic indifference, and while remembering its pleasant associations, to hear his favourite rod abused and damned off-hand?

There is much to be said for the inborn respect of the Britisher for antiquity. But in Salmon-fishing ours is an age of *reason*, and we must be prepared for a quick march towards the absolutely, the ideally best style of rod. In short, sound reasoning on the facts, and not taste, however legitimately and respectably begotten, should be our guiding light. We must fall back on open facts.

The question is first, What is the best all-round style of rod?" and then, "What modification or adaptation of this is best in each individual Fisherman's circumstance?"

In discussing this question in a preliminary way, I seek not only to take up unassailable ground in giving expression to the convictions born of my own experience, but also, whether I personally am right or wrong as to the style of rod I advocate, to arouse some of the rest-and-be-thankful school to the necessity either for progress towards a better weapon than the old-fashioned one, or for a justification on grounds other and better than those at present commonly held for the continued use of the very inadequate, cumbrous implement handed down from the fathers.

Manufacturers move on, and such vast strides have been made in the last few years in almost every part of the Angler's outfit that it was by no means unreasonable to expect some improvements in our rods. Our expectations have been realised. Very considerable improvements have been made, although there are rods still in stock that might be called fossil rods and go very well in use with the proverbial fly in amber.

But putting aside, for practical argument's sake, any predilection to taste and opening our minds to impartial conviction we had better ask, *What is the best style of rod for Salmon-fishing?* The obvious answer is—that style of rod which is all-round best, which executes best all the several kinds of casting practised by skilled Anglers—the style that, on the whole, best meets, most powerfully, easily, and pleasantly, all possible exigencies of place, time, and circumstance.

Surely this style of rod is equal in trained hands to make the "Overhand," the "Spey," the "Underhand," the "Flip," or even the "Wind" Cast—each as required. This certainly is the beau ideal of a rod for a skilful Angler whose fishing lies *in a great variety of water*.

But on the other hand, there is a legion of Fishermen, keen on the sport and fully alive to all improvement, who, naturally enough, contend that the waters they fish do not call for such a variety of skill on their part, and, therefore, such a many-sided action in the rod. They rather look for certain special qualities in the rod, because their practice is limited to one or perhaps two varieties of casts. One may possibly often have to adopt the Spey cast, and fishing only that river, content himself with a local model which carries a lightish line; whilst another, in an exposed run of catches, has as often to contend against a head-wind and otherwise must use the Wind Cast, which demands a maximum of lifting power in the rod and plenty of butt action, or leave the water unfished.

Such and similar considerations must modify the ideal rod by giving prominence in its style to the particular needs of each individual case. But this opens no door for the exercise of haphazard taste. If the Fisherman allows that intruder in, he will defeat his search for the best rod. He must determine what modification of the ideally best rod will suit him, and educate his taste to that ; then, taste is good, it is founded on reason and fact, and the result in practice must be sound.

Rods of this calibre are built of well-seasoned materials, and are, however, not merely ideal, but are to-day realities in actual existence and use in several well-known hands.

In proceeding to adduce facts and to reason from them, I wish to emphasize what I have already implied, that, our aim should be *sport*, not mere prowess. There is, I think, a material difference between the two. Sport includes comfort and a more or less continuous and pervading sense of direct pleasure—elements that are often wanting in the display of mere prowess. In the best style of rod, therefore, its capability to promote sport should be thought of before all else.

In determining the absolutely best type of rod, to be deviated from only in the particular feature and to the particular degree ascertained to be needed in each case, we must repeat a first great general principle. It is this :—that muscles, rod-butt, middle, top and line right down to the fly itself shall form one instrument—" compound organ," so to speak—harmonious and unbroken in action, and imbued with ready obedience to the Angler's eye and brain—an organ adapted right through for one purpose. Practice, and that alone can give a man the power of so exerting his brain and strength. The rod and line are to be, as it were, part of the man, though distinct from the man, and they are to be in such unity, so well adapted to each other, that, such a rod and line in this or that man's trained hands on his particular water shall give for him better returns than any of the others.

Now let us see how and why our old acquaintance the " trouty " Salmon rod with its light line has been of late years left in the lurch, just as the breech-loader has displaced the old-fashioned muzzle-loader.

The general requirements of Trout-fly fishing have necessitated that the rod for that branch of sport should be adapted for throwing a comparatively light line and that mainly by action from its top. Here is the fundamental and generic difference between your true Trout rod and your true Salmon rod. For the latter, to achieve its specific purposes, should be worked with a line that is out of proportion heavier than the Trout line,

The accompanying illustration of a corner in the extensive premises at the Standard Works, Redditch, will give the reader an idea of the care

GREENHEART LOGS.

taken by Messrs. Allcock & Co. in securing and seasoning, for wholesale use, the logs of Greenheart in this department alone.

and it must develop its wave of casting-force less from the rod-top than from the butt. The two actions are totally different, therefore the rods and the lines most suitable are different.

In laying down this doctrine I refer for support of it to the records existing in the public prints of recent casting tournaments, a testimony open to all and of irrefragable character. In the "Overhand" method of casting, in which mode alone the "trouty-rod" is of any use at all, the slight top and the stiff butt have caused it to be hopelessly left behind. And apart from these competitions, this style of rod has been conclusively proved to be wrong in every-day angling experience.

As to the "Overhand" cast, beloved by all, and well suited as it is for places with plenty of room in the rear of the Angler, it is supposed by many to be the easiest cast of all with plenty of wood in the butt. This is also a misconception which may be often traced to the misleading influence of the earlier acquired habits of Trout fishing. It is not that the Fisherman is unable to make the cast, but is unable to make it perfectly; and, as I have said, this rod is almost, if not quite, useless in other modes of casting and especially so on all occasions when length of line is required in windy weather.

As an instance here I will quote words which I wrote some years ago:—"Too much importance is usually attributed to the Overhand cast and consequently some of the most favourable pools are passed by because the Angler is inexperienced with other casts. Take for example, a pool where you wade, with three 'catches' in it. No. 1 would be an easy station but for a high tree immediately behind you. Here the 'Switch' would be necessary. No. 2, some yards further on with a large bough overhanging the water low down, and no stream to carry the fly beneath it owing to an eddy beyond the bough, would demand the use of the Flip Cast: and No. 3, which you reach after turning a sharp corner, has the wind in your face, and this brings the Wind Cast into operation. In these situations, the old fashioned, stiff-butted rod with a fine top, noted for throwing a light line from the point, would be as useless as it would be for holding a fish from rocks, dead trees, weirs and similar dangers. . . . Where Salmon can be captured without the display of skill or much perseverance, and without having to resort to the 'Spey,' the ‘Wind’ or the Flip Cast, any ordinary rod might be used, and with a certain amount of success. These places are few and often far between and are as often bordering upon many ‘awful places,’ in which the veteran will present his fly as if by magic. To do so he must be well appointed. A rod for general purposes may be ever so perfect, and yet prove almost useless with a line either too light or too heavy. The action of it is made manifest by comparison with a Trout rod. In direct contrast, it will propel a heavy line from the butt without perceptible effort of the Angler.”

The reasonableness of what is now being urged with, I fear, too much repetition, is clear. To be able to cast far, to cast against wind successfully, to “Switch” or “Flip” properly—in short, to be able to hold your own in Salmon fishing, you must not use a line too light, but one that demands plenty of lifting power in a rod having plenty of stuff in the upper part even to top-heaviness.

To objectors it may be also replied that a light line is no desideratum in fly fishing for Salmon. On the contrary, it is well to fish fairly deep; and, moreover, line and gut trace should taper as explained elsewhere. To the more plausible objection as to increased weight in rod and line, this must be emphatically said:—First, that owing to modern improvements, especially in all fittings, rods are made much lighter in proportion to length and strength than they used to be; but, apart from that (and here the emphasis lies) the great question is not so much whether a rod is actually heavy or not, but whether or not it *fishes* heavy. When once its proper use and available powers have been acquired by a few days' training, the modern rod, of the style described, fishes infinitely lighter than the old style. “The rod casts of itself” is an opinion often declared of it. The question is one for the muscles, What is it that tires? Not *weight* absolutely, for it is manifestly true that, even with two old-fashioned “Trouty” rods, the heavier, if the better in balance, is far less tiring than the one of lighter weight reckoned by lbs. and ounces.

We should not be misled by the adjective “light,” as applied to rod or to line. The term must be regarded as relative; and determined practically in meaning not merely by weights and scales, but also and chiefly by the final verdict of nerves and muscles. Weariness comes far sooner from the active exertion of doing all the work oneself with a light rod, than from the semi-passive labour of carrying and controlling a heavier rod that does for the Angler most, if not all the work within certain limits. This principle is of intensified application where the more special modes of casting are involved. In a moderately strong head wind the old-fashioned rod must give up altogether and look enviously on its modern rival rejoicing " in the battle and the breeze." In short, it may fearlessly be affirmed that, under any conditions of wind and weather the man who has once found himself able to cast his fly upon the desired spot with the scrupulous accuracy and reasonable delicacy and lightness, easily acquired with the modified Castle Connell rod I advocate, will never again return to the old combination of tackle. Nor will he regard as draw-backs or defects the superior strength added in the new type of rod, which secures the virtually sky-high immunity from banks, bushes and other traps behind him.

This particular modified Castle Connell is perfectly made in green-heart, and is called the " Kelson Rod." I do not know of any defects to set off against its merits. Its merits are—power of steady endurance in holding a big fish in a strong stream ; power of lifting and propelling a long line by every method of casting in any kind of weather or place in which one fishes ; and—what is even more useful where the " Spey " is imperative—power of making the thrashdown by *throwing*, when, in awkward winds, *casting* is impracticable. (Spey rods cannot do that.) By its action alone one is capable of commanding with this rod thirty yards of water ; and, when necessary, it can be made to command without much force over forty by employing the " Overhand " and of course much more by the " Governor."

The superb rod on the Shannon, known as the Castle Connell, is the parent of this rod, which, after a long and varied experience in rod using and rod making, I have found the most pleasantly powerful and generally serviceable. In all-round competition, and this includes the making of all the known casts, except the " Overhand," the Irish rod is indisputably the most successful of all the ordinary types.

The distinguishing improvements in our rod have been introduced with the intention of curing as far as possible any tendency to repeat the faults in character of the original. They are said to be instantly recognised by the Angler who adopts only the "Overhand."

That the failures of certain Anglers to secure with the Shannon rod all they want argues nothing against its several virtues, but only emphasises the need and the inducement that struck me for making an effort towards the prospective amelioration of their lot. The "Kelson" rod was not introduced into use hurriedly, for in doing my utmost to discover what kind of rod would best execute *all* the casts with the minimum of exertion and the maximum results, I made various experiments with many other types differing in circumference as much as 1/16th of an inch. In those experiments lines of different degrees of weight were used. The outcome is that the ordinary Castle Connell—famed chiefly for Side casting, Spey casting, and for holding heavy fish without fear—has been modified in a marked degree by being built somewhat stouter in the butt on such a scale as to considerably improve the action for all-round fishing with ease and comfort. The holding qualities are not perceptibly interfered with. The taper, be it noted, falls off not nearly so rapidly as in the old Trouty rod, and only slightly quicker than in the parent.

Any further stiffness in the butt, produced by a yet increased allowance of material than that given in the modification *would defeat the whole object in view.* On the whole, the Shannon rods may be summed up in the familiar formula of "As you were," for they always fulfil the expectations of their most sanguine supporters.

As to particular deviations from what I judge to be the best all-round rod, I may instance, as instructive, the "Traherne" pattern. This particular style of rod is decidedly stouter in the butt, and is more widely known at present than my own. The "Traherne," in the hands of Major Traherne, calls for no praise whatever here. It is sufficiently recommended in the *Badminton Library*, which tells us that the author of the *Habits of the Salmon* himself made an Overhand cast with it of no less than 45 yards 1 inch. But were I asked to pronounce an opinion on its merits, all the praise the rod would get from me would be conveyed in a very few words, viz.—That all Anglers who invariably adopt the "Overhand" should not be without it, for the simple reason that on stormy days, when they usually have to knock under, this rod enables them to continue fishing in their ordinary way. It is, in short, just the very opposite of a Spey rod, which in windy weather is useless.

It has just been said that my own rod is found the most pleasantly powerful and generally serviceable. Lest there should be suspicions arising of a possibly mischievous severity upon the fish's mouth due to the increase of material in the modification, it may safely be promised that there is no ground whatever for fear. A crucial instance may be adduced here in support of this statement, apart from what is urged elsewhere on striking and playing fish. It occurred early in the experience of a friend when using a rod selected for him by myself. This is his account of its conduct in his hands, with one of my own lines lent upon the occasion:—

"At first I was quite disappointed in the rod, and though you described to me intelligently enough how to use it, especially in casting 'Overhand,' it was not until the third day—call me duffer, if you will—that it ceased to be tiring and I began to acquire the knack of it. Now I would never wish to go back to the old style. I really think I should lose all pleasure in fishing if I did. The sense of power and of scope for skill are vastly greater with your pattern. I astonished myself when I came back to the old Spey cast, and popped out a good line in gusty weather. The latest triumph, however, was this. Certain friends here who use light rods and lines have looked rather askance at the rod's action, and suggested that it would be sure to tear fishes' mouths badly. If yours did so, what about Major Traherne's? But facts, happily, are surprising things, sometimes the right way, too. What mouth among the *Salmonidæ* is tenderer than a Grilse's an hour or two fresh from the open sea? It is like a grayling's almost. Well, on the 15th August I hooked and ran within 200 yards of the open North Sea thirteen Grilse, and saved eleven of them without assistance. I struck them off your pattern reel from Farlow's. It seems to me that even without other experience this proportion of eleven out of thirteen played should for ever put an end to any charge of severity against your system of rod and line. . . No more broken tops this season either. Bravo modified C. C."

The saving of "tops" referred to a little hint previously given not to hold the rod *too* upright in playing either Salmon or Grilse. Passing now to other particulars, and first to materials, I do not care to mention more than four—Greenheart, Cane, Blue Mahoe, and Washaba.

Mixtures—"Composites," as they are called, of which the worst is a combination of ash and cane—are not to be commended, except in Spey rods. Cane is very quick in return; ash very slow, and not powerful in action.

Experiments extending over a long period have satisfied me that honours are divided between the cane rod I possess and those of my pattern in Greenheart. Everyone knows, however, that it is no easy matter for a maker to bring out the desired action in cane. The surface will bear no planing, so when the pieces are glued together the joints themselves cannot be reduced or interfered with. Mine never required it, for Hardy soon succeeded in securing all the harmonies of action, balance, and good workmanship. The action for my work—that is to say, the action wanted for successfully making any of the known casts—is exactly as it should be; I do not wish for any alteration. Good action in cane means *nothing less than durability*, and no better proof can be given of this than the fact of my having taken with the rod considerably over one thousand Salmon, kelts included. Perhaps I need hardly remark that it is *without* the steel centre. A *real* "Kelson" in cane will not break, and though costly, cannot be said to be dear. To begin with, it is infinitely the best kind of rod for the Wind cast; and in casting Overhand, the Angler is less fatigued than with any of the others. These advantages arise from the fact that he has not to dwell so long in the motion—a feature of no inconsiderable moment as old age creeps on one, or even as regards one's comfort and pleasure during the first few days of fishing before the muscles get fit for work.

My favourite greenheart—if, indeed, any one of them is better than another—is a Farlow, more than thirty years of age and looking as young as ever. On this subject it is difficult to write of this firm in words of becoming praise, and without giving the impression of some conscious exaggeration of language and sentiment in one's endeavour to do justice all round. It is, however, the literal truth that the correct action in greenheart may be implicitly relied upon by the purchaser. For when these rods are first put together the surface can be worked down until the desired balance is secured; and in this important detail the maker has never failed to give me satisfaction. What is equally pleasant to record and equally appreciated by his customers, one and all, is his punctuality in executing orders within the time of promised delivery.

Apart from all other advantages of this style of rod, be it of cane or greenheart, the usual weakness caused by the continual use of any one cast may be quickly counteracted by the adoption of another cast. The "Spey," for instance, produces an upward bend, and this defect is soon rectified in working by the "Overhand."

Blue Mahoe is here and there the acknowledged king. But sound as his title is said to be, his crown would be much firmer if he had not an ugly trick of unaccountably and unexpectedly "striking work" on very little provocation. In spite of all care in the selection of matured, straight-grained wood from butt to point, the upper joints will sometimes snap asunder like glass. I had one of Ogden's in use for a few years, and prized it immensely. It had shown no signs of wear and tear until one fine day a young friend, casting only a short distance with it, broke the top joint clean in two by lifting the line before it was thoroughly extended. Any rod is liable to fracture under this condition of treatment, though as yet I have never seen cane surprise anyone by such sudden misbehaviour. Blue Mahoe is nevertheless a remarkably light, if not the lightest of all rod woods, and in skilled hands fully justifies the claim Ogden makes for it.

Washaba differs in this respect, for it is the heaviest of rod woods. Washaba rods are very "steely," and never seem to wear out. I have seen one at Usk as old as the hills and as straight as an arrow despite the severe trials it has looked full in the face.

There are many other rods besides those to which reference has been made. Manufacturers in Ireland and Scotland finish their work well, and find plenty of local support for their wares. As a rule, these are built purposely for the Overhand cast only.

The rod liked on one river is detested on another. The Spey rod, for instance, in the hands of a purely local performer on the Tweed would meet with the utmost condemnation; whilst a Castle Connell pattern for the "Overhand" would be equally disliked by any of Forrest's customers at Kelso, or Malloch's at Perth.

In making his purchase the Angler must determine for himself the sort of rod required to meet and suit his own purpose or purposes; and here one difficulty arises over which no living mortal has control. It is this. There is no occupation of ours in which a man has greater need to have his wits about him than that which has for its object *the choice of a rod.* Even expert Fishermen are frequently mistaken on these occasions. I have, however, endeavoured to cope with the difficulty by giving those who wish for the *modified* Castle Connell the information required for its purchase.

(In use the ferruled greenheart is tied at the joints with purse silk—Pearsall's "Typhast." The joints of the spliced greenheart are often glued together and bound with fine hemp. In binding mine, I varnish the hemp, say, two yards at a time, before I proceed; and give the splice so made a final coat when dry. But Farlow has recently introduced a *band* for the purpose. Each lap adheres to the wood, and, in finishing off, the upper lap rigidly sticks to the one placed beneath it, and remains so. By the employment of this band the rod can be "put up" in three minutes, and keep firm for the whole season. It is the neatest form of "whipping" as yet introduced.)

The cane rod being furnished with lock-fast joints is simply put together when the stoppers are removed. How lock-fasts would behave on greenheart I do not know, but I find them convenient and deserving of much praise on cane.

With regard to *weights*, the $4\frac{1}{4}$ aluminium winch holding 150 yards of line weighs $18\frac{1}{2}$ ounces.

	Length.	Weight.
Ferruled greenheart -	17 ft. 4 inch.	2 lbs. 11 ozs.
Spliced greenheart- -	17 ft. 4 inch.	2 lbs. 10 ozs.

and a little less when the new band is used instead of the hemp.

Built cane - - -	17 ft. 8 inch.	2 lbs. 11 ozs.

As regards *length* of rod, the build of the Fishermen, the breadth of the river, and the average size of the fish are items to be taken into account; yet it is very easy to so exaggerate these conditions as to err in favour of prejudices, either for undue length or undue shortness. For myself, I am inclined to think that for general purposes, having in view, on the one hand, the length of line, it is *possible* to cast by any of the methods with advantage, and on the other, the time occupied in killing a fish, that 17 feet 4 inches in greenheart, and 17 feet 8 inches in built cane is the most serviceable length for Salmon in river fishing. For lake fishing for Salmon a much shorter rod is an indispensable condition.

The bottom joint should carry three rings, the lower one being 2 feet from the upper end of the winch fitting. The old-fashioned drop-ring should be discarded for the upright revolving ring, having phosphor-bronze centres, with brass wire to prevent rust. Perhaps for this improvement a small extra expense is incurred at first, but the diminished wear of the line—a perfectly natural consequence—assuredly makes revolving rings the cheaper article in the long run. The chief object of the Angler in this connection is to secure a free run through the rings so as to be able to "shoot" a good length of line. By shooting line (fully described elsewhere) is meant the useful practice of holding lightly between the thumb and forefinger of the upper hand, several coils of the line either drawn in from the water, or direct from the winch, and letting them go free to be taken out by the momentum given to the cast in the thrashdown.

On the question of ferrules, little need be said.

Serrated ferrules, graduating as they do the strain that arises at the junction of the pliant wood and rigid ferrule joint, have been highly spoken of and strongly recommended. Good sheet brass, hammered until it becomes almost as hard as steel, is the best material, and, in my judgment, no ferrules equal those made on steel triblets, but they should only slightly taper and have bell-mouths.

The chief point for the Angler's consideration is that, as ferrules wear loose with lapse of time, the rod is apt to meet with serious injury if used in that condition. To detect loose ferrules put the rod together and test each joint in the following way:—The rod is "played" by one hand, whilst the forefinger and thumb of the other hand hold it at the union of wood and ferrule. In this way any shakiness is easily detected. Put on with Le Page's glue, they seldom require attention.

Under bad usuage a rod may become either racked or strained. "Racking" means disablement for the part affected. A "rack" is a kind of strain concentrated in one spot and is so bad an injury in itself that it can best be defined as "incipient fracture."

A "strain," distinguished from a "rack," is rather a warp inducing a temporary curve in one direction.

"Racking" comes from lifting a line too suddenly; from making the thrashdown too soon, or too late; from catching the hook in boughs, &c., in the rear of the Angler; or from using a line too light in weight.

"Straining" results from continually fishing upon one side of the water; from standing the rod against a wall in a damp place; from working with loose ferrules and sometimes from using a line too heavy for the rod. The defect is one that can be cured by a skilled rodmaker; but racking is incurable.

PART SECOND—CHAPTER VI.

"He only sees well who sees the whole in the parts, and the parts in the whole."

LAVATER.

THE LINE.

MANY and various instances in mercantile and industrial enterprise give rise to the current belief that, real progress does not depend so much on the perfect knowledge of the abstract sciences, as on the extent and perfection of those simple arts which minister to the daily wants and comforts of life. However this may be in the ordinary course of things, we are perhaps not concerned at the present moment to inquire; but no doubt whatever exists in angling minds that the progress of a Salmon-fisherman does not depend so much on the perfection of fly-work, as on the way the fly is put before the fish. That being so, it may not be altogether out of place here, first, to draw attention to a certain art in fishing the fly, the achievement of which considerably depends on the make and quality of the line in use.

Who, for instance, ever heard of the scheme, or even recognised the necessity for *mending* a cast five and twenty years ago?

Now this is just one of those important measures that may come to us in actual fishing by mere chance. Accident, say perhaps a stumble in wading, might cause one's well-balanced rod and properly weighted line to do something or other, which does not fail to be noticed, and then, feeling an immediate tug of a fish, one makes a special note of the unexpected effect so produced.

In point of fact this is exactly how the "mending" business originated with me. But the chance for discovering any such new method of treatment as this seldom occurs now as the opportunity hardly ever comes. Comparatively unwary, vigilantly on the watch, fish used to follow the fly bustling across the river anyhow, and leave it alone until the water, not the Fisherman, compelled the lure to, sooner or later, assume that natural position, which, in these days, is absolutely required from start to finish.

Eagerness on the part of the fish in that direction is the exception at the present time, not the rule, so in the matter of presentation has fishing long since undergone a fundamental change.

The object of this practice in presenting the fly, clearly, is to incite immediate action on the part of the fish rather than encourage indolent inspection. It happens to be a delightfully simple performance, if the Angler is provided with a line so constituted as to instantly respond to the turn of the wrist. We do not propel the fly, as of yore, and leave it to fate and fortune; on the contrary, we take care to promptly counteract the instant effect of water which occasions the line to take a snake like course, by *mending* the cast; that is, *by lifting the rod with telling effect, and by a simultaneous turn of the wrist, to the right or left as the case may be, switching over the belied portion of the line (caused by the lifting) by which means the fly is compelled to fish straight throughout the area of the cast made.*

This latest art-achievement in fishing—it is new to many—may strike the inexperienced as being an extremely insignificant matter, but in reality, it is the essence of "presentation" and on most rivers the very foundation of success.

No; fish do not follow the fly as they did "when the novice hooked them at the first bungling throw"—not one in fifty. Those halcyon days—the true time when it was "never too late to mend"—have gone like the May pole and the dancing on the village green. Long since that innocent era Salmon have been taught to better use their eyes and other organs. Their constantly declining to follow flies across the water, as they did, is a fact that has forced itself upon our recognition; and driven us to prepare for this and other propensities which originate in that "thinking apparatus" of theirs.

The question therefore arises: Can we properly "mend" our cast with the line of the period? No, but out of this evil, good has come, for our amicable conflict with these difficulties has obliged us to consider the matter of lines in all their varied uses and relations, and our investigations have turned out fruitful in precious results. We were not long in finding out that a line should be possessed of certain qualities, and, that those lines commonly used failed us in respect of pliability as well as in weight unless possessing an outrageous amount of bulk.

The essential qualities which stamp a good line are four in number—*Compactness*, *Suppleness*, *Evenness*, and *Durability*.

Our list of demands may appear somewhat formidable, but it is impossible to charge a single item with superfluity. No practical Angler will question the signal merit of a line possessing these valuable characteristics. *Strength,* though generally regarded as being of material importance, is not included in our list. Personally I have always looked upon this quality with indifference, from the fact that even the thin end of the taper of a line, fit for use, stands a far heavier strain than the gut attached to it.

In my report, as one of the Judges of the Fisheries Exhibition of 1883 (see *Field*, 27th October, 1883), I made the following observations:

"In judging, the lines were tied to a steelyard. The highest "pull" was 59 lbs., the lowest 24 lbs. After many years practical experience, and, having for the sake of experiment made various lines myself, I am convinced that a tightly plaited line is by far the best for fishing purposes. Yet a tight plait under the weight test would pull considerably less than one loosely plaited made of exactly the same quantity and of the same length. . . . There is greater weight in it for the same circumference of loose plait. . . . . I am fortified in this opinion by the entire concurrence of the leading manufacturers in the trade."

Now, *weight*, brought about by the quality of *compactness*, is very desirable, but any undue increase of *bulk* is most detestable. Burdened by loose, over-gorged plaits, culminating in a distended corporation, the line offers too much resistance to the air, splashes too much, is lifeless and ungovernable in the water, necessitates an extra large winch or a dangerous shortening of back-line, and above all requires a stout, unwieldly rod of a kind I would call "an unmitigated enormity," which, for taxing the powers of endurance, robbing anticipation, and dispelling keenness, it would indeed be hard to surpass.

On the other hand, a line too light in weight, and too small in circumference, is equally bad and sometimes worse. In contrary winds, for instance, it is almost useless, whilst in long casting, the rod, suited in every way to fulfil its proper functions, is completely spoilt by the extra force required.

In proceeding now to deal with the qualities enumerated above, it should be clearly understood that the most essential characteristic in a line is *compactness*. In plain language, this means the maximum of weight combined with the minimum of bulk, the significance of which only those well acquainted with high-class Salmon-fishing can fully appreciate. Compactness ensures a fairly smooth surface, else the ordinary way of riverside dressing is ineffective from the very first. With this quality as a substratum the line should never become too stiff or too supple. A hard stiff line neither casts well, fishes well, nor wears well. If made stiff by improper dressing when new, the line soon "knuckles," and no sooner are the early defects made good than the complaint breaks out in I know not how many places. They shall, however, receive attention presently.

Suppleness may be carried to an extreme. In some waters—in those, for instance, that break and chop about in all directions—it is impossible to have any contol over the fly with a line as supple, say, as one that has not been waterproofed. A loosely plaited line very soon becomes too supple for second or even third rate fishing, dress it how you will. A tightly plaited line, unless thoroughly saturated at first with the right material, comes to grief as quickly by knuckling, whilst both the one and the other are apt to get water-logged and then go permanently to the bad.

Such a degree of suppleness is to be sought in a line as not to interfere with the other good qualities. This can be secured and every evil defied provided the line is plaited closely, dressed under a system detailed in this chapter, and properly cared for after use.

Evenness is an important factor in commanding distant catches. A waterproofed line having a perfectly level surface, of proper size and weight, and a flexibleness combined with a certain amount of stiffness, passes so readily through the rod rings and air that to "shoot" eight or ten yards of it is a profitable achievement soon mastered. At all events the Angler profits in saving himself from over-fatigue, and his rod from severe treatment. In "mending a cast" an uneven line forms a wavy, cramped curve in the air and spoils the business; but this irregularity is never seen at all with a good line. When evenness prevails the ease with which the line can be lifted, or the cast effectually mended is noticeable at once. Another advantage is derived from this quality, in that the smoother the dressing the longer it lasts. The American machine, working American ingredients, produces a smooth, bright appearance for a *comparatively limited* period, no matter how even the line may be. In respect of polishing nothing beats handwork.

Durability needs no justification and very little explanation. It should not, however, be forgotten that silk lines as a rule do not last long unless made of the best material, dried thoroughly after use and dressed properly when new.

As for using undressed silk lines, I should never think of such a thing. I am puzzled to find any reasonable and sensible conclusion for the strenuous recognition they receive, though a deeply-rooted mistrust of them in some places is established. But still, lines of this description are recommended by authorities to whose testimony we cannot fail to listen with respect, whether we agree with them or not. According to my experience and conviction the pleasing theory of these amicable mentors has been rebutted scores of times in actual working practice. The broad charge I would record against lines undressed is that they are far too supple and too light in weight; for even by the aid of upright revolving rod-rings, a serious effort is needed to get them to "shoot" at all. They are moreover liable to get into a confused mess, and, besides being prejudicial to success, owing to their obvious conspicuousness in the water, are far more troublesome to use and to dry. If there is any good in them I cannot detect it.

Other materials have been tried. Hair lines, and those of silk and hair together, are too rough, too loose in plait and too light in weight. Besides, it is useless to attempt to dress them.

Plaiting is better than twisting. A plaited line is less liable to kink, takes dressing better, and, what is still more important, is easier controlled in the water. I often meet with twisted lines, but never once have I seen any "tricks of the trade" performed with them at work. The plait may be either round or square. The former results in a more even surface at first, whilst the tiny hollow centre running through their entire length can be filled up by a certain process of dressing—a solid continuous core being thus permanently formed. Managed in the old fashioned way with any sort of dressing, this small channel soon holds water and then the silk begins to rot. When this fact became known, lines plaited over a manufactured core were introduced into use, but in our branch of the sport they afford no practical benefit.

The lines I use myself have often been submitted for trade inspection, and it is gratifying to announce that Mr. Carswell, 90, Mitchell Street, Glasgow, a wholesale maker, has so far succeeded as to be able to supply retail dealers with something that will assuredly find favour and please critical eyes—with a line, at all events, that considerably reduces every difficulty in high class presentation. As may be supposed, I have given several of these a good trial and find they differ in a great degree from the ordinary stock in trade. They, moreover, possess exceptional qualities which are at once serviceable for the Salmon-fisherman. They happen to be christened the "Kelson Enamelled." Their salient features are:—A fairly tight plait, a smooth surface, more weight for bulk than usual, whilst the quality of evenness and of material cannot be surpassed. They are made in several sizes, the choice of which is necessarily left to the judgment of the purchaser from the fact that rods differ so much in action. The "Kelson" rod best carries a No. 3.

From this we begin to see the advantage derived from having a standard line in the market fit for a rod so balanced as to admit of the various casts being made without the chance of disappointment arising.

It may be useful to note that these lines can be bought at the tackle shops dressed or undressed, but I shall deal with that matter presently.

At this point I would mention that, from time to time, I have put both round and square lines under severe critical test and after full consideration finally decide in favour of the former. But the latter sort are not without their merits. For instance, they are solid from end to end and so do not require quite the same amount of care in the out-door principle of dressing. On the other hand, the second process in that system, viz., that of polishing—when applied to their less regular surface quickly loses its effect, and this will be found to be so until the line has had considerable wear and tear.

Tapered lines are better for making all casts except the "Flip" and the "Governor," and perhaps the "Spey" with the Spey rod. The tapered ends measure ten feet, six inches, and the whole line itself measures forty-two yards. These measurements were fixed for particular reasons and by no means in a haphazard or arbitrary manner; the size of the winch, distance and cleanness in casting by all the methods, having been studiously consulted.

The entire length of my own tackle runs into one hundred and fifty yards. But seeing the whole in the parts is *not* seeing the parts in the whole. Many would object to using a line so thin at the back end; but when this part is brought into use, Trout tackle would be equally effective. Seen in the parts "idling" at home, my tackle would not please one in ten, seen in the whole, "busy" at work, every member of the fraternity would "see well," and instinctively feel not only the necessity for the qualities which have been assigned to the casting line, but also the desirability of trimming the winch under the following system, by which arrangement I have saved more than one Salmon in my time.

The casting line is "married" to about seventy yards of *No. 3 or E* of the "Standard Waterproof Braided silk line" (Allcock & Co.), the remaining portion consists of the same standard article *No. 4 or F*, which is, one degree less in size. By the same process (marriage) two and a quarter yards of plaited gut, tapered, having a small loop for the single trace, is attached in front. In its complete form, as explained, the combination "packs" a $4\frac{1}{4}$ inch aluminium winch.

I have never yet experienced a fish running out the whole of this length; nor has it ever been my lot to fear the strength of the line from end to end, though it has been well tested on numerous rivers. The whole of the back line should be packed on the winch tightly, not wound loosely in disorder, but firmly, in even close coils, after the fashion of the tinsel upon a silver-bodied fly. Thus packed, all "jamming" in running a fish is entirely obviated.

Not many years ago I explained my ideas to Farlow of a contrivance for drying lines, with the result that the "Skeleton Line Drier" was made and patented. Constructed so that the air passes through to every portion of the line, this machine is fixed to a mantle piece by a screw clamp grooved to steady the winch in winding off, as shown in the illustration.

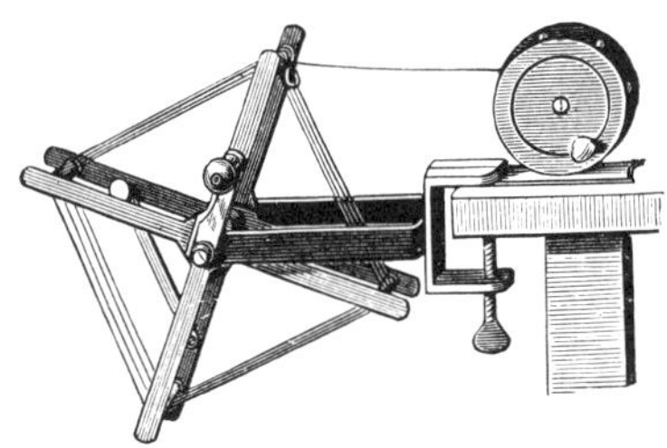

THE LINE DRIER OPEN.

SHUT.

One amongst other advantages gained in using this Winder is that all "kinking" is prevented.

It is quite as needful to dry the line in safe custody after use as to saturate the gut trace before use, and perhaps more so. If left on the winch, even in a damp state, the line soon becomes worthless.

In the matter of "knuckles" (which invariably come with bad dressing), so far as remedial measures are concerned, the sooner they are doctored the better. But when once these sores break out, the seat of disturbance is of a magnitude that makes the prospect of cure exceedingly remote. The wounds may be healed, but sooner or later will renew their assaults with redoubled energy; besides, the disease carries perpetual contagion with it. Every day the infection brings fresh trouble. However, for the purpose of a local application, prepare No. 1 Dressing mixture (mentioned presently) by heating it in a saucepan or by immersing a jar containing the liquid in boiling water. When rather hot, paint with a camel's hair brush each plague spot, and coax the stuff well into the silk by bending the knuckles to and fro until they present to the eye a white, frothy appearance. Rub off the froth and allow the line to dry. But the best plan is to steep the line in methylated chloroform for a day, and with soap and warm water wash off the whole of the old dressing (which never penetrated the silk at all well) and re-dress it in the manner described hereinafter.

It has been reserved for the ingenuity of Mr. W. Wells Ridley to bring out for himself and friends the best line, to my thinking, ever wetted in a Salmon river. In every detail can be traced the result of extended experience and exhaustive inquiry. The way they are plaited is simply perfect. Compactness is obtained by using the best silk, freed from all natural gum, and by employing unusually heavy weights on the plaiting machine. The strands are packed as closely as they can be without incurring the risk of a "curl," which is worse than a "kink."

Mr. Ridley once informed me that his lines contain one-third more silk than any others of the same length and circumference, and that this is entirely due to some special process adopted by him. There certainly is here an art of preparation and a measure of success which I think no manufacturer possesses except Carswell. The very look of them is enough, and they are no less surprising for their appearance than for the facility which they afford in casting and in "presentation." So far as durability is concerned, I have had a line in use since 1878, and in spite of hard wear, it is as sound and, if possible, more serviceable than ever. A small case of these treasures was on view at the Fisheries Exhibition (1883), and attracted general admiration. If only from a feeling of personal obligation, I would add that the Salmon-angling world at large

MR. W. WELLS-RIDLEY, J.P.

is deeply indebted to Mr. Ridley for proving that the ideal line is a practical possibility, and for giving me sufficient information to enable me to get it on the market.

I have only a few more observations to offer to students before we consider the question of dressing lines.

Salmon lines are imperilled and injured by many causes; now by Spey casting in close quarters, where it is impossible to keep the line from skirting rocks and other traps in the way; now by the wrong dressing; again, perhaps, by not polishing when necessary, and frequently by being left wet on the winch.

I use the word "perhaps," as line-dressing is a subject I hold an open mind upon. It all depends upon what a man wants and how much time he has to get it. If he wants an ideal dressing it is to be had, but not in a hurry. The time is not far distant when everybody will learn to waterproof lines with a lasting preparation that improves them from the very first, one that will permeate the *whole* texture and provide a smooth, elastic, and protecting surface that will not deteriorate. Only after years of attention and personal experiment did I hit on certain reliable methods and ingredients which I employ when fishing. The evidence of others, however, had been carefully considered, and their various materials tried and exhaustively tested.

The plan I recommend for river-side dressing has a first and a second process. In the preliminary work the oil penetrates round lines, makes them somewhat solid and, with subsequent care, permanently waterproof. The final touches result in such a smooth surface with a new "Ridley," or an old ordinary, that no sign of roughness can be seen or felt. An equally happy result can be relied on with the "Kelson Enamelled" line. This fact of itself goes to prove the similarity between the "Ridley" and the "Enamelled."

As Mr. Ridley's lines are distributed throughout the country (gratuitously, let me add), the best method of dressing them and my own, when wanted in a hurry, is as follows:—

Soak the new line for forty-eight hours in the "Dressing for Fishing Lines," sold at Apothecaries' Hall, Blackfriars, London. Then tie it up at each end out of doors, full length, and allow it to remain untouched for about sixteen fine, warm days—or at all events, until the "dress" is set and sticky.

In fixing the line, do not wipe off much of the material. The plan is to marry on spare string at each end to tie with, and so prevent a certain waste of taper. Running and back lines are married to each other by first fraying out nearly half an inch of the two ends with the point of the stiletto. After the strands are thus well separated, divide the part frayed out into three portions, so as to form three "legs." These portions are twisted to a point, see Fig. 1 and 2.

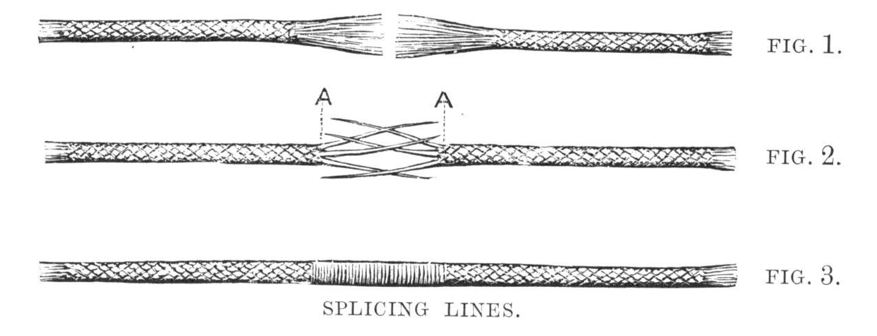

SPLICING LINES.

They are then interlaced. The forks are fitted together until the original thicknesses meet at A—A. The six legs are spread out so as to surround the line, see Fig 3. Then, with double tying-silk (waxed), the whole splice is bound down in the ordinary way with close coils, tapped with the back of an ivory-handled knife on a table, and then varnished.

On taking down the line for use, be careful with the married points, as they will marry again and again in making up the running tackle.

The best season for this dressing is in summer.

The liquid in which the line is soaked is previously made rather hot. When it sets, take more of the warmed dressing in the fingers, and with them give the line another good coating. It will have already absorbed the previous coat, and present a bare appearance. In a few days from this (locality and weather upset all calculation as to the *exact* time) the second application will be ready, and the rubbing process begins.

I rub the dressing when obliged to adopt this method with my fingers, as my hands soon harden in fishing; but a piece of thick felt answers the purpose equally well. The line must be rubbed backwards and forwards over and over again, day by day, until the dressing is almost hard.

The first process having thus been completed in its entirety, the second one is at once started. This consists simply in hand polishing.

Take a piece of linen about six inches square, make it into a pad, and dip it in spirits of wine, squeeze the pad, and on the damp face of it put three drops of old linseed oil (from Apothecaries' Hall) that has thrown off many sediments, and smear them over the pad. Now rub to and fro two yards, little by little, lightly and quickly, imbedding the line in the pad. Continue the rubbing for about three minutes. Dip the pad, as before, into the spirits, and, with three more drops of oil, proceed in the same way, two yards at a time, along the whole length of the line.

The hand, or the felt, rubbing will have deadened the appearance of the body dressing and made the surface smoother, but after a few days' work with the pad—which should be used only once in twenty-four hours—streaks of polish will appear visible, and increase daily in number and size. In seven or eight days the line will be finished; and it is gratifying to know then that, whatever trouble the system may have involved, the line *can be used* after it has remained in the sun for two more days. Do not underestimate this advantage.

After the line has received its second coat of polish, which it will require in six weeks time, it will maintain a fair face upon it for the whole season. In use the secret is *never to allow the polish to get too dull.* In order to prevent knuckles the line must be watched and polished when necessary, the necessity being increasingly apparent to the observer as dulness sets in. On the second occasion, the linen pad will effect its purpose in about half the time. When due attention has been paid to this, the body dressing, so far my own experience extends, is never wanted again.

Ordinary lines necessitate a somewhat different treatment. As a rule their surface cannot be made sufficiently smooth by the first process, so as to effectually secure, at an early date, the best results of process No. 2.

To attempt to secure this by daubs of dressing is to fly in the face of that enemy best known by the term "dandruff." Too much body dressing is just as harmful as too little. An extra coat for rough lines is, however, advisable, and when quite dry the surface is best worn down by using them.

In all cases, Anglers will decide for themselves when the surface is ready; but, after fishing with the line, another thin coat is needed in order to start the polish before the liquid sets hard. We cannot, however, escape from the cold fact that, with all our dipping and rubbing and subsequent care and attention, this treatment involves us in clouds of doubt and apprehension. But let me turn for a moment to some brighter prospect—something else which has escaped most line dressers hitherto.

What Salmon-fishermen want, and what I understand can now be found in the Alnwick market, is a waterproofing that will, at all events, stand the test of time without cracking and knuckling. We know to our cost that knuckles always constitute a standing menance to all endeavour to reach a high branch of efficiency, and, in consequence, to attain good angling records.

What the uninitiated line dresser wants is a means by which he can ensure Salmon-anglers the full enjoyment of their privileges, by not allowing those dark clouds to overhang perpetually their paths of progress. If he obtains this, he will, without doubt, find ample support to back him up in his own neighbourhood; if not—?

A happy opportunity for welcoming a widely proclaimed creed presents itself. It is a maxim of law that there is no wrong without a remedy, and unless line dressing is to confess a humiliating inferiority to jurisprudence there must be some curative agency by which the removal, or rather the prevention of all previous drawbacks can be triumphantly overcome. In point of fact, I have long since satisfied myself that the AIR-PUMP is our only guarantee—a statement confirmed in the best school of Trout-fishers and verified in Salmon-angling by prolonged and unfailing tests.

Good and satisfactory as the out-door dressing is in comparison with other make-shifts, a line is not, and never can be, impregnated with nearly as much oil as the air-pump drives into it. The material, be what it may, never enters those numberless interstices in which air settles and remains. As I have pointed out, our security is of a temporary nature, dependent on care taken in polishing and repolishing; and perhaps not one Fisherman in a hundred is gifted with that imperturbable temperament for the undertaking.

Seeing, however, that a thoroughly saturated line keeps nearer the surface of the water, it would appear that, to a certain extent, some compensation exists for those tiresome knuckles. Air-pumps are, moreover, luxurious articles, expensive to purchase,* and troublesome to take from place to place. But to those who like to take the hint and snap their fingers at all such trifling difficulties, I must say the air-pump is simplicity itself and a luxury indeed.

A few plain directions for its employment will suffice.

To begin with, "the dressing for fishing lines" is not suitable in this case. Better it is by far to use the *Clarified Oil* specially prepared by Naylor Brothers & Quick, 12, James Street, Oxford Street, London. This firm of merchants have devoted ample attention to our wants. By a process of their own they have succeeded in removing all flocculent matter which can always be traced in the finest sample oils. In order to clarify the oil completely and make it stable they keep it in cisterns, on hot water beds until the liquid is ready for our purpose.

Secondly, the lines can be dried artificially; this is an advantage in the South, though in the North-east of Scotland they dry in the open air.

With regard to my more recent experiments with various dressing ingredients under the air-pump, it has been my privilege to consult gentlemen who have had the wisdom to work out the problem by the excellent method of practical common sense. I allude to my friends Mr. Halford and Mr. Hawkesley—both well known for their skill in dry-fly fishing and for possessing Trout lines that never knuckle. To these lovers of art and science we are entirely indebted for the pains taken in finding that infinitely more suitable waterproofing for this particular system.

---

* Since writing these remarks, Messrs. Baker & Co. have brought out an inexpensive air-pump that answers the purpose admirably (*see engraving*).

THE AIR-PUMP.

Mr. Halford, in his admirable book on Dry-fly Fishing (Sampson, Low and Marston), directs us to "immerse the line in a flat vessel containing pure boiled oil,* place the vessel under the receiver of an air-pump; exhaust until all air-bubbles are drawn to the surface; do not remove the line until after all the air-bubbles have broken and vanished. Take the line out of the oil; draw it through your fingers or a piece of flannel or felt lightly, so as to remove all superfluous oil. Then wind the line on a frame which is about 18 inches long, made of two side-pieces of wood, with two pieces of iron wire across the ends. There are saw-gates cut obliquely on one of the wooden sides of the frame. One end of the line when covered with the first coat of oil is fastened in the saw-gates marked No. 1, and the line wound on. The frame and the line is then placed in an oven,† heated to the temperature of a 150° Fahrenheit and baked for about ten hours. The line is then taken out of the oven, and, when cold, all the irregularities are rubbed off carefully with very fine glass-paper, taking care not to abrade any of the silky fibres. After all irregularities are rubbed off and the line made as equal in size as possible, it is again put into the oil, under the air-pump and the air again exhausted. The line, when all the air-bubbles have broken, is taken out, and again wound on the frame being fastened at the saw-gate No. 2, and so on; so that the line should have a different point of contact with the iron wire after each coat."

Mr. Halford tenders further advice, and presents us with a number of reliable details, which are of solid value in the completion of the system for Trout lines. He has, moreover, a happy knack of showering many other blessings on the heads of his followers; and (to adopt the appropriate expression of Mr. Dagonet) though the book is going like "wild fire," the next generation will have nothing to fear on that account from the simple fact of its being *stationary*. Mr. Hawkesley being versed in practical

* The Author meant the Clarified Oil.

† A tin box over gas.

mechanics, has attained the mastery of this system. He is of the opinion, and wisely so, that to make a Salmon line absolutely solid it should be immersed three times and baked in a temperature of 130°, allowing on each occasion a little longer time for drying.

This is pretty much what I have found in my own experience; but I rub the line with powdered pumice stone, dry it in the sun, or, better still, on the plate-rack over a kitchen fire, and polish it before use. By this process a line holds double the amount of oil and therefore it takes much longer to dry.

The air-pump suggested itself to me many years ago while repairing knuckles. In so doing, the froth or air-bubbles that quickly appeared made room for the drop of dressing to disappear as quickly, and this spoke volumes. Although not wanted as a safeguard against knuckles when the air-pump is used, the second process of mine is still beneficial insomuch that it favours those who pride themselves on "shooting" line.

Eton and Deller, I understand, have brought out a salmon line for Mr. Halford, whose name alone is quite enough to recommend it.

I have pointed out the little debt to the air-pump which ought to be paid—in fact, I may say, liquidated in full—by subsequent patience; and with that condition fulfilled, the machine may have an ideal career for the Fisherman, who, by its aid, should escape that acute unpleasantness of being "under a cloud."

PART THIRD.—CHAPTER VI.

"Wind up your watch as you please, but, in bringing a fish to bank, wind quickly when you get the chance."

THE WINCH.

At a period well within the memory of the middle-aged Fisherman the winch was an ugly, heavy, barrel-shaped article, without any check and having sharp shoulders to the cross-bars, square edges to the plates and a crank handle attached to the spindle. In dimension it was large enough to hold over one hundred yards of silk and hair line of one size throughout—a clumsy, cumbrous thing, well in keeping with other primitive appointments of the time.

How different is the winch of to-day! The weight has been reduced by more than one half; the shape perfected; sharp shoulders and square edges have disappeared, whilst the old crank handle (always unsightly and liable to work loose) has made way for the revolving disc with the handle attached to it.

Passing over the period when multiplying winches were in favour, and saying nothing of the difficulty in winding in a fish with them (they were from their complicated mechanism hardly ever in order), we arrive at the time when a decided advance in winch mechanism took place. Over thirty years have elapsed since a prominent London firm engaged a noted workman to devote his time entirely to this special branch of the trade. Other firms followed its lead, and many and varied are the winches to be seen in the fishing tackle houses of to-day, the Moscrop among others, for instance, all displaying vast improvements upon the original invention.

Some few years later I devoted considerable attention to further practical improvements. I had often observed, especially among average Anglers, that fish were lost either in striking or in the final struggle under the gaff. But this was not all, for the great majority of fish which were landed by good men had their flesh badly torn by the hook. After much thought I came to the conclusion that this flesh tearing must originate in the "striking," and that, therefore, there was something radically wrong with the system of holding the line as practised at that period.

There are Fishermen and Fishermen, but how many are there who would fairly be classed far above mediocrity? How many with even twenty years' experience can conscientiously tell you that, under the old method of holding the line, they knew exactly what force to use in striking without ever meeting with an accident? Under the new method as described elsewhere, accidents are almost impossibilities.

Accordingly, in my experiments, I set to work with screw-driver and pincers, and made the break in some of my winches reasonably stiff and in others reasonably loose. In "striking" I gave up holding the line altogether. After a little practice in adjusting the strength of the break to suit particular waters I lost so few fish, and found the flesh so little torn, if torn at all, that now I adopt no other plan. Convincing myself at the time that the general principle was the right one, I commenced to design a winch with an adjustable check constructed so that *the power of resistance in striking, as well as in the line running, could be graduated at will.*

Having given up my country residence and come to reside in London, workshop experiment being doomed, I put myself in communication with the firm spoken of above. A lengthy correspondence took place, relating principally to details in the construction of the lever, with the result that a Winch was patented, and to this day is sold at 191, Strand, under the name of THE PATENT LEVER WINCH. The neat and skilful way in which the work has been executed at this establishment is in every way a source of satisfaction to me, and a transport of delight to all my friends.

THE WINCH (Fig. 1).

This winch, the special object of which is sufficiently indicated by its title, has sometime since entered upon the first decade of its existence, and one is able to point to highly interesting results attained with it by good, bad and indifferent Fishermen. As soon as it became widely known several hundred were sold, and the sale has been steadily increasing ever since.

The lever, responding instantly to the turn given by the fingers to the external screw, renders the spindle capable of revolving at a high rate of speed *to the very last of the packed* line. All danger is thus obviated when a fish, having a range of, say, one hundred yards, yet makes a determined run. Upon such occasions we had formerly to use considerable force in pulling the last fifty yards of line from the winch so as to allow the end coils to run at all, whilst it was impossible to wind them back quickly.

To sum up its other merits the course of instruction necessary to master this winch is easily understood.

The handle is fitted into a counter-sunk bearing and so the line cannot get beneath it; nuts are dispensed with, one end of the pillar being screwed into the outer plate, the other drilled to receive the screw. Properly set it never over-runs, and, therefore, cannot become choked. It is easily adapted to different catches; set lightly for rapids, and sufficiently stiff for sluggish pools. The lever instead of weakening the winch actually keeps the plates and framework so firm that they never become loose or shaky.

There is really nothing to be said in disparagement of its qualifications or of the system of striking, provided single gut casts are in use and the flies are in sizes *under* 2/0.

Fig. 1 represents the winch and the relieving screw which passes through the handle plate. By turning the screw from you the break power is reduced, by turning it backwards the power is increased. Thus, while playing a fish, the winch can in a moment be made to run as easily as the Angler pleases. The head of this screw is flat-sided, resembling half a sixpence, and is easily regulated by the fingers.

The handle side of the winch consists of three discs—the outer, centre, and inner. Of these, the outer and inner revolve with the axis to which they are attached. The centre forms part of the fixed frame and does not revolve.

Fig. 2 represents the inside face of the handle plate. The break, or fraction lever, is a piece of suitably tempered steel fixed at one end by a screw to the handle plate; through the centre of it a hole is drilled for the axis of the winch. To the other end of the break a screw is attached (see also Fig. 1), which passes through the handle plate. The middle, or broadest part of the break, presses upon a raised "boss," formed in the middle of the fixed centre disc, and thus retards the rotation of the handle plate and the axis to which it is attached. There is a hole in the outer disc for oiling purposes.

THE WINCH—INSIDE FACE OF HANDLE PLATE.

The one I use is silent and without the usual rachet or "noisy corn-crake," which, in spite of its poetical associations, is alike useless and injurious. In winding up line, for instance, it rouses fish by "telephoning" to them in a series of maddening jars, and this serves as an inducement to them to drop down rapids and even weirs. Without this rachet, the mechanism is simplicity itself. I have reeled in many and many a fish close to my side in the water without noticing a kick or a struggle, thus saving much time when time is precious.

The "Kelson Patent Lever" met with further improvement in 1889. By the substitution of aluminium for hammered brass the weight was considerably reduced. The one I have in use, packed with 150 yards of line, weighs less than twenty ounces! Time has disproved the old axiom that a heavy winch is wanted to balance a Salmon rod. This, in days gone by, was nothing but a deeply-rooted prejudice. In 1890 I used the lighter winch much to my comfort, and found no difference whatever in the action of my rod. Nor did I expect to. In fact, I demonstrated by subsequent experiment on grass that the line can be cast just as far and just as easily without any winch at all. Naturally enough, the centre of gravity in the rod will be slightly shifted by changing the weight of the winch; but this is met by placing the upper hand a trifle higher on the rod than usual—a measure which is rather a relief than otherwise.

It need hardly be said that a good winch deserves careful treatment. In use it should be regularly oiled with refined oil, and cleaned inside and out from time to time. Upon every Salmon river we meet with banks of sand, particles of which are apt to be blown in between the outer and inner discs of the winch. When this mishap occurs, a grating sound will notify the coming mischief. Then is the time for the inside to be thoroughly cleaned with paraffin and oiled with the best oil. This winch is specially recommended to Salmon-anglers in the Badminton Library.

The "Sun and Planet" winch introduced by Malloch has its admirers, but I do not know of it from my own experience.

The "Moscrop" is a ventilated winch having a lever made under a different principle. The inventor claims for it that the Line Drier is unnecessary. At all events, a line which I once left on after use was perfectly dry the following morning.

There is another, brought out by Holbrow, which is a vast improvement on the old sort, if only because it is made of aluminium.

CHAPTER VII.

THE ROD AT THE RIVERSIDE.

"Age has experience behind it, Youth has promise before it; and this promise is soonest realised by men who refrain from the employment of what, if old in fly-work, is not altogether good, and who remember that most of what is good in the various ways of fishing is not altogether old."

NOTHING is more capable of filling the mind with noble thoughts than the scene viewed from some airy point beside a Highland stream. Would that my pen could describe those charms of Nature in her grandest plenitude, those enchanting panoramas which are the delight of all fishers and other sons of man.

Picture the majesty of a distant Ben standing out against the deep orange of the western sky, its crowned head a gleaming mass of snow, and the broad plain, irradiated with sunlight, spreading like a golden carpet at his feet. Imagine the outlook on the southern side, partially broken up by the rich fulness of waving woodland bordered with trees of various species and appearance, each differing in glory like the stars. There is one glory of the birch, so elegant in the midst of its silvern tresses; another glory of the yew, whose eager arms are driven round and tortured by the many scolding winds it faced when young; another glory of the rowan-tree, whose orderly array of berries are supposed to possess the magical power of charming away the wizards and the witches; and another glory of the sycamore that "spreads in gentle pomp its honeyed shade " o'er cooing cushats and mossy banks, where Sabbath couples love to roam and linger.

The attentive eye is deeply moved by the pale blue of the heavens visibly melting into a still paler gold that dies away in the orange towards the horizon, over which hangs a thin veil of flame-tipped purple cloud, letting a little bit of warm ground show through with variegated effects of light. As a centre to the composition, a virtuoso is busily engaged on the knoll in the foreground with his precious samples of potstones and pseudomorphs. At uncertain intervals are groves of lofty pines, whose weird gloom fittingly adorns the grandeur and mystery of the hills. Cleft out from them is a half-choked ravine bedecked with budding green and little streaks of water that sparkle among the sedges of the bracken-covered banks. Drip, drip it comes in icy crystal drops from wreaths of tangled moss; and, here in baby jets and there in tiny trident falls, forms a burn that gathers way and cuts through parish tiends and stubbled land dotted with beehive huts, in which the Crofter, with happy abandonment, wakes to the voice of the " wasteful cascade " below.

Suddenly the peaceful scene is invaded by the pinions of a hungry and hateful cormorant. Warily advancing inland, watchful over the watercourse, he is, after all, only the acknowledged portent of bad luck; and, caring for nothing short of four drams of powder and an ounce and a half of " No. 5," steals away with the international blessing, " Tubaist air an eun mohr dhubh sid! "*

Meanwhile, hope springs eternal—the fine splashes of a fish are heard and the rings seen. In the lowland the flowers rise in clustering beauty towards the towering rocks that cast an awful look below. From the clefts in their sides a few straggling geans blossom out into rampant trees, and if so be a wandering branch bears down, split and torn, it still holds fast to the parent stem, and shelters beneath it the tesselated pavement of Anglers' diverse beliefs.

A little further round riverward on the bosom of the brown moorland extend the Butts, now and again emitting little puffs of white smoke and sharp tongues of fire that tell of fellow sportsmen's doings not far away.

---

* Bother that big black bird there.

Midway, seated under a rock, an old shepherd and his dog are resting, yet both alert that none of the flock stray beyond bounds. Hard by, with its ivy and its daws, the ruins of an abbey (scored by the terrible mandate of Cromwell) moulder away. Over the water Mr. and Mrs. Venerable Goat peer at us wonderingly, while their two fair "children of peril" gambol in frolicsome mood and munch the grey-green herbage on rugged heights inaccessible to feet bebrogued. Below, in the river that we love, a solitary stag, alarmed by the grouse shooters, pursues a tranquil course through the tail of our own pet pool, nodding his royally plenished head the while. And as yon level sun sinks lower and lower and the silver sheen of twilight fades from the darkening current, all these, save for the music of rumbling waters and rustling trees,

> In sweetest silence seek the shade of night,
> And fill the pause the Salmon's leap made bright.

Then the moon glides, queen-like, into her great throne-room of the heavens.

How vivid and how full of pleasure is the memory of such scenes! And yet how temperate is the emotion compared to that which the Fisherman experiences when he stands prepared for the fray on the marge of faultless pools stocked with fresh Salmon on their way from the sea!

And the Salmon, the monarch of the river, what of him? For though there are several species of *Salmo*, from our standpoint there is only one Lord and King; the rest are offshoots of a noble family.

He is a picture once studied never to be forgotten. His proportions cannot be taken in at a glance. He is courageous in the dead calm, and bold as a lion in the very tornado itself. He shows no fear of men who show no designs upon him. Like his captor, he varies in temperament—he is shy, volatile, determined, impressive, and forgiving, yet sometimes very sulky. He has his own innumerable havens of rest, sometimes shaded and shut in by feathering trees where sunbeams glimmer fitfully—the very place for a water nymph discreetly shut out from the gaze of man. And in rivers that know no impurity he reigns in all his glory.

But our object is to catch him—not with a prawn, not with a worm, not with a "colley," nor with a spinning-bait. Not to any of these second-rate subtleties should he succumb. *He should be caught only with a fly.*

Occasionally he allows no fly to pass him. Occasionally he refuses all flies; and in this respect he passes all understanding. Only the expert himself, familiar with the peculiarities of every river from varied experience and persistent observation, who knows and practices all the casts, sits and dresses his own flies, and with them makes experiments wherever he goes—only such a man can be assured of anything like general success; and, even for him, an endless variety of patterns is an indispensable condition.

Now in using a fly, men's ways are wonderfully diverse; but if the student aims at taking high rank in the art, the first step is to learn to propel the fly by every recognised method so as never to miss, never to pass by, but to cover and command each and every one of those "innumerable havens of rest," either by the "Overhand," or the less tiring "Underhand"; by the "Switch" with the "Peter"; or (among other methods special) by the scientific "Spey."

Having frequently instructed friends myself, I learnt in teaching to observe carefully the motions necessary for the successful accomplishment of the casts most commonly used, to what faults the inexperienced are prone when attempting them, and in what manner such faults may be corrected.

THE OVERHAND CAST.

I may here refer to an incident which will illustrate my point. It took place on the greensward, and with a pretty "toy" made by Farlow after my own pattern. By my directions my pupil proceeded to make a plain Overhand cast, and in doing so was not long in betraying his antecedents.

"A Trout throw," I ejaculated, watching this his first effort. "You are throwing from the point instead of casting from the butt."

"Kindly show me the practical difference," he replied, handing me the rod.

"Toy" though I called it, I complied with his request, and sent out thirty yards of line with it. My "trouty" friend then reeled up to about four and twenty yards, and yet he was not happy in his method.

THE OVERHAND CAST.

"Stay," I said, "don't jerk the rod in lifting the line at starting, but with the point of it held down towards the fly (not over your head), get the rod well bent by rapidly increasing the upward pressure; and look at your line as it goes in the air behind you. . . There it flies, not away to your right rear, as it should do, in a direct line up towards that cloud there, but sweeps round, mowing the grass actually behind you. Do not let the point of the rod decline from you in lifting the line; bring the rod *straight up* past your right shoulder, and instead of swinging it round behind you, check it sooner; when, to make sure you have done right, you can let the line drop on the grass to see if you had given it the tendency to turn from a straight course."

"Thanks; fault No. 1," my pupil said, with a look on his face as if he expected other corrections to follow. "And I suppose you don't approve of the way I make the 'thrash-down'?" he added inquiringly.

"I was coming to that. You don't 'thrash-down' at all, but give a sort of side cut with the rod, and at the same time commit what, though proper to Trout fishing, is a radical error in Salmon-angling, viz., trying to make the top joint do the work."

"Then you wish me, as it were, not only to work from the butt, but also to thrash downward, if I understand rightly, in the destined direction of the cast."

"Exactly so, and in no other way will you be able to get the full length of line straight out in front of you by this method."

I then proceeded to correct his attitude, getting him to advance his left leg sufficiently forward to secure firmness of balance, and to warn him to avoid labouring and swaying backwards and forwards, instead of preserving a soldierly, erect position—a position which, grown into habit, becomes to the Angler a source of ease in action and economy in force.

"Then," I continued, "in the details of the cast, I notice two other points to which you must pay special attention. First, the action of the two hands, as you attempted to make the cast just now, was suggestive rather of whipping than of casting. Maintain the hands throughout the cast in their proper relative positions, so that in the back motion the lower hand does not become unduly raised towards the front, or the point of the rod will descend too far behind you. . . . As I said just now, you must check the rod-top sooner. Secondly, you fail to grasp the idea that in order to achieve my method you must turn your head to watch the line behind, not only for the purpose of seeing that it is sent straight back at the right height and angle, but for seizing the exact instant for making the thrash-down."

"But how shall I know that?"

"You will soon know, if you never fail to look and see for yourself. When you observe the fly end of the line extended in the air a little higher than the top of your rod you will *know*; but bear in mind the operations of gravitation, so, in extending it, take your aim high enough at the outset."

"I am determined to learn the right way, if I can, but I confess I find it difficult to follow the line with my eyes, for I cannot turn my head."

"You will not find any difficulty if you send the line upwards in the *right* direction. When you cannot follow the line with your eyes by a slight turn of the head you may be sure you have sent it too little to the right and too much to the rear, and that you have not brought up your rod sufficiently straight."

"Now let me clearly understand how to make the thrash-down explain to me what you meant by the 'exact instant.'"

"When you have checked the rod in the upstroke, dwell until the the line is nearly extended in the air; but if you allow the fly to travel further than within three or four yards of its full distance by dwelling too long, the middle part of the line will be falling to the ground, when you will not only fail to cast it, but very likely break the rod in trying to do so."

"Why?"

"From the fact that the 'tug' of the line on the point of the rod has died away. In setting up the tug, if you *snatch* at the line the rod will probably break; and this applies to the upstroke as well as the down-stroke. Whatever you do, don't forget to check your rod early enough in the thrash-down. It should not be allowed to reach beyond an angle of 55 degrees, and then you can *lay the line down* rather than let it fall on the water as in Trout fishing."

"I think I understand you from beginning to end, but practice is the thing I want. I mean to master the lifting first; it won't take me long to send the line 'up towards that cloud,' and then I'll try and perfect myself in the thrash-down. The method must be learnt by degrees, or else I'm mistaken."

"That is an excellent conclusion to arrive at; but remember—here is the chief point—remember the necessity for *looking behind;* you understand the object of it, and believe me, your progress towards efficiency and your complete success entirely depend upon it. Practice it even when you become proficient, or you will soon fall into bad habits."

* * * *

Now, I refer to this lesson not only because it illustrates the difficulties which the novice encounters in attempting the cast, but because it also explains details which are not given, so far as I am aware, in any book hitherto published on the subject. Modern authors, as we know, abound with information on playing, striking and gaffing, all of which might be learnt and written by a punt Fisherman with merely Thames experience.

The first point for beginners to study, is the position both of the legs and body. This varies according to circumstances. On land, or in easy flowing streams, the Angler should stand fairly upright, his body being sideways to the run of the stream and facing the spot on which he desires his fly to alight—that is to say, alighting across the current at an angle of 45 degrees or thereabouts. The left foot in right-hand casting should be in advance of the other and point in the desired direction of the cast, while in left-hand casting the right foot is similarly advanced. This position ensures the proper balance of the body during the effort required to make the cast. But in rapids *safety* has to be considered before *convenience*. It is frequently dangerous and at times impossible to fish in rapids unless the Fisherman stands altogether sideways and leans against the current, the up-stream leg bent, the foot pointing somewhat that way, the down-stream leg extended and the foot pointing almost in the direction of the current. In moving onwards the up-stream leg should always take the first short step, and when it is firmly planted, the other should feel its way to a secure position. If the down-stream foot is

MAJOR J. P. TRAHERNE.

first advanced, a concealed boulder may give the Angler a sore shin or an untimely bath before the up-stream foot can obtain a firm hold. The body should be held fairly erect throughout the cast. The novice who imagines that he can propel his line to a greater distance by throwing forward his body in making the thrash-down, must never think of doing so in rapids. A mere glance at the man who understands the work would soon satisfy him of this.

The whole of the work must be done by the arms and the rod from the butt upwards. It need hardly be said that, if the current flows from the right to the left of the Fisherman as he stands facing the stream, the rod is grasped with the right hand eight to twelve inches above the winch so as to effect what is called "a right-hand cast." When the current flows in the opposite direction a left-hand cast is required and the position of the hands is reversed. The exact distance of the upper hand from the winch is determined by the balance of the rod and the convenience of the Fisherman. The novice will speedily discover for himself at what point he should place the upper hand so as to obtain the best result with the least expenditure of force. (Fishermen should accustom themselves to use either the right or the left hand as the upper one with equal facility.)

Having placed himself in the appropriate position the Angler proceeds to get out his line by taking a yard or two from the winch and making what is termed a few "false casts" each time. As soon as sufficient line is thus extended down stream, in lifting the rod back into the air, the Angler gradually gets the point well bent before the smart backward turn of the wrist of the upper hand is given. The lower hand, holding the rod just above the indiarubber button, is at the same time brought across the chest, swinging, as it were, with the right. If the lower hand is not brought back in that way, the rod will be slanting too much at the time it is checked. Any undue raising of the lower hand in front of the Angler, and the line falls too low in the air behind him—perhaps strikes the ground, in which case the hook is invariably broken or blunted at the point.

The back sweep of the rod describes in its track the outline of a narrow oval. It is *not* semi-circular, as we are often given to understand. The rod barely declines to the right in ascent, nor inclines to left in descent. Indeed the nearer the course of the rod's point to its course taken in the thrash-down the better will the line be sent back in the air, and the straighter and farther will it be laid on the water.

(The "recovery" of a rod in the back part of the cast depends for the most part upon its material and make: in other words, one rod straightens quicker than another. The action would, of course, be delayed were the line in use too heavy for the rod; but, apart from that, a cane is quicker than a greenheart, and, in my opinion, a "Kelson" is quicker with a long line than one having a steel centre, therefore the delay spoken of is of less duration. The consequence is that the Angler is less fatigued because he has not to hold up the rod so long in the air.)

I have referred to the mishaps to which the unwary Fisherman is exposed who may attempt the thrash-down before the line is sufficiently extended; but sometimes the series of troubles is increased, and especially so when the wind blows down stream. More flies are lost on those occasions than on any other. This is occasioned by the resistance of the wind against the line in its backward course whereby the "tug" is lost. It is just here that a semi-circular sweep of the rod *is* advisable before the thrash-down is made, in order to prevent the fly and perhaps some of the gut being "snicked" off. The radius of the necessary semi-circle depends on the velocity of the wind. There is, however, another expedient by which all mischief is obviated, and it is far better for the novice to adopt. He may put on a second fly (or "dropper") three feet above the other, and find it act as a perfect safeguard; and then he will find that far less care in making the sweep of the rod is needed. Personally, I never work with two flies, as I support the view that the practice separates one from the proprieties of usage conducted on the lines of true sportsmanship. If an expert were Spey-casting left-handed, and a high down-stream wind sprung up, he would renew the cast right-handed. After shifting the rod, he would drag the line towards him on the near side and switch it out immediately dead across water. But in the event of a long line being requisite he would make a similar switch and then pick up the line and cast it across by the "Overhand," leaving the wind to carry the fly to its proper quarters.

It remains for me to describe how the *length* of a cast may be increased by "shooting" line; and I have a word or two to say on a different matter. The subject of shooting line has been referred to in another chapter; and but little practice is needed to master the method.

The feat consists first in the Angler drawing from the winch the length of line required, and, while so doing, making and placing coils of it, one by one, between the point of the forefinger and thumb of the upper hand. These coils, of about a yard in length from end to end, hang down in front of the winch and are lightly held there until the point of tension in the thrash-down is reached. If at that instant they are dropped they will be dragged out by the rest of the line; but if dropped

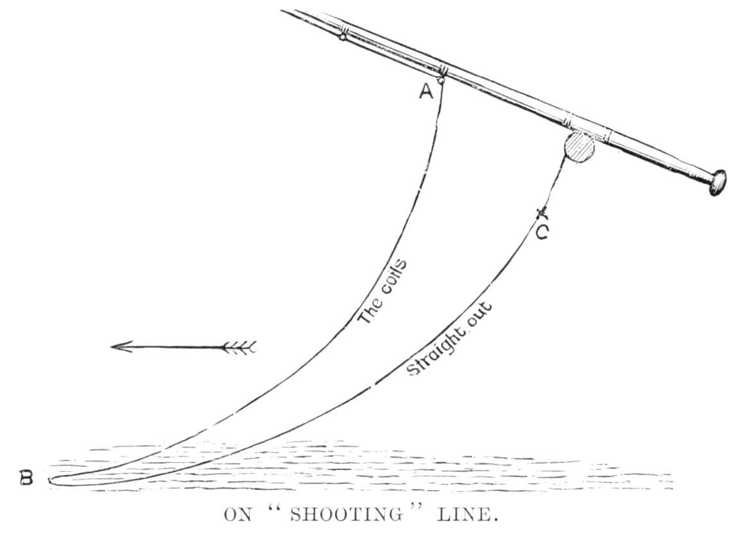

ON "SHOOTING" LINE.

too soon, the middle part of the running line will belly down towards the water, and the "slack" will not be taken out at all. In making, say, a thirty-yard cast, a four-yard length should be shot; a thirty-four yard cast a six-yard length, and so on in proportion. To shoot ten yards with upright revolving rings is no great feat provided the line is smooth, properly dressed and of the right size and weight.

But in wading, when the coils fall from the hand, the current takes them out of position as shown in the accompanying diagram, thus forming an acute angle in the line at the point A as well as at point B. The force of the water at the lower part B prevents the feat of shooting being accomplished. This is easily remedied by the Angler seizing the winch end of the dropped coils at the point C, and giving with his lower hand so placed a good snatch so as to bring the whole of the slack part back under the bottom ring of the rod, when it will all shoot out as readily as on land. Thus it will be understood how much the action of the rod can be preserved, and, by this cast, how much more water can be covered.

This extra length of line, however, often results in a good deal of it getting "drowned"—sucked to too great a depth below the surface. When this occurs, the excessive resistance offered by the water impedes the recovery of the line, which refuses to be lifted; but this opposition of the water is counteracted by what is known as "fiddling" the line. Fiddling is accomplished by beating the point of the rod up and down, just before the fly gets to its final station in neutral water. The process may be best described in the following way:—

The short, sharp beats are continuous and are all strong enough to kill a small bird perched on a post at a convenient distance from the Angler. They cause a sort of coil in the line, which seems to run along the surface of the water, and so raise or keep the fly-end near the surface. This explanation may be taken as the practical interpretation of "fiddling" the line, and unless the Angler is using such a rod as the "Traherne" pattern, which is noted for its power of lifting, he should hardly ever make a long Overhand cast without as much of the performance as the nature of the stream suggests.

In quitting our remarks on the "Overhand," I would remind the student that, apart from questions relating to stature—whether the man be very tall or even very short—the line should be made to whistle through the air and that the least amount of strength should be applied for the accomplishment. Whatever the line may be, the action of the rod is an all-important consideration, as I have already endeavoured to show. The Angler *must* be properly appointed. No decent Overhand cast can be made, for instance, with such tackle as that commonly used on the Spey. The Spey rod is exceedingly whippy and useful, and as

MR. HENRY KELSALL.

unsuited for the "Overhand," as the all-powerful "Traherne" is for the Spey cast, or for killing fish in low, bright water with fine gut.

THE UNDERHAND CAST.

It seems but yesterday that I was reading, I forget where, of the folly of using more than five and twenty yards of line. But I believe the writer was no approved authority; at least, his reasoning appeared to me as remarkably suggestive of the fellow who would attempt to describe the habits and customs of mankind with only a knowledge of those of one nation.

Five and twenty yards by the "Underhand," is, without doubt, a pretty little length to get out fair and square; but I have been, I am and always shall be, of the opinion that a long line in Salmon-fishing is often as necessary as a short one. The question seems to be disputed only by those who, from some fault in method or tackle, are unable to cover or control a fish in the distance. To propel a really long line by the "Underhand" is, however, impossible, yet the cast is as popular in places as the "Overhand" is worshipped. This may be accounted for by the fact that it frequently satisfies the requirements of men getting on in years who seek entertainment with the smallest degree of exertion.

The "Underhand" is far less tiring than other methods, and will exact from the novice a minimum of intellectual effort for its comprehension.

The leading features will be brought before the eye and mind of the student, by a mere casual study of the accompanying illustration. With the picture before him he will comprehend, without verbal instruction, the simple method that dominates the cast. Perhaps a little explanation in regard to certain details may be of service, but I fail to see the written description that would answer the purpose so well as the picture.

Let us first take the way in which the Angler should stand to fish; for whilst the "Underhand" demands from its devotees a good attitude, they are, at any rate, released from the duty of "fiddling" the line as they proceed.

THE UNDERHAND CAST.

It is important for beginners to possess the most accurate ideas of the position of the feet and legs. This varies more or less in accordance with circumstances. For instance, on land, as in easy flowing streams, the Angler stands fairly upright and less sideways than in Overhand casting, as shown by the sketches. He, moreover, places his feet to suit his own comfort and convenience, though, as a rule, the right foot in left-hand casting is a little in advance of the other, and generally faces the ultimate direction of the line. But in rapids this is not so, because, as I have said, safety must be studied before convenience. It is simply dangerous, if not utterly impossible, to fish in rapids unless the Fisherman stands altogether sideways and leans well against the current—up-stream, leg bent, and facing rather that way; the down-stream leg extended, and the foot pointing somewhat with the run of the water.

It may be said that, on land, the sole object of the Angler's attitude is absolute freedom—an easy working, unattended by any intermediate tax on the workman as in the case of the "Overhand," *e.g.*, the looking behind.

In the present instance, *i.e.*, in rapids, the position is decidedly cramped. The Angler is, so to speak, limited to the use only of his arms; the firmer and the more rigidly he holds himself the better. And here, I would repeat, that in moving onwards the up-stream leg always takes the first short step; the other then feels its way before the foot is planted.

Now in propelling the fly, the Angler makes the back sweep of the rod with unwavering confidence of success. He *feels* rather than *sees* that the line is dragged from the water, that it travels round in the air far enough behind him so as to tug the point of the rod, the action of which alone propels the fly. This is equal to saying that the line is steadily *drawn* from the water rather than hurriedly lifted, and that the thrash-down is made without vigourous muscular exertion.

In lifting the line, the rod may appear to the eye of a spectator to bend considerably, but provided all jerking is foresworn and a steady swing of the arms pursued, its action is, nevertheless, so even and regular that failure is almost impossible. So far, however, as regards the force to be applied, we must bear in mind that the line is only partially extended behind the Fisherman. It follows that much less strength is needed than in the "Overhand," in which case the line is fully extended.

Observe the shape and position of the rod in the picture, wherein the fly is supposed to be just leaving the water. If the Angler does not permit the rod to take a lower or more slanting course, and if sufficient yet not too much force be employed, the fly can scarcely help taking the track depicted.

We are told, I need not say where, that long casts can be made by the "Underhand"! To my thinking, the mind of the writer in question could not have been directed to the "Underhand" proper. He may have been speculating upon the results attained on the Spey, for in his arguments set forth—if my memory does not strangely deceive me—he suggests that the rod there in general use is originally made in a curve to strengthen its lifting power. Really the statement involves questions for solution, which must be traced to their source and accounted for here, as it has ended in the loss of much money, time, and energy. Rods *have* thus been made, tried, and thrown aside. Even rod-racks, constructed on a principle to preserve the curve in the hope of strengthening the rod, have been established. But what a mistake! In the ordinary Spey cast, *length* is a more important factor in a rod than *strength*. You cannot lift a long line with a short rod; and what a Spey rod lifts it casts. Besides, you want no special strength for lifting the line; in the "Underhand" you do; and, in the Overhand—the remarks bear repetition—you want still more.

Perhaps I need not enlarge upon what has been urged in this chapter with regard to the distance the fly can be propelled by the "Underhand"; but I especially wish to observe that the Underhand cast is separate and widely different from the "Spey." The two methods differ; the results attained differ; the local conditions compelling the adoption of the one absolutely prohibit the adoption of the other; the one is mere child's play to master, whilst the other is known to master men.

As to the origin of the curve in rods, we may think as we will, but we cannot get away from the solid fact that the most common cause of a rod bending up or down is *use*. I am convinced that this curve, come how it may, is a downright defect, a positive weakness. Just for instance,

COLONEL RICHARD ROCKE.

as the upward curve proceeds from Spey casting, so does the downward curve from Overhand casting, and the explanation of it is simply this :—

In both methods there is the *up* and the *down* stroke. The principal strain on the rod in Spey casting is generated in the *down* stroke, and, as a perfectly natural sequence the top joint, in due course, bends *upwards ;* on the other hand, the principal strain on the rod in Overhand casting is generated in the *up* stroke, and so, just as naturally the top joint bends *downwards.* But from a comparative standpoint, the difference between the up and down strain is greater in the "Spey," and so it takes less time for the "Spey" rod to get bent than for the "Overhand" rod.

It is quite immaterial what the rod may be ; in every case, Salmon rods are affected in this way when persistently used for the one or the other method only. The remedy for such weakness is very simple :—Spey casting cures the Overhand weakness, and Overhand casting cures the Spey weakness ; but this treatment is, of course, recommended to Anglers who use the tackle advocated in these pages, rather than to others whose rods are not built for making both casts.

As, however, the novice may entertain some doubt in regard to the final position of the rod engaged in the "Underhand," I would now submit a few further details for his guidance.

The Angler completes the forward movement, or "thrash-down" as we call it, without that sudden checking which is imperative in the "Overhand." The rod is thrashed *through* and reaches quite a horizontal position. In making this cast even experienced men sometimes beat the surface of the water with the rod at the finish ; but is not the practice one that shows a want of order and neatness ? I think so.

It is a proviso, which perhaps may be attached with advantage to these details, that in whatever way the line is propelled, "playing the fly" in the water as subsequently explained should be generally observed.

Suffice it, however, for the present purpose to state that, in working the fly round over the area of the cast made, the rod pointing to where the fly fell, maintains a somewhat horizontal position; at any rate the rod should be only slightly elevated. This is for two reasons :—first, the fly fishes deep and the Angler has a better chance of striking and hooking properly; and secondly, the lifting the line for another cast can be better accomplished.

Now the only element of uncertainty in connection with the "Underhand" turns upon the question of one's appointments. The cast, for example, with a line too light for the action of the rod, cannot be made to the satisfaction of critical eyes. The principle of the method is a safe and sure tell-tale of a light line. Unless the line is heavy enough the tug dies away, in which case, obviously, considerable force for the thrash-down must be employed or the whole thing fails.

The general principle under which the Angler can best judge of this matter for himself, is simply to watch for a certain symmetrical form of the rod, just before the line leaves the water. The picture, however, here comes to the rescue. It should convey to the observer a thorough idea both of the form of the rod at that moment, as well as the effect of its action consequent therefrom. If the rod were less bent at that moment, the line would in all probability be too thin or too light; if more bent, too bulky or too heavy. As regards the action of the rod itself, here, likewise, I am conscious of the somewhat indefinite nature of verbal instruction. It is too well known that in selecting a rod from the maker—even with that "other eye," like Sam Slick's artist's, which takes the view before the act of vision is completed—many questions will arise which are extremely difficult of solution. What an unnamed rod will be like in use, we cannot tell with exactitude in a tackle shop, for there is absolutely no criterion to go by. In short, no human ingenuity can devise a plan by which we can make sure even of a greenheart rod, unless it were one of the few that are christened by men whose names are, in themselves, a guarantee—the very few of which, in the hands of experts, the one is equal to this cast, this to that, *and the other to them all.* And there it must end.

To sum up my remarks, if the patient pursuit of excellence in Underhand casting is not uniformly rewarded in rapids or under falls, it meets with its full share of recompense in pools, and particularly in ruffled but steady and straight flowing waters. With that observation we will pass on to the method adopted in the Highlands.

THE SPEY CAST.

It is remarkable how great is the difference between ideal impressions and the truth established by practical experience. I am reminded of this by reference to a communication which I received from a Scottish gentleman of great authority who says that "An ounce of demonstration is worth a pound of theory." . . "But the glory and reputation of the 'Spey,'" he continues, "is positively demolished by Mr. ——, who flings at the unwary, not one apple of discord, but a whole orchard full. Fancy an author of an Angling book estimating our method as the best to adopt in *boisterous* weather! Not for the sake of twenty books or for the fame of twenty authors must such a false impression of this beautiful cast be allowed to remain an enduring reality, seeing that practical Anglers are still to the fore who can and will refute his delusive assertions." No doubt there are many who could do so; at all events the rising generation of Anglers may safely understand that the time mentioned in the book alluded to for the adoption of the "Spey," is precisely the very time when Spey men desist from its use.

Although the intricacies of this cast, as commonly made, may be set down on paper with considerable probability that the explanation will be sufficient for bright intelligences, it is scarcely to be hoped that verbal instructions will have much fruit without considerable practice at the riverside. But in explaining any of these casts, I feel greatly assisted by illustration obtained by processes not disclosed to writers up to this time.

The "Spey" admits of many variations and, without exception, produces signal results. It is, therefore, just one of all other casts to master and apply in places for which the system is adapted, as, for example, where the line cannot be fully extended behind the Angler. But although more or less complicated, the cast does not seem at all bewildering, even in verbal description.

To better follow me throughout the details, which I may say are authenticated, it is necessary to agree very carefully as to some precise situation in which I am supposed to be fishing. The reader may take it that I am at work on the bank of a river which flows from north to south, and casting right-handed.

MAJOR AND MRS. GRANT.

Some of the particulars to follow will derive much of their interest from the circumstance that they emanate from an accomplished executant of the "Spey," whose name will at once occur to brothers of the rod. For I am fortunate enough to possess a plain and effective argument from Major Grant, and am also at liberty to give the reader the text of his communication. Indeed, the information must be infinitely more acceptable than anything I could write myself in my own conventional vein.

"I hardly think," says "Glen Grant," "that the cast can be written of so as to unveil the mystery from end to end. Comparatively speaking, the riddle of the Sphinx is a contemptibly easy conundrum. Do not attempt to enter into countless matters incidental to the method. Simply state that at times every cast varies—now from the run of the water, out of which you take your fly; now from the length of line you want; again from making your fly alight on a particular place; and still more, perhaps, from the strength of the wind and the way it blows. The beginner soon masters all this if left to himself, I know that of old from personal observation. Doubtless there are difficulties to overcome in mastering a new cast and making it familiar; but merely explain the essential principles, that is all that's wanted. In the natural order of things, the minds of your young pupils will, I feel sure, take a wider range and soon learn for themselves that nothing is denied to well-directed effort and very little obtained without it."

Here we have a definite, accurate, separate, and entirely practical testimony which the student of the "Spey" would do well to consider.

Before proceeding further, I cannot but express the hope that all the complications, which to the merest child on the Spey are not complications at all, may be eventually estimated by the student in their true relative proportions, and that the arguments submitted are easy of comprehension.

Now the great thing in this cast, the pure essential part upon which it entirely depends, is to compel the line to strike the water after lifting it out instead of sending it back in the air. Bearing this in mind, let us fix our attention on the special features of the procedure from beginning to end.

Plate 7

The Wasp Grub

Louise

The Hop Dog

The Ghost

The Blue Boyne

Bo-Peep

Lorne

The Inver Green

The tackle being extended down stream, you first get a *downward* curve in the portion of line out of water, by raising the rod somewhat gently towards the position seen in Illustration No. 1 ; then, without any intermission, you get the curve in the contrary direction (*upward*) on the eve of lifting the fly-end out, by slightly dropping the rod-point when near the perpendicular, *outwards* ; and, still carrying the rod easily and regularly back and round *inwards*, so that the point of it forms the outline (see Illustration 1) of a reversed letter S, you finally complete the cast, just as the fly-end of the line is lightly striking the water near your outer side, by a hearty " thrash-down " aimed at the destined direction of the fly, as depicted in Illustrations Nos. 2 and 3.

The student should get these few words fixed in his mind and be able to follow their meaning before perusing further explanations. When he has succeeded so far, having, I take it, become intimate with the " Underhand," if only by the association of ideas, he can mentally draw comparisons between the early part of the two casts, and form a clear notion of the design and purpose for which each is done He will realise that in the Spey cast instead of the fly being drawn out of water higher and higher from its surface until it turns up and round in the air behind the Angler, it has (with one brilliant exception) to be drawn no further up-stream than beside him. And he will understand that by the law of mechanics as the fly has to strike the water beside him, the point of the rod *must* descend for that purpose before it finally rises to make the thrash-down. The very fact of this descent and ascent compels the fly to take an up-and-down course in the air before it strikes the water.

What would be the result of making the first part of the " Spey " without dropping the point of the rod outwards as the first part of the " Underhand " is made ?

Simply defeat, from the fact (1) that the line would not leave the water, and (2) that it would be dragged *in* the water towards the Angler only a limited portion of the desired distance. But, in spite of this, I am inclined to the opinion that the easiest way of learning to make the line strike the water as stated, is to fancy you are making a *sort* of " Underhand," not failing to slightly raise the point of the rod at starting, and to

THE SPEY CAST (Illustration 1).

THE SPEY CAST (Illustration 2).

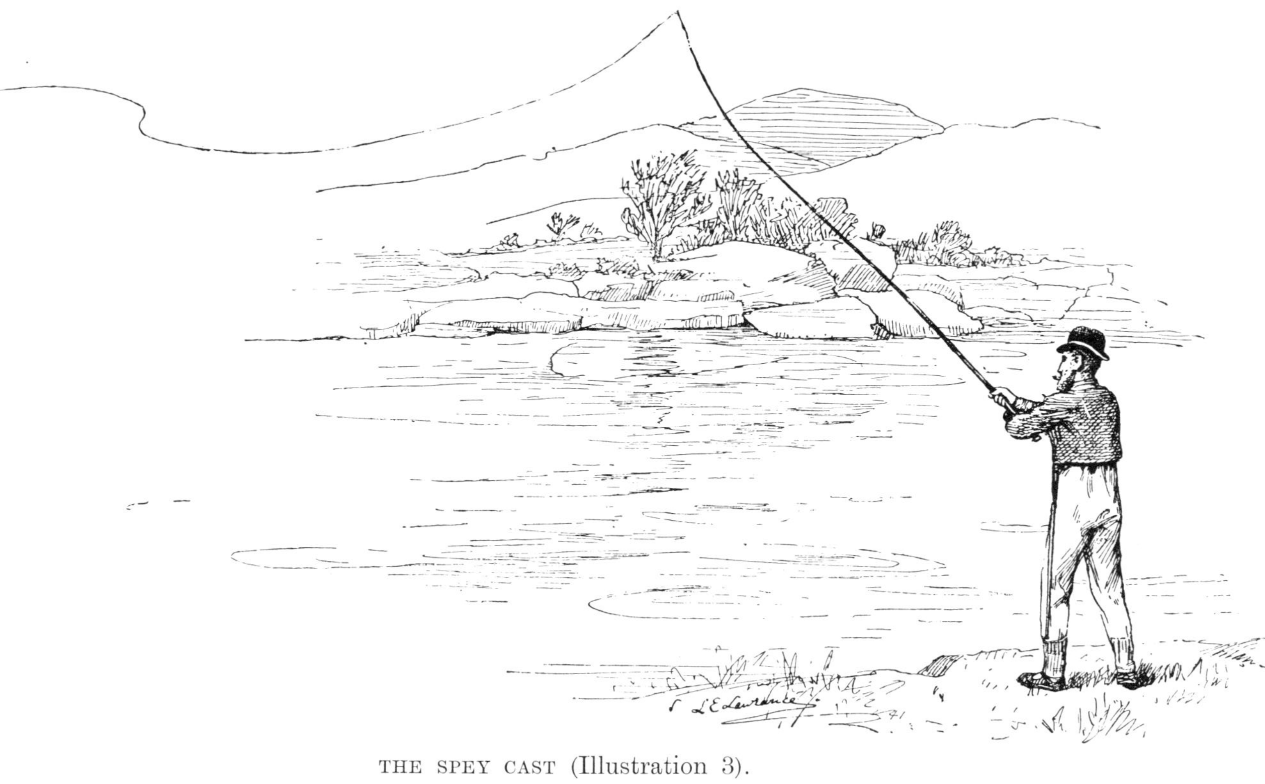

THE SPEY CAST (Illustration 3).

bring it round in an "O.G." fashion before making the thrash-down in continuation of the sweep of the double curve.

However, the young aspirant who, with an intense desire to obtain the key to Angling knowledge, has cast a longing eye upon the "Spey," and secretly wonders at the result incident to the method, should clearly understand that the principle owes its success to that one bold, urging, persistent movement of the rod which refuses to be hindered in making progress by quasi-jerks, or, in fact, by anything that shall check, bias, or alter its even undulating, progress, and finally vigorous action.

The cast is made in one motion, without intermission, and not in two. The point of the rod keeps steady. If the rod does not maintain its bend, the point quivers and shakes, the very symptom of which forbodes defeat. Neither can it be impressed upon the beginner too strongly that the rod, *not stiff in action,* must be sensitive to the tug of the line, the loss of which influence absolutely destroys the intended effect of the whole proceeding. Although the "Kelson" covers 40 yards and more, the rod I like best for this business is built by Farlow on the lines of one altered again and again at the riverside and fashioned by myself. I like it, not only because a long line is easily worked, but also because the rod possesses a certain power that comes to the rescue at those times when the wind renders Spey-casting almost impracticable.

(Sometimes we are obliged to change the position of hands. As an instance of this, when the wind crossing the water blows the line much towards the bank, we put the left hand above the right, lift the line as before towards the right shoulder, and, after bringing the rod well round overhead to the near side, make the downcast left-handed. It is eminently desirable to exercise this extra care and judgment, inasmuch as some people exhibit on these occasions a curiously elaborate capacity for hooking themselves in the cheek; whereas if they shorten the line, put on less steam, and proceed in the manner described, gradually increasing the length of the line, the operation of cutting off every atom of material from their imbedded fly before the bare hook is removed from its hold point first, would never be required. Sometimes one or two, or maybe three, false casts are necessary in order to "pick up" the line properly. These are made as far as possible away from the fish, inside or outside their lay-byes. And, it may be incidentally said that, in fishing from, or very near, the bank, visible signs of wear and tear of the line soon become apparent. The mischief proceeds from hitching up in bushes, or coming in contact with other more serious obstructions—pebbles, rocks and the like. But as soon as the general principle of the cast is understood, the method might be practised in one's room with a stick and a piece of string, or on one's lawn with a rod and a short line.)

By our ordinary way of bringing the rod round, the delaying influence of the water upon the portion of the line that strikes it helps to make the tug perpetual, the immense importance of which is instantly realised at the critical moment of making the thrash-down. The veriest tyro will understand what I mean by attending closely to the following minute particulars. He will understand :—(1) That the mere fact of bringing the rod *back* must cause the line to tug the point of it. (2) That the strength of the tug, though moderated in slightly lowering the point of the rod *outwards*, is yet compensated for by the reduced speed of the line caused by coming in contact with the water.

From a nearly perpendicular position the rod slightly ascends before descending, and is brought round so that at no time it reaches more than the angle of about 45 degrees. Brought round at a lower angle the rod causes an unnecessarily large backward bow in the line. If, however, a cast has to be made actually across the water, the fly must strike the surface much further out than usual, in which case the line forms a very large bow almost opposite the Angler rather than behind him.

Speaking generally and familiarly, if you don't pick the line up clean and don't place the fly sufficiently up-stream, the line splashes the water in reaching its final destination. In fact, when the cast is made perfectly the fly beats the rapid current a little higher up than the Angler, and then he is able to propel the line, not *along*, but altogether *above* the surface, if he wishes to do so. The faster the current the less time must the line rest on the water, if, indeed, it should be allowed to rest at all, even in the steadiest stream. And it stands to reason that an accelerated current demands a proportionately quick effort to make a suitable cast over it; but this quicker cast will not be found as difficult as that suited to the slower stream.

Let us now consider the question of force usually required.

The Angler makes no violent effort, he uses little force, and yet brings the rod round quick enough to reanimate and keep in swing, say, 35 yards of line, so that it tugs the point of the rod as uniformly as possible up to and during the time of the thrash-down. It need not be said that the extra force employed in actually propelling the line just while it strikes the water makes the tug considerably greater—everybody understands that.

There is, perhaps, a little speculation as to how much force is applied in bringing the rod back and round. In this one detail (so much depending on the wind as well as on the water) I fail to see the value of written instruction from which the student could take his cue with any degree of confidence and suddenly reach an immediate satisfactory result. The very nature of the thing prohibits it.

In such a contingency, having no instrument to measure the degrees of force applied in lifting the line, how am I to estimate it? The true force is ascertainable by comparing various facts, and this is the only way out of it. It is perfectly obvious that, in lifting the line, the proportion of strain on the muscles used in the "Overhand" and the "Underhand" respectively differs in ratio, neither more nor less than do the respective proportions of strain used in the "Underhand" and "Spey." For instance, in the "Underhand" the force is less than in the "Overhand," and yet sufficient to compel the fly to travel about one half the distance in the air at the rear of the Angler; whereas in the "Spey" that force is so reduced as to bring the fly no further than beside the Angler, or even a little in front of him. Hence the proportionate decrease of force needed, and the necessity for much more lifting power in the Overhand rod than in the Spey rod.

But taking any one particular condition of wind and water, is the force definable?

This question is, I think, to be answered in the negative. It seems to me to be purely an affair of judgment. But if by the comparisons just made and conclusions just drawn from the three distinct methods of casting the student has succeeded in gaining a clue to the amount of force wanted, his study of the Illustrations will surely lead to further knowledge ; at least, I hope so, for while arranging and adapting them to our purpose, I had this one important particular in my mind's eye. Let him examine closely Illustration No. 1, for it clearly suggests that in thus lifting the rod and bringing it back and round in such limited space the force cannot be very great. I am, in short, clearly of the opinion that if the Spey rod were over-powerful, the action of it alone would compel the fly-end of the line to travel much too far up-stream after the line is lifted from the water.

In making the cast, the impetus is given to the rod almost entirely by the right hand. The pear-shaped figure which the point of the rod describes is depicted in Illustration No. 1 just as it appears in the original photograph. But in point of shape this figure varies, sometimes for one reason sometimes for another.

First, in wading, or we will say, working on ground free from all obstructions, the rod descends not much outward, but nearer the right shoulder, backwards ; at any rate, in a far more continuous line with the casting line. Here, then, to get the necessary sweep of the rod in bringing it round afterwards, the point must come more over the bank actually behind the Angler, consequently the part of the figure in No. 1 Illustration, where the line seems to cross or intersect itself, leans out *over* the water, whilst, of course, the base of the dotted line is more round towards the bank. By keeping the above considerations before us we shall best attain our object to fish often with as little fatigue as possible.

For a second example, we will take for illustration the cast made across the water. Here, as intimated, the rod, in descending, reaches an angle of 35 degrees in order to place the fly well out upon the water, therefore the figure differs in shape. But this variation in the "Spey" is often adopted in order to keep the part of the line which curves round astern of the Angler, from boughs hanging over the water (up river) almost within reach of the rod ; so, in forming the first part of the figure, it is imperative to give considerable *outward* impetus to the rod in its descent by *wrist action.* The natural sequence from this detrusion is that the fly strikes the water, not close in, but far out upon it, and that is why the rod can be brought round for the thrash-down nearer the perpendicular, instead of deviating in a greater degree than usual from the

Angler's right side. The point of the rod has described, we will suppose, the outline of an ovoid athwart the river, just on the right side of the Angler. If the point of the rod had left some mark to indicate the track pursued, the figure would appear to a spectator stationed in the water above or below to range between east and west.

The due formation of such figure and the effect it produces on the line will probably involve the student in complicated embarrassments more difficult to surmount than any that he will experience. The whole cast, in this instance, must be made quickly; and, although difficult, it still appeals irresistibly to the Fisherman because no other means of commanding a fish in such awkward situations are forthcoming.

To introduce that one "brilliant exception" to which I formerly alluded, I would first remark that, in passing from quiet to rapid waters, we find it necessary to make the fly strike the surface in a different place altogether.

The instant the fly-end of the line is placed on the surface in a rapid it is swept away out of the position by the torrent, and to meet the case the fly must strike the water, not *beside* us, but at a spot five to seven yards *above* us. It is in rapids only that, during the thrash-down, the rod almost hits the fly as it rides past the Angler in the air up-stream, heedlessly, yet under perfect control. This is practically equivalent to saying that the thrash-down takes place sooner than usual—certainly somewhat before the fly alights. It is so, and consequently this variety of the "Spey" is also made quickly; and in obedience to the quickened movement of the rod in its backward course, the fly travels further up the water before reaching the surface. But this is not detrimental to the proceeding. On the contrary; for in working its way round the rod keeps pace with the line with mathematical precision, and so the whole business is materially simplified. We also find that in making the thrash-down there seems to be less need for the delaying influence of the water, yet we know that it has occurred, not necessarily by an instantaneous act of the mind, but by the constant co-operation of the rod and line, detected by the sense of touch at the time being. From these facts the student probably comprehends how much easier it will be for him to learn the Spey cast in rapids than in quiet waters.

There are many debatable points, but perhaps the reader has formed a fair estimate of the system already; still the subject has not been yet by any means exhausted.

At this stage I should like to call for special attention.

We have said that the Spey cast is not a method of fishing to be adopted with a Spey rod in boisterous weather; we have had the nature of the cast revealed, and have read a series of comments relating to certain observances in the system; but we have yet to follow it from the Illustrations.

In proceeding in that direction it will be my endeavour to analyse the cast by a separate process, in the hope that the understanding may be enabled distinctly to follow up the method through its different stages.

Looking now at these Illustrations, the point of the rod in No. 1 first describes an outline of a contorted and reversed letter S.

I say "contorted," and I am well advised, as the shape is not that of a reversed letter S on a flat surface; for the upper part soon twists outwards, while the lower and very much longer curve turns inwards.

At the very beginning of the cast, I would repeat that the rod is raised. This makes the line belly downwards, as shown, and brings the "tug" into existence. Without pause the rod still ascends, and then slightly descends outwards, circles round, as it comes inwardly towards the Angler's right rear, and pursues its course for the thrash-down to a point where, if the line is to be propelled above the water, as in No. 3 Illustration*—a better plan than allowing it to run its course along the surface of the water in the customary way—the rod is to be checked as set forth in the details of the "Overhand."

The explanation here is simple and will not detain us long.

Casting the line above the water is a justifiable measure where fish are shy; for the very splash of the line disturbs them to such an extent that I have seen it result in driving both Salmon and Grilse from pools altogether.

For this reason the departure from the old custom, at times and in

* This improvement in the system is not one to be recommended to the novice. Let him become familiar with the ordinary way of propelling the line and he will have far less trouble in learning the cast and mastering its various features.

places, cannot be insisted upon too strongly. But in more than one direction the improved and creditable method affords great pleasure to the artist engaged. For, if while fishing a shy pool over again, he reaps no benefit by reason of his former care and dexterity, he certainly retires with the satisfactory knowledge that his successor on it will fish in water comparatively undisturbed. We ought all to hold the opinion that this is no trifling satisfaction to veterans ever mindful of the interests of others. There is yet another practical advantage derived, for when propelled above the water, the line carries out coils drawn from the winch for the purpose of "shooting." Perhaps the chances for the novice using a Spey rod of coming to grief in this respect are somewhat numerous, for as it happens the most diligent enthusiast would not pledge himself to manage more than half the length accomplished with ease and success by the Overhand method with our style of rod. Still a yard is a yard, and must help to preserve the rod's action.

But to continue. The "S" motion may be said to terminate and the down-cast to commence at the same point as in the Overhand Cast. And, to be very explicit, the course of the point of the rod almost from start to finish is distinguished by the dotted line.

The reader will observe, that to bring the line under efficient control it has been first raised from the stream as much as possible by lifting the rod high in the air. But it should be borne in mind that the Angler then proceeds without delay, and uses just sufficient power to bring the line from the water (by the motion of the rod as described) so that it strikes the surface momentarily at the mark **X** in No. 2 illustration.

The benefit generally derived from so lifting the rod in the preliminary process is manifest—the less line in the water, the less force in withdrawing it, and the less chance of failure in propelling it, because the fly-end strikes the water at the proper place. The long Spey rod, therefore, claims a slight advantage over ours when any great length of line is in use. But in actually propelling the line, our style of rod has far greater power against a breeze (in fact, a Spey rod has little or none), and you can either *cast* or *throw* with it—an advantage that can hardly be over-estimated in certain cramped places on unfavourable days. *Throwing* a Salmon fly is, however, a practice passionately denounced on Spey side as being not precisely sportsmanlike. I referred to this matter before, but sometimes it is not possible to get out the line by any other method.

If a swirl or undercurrent should happen to bury the line so as to suggest undue force when first lifting the rod, an inner false cast or two must be given, and as soon as the line by that means has been fully extended, the cast is made before the mischief again sets in.

The centre course of rod and line simply shows the effect produced on them *in rapids* where the current *holds* the line and sets up an increased action of the rod. If the cast is commenced too hurriedly, or, in other words, if too much force is used to start with, the fly-end is sent too far up-stream, in which case the tug of the line is often lost, and this means defeat. The Angler would be more likely to be spared this dispiriting occurrence if he rather under-rates than over-rates the force needed. The action of the rod should do all that is wanted without using force.

The rod and line with the mark X in No. 2, show the usual position of the tackle at the beginning of the thrash-down. But sometimes the fly has to strike the water further up-stream than the spot thus marked; still, in either case, the practised hand can instantly tell whether or no the fly has taken a right and proper course.

In describing the down-cast or thrash-down, any increased power needed is dictated to the Angler by the length of line about to be used. He will, if necessary, gradually augment the pressure at the butt of the rod, mostly with the upper hand. The force generated in and emanating from the centre at the butt where the strength is applied, serves either to drive the line along the water or propel it in the air, and exhausts itself while the fly is alighting at its ultimate destination (see Illustration, No. 3). Thus may we discover some few points of similarity between the Highland style and the ordinary "Overhand."

Strictly speaking, no method of casting takes so long to acquire in the general way as this one; but things laboriously learnt at first soon come to be done without the feeling of effort. It is true that once in my experience I have seen the cast learnt in thirty-five minutes; half an hour of which was occupied in listening to verbal instructions and in putting questions and pondering over answers. The fact is, a man must *think* for himself. He must put two and two together, and with our

Illustrations before him, let him *reason*. Let him in his independent spirit of inquiry penetrate deeply into ultimate causes and find out mentally why This or That is so. Then let him come with his rod and put into practice the theories he has set up for himself by correctly following this book and not hastily tire in the undertaking. It would indeed be useless for a man to go to work with a feeble, irregular, vacillating idea of the system and expect the attainment of excellence off-hand.

The reader is by now sufficiently at home with various systems of casting to have formed for himself one particular conclusion, as most Fishermen would. What is this one particular conclusion?

That the achievement of any individual cast is an art, and from the very nature of it, the achievement of the much-coveted "Spey," the highest art of all—is an art endowed with an irresistible fascination peculiar to itself and so enjoyable that I may leave it without further comment. But in truth, the "Spey" is to fishing what words are to thoughts, for without it certain waters cannot be commanded, and without words certain thoughts cannot be expressed. To sum up. What is the chief end of the system?

The "Spey" system's chief end may be briefly put thus:—That men who are practically conversant with all the circumstances which render the cast necessary, and with all the various ways of making it, are so far removed from the struggling rank and file, as to frequently meet with the highest success on pools which, to others, are positively unfishable.

THE WIND CAST.

In all sport the great secret is to know beforehand what one really wants to accomplish, and then look sharp in making the most of one's time, place, and opportunity. Time and tide wait for no man. Neither will a nice porter-coloured water, when the bailiff draws a long face and says:—

"Oh, lud, lud, this wind! or she'd no fush that bad the morn, sir."

And here it is indispensable for the man who has the laudable intention of distancing friendly (or unfriendly) competitors, to bear in mind that certain ideas—plausible fallacies, I call them—which have become rooted in the popular mind, may yet be pregnant with disastrous consequences in practice.

I say, "to know beforehand," for the simple reason that, after much experience of "shy" waters, I find that changing front in face of the enemy is a most difficult operation to carry out, whilst there is some little chagrin in the mere fact of altering one's plan of campaign. Naturally this of itself would be inimical to all pleasure for the time being, for no Angler likes to feel that he has not been prepared to immediately make the most of his opportunities.

Old-time practices, once of daily occurrence, come vividly crowding back on one's memory. Take, as an example, the way of fishing in a gale of wind in by-gone days when there was a total absence of all principle, and compare it with the present style of making a cast against the wind. To fancy the "Overhand" the right and proper method, is a fallacy indeed, and yet it was once the fashion. I remember following it myself through the years of my *calida juventus*. I used to pursue the work with vigour and enjoyed it to my heart's content in spite of defeat again and again. The mere gratification of having a rod in my hand and trying all I knew, was enough. No matter how the fly fished or whether it received an "acknowledgment," so long as I covered a Salmon, say within fifteen or sixteen yards, I was satisfied. Naturally in those days, if the fish refused, I fancied the game was up and my chance gone! It is true I had scarcely begun to inquire into the subject of "presentation," its motives and effects, and remained for long uncertain of its advantages. And my want of success deluded me into the mistaken notion that fishing in strong wind was impracticable.

But at length the Overhand practice became too dull and dreary, and as I grew too keen to sacrifice fishing for fun, and acquired the conviction that, in a hurricane, the "Overhand" was alike a restriction and a fallacy, I weaned myself from delusion and set about devising a better and surer means of commanding the water. I investigated these matters some five and twenty years ago, and finally grasped the principle which, without more ado, we may well proceed to examine and analyse.

In my opinion the "Wind Cast" (as I determined to call it) is of mmense value on its day. No doubt the practical demonstration of the

MR. HENRY J. DAVIS.

method is a bold undertaking, and demands a ready ability on the part of those who would become proficient in it. Capricious incidents render the work always difficult and sometimes impossible, as no one will be found to deny. And yet, considering all things, perhaps it calls for more close attention than for extraordinary skill. I noticed this particularly a few years since on the Upper Wye, where I was much struck by the skill displayed by quite a young Angler.

The great and indeed the only objection that I have seen brought forward against the Wind Cast may be summed up in one brief statement :—The experiment is costly. It is said to favour the tradesman more than the Fisherman. Rods *will* break—but may not this be attributed to the fault of the wood, to personal inexperience, or more probably to the sudden vacillations of the wind, which, by-the-bye, beginners are apt to forget. There are rods and rods. Some crooked grained ones break at little provocation ; others cleaved from the plank like my own stand the roughest usage. It certainly is "rough on a rod" to hurriedly lift a buried line, as examination of the method will soon show. It certainly is still more rough on a rod to undergo excessive pressure in the thrash-down, particularly when its action is not steadied by the counter influence of the tug of the line. And this, unfortunately, is of no uncommon experience. But where should we be unless the line were lifted quick as thought (if I may adopt the expression) ; or again, in the absence of that indispensable pressure needed to procure sufficient action of the butt.

I have seen novices, irritated to a degree, break rod after rod simply because they forget these facts. But I always notice that close attention and a constant repetition of melancholy failures is, at any rate, a means of fixing them indelibly in their memories. Old Fuller says, that to try and remember a forgotten condition, a man should scratch his head. Another literary authority writes :—

> "No wonder that our memories are bad,
> We neither bite our nails nor scratch our head."

But would not these morbid expedients be waste of an Angler's time ? All we can do is, to keep our wits about us, for, whatever may happen, the cast *has to be made;* and that too, in the midst of latent dangers and probable interruptions. We know full well how the rod smarts under the loss of the tug. We feel the tug's restraining influence; we feel that it creates, that it constitutes an instrumental, nay, an essential element and we thoroughly understand that, even with the utmost practice and attention, the chance of sustaining that needful counter influence, is wrapt up in doubt and uncertainty. That's just it—just the very detail too, in which our memory must not fail us.

For the intensity of the wind the expert cares nothing, so long as it does not play tricks by fits and starts; when it does this, thoroughly reliable work is impossible.

But now let us consider how to excel in an undertaking frequently deemed impossible, even when the wind is not specially unrestful. In spite of all drawbacks, we find six points for success against half a dozen for failure. The chances therefore are equal, and this is somewhat encouraging.

The next encouraging fact is, that although the wind blows so strongly as to try one's strength to stand steadily, a fish lying from five and twenty to thirty yards away may be covered. Nay, more, the fly can be presented so straight and well, as to yet further astound the uninitiated. Hence the superlative value of this cast.

To clear the way to a methodical illustration of the principle of it, let us touch on one or two specific conditions, which must be neither overlooked nor under-estimated.

First, the direction of the wind. It is only when the wind comes pretty much from the destined direction of the fly that the cast can be made in any degree of perfection. Secondly, it is impossible to excel in the undertaking with a light line, or a rod with a stiff butt. A heavy line is indispensable; not only for making the rod "bend double" in raising it into position, but also for cutting through the wind in obedience to the thrash-down. This point cannot be too strongly emphasised.

In this particular method our object, to begin with, is to lift the line no further than overhead, in such a manner that it represents to a man located on the opposite bank, a regular letter S in the air. To baffle an opposing wind of considerable force and speed, requires the employment

THE WIND CAST.

of considerable power, both of rod and Angler, in lifting the line properly. A peep at the dotted line in the Illustration reveals the action of the rod while forcing the line into that one position from which alone it can possibly be controlled and propelled.

Provided the student refrains from working in swirly waters, and provided he uses suitable tackle and is not baulked by the sudden changes of wind when the line is in the air, this first part of the operation depends for its success upon strong arm power combined with a certain action of the wrist. The arm power, though inevitably considerable (far exceeding that needed in ordinary casts) is not suddenly exercised, for the line must not be *snatched* from the water. The rod is brought "straight up," as we say, the point neither leaning outwards nor inwards; and perhaps an idea of the necessary wrist action may be best conveyed to the mind of the novice by inspection of the accompanying Figure. The method of lifting

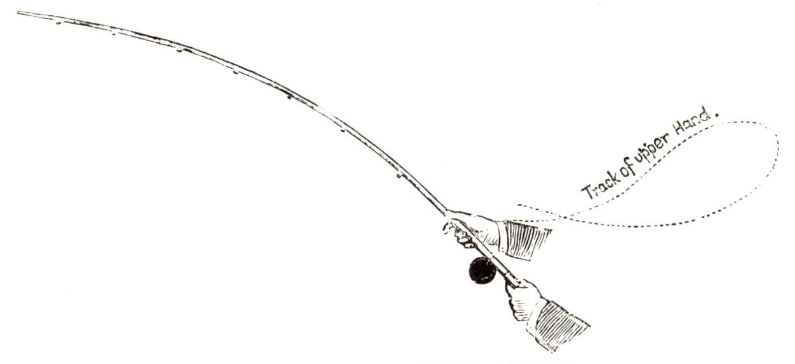

TO ILLUSTRATE WRIST ACTION.

the line very soon commends itself, and then the impulse to diligently obey the rod is too strong to be resisted. The motion of the rod is continuous, and is not checked until the finish. By bringing the upper hand in the track represented, the student can well imagine that the wisdom of using excessive pressure is justified and more than justified by the result attained.

I would, however, remind him that, when unimpeded in its aërial course by the sudden fall or blast of wind, the line is *easily propelled by butt action.*

It is not easy for the untrained eye to actually see what is being done or what has taken place, though the educated eye and touch of the seasoned veteran enable him to immediately form a definite opinion for himself. If in lifting the line, the student is uncertain, what then? If a wise man, he will cease, let the whole thing "slide" and begin again; for he should be alive to the fact that, having lost the "tug" the thrash-down would ruin the rod for good and all. And so the decrees of Fate are accepted with a resignation becoming an instructed sportsman.

How often on these occasions have I witnessed a little sympathy shown in a few encouraging words uttered in the presence of beginners, and observed the immediate effect! In fact, nothing is more odious to me than meeting with that indifferent individual, so wrapped up in himself and his own affairs, as to prevent his being moved with either the failure or the success of others. It is hardly within the power of novices to quickly discover or dodge these difficulties by the aid of the eye, or by the sense of touch, the very force and fickleness of the wind tend so much to deception.

Now we come to the thrash-down.

This terrible "stroke," easier to demonstrate than describe in a cold written page, differs considerably from that in other casts; yet it has intrinsic merits and is entirely orthodox in principle. In point of fact, the line is made to cut *through* the air, not by merely checking the rod in the usual way, but indeed by absolutely *nipping* it at the butt, so as to arrest its course instanter. Now this "nipping" is a rather difficult and precarious experiment for the novice. I have heard old people say:—"It is so easy," and tantalise one by winding up with, "but you've got to know it first."

In all cases our nerves brace themselves up to an effort or they do not. The Wind Cast is not beset with grievous complications to the nervous system, yet "nipping the rod" properly, is in a great measure dependent on good nerves; and nipping in this cast is a feature of the first importance. The enormous *upward* strain of the rod in raising the line results in a corresponding *downward* strain set up voluntarily; or, in other words, the rod bends back so far that, in propelling the line, its action reduces the strain on the muscles of the Angler.

And what is the meaning of "nipping"? It means checking with a vengeance. Nipping expresses that almost indescribable action of checking the rod violently, which is often but very inadequately expressed by the unbearable word "jerking."

For the behoof of novices I feel obliged to travel over old paths once again; and let it be understood at the onset that the words "tug" and "counter-influence" are synonymous terms.

Now it is a fact that the full power of the tug's real influence can be, and is, engendered in the lifting of the line. It, of course, varies according to the degree of strength used. The tug is less felt in the "Overhand" than in the "Underhand," because the strength used is greater. In any ordinary cast the Angler *feels* the tug, and delights in it when making the "thrash-down" at the right moment, though, if too late, he feels nothing of it at all. Lose any of this influence and the loss, in most cases, is detected at once; *but not in the Wind Cast at any time, or, at all events until too late.*

So entirely does the issue in the Wind Cast depend upon this counter influence that, were it dissevered or dispelled, the most dexterous man alive could not possibly get the line out. But above all it must be repeated that any such disseveration brings in its wake a far more serious trouble; for that *nip* without that identical *tug*, and the rod is doomed to all intents and purposes.

For all its difficulties the judicious beginner will not hurriedly condemn the Wind Cast, nor hesitate to try to master the method. For me, many fond memories surround it, and I believe it destined to the honour of circumventing fish, when all other known methods are impracticable.

The cast is, in short, a triumph of ingenuity and skill and high-spirited endeavour following the dictates of much thought and consideration. And, judging from what I have myself seen hastily done by novices, I would say, "search *slowly* into it; for, as experience teaches, those who are quick in searching, seldom search to the quick.

THE GOVERNOR CAST.

Once upon a time—not so many years ago either—on returning home after a hard day's fishing in the rain with an old attendant named Ewan, who at different times in his chequered career had served me as valet, groom, gillie, and factotum generally, we came suddenly upon the whole *posse comitatus* attached to the hotel, which happened to be, for the time being, my headquarters in the North. There was "long Sandy," than whom no Scotchman e'er cast a much longer line, or tied a more killing "flee"; and Robin, who seemed by instinct to know the "lie" of every running "fush"; and Jamie the untiring, whose muscles were of steel, and for whom no day was too long or "bag" too heavy; besides a few others, whom to name were needless. The sudden appearance on the scene of my trusty henchman with a frail on his back that evidently contained something weighty, instantly took these worthies by surprise. Knowing themselves the hopeless state of the water, it roused their curiosity to the highest pitch. Robin first opened the ball with :—

"An' hoo mony heads hae ye gotten the day, my braw laddie, for I see twa tails whatiffer?"

The rougher element had already thrown out some noisy misgivings amongst themselves and were now shouting impromptu verses on the "common or garden" fly.

"Order!" cried Ewan.

"Order anything you like in the way of whisky or baccy, no worming for us," rang through the air.

"If Ewan is to tell you he must have silence," I remarked; when Robin, with a knowing wink at the others, repeated his query as to how many heads, etc.

"'Hoo mony heads?' Hoot awa! De'il tak ye, there's as mony heads as tails, and, ye daft creeture, it wad hae been a lesson to ye had ye bin there wi' us the day," answered Ewan, as I thought rather impatiently.

"'Deed then, an' that's no altegither improbable," drawled out Robin in a tone of more than usual solemnity.

"Weel, but," continued Ewan, "I tell ye it is sae; it's nae man in these parts but the Maister that kens how to fush siccan pool as 'Pol-o-dour' ava."

And with a few more disparaging remarks of a similar character, Ewan took himself off indoors to get rid of his burden—of course, at the bar.

"Pol-o-dour," I may here state is the local name of a certain deep pool on a river, the name of which I withhold for various reasons. It has the peculiarity about it that the catches are fishable only when the river is at its very lowest. As a matter of fact, the place never comes into ply until the rest of the "Casts" look as ludicrously small from want of water as the local men look from want of sport. All the fish in the immediate neighbourhood make for the pool and congregate there by the dozen, but the Fishermen never could command it. The pool itself is long, still, and broad—perhaps seventy yards in width and very "dour." It is fished from one bank only, high, over-hanging rocks fringing the opposite side. However, in the course of a few minutes Ewan returned to the front of the house where the others were sitting, and the conversation was resumed. In the meantime he had tossed off a "caulker" of whisky at my request, for he was wet to the very bone, and was now disposed to be still more communicative.

"Hech, sirs," he began, addressing his audience generally, while I sat finishing a cigar after getting rid of my waders and the "wee drappie" left in the flask, "it wad hae done ye hearts gude to hae daunered alang the banks wi' me the day and seen the maister bang oot the flee, mair by token that ye wad then ha' been able to joodge o' his seestem."

"'Seestum'—that's a deectionary word, and what maun that be like," asked Sandy, jumping on tip toe.

"Whist, mon, he joost has a plan o' his ain, and covers 'Pol-o-dour' frae the top to the bottom o't."

"Ye'll no mak me believe that Ewan, it's na' in the power o' no fusher whatiffer."

"'Deed ay, but I will, Sandy, an' if ye'll come wi' me in the morn, I'll be bound the maister will be right pleased to show ye the seestem his ain sel."

Then I ordered more " caulkers " upon the festive scene. The conversation shortly glided into other channels, and, among other songs which were most entertaining, " The lass o' ' Gowrie ' " was befittingly rendered by one of these honest souls.

The " Governor " is a singular cast, sound in principle, though quaint in its inception. In practice it works admirably. Without it I, at least, know no other way to reach fish lying fifty yards or more across stream, and for no other purpose did I originally intend it. The cast is withal simplicity itself. A mop handle, five feet in length (shod) is pushed into the ground and remains fixed at its back merely by string attached to two tent pegs. A small staple has been previously hammered in at the top, through which an elastic band is adjusted. The fly must not penetrate the elastic itself; the hook should merely hang through the ring. All the Angler has to do then is to walk right away to the riverside *in the line of the cast,* letting the winch "run" as he goes, until he has sufficient casting line out to cover the distance required. Of course he will have previously made himself acquainted with the particular catch he desires to command, and have taken precautions as to measurement and direction, by shifting the apparatus beforehand. By this simple yet judicious method, any novice—lady or gentleman—can get out a tremendous line, without any previous knowledge, in half a dozen trials.

When an extra long cast is wanted I invariably use a line which has been spiced for the purpose, for it is a drawback to have any length of thin back-line at the point of the rod.

The next step is to make the " thrash-down." This breaks the elastic band, releases the fly, and away it goes. But it is necessary to bear in mind that the rod must always be dropped back, as shown in the drawing, so that the line almost touches the ground when the operation is about to be performed. The more the rod is checked at the finish, the greater is the line under command.

If the first cast does not raise the fish, all you have to do is to wind up, walk back to the mopstick with the fly in your hand, put on another band—the band is partly pushed through the staple and looped through itself—and muttering to yourself "better luck next time," at it you go

THE GOVERNOR CAST.

again. It is really astonishing how many fish in the course of a season can be picked up in this way on certain stretches hitherto deemed quite inaccessible to rod-fishers. I know this by my own personal experience; and therefore in future it will be the sportman's own fault if with the aid of the "Governor" cast he does not cover fish absolutely out of reach by any other method as often as the necessity and the opportunity may arise.

The little party of quidnuncs soon afterwards broke up. Old Robin led the way apparently engaged in prayer. He had been the most attentive listener of them all whilst I was expounding the above precepts, and now he was "snooving" off, "his lyart haffets wearing thin and bare," muttering to himself something about "the principle o' the thing having been in his head for years, and was quite the idol of his adoration," whatever that may happen to mean.

Of course, this cast will be found available only in a clear space and not in one bordered by trees or bushes. The fly placed inside the band when freed flies through the air like a stone from a sling, and alights at the farthest point the line can take it. The only element of uncertainty to be found at all, is the strength of the bands in use. Bands breaking on a steel yard at a pull of nearly 5 lbs. are required for very long casts. But so recently as the commencement of the Angling season of 1893, in a series of experiments carried out on the river Beauly, I made two casts, measuring fifty-two and fifty-three yards respectively, with bands pulling from 3½ to 4 lbs. apiece; and was present at some other trials on the Tay when I saw fifty-seven yards covered again and again by Mr. Barclay Field.

Singularly enough the method has not proved attractive to the angling public in any marked degree, though it was personally introduced to public notice first in the year of the great Exhibition of 1851, and afterwards illustrated and described in the *Fishing Gazette* of 1884.

THE SWITCH CAST.

I shall not attempt any laboured enconiums on an authority—I might almost say the *one* authority of his day—nor endeavour to summarise his time-honoured principle of switching; for, just as the

MR. BARCLAY FIELD.

future obliterates the past, many of these so-called settled rules of action die out or vary in course of time. He himself, poor fellow, has long since ceased to fish—and to live! But a letter in his handwriting, now lying before me, would have us believe that "the theory of a cast is a science, the practice of it an art."

My informant, whose name and rank I am compelled to withhold, laid down the grand principle, that the method of the Switch being too rigidly inelastic for general purposes, remained for years undeveloped on its strongest side.

These judicious opinions call up ideas more enlarged than the mere sound of words at first convey, for on attentive examination of the Switch Cast, one will easily see how incomplete it is without the "Peter," which, though young, was not discovered yesterday.

Modern Anglers would hardly credit the countless improvements in ways and means of casting which have only recently been more or less adopted; but it would be interesting indeed were we able to trace the progress of each art through its stages from the classic days of Walton right up to the commanding position it occupies at the present time.

In the case of the "Overhand," what do we find? As practised from a time (which may be called immemorial since no one can fix a date "to the contrary") the system of *throwing* with a light line and fine-pointed rod scarcely lingers in the Angling mind now; indeed, the old-fashioned method is almost forgotten. With other appliances the "Overhand" still holds its ground.

But doubtful as the policy of the "Switch" was, save on an emergency, no one can say that the scientific founder of it did not trust to reason, nor that the wise reformers of the method trusted only to imagination. No discovery of a system of casting is made without some previous conjectural effort of the mind, nor is any amendment in principle inculcated without some exertion of the reasoning faculties. Practical experiment should do the rest. No doubt that in the case of the "Switch" the one chief object was the discovery of truth, and this has, in my opinion, been undoubtedly attained.

Say what we can of the "Switch," the cast will never hold its own in a race with the "Spey." The "Spey" would give the "Switch" a beating; that is to say, as far as the matter of distance is concerned, the former would cut out the latter in competition by at least twenty-four feet without being extended.

The great advantage which this old-fashioned cast has over the "Spey" and all others is particularly its own, and counterbalances all its failings in those places where the "Switch" only is suitable—when trees, shrubs, or other immediate obstructions handicap the different, and more water-covering modes of propelling a fly.

The "Peter" is an intermediate and auxiliary movement of the rod in aid of the final effort to get out the line.

To properly explain the method of the "Peter" and "Switch" combined, the student should understand that the former is a *dodge* or *scheme* resorted to only in connection with the latter, with which alone it is associated. The Peter was simply born for the cast and united to it long ago. It is, moreover, a commanding feature of the cast, which, in its absence, is at times absolutely unpracticable.

The "Peter" has developed the "Switch" to such a degree that the cast may be fairly ranked among the favourite formulas of the day. And although the performance is said to be somewhat difficult to master, the merest tyro will, if he persevere, soon be gratified by the progress made and quite convinced of the value of it.

How then is the cast to be made by the Angler (fishing right-handed) whose line is extended down-stream?

The brief instructions for making the Switch, with the Peter in one continuous action, are:—

(1) "Elevate the rod steadily but with a rather increasing movement: (2) now twitch the point of the rod forward (Fig. 1) by a smart, short action of the upper wrist, from right, overhead, to left, to form a narrow oval: and (3) finish with the thrash-down."

By No. 1, the line will be drawn to the surface and belly *towards* you. No. 2 (the "Peter") causes the line to bow in an opposite direction. (See dotted line Plate 1.) The "narrow oval" is completed by a bold sweep of the rod taken round to the right. (3) Is effected vigorously and additional impetus is given to the line by forcing the arms forward during the thrash-down to their full extent. On reaching an angle of 45 degrees

THE SWITCH CAST (Illustration 1).

THE SWITCH CAST (Illustration 2).

the rod is checked by a firm grasp (Illustration 2), when the line is left to work its own success or failure.

With these instructions before him the reader will probably recognize that the object of the "Peter" is to clear the near portion of the line from the destructive influence of eddying waters, and to compel the line to tug the point of the rod in order to regulate its action, keep its point within bounds, and render the thrash-down practicable and efficient.

(The situations in which the "Switch" is necessary are few. They are when neither the rod nor the line can be extended for more than eight or ten feet in the rear of the Angler.)

In proportion to the effect of the "Peter," the calculation is made of the force wanted for the thrash-down.

Now and then, for instance, the current, by flowing in all manner of ways, causes the line to lie on the surface in a zig-zag form, whereby it is rendered uncontrollable. In such a case the "Peter" is simple and immediately successful, and the thrash-down is effected in the usual manner of the cast. But where we encounter a sharp eddy, swirling under the rod, outwards, a satisfactory result is not so readily attained, or, at all events, without a much more forceful "Peter" than in the former case. Even then, unless effected in time, only a portion of the disarranged line, which the eddy has seized, may be cleared from the mischief, and in that case the force needed for the thrash-down must be increased accordingly. If the still greater mischief should arise from a swirl that dashes the line inwards, the *modus operandi* changes.

Take by way of illustration, a man fishing right-handed. The line having been thus hustled towards the bank, the Angler shifts the rod like lightning into the left hand, hurries the "Peter," and, without further change or perceptive cause, completes the whole business, then and there.

What I very much want to point out in Petering is the one risk the inexperienced run. In all cases, the greatest care must be taken lest *too much of the back portion of the running line be removed from the surface*, or the second state will be worse than the first. The line has to

HON. SIR FORD NORTH.

be cleared from swirling eddies, that is certain; but it is on these very occasions that the rod is liable to act upon it in a most prejudicial way; for the instant the line gets clear, the deplorable mischief of undue power, so frequently used in the experiment, reveals itself and absolutely arrests all further progress. To those who thoroughly understand switching, the force of this argument is obviously manifest.

But as against this argument the more one makes the line bow *from* him in Petering the greater will be the tug on the rod, which fact is sufficient of itself to ensure the thrash-down always proving effective. The secret is not to allow the butt to assist in the Peter at all. The work must be executed by the point of the rod, the action of which is brought out not so much by the strength of the arms as by a free use of trained and flexible wrists. Indeed, it must be distinctly understood that any muscular exertion would mar the experiment and defeat the object in view.

I have a few words to say in hope of removing a slight prejudice with respect to the cast, and making it more available for free use than in times gone by.

Common opinion declares the "Switch" to be good only for false casting, but with the "Peter" it presents, in my estimation, much ground for thoughtful consideration. I would add, for the instruction of the uninitiated, that the "Peter" is unnecessary in streams or other straight running waters, and that the measure of its success largely depends on the varying circumstances under which it is employed. And it would appear to me that the student should view at all times, with perfect coolness and accuracy, the various circumstances of the situation, so that each of them may produce its due impression on him without any exaggeration arising from nervousness or lack of experience. The influences surrounding this cast are self-registering, and unconsciously write their story in all its fulness on the mind of the student who, watching a clever performer, sees the combination of all its elements at once. Clear vision is, however, a *sine qua non*.

Some slight inconvenience may possibly arise from a too rigid obedience to our preliminary instruction. If in elevating the rod steadily at first the line does not "come freely" the process of "fiddling," as previously described, must be consistently adopted. You may, however, rest assured that the remedy will not be required often, provided the interval between each cast be not unduly prolonged.

Coming now to explain the thrash-down, as shown in Illustration 2, the method differs but slightly from that employed under ordinary circumstances. The process from gradual becomes rapid, and looks like developing what the meteorologists are accustomed to describe as "dangerous energy." It would be perhaps safer for the novice if he made a sharp *thrash-through*, and not attempt to check the rod at the usual angle of 45 degrees. But all fear of the rod is soon reduced to a minimum, save perhaps in the case of too much force being used on those occasions when the wind counteracts the effect of the Peter by blowing the line out of gear.

One of the commonest errors may frequently be traced to the inherent desire to bring the rod, in the "back sweep," further than at an angle of 45 degrees—any such propensity should be strenuously avoided. And, moreover, I would strongly caution the Angler in accepting all hurried instruction that would induce him to bring the rod round by his side too low. The loss of the tug of the line might lead him to do so; but, in my opinion, following such advice as that is wrong in any case, though it requires no little courage to say so.

The *thrash* of the rod, when executed as described, forms a sort of loop in the line (see Fig. 2), which seems to rush along the surface of the water until at last the fly drops over and alights at its proper destination.

THE FLIP CAST.

The Flip proper is a sort of side cast—*side flip*, in fact—which the practised Angler can learn in a day.

I say a *sort of* side cast, though it in no way resembles the Side Cast as practised on the Shannon and elsewhere. The Irish claim to be masters of that method, and there is no doubt that their tackle is eminently adapted to the purpose. For making the Side Cast no rod quite equals the Castle Connell, but I am inclined to the belief that, apart from the clever way in which our neighbours are accustomed to use it, their system, when adopted by us, is more for the sake of a change than for a necessity.

To extend and propel the line in the air as they do by moving the rod in a horizontal position from first to last is less tiring than the Overhand, which, with this Irish rod, is more difficult and less effectual. I have not deemed it necessary to illustrate and describe the Side Cast, but I wish to record the fact that by employing it a very long line can be controlled even with our own style of rod. Also that the cast is by no means to be despised under boughs and such places where space will admit of it.

The "Flip" has two variations which assume the names of the overhand and underhand flip respectively. The overhand flip requires a certain amount of room overhead in front of the Angler, and often comes into use where willows weep over the water with sufficient height between the water and the branch from which the weepers hang, and sufficient room between the weepers themselves. The underhand flip is adopted when the space just mentioned is limited. Although some men fish for years and think nothing of either of these variations, yet they will in many instances be found his only salvation. Indeed, by no other method than the Flip can certain catches be commanded.

The Flip Cast is generally said to be the easiest of all to master. I have heard it extolled to the skies and condemned to the lower regions in language strong, if original. I have also heard it said that the easiest methods of Salmon-fishing, like the happiest women, have no history; at all events, to the Flip I owe some of my greatest summer successes. Surely it is just as necessary to master one system as another, else we are comparatively helpless when some unusual condition for action arises. Shakespeare tells us that there is a tide in the affairs of men which, taken at the flood, leads on to fortune. We must, however, "take the current when it serves, or lose our ventures"; and an Angler will look very foolish if, by neglecting to learn the Flip, he has to pass by a shaded spot holding plenty of fish which cannot be covered by any other means. The usual place for flipping is under trees whose lower branches have been levelled off and cleared away by flood water. The rushing torrent, together with the debris it carries, so levels overhanging branches and twigs as to make them appear like the under parts of trees which, in parks, have been reduced to an equal condition by cattle.

Though easy to learn, the Flip is not so easily described. Affairs in

MR. F. M. MACKENZIE.

general, simple enough in themselves, are often the least capable of definition in terms simple or abstruse. But I am content to leave the student with the few following details.

When flipping left-handed the rod is to be held in the right hand. The Angler gets into the water with his fly hitched as usual to the bar of the winch. As soon as he has taken up his position he proceeds to draw forth a few yards of line, which he coils and holds between the finger and thumb of the hand working the rod. Pointing the rod a little down-stream and holding the butt firmly against his hip, with the winch facing sometimes one way and sometimes another for the sake of the action of the rod, he unhitches the fly, shortens the line a trifle by pulling it in, makes the rod bend all he can by fully extending the left arm and hand in which the fly is held, and suddenly lets go, allowing the coils to depart in the manœuvre.

The instant the fly is freed additional propelling power is given to the line by sharply swinging the rod to the point B and bringing it back into position. This helps the action of the rod considerably.

As the reader may suppose, the line is previously shotted. About 14 or 15 inches from the fly three or four swan shot are fixed to the line, above which, say, about 4 feet, another shot a little smaller in size is attached.

To renew a cast in close quarters, wind in line, turn the rod up-stream quite behind you, and the line can be easily reached and picked up.

I have now completed, to the best of my power, these illustrations. To say that I am absolutely satisfied of the exactness of every detail would be to admit what I scarcely feel. The *exact* picture of the tackle from the beginning to the end of any cast cannot possibly be obtained until Mr. Edison has perfected his Kinetoscope for the continuous photography of objects in motion. Then, and most likely not before, will a series of pictures become in effect but one picture. I would nevertheless strongly urge the student of these seven different casts to note down with accuracy all the circumstances of each particular case, for just as by far the most valuable of the two educations man has is not that which is given to him, but that which he gives to himself; so, indeed, must the

THE FLIP CAST.

young Angler work out and resolve all these knotty points for himself. The secret is, not to fall into wrong habits at the beginning, but to make sure of every step taken, bearing in mind that most things to be learnt are very simple, and that some books do their best to render them obscure.

We have had to travel over a lot of ground in our preliminary combat, to smooth the way for safely manœuvring in every nook and corner at the riverside; but our tussle with the "tug of the line" is over now, and gives way for that other tug—the veritable *tug o' war*. The foregoing illustrations and descriptions will soon show the student how to cast, but I now propose to show him how to fish; and I shall endeavour to give him some valuable hints connected with this branch of the subject.

In Salmon-fishing there are two principals—the Salmon and the Salmon-fisher. Their interests run counter to each other. The one is fully equipped with deadly weapons in his hand; the other with only a good broad tail which is his sole resource to fight with, in defence of life and liberty. The conflict sometimes is very hot, and, after all, the match is not so particularly unequal. But in order to pilot the tyro to victory he must be possessed of certain further information. He must first know the "Catches," and then how to fish them. Let me explain that Salmon are caught in Pools, Streams, Flats, and Rapids. The places they haunt in these are called "catches" or "lay-byes." The catches vary in size and consequently vary in regard to the number of Salmon they hold. On one day twenty to thirty tenants may be found at home, on another day none at all; and this difference largely depends upon the time of year and height of water. It comes to this then—the stranger must ask, he must court local opinion and advice, or he will most likely find himself at work, as I myself have been, in barren waters.

Some pools in certain rivers are fishable at any height of water; whilst in others a slight rise or fall might spoil one's chance altogether. I have, for instance, had good sport on the Lochy in twenty feet or more of flood water, but only in the pools situated at the various bends of the river. And even then a good deal depends upon the nature of the shallow or fishing side. Slanting ground from there, covered with gravel or boulders, generally turns out well in high water. As the waters rise so do all the fish remaining in them come across from the deeps and take up new stations on the shallow side. The catches are known to the ordinary gillie in attendance. Where the river runs fairly straight, pools get out of order, and, as I say, an inch, or even less, makes all the difference so far as sport is concerned.

With regard to streams, it may be taken as a rule that rain soon puts them out of order. Salmon rarely stay in them when the waters rise to a certain height unless boulders large enough to form an eddy are imbedded in the river.

Flats, on the other hand, call for closer inquiry. Although, in rising water, fish invariably like to go ahead, they will occasionally drop back and stay in the lower part of such reaches as these, till at length they are forced by the torrent to make for shelter elsewhere. This propensity is especially noticeable in a long straight piece of water, in the lower part of which, at normal height, the current scarcely moves.

As to rapids, the Angler *must* bide his time. If the top part of a rapid is in ply, even so little as half an inch rise will ruin every lay-bye in it. But when fishable, rapids are by far the freest taking places, though by no means the freest rising places; at all events, they are the surest and the easiest for the novice not wanting in nerve. I have seen men at first almost frightened to death at the mere sight of a rough-and-tumble rapid. The feeling soon passes away--at least, if one may judge by the show of daring that often follows a fit of nervousness, and confidence restored by greater familiarity with purely imaginary dangers.

I have given a somewhat curtailed description of the above resorts by way of preface to the more elaborate details which are to follow. The student finds out exactly where the casts are, and should devote his attention to those which happen to be best in order and best suited to his capacity. It would be labour lost to persevere in any Catch where more line is required than can be controlled—where, in short, the fly can be presented to the fish in a proper and alluring manner ; and this part of the subject shall be dealt with presently.

Fishing is not what it was by any means ; and when you come to look into the circumstances under which it is now conducted you would not be surprised at the extreme care taken by our best men in casting straight, in "mending" casts when necessary, in playing the fly, and in the easy, apparently indifferent and undesigning attitude which they assume towards the fish.

Great as is the divergence of principle and method adopted in fishing the various places just mentioned there is a singular resemblance in respect of casting straight. The thing is this—always endeavour to let the cast be made so that the fly may be "fished" at once. When this can be attained without "mending," you may be sure that your cast has been made by a suitable method. The fly cannot fish at once by, say, the Spey cast, when the line is propelled along the surface of the water, because, by the time the fly alights, the current has carried down river the middle part of the running line, and instead of the fly fishing, it will be drifting ruthlessly across stream headforemost. I strongly recommend the employment of the "Overhand" wherever it can be made.

The word "stratowa means not merely that the line itself shall be pretty straight when laid down on the water, but also that the Angler aims straightight 'rds such a point that the line shall reach the water at

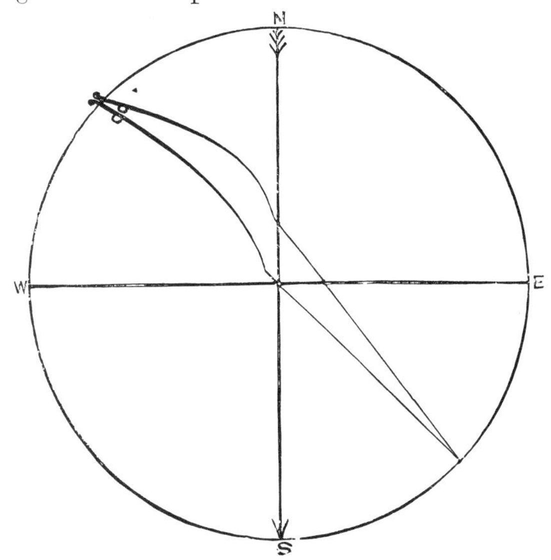

a certain angle from him. As regards the scope of that angle people differ. Some cast across the water, but I never do so if it can be avoided, for the best of all reasons that, as a rule, I kill far more fish when, for example, the fly falls S E from N W as shown in the diagram. (For Salmon, it is sometimes necessary to break the rule, but never for Grilse.* If, for instance, a fish is lying in the bottom part of a stream in summer-time, or even beside the more rapid water on the far side nearer the neck, at any time of year; or, briefly, if you cannot work the fly sufficiently fast, the rule does not apply.)

Speaking generally, as soon as the fly reaches the water at such an angle, it will sink and fish immediately, by bringing the rod (horizontally) a little more up-stream, *and working it there.* The stream instantly tightens the line, if, by accident, there is any to tighten. Do not alter the position of the rod; but, keeping time with the pendulum of an imaginary church clock, move the point of the rod (as with one beat of it) some 18 inches towards S, and a little faster than the pace of the stream, returning (as with the next beat) by a similar but slower movement. Continue these backward and forward movements steadily and regularly till the fly has crossed S, when the point of the rod should be brought round with each beat towards S and past it, in order that the fly shall fish on and reach the point midway between S and W.

If the water flows so slowly that the fly dwells too long in front of the catch as it passes, assist the pace of it by bringing the point of the rod round earlier with each movement. But on the other hand, if the water runs so quickly that the fly is swept hurriedly across the catch, the rod held still (facing eastward) or, maybe, that a very little playing of the fly will suffice to put matters right. Bear in mind that the "Eagles," and other flies with such long hackles as the Hen Pheasants and Herons (black, grey, and cinnamon), are more alluring to the fish when not played at all.

The diagram should, I think, be sufficient guide for the student to determine at what angle down-stream he should cast his fly. As regards "mending" the cast, it may be unnecessary to enlarge upon what has been said. Nor will I detain the reader by making further allusions to the choice of flies than occasions demand as we proceed.

---

* Grilse fishing is not what it was. I remember Craven (Keeper to Lord Arbothnut) holding a little croft beside the Bridge of Feuch some thirty years since. It was he who killed no fewer than fifty Grilse at the foot of the Falls in one day. Deeside men know this favourite spot of old.

In fishing, the underlying principle for the Angler is to convince himself what flies others have used unsuccessfully, and in what way they have been fishing, *i.e.*—where they stood, what method of casting they adopted, how long they persevered under the conditions which, presumably, remain unaltered, and, above all, whether by their untutored demeanour in the water or out of it they were likely to scare the fish, and, for the time being, put them "off" altogether.

In all these respects the Angler should choose the opposite tactics as much as he can. If, for instance, small, light flies have been used with short hackles, he should select a pattern larger, darker, and longer in the hackle. But whatever may have been done in other respects, a pool that has been long thrashed with gaudy patterns requires considerable rest, and even then, a couple of casts over a fish is sufficient before passing on. In passing on, or rather fishing on, *see* everything but *look* at nothing; for you will give yourself away if by your manner, you arouse the suspicions of the fish.

Whatever be the general opinion it is certain to my mind that Salmon have an instinctive dread of an *inquisitive* Fisherman. If he "behaves himself" a man may catch a Salmon under the very point of his rod; I have often done so, being fully alive to the fact that, as to "behaviour," the susceptibility of the Salmon does not materially differ from other creatures. Rooks and gulls, we know, will pick up worms out of the very footsteps of the smock-frocked yeoman who trolls a song of the soil between the handles of his plough. Shy mountain sheep take no notice of the shepherd who warbles an old-world ditty along the hill-side; nor will the most spiteful thorough-bred be affrighted by the smith, who, while singing at the forge lifts its leg on his leathered lap as a matter of course.

Almost all that is necessary on the subject of a man's manner can be said in a few words.

Stand easily and erect, do not peep about, do not assume a defiant demeanour, and move as naturally as though there were no fish in the water.

Now let us first see how to fish "that pool there," whose shallow waters at the neck, this early spring morning, ripple less and less as they change their course; now making towards that large deep eddy on the far side, now increasing in velocity and forming certain little curls below until the Angler is forced to wade or retire—a veritable low water catch, this!

First, the question forces itself upon us, Where are the fish? Well, the gillie will decide this for you, as, sometimes they take up their places at the neck of the ripple, sometimes at the near edge of the large eddy, and at other times at the lower part of the pool altogether. But let us consider how best we can proceed from the eddy downwards; for the streamy part at the neck will hold not one single fish until quite the middle of the month of May, unless the weather has been abnormally warm.

The chief object here is not to allow the fly, which must be cast well into the eddy, to be dragged too quickly past the long narrow catch by the force of the water upon the bellying line. (These catches are generally long and always narrow, for the fish lie in the small space between the stream and the eddy, which may be even twenty yards in length.) If the fly comes too quickly, the rule of presentation is broken from the fact that the fly travels head first past the fish. And yet, in this case, it is impossible to rigidly obey the rule, unless the length of line in use is so limited that the Angler can work the fly at almost any pace he likes, by holding the rod high in the air. Still, there is usually a way out of these difficulties, and, maybe, the remedy is simply to "mend" the cast immediately it is made.

It would be a very strange place if that remedy did not have the desired effect all down the eddy and cause the fly to work before the fish in true orthodox form.

When the first cast is completed and previous to making another, as your gillie will tell you, walk one yard on, or, if the water is coloured much, half a yard will do, and continue casting and "mending" as before. But should you raise a Salmon and he should happen to come short, walk away, change the fly for one a trifle smaller, or, if you like, cut out such feathers as Jungle fowl or Summer Duck, and use the same one again. In about four minutes make a couple of casts over the fish from where you stood before, *but not lower*. Should this fail, select a fly a trifle smaller still and very different in colour and type. Two casts with each fly are sufficient, provided the water is not discoloured. In giving the fourth trial having rested the catch for ten minutes, put on a Grub, one or two sizes larger, or the fly that first raised the fish. And before finally giving in, try a fly in character with the river both in colour and make, three or four sizes *larger* than any one previously presented.

If, however, you have an "interview" with a Salmon—*i.e.*, prick him, it is not worth while trying again. Only once in my career have I succeeded after an "interview," and then the fish had shifted its quarters. A Salmon at the bottom of a pool on the Wester Elchies water had run me foul, broken the line, and taken away fly and gut length. On resuming operations at the *head* of the pool, I found to my astonishment after gaffing a fish, the very fly in his mouth I had just lost below. Shortly after this capture, on working my way down the pool again, I lost, for the second time, the self-same fly in the same place and way as before.

How well I remember the joyous chaff of that eventful evening!

But is there not very often a reason for merely pricking fish? I think so, and have many a time traced it to some fault of the fly. The pattern, for instance, may be overdressed as regards the actual amount of materials; your conspicuous feathers, Jungle, Summer Duck and the like, too large; your long hackled fly too much played; or your pattern too large, too gaudy, or altogether too fanciful. Under any such circumstances, it should be changed for something quieter in tone, smaller in size, different perhaps in type, and not played at all. Reverse the whole process in fact.

After fishing the eddy you pass on to the catches below it; the first of which we will suppose is created by a boulder causing the current to flow from it on both its exposed sides, and making the water "sail back" in its immediate wake. This wake perhaps increases in width until the waters join again. Salmon will not lie behind an obstruction of this sort, but take up their quarters on either side just on the verge of the downward current.

"Ah! there he is, sir," says the gillie, betraying no emotion—moving not a muscle of his wiry frame. "See that 'heads and tails'—no splash, no noise, a sure taker he is. But I say, sir, look at this nasty, drowsy haze coming on ; now we do know what to pick out ! Here's the very thing—a little 'Black Doctor.' Look alive, it's time now, three minutes is always enough. Cast over the middle of the rock, bring your rod sharp round this side of it and lower the point for the stream to catch a bit of line, so that the fly comes in front of the fish at once. He'll have——— bless me, you are hitched up this time! Don't pull, don't pull, stop a second, you'll never get it clear, give me the rod, and just observe how I do it."

It is to be feared that, in these cases, the novice, unaccompanied by an experienced hand, had better choose the lesser of two evils by pulling the line with his hands for the fly to give way or be broken off. I never like losing a fly, but would much rather lose two than my chance of a "heads and tails." But still it need not be supposed, when the fly is merely hitched up in a rock by the influence of the current alone, that it cannot be cast adrift ; for the process of clearing to adopt, though decidedly of a nature calculated to disturb fish, can scarcely fail, provided the line be not pulled beforehand.

The plan is to get the line well over to the farther side of the mischief ; so walk back, letting out as much line as you think you can switch, and, by the usual down-cast, send it out beyond the rock, when it will be taken below by the stream while you make towards the rock. As soon as it has been carried ten to twelve yards, hold on. If the strength of the current itself has not the effect desired, lay aside the rod, and, catching the line in your hands, say three or four feet from the point of the rod, give a sharp, long pull. Should this fail, allow the line to be carried down again while you walk ten or twelve yards below the rock ; wind in spare line and pull as before.

But for the purpose of our programme, let us suppose that the gillie in question cleared the line from the snag, and that in two minutes afterwards the little "Black Doctor" had met with a downright refusal on the part of the fish.

The gillie, let us imagine, was new to the neighbourhood—had only recently been engaged owing to his remarkable success in the South.

"We have," says he, "not done much to boast of in this pool as yet, and the dreams of a good day which we cherished remain dreams still.

Look here, sir, if you won't wade, let me. There are plenty of fish about, but somehow I don't like the way they show themselves. I wonder what's up with 'em; I'll find out before I've been here long. I 'scarce' know the way of the river yet. How rivers do vary! Fish such a pool as this, and no sport! Extraordinary! Is the water falling quickly? No; then what is it? Fly wrong? Can't have a better than a little black one in a haze. Pool out of fettle? Can't be, according to the run of the water. Glass rising—what can it be? Fishing wrong side? No; I always prefer casting from the shallow towards the deep. The fish *might* not have seen the fly; the weather is boisterous enough to make him settle in the very neck of the eddy, so we are safe there. Then there are no big white clouds rolling about. I don't notice any 'muck' in the water. Pollution makes Salmon travel, and those which are not that way inclined rise, but won't take. Nor do I see any trace of Otters. Dismiss the question as unanswerable is an easy way of escape, but that don't suit *me*. Here comes the superintendent, he'll tell us, no doubt."

"Good morning, captain, good morning. Jim, take my dog in the slip and tie him to yonder gate, for in fishing dogs are as bad as Otters. What luck, sir? Goodish day this, and plenty of fish 'going.' Sorry I couldn't be with you before."

"Luck isn't in it my way, MacGregor."

And the captain relates all that has transpired.

"Well," continues the superintendent, "that chap Jim ought to know, else he shan't stop long with me. He seems to have told you right so far. We don't know *everything*, and never shall. Yes, yes, all that seems right, but common sense doesn't look to these matters alone. Jim, just take the cup out of the frail and bring us a sample of the water (tasting). Ah! thought so, by the greyish look of it; this bitter taste is enough for me. Never mind the waders yet; come back with me, I know what's the matter—*it's heather water!* There! There! Look at that caterpillar going down. You must try the 'Heather Dog.' I got this tip from *Land and Water*, and it finds 'em out sometimes, I give you my word. But I say, captain, as the eddy has had such a doing, you'd better have lunch first; besides, the haze seems to be lifting, and that'll help you considerably with this style of fly."

Let the angling reader clearly understand that this picture is drawn from everyday work, so to speak, and may be accepted as a fair specimen of Salmon-angling and the system of procedure. The success of a particular fly on some special occasions is of no uncommon occurrence. As to how the captain hooked, played, and finally secured his fish we will not inquire, for the reason that these matters will be practically treated presently in accordance with my original plan of arrangement. Of course, he waded, or left the bottom part of the pool "maiden"; but this also is a subject I defer.

In reference to streams there is a general disagreement of authorities as to the size of the fly. The little fly theory is, in places, much maligned, whilst the most plausible reasons are advanced in support of the large one. Veritable champions, few though they be, come and catch sulky fish with large sized patterns on those particular occasions when other men have failed; and even then their success is invariably attributed to the *humour* of the fish. This old exculpatory plea will not do at all. Their victory is entirely due to the principle adopted in presenting the large fly. Let us take a case in point.

The man fishing a small pattern in a stream, takes up a position in close quarters with the fish, and I shall explain why very soon. If he be inexperienced in approaching Salmon, his manner alone, as I have before observed, may spoil his chance. It is certain that the untrained novice had better stand back and use a large fly, than wade in and fish with a small one.

Success in either case necessitates a due obedience to the laws of presentation. For instance, a small fly must dwell longer over the fish than a large one. In order to ensure this, wading is imperative. On the other hand, a large fly can often be played properly from the bank, the expert being fully alive to the fact that such a lure in most streams must be worked quickly and not allowed to dwell at all.

It would be manifestly unfair towards brother Anglers who fish after one, to wade in and thrash a stream with a large fly. The mere fact of punishing a stream in this way prohibits the use of a small fly on it, put by the hand of a novice. Fortunately, however, this practice, and others—that for instance of "skimming pools"—is quite the exception and rarely if ever witnessed on other than Association waters, whose list of members, forsooth, sometimes includes the names of persons ever more on the alert for jealous competition than for the enjoyment of true sport.

At all events, before closely examining stream fishing, it must be said that some of these "rippling runs" abound with "tub" catches and may be bordered with one or two eddies. This chiefly determines the choice of flies, their size, and the characteristics of their dressing. The essential difference between a "tub" and an ordinary dip in the bed of a river is this:—A tub catch is always protected at the head by a boulder, immediately behind which, yet in the hollow itself, a fish will lie; whereas in the ordinary dip, arising from some peculiarity in the flow of the water, the unprotected fish will take up its quarters at the tail of the dip rather than on the rising ground. (Salmon will lie on the rising ground when the so-called "dips" are out of all proportion larger than the places which I am alluding to, and lead into very deep channels.) It is an invariable rule with me in fishing "tubs" to mount a small fly, dressed with over-sized Jungle "sides," or well-marked Summer Duck serving the same purpose, and fish foot by foot rather than yard by yard. In the case of fish coming up from deep water, and lying at the very head of a long dip, the size of the fly is not so important as the way it is presented, whilst the question relating to Jungle and Summer Duck does not enter. One wants to fish close, in other words, to take short steps, with a view to getting the fish to come sharp at the fly when he sees it at a distance.

I have always noticed in stream fishing, when the bed is formed of gravel, that the more the district is overstocked with Rods, the more readily well matured fish fight shy of gaudiness, and exhibit a special preference for common looking, plainly dressed flies; and this is, in my opinion, the very reason for so many of our Standards being blessed with so many variations here, there, and everywhere. In unfrequented districts, the very opposite ruling applies to streams of this sort; and, if I mistake not, it was for one of them that "Jock Scott" was first dressed with a blue silk section, and its reputation made at once.

There are circumstances connected with the temperature of the water, its height and colour, atmospherical changes, and the influence of local surroundings—all of which puzzle us now and again, and I desire to urge that these matters must be separately considered in stream and other fishing, else the flies chosen will serve only to catch the eye and not the fish.

It will be apparent that, in the economy of nature, heat and cold play parts of the utmost importance to the Angler, for the disposition of the Salmon is amenable to all climatic vicissitudes. Certainly a rapid change to cold, if taken in time, is not so productive of mischief as in the case of the weather turning suddenly hot. The fish will *cease to show, but not to take;* and it will be found that, for sport, the morning is better than the afternoon. Sudden heat, as I will explain, has a different effect upon them.

Now, the safest principle for the Angler to adopt, according to my experience, is to increase the size of the fly, and decrease the gaudy materials in proportion as the air gets suddenly colder. This is my rule, and it appears to hold good at nearly all seasons of the year. But when the day turns suddenly hot, in which case with a rising barometer Catches, hitherto barren of splashes and rings, show signs of life and animation, the occupants, as a rule, are restless and seem indisposed to look at any fly for the time being. They will leap high out of the water to fall back tail first, flounder sideways to come down with a smack often heard two or three hundred yards away. Still, however much some fish may be thus inclined to revive themselves, it would be quite an error to consider that the difficulty is very much increased in catching others, which, though located in the same pool or stream, are not quite so restless. It may be taken that any sensible degree of rise, as measured by the thermometer, should lead you to adopt widely different plans. You reduce or enlarge the size according to circumstances. For instance, up to the end of March, not once in twenty years will you have occasion from the exigencies of increased temperature alone, to come down more than two sizes. But the change coming in the month of May, when fish generally begin to "sport" is a signal pointing in two directions; (1) to reduce the size of the fly on most rivers by more than one half; (2) to increase (as much as you can in reason) the comparative gaudiness. Once on the Dee, when fishing under such conditions in May, 1895, I came down at one bound from a five-inch hook to a "dress" measuring only three quarters of an inch.

As regards the height and colour of the water the one standard principle applies everywhere:—In high water you use a larger fly than in low, but in the event of discolouration my tactics are these; (1) flaked water, silver bodies; (2) road washings (of any colour), Seal's fur bodies well picked out; (3) porter colour, blue hackle over black body; or a claret body, grey Heron hackle and cinnamon Turkey wings for choice. (These remarks apply more especially to those rivers on which fancy flies are in general use. Nevertheless, on the Spey, where a peculiar variety of the strip winged fly is and has for long been popular, the bright fly system holds good on bright days, though perhaps not to any particular extent in point of gaudiness. The claret (or fiery-brown) body and cinnamon wings is, however, a typical pattern on the Spey for porter-coloured water; and until the summer season, when Cock's hackles take the place of Herons, an almost universal system in the selection of flies prevails for various conditions of weather and water. That is to say, the "Rough Grouse" is invariably reserved for a dark, drizzly day; the "Brown Dog" for a bright day in dark water; whilst the "Purple King" is estimated as being the best general pattern on the river.) In any place, I would impress upon the student the necessity for studying the effect of long hackles. Responsive as they are to the slightest movement of the rod, in the water long hackles are, under proper management, far more telling in still pools and lagoon-like reaches than short ones more or less stiff in fibre. The secret is never to encourage them by movement of the rod to make grotesque and irregular gambols, be the water what it may. Perhaps they are less valuable in "maiden" streams than in other Catches, yet may be the only sort the fish will notice. Many a time have I seen men dwell beside a favourite stream and from want of knowledge put fish down with the short hackled flies to such an extent that nothing but long hackles would stir them afterwards.

This being so, we arrive at the reason of that success which attends the man who comes with a large fly and picks up sulky Salmon to the astonishment of those who have gone before him fishing small. It may be assumed that his whole system differs from that of his innocent predecessors. He had well understood the failure of the small, short-hackled fly, how, amongst other faults, it was played, not with clock-work precision, but by shaking the rod about as though a wasp had settled on the top ring; he stands well away from the fish, aims more across the water than usual, in order that his fly should not unduly dwell over the Catch, and "mends his cast" immediately it is made. Should his fly be of an ordinary type, he uses an extra length of line, *and never plays the lure till it reaches the middle part of the stream.* He uses the ordinary type, and trusts to other principles in his method for those streams which are very open, not a tree or a bank to shelter them, upon every occasion *when the day has grown brighter*, not forgetting to have plenty of tinsel round the body—silver in the morning, gold in the afternoon—and plenty of Grey Mallard, or Teal, or even Summer Duck in the wings.

Of course, there is a limit in all things, and when we say "Use the fly which shows best under certain conditions," the exact signification of the word "best" can only be realised by correct calculations and observations. Flies which look well under a clear sky with the sun behind them look wretched in rain, and yet, as it may now be understood, circumstances sometimes compel us to use them.

In connection with rain, the worst of it is, and the truth of it is, we know very little about the effects of it on fish; but having had my mind directed to the subject, I have obtained a certain advantageous knowledge. I shall, however, make no endeavour to satisfy the exacting demands of the serious student of the problem for a complete exposition of the details—that would be a feat of no mean order for any Salmon-angler. Yet it is certain that rain may either make our fortunes or leave us worse off than before. A good flood in an uninhabited and uncultivated district is invariably favourable to sport in *certain parts of the river;* but a heavy thunderstorm often thickens the water without raising it much, and keeps it altogether out of ply, particularly on slow-running rivers, for many days.

I have known a man fishing in heavy rain under a wood, at that season of the year when the sap rises, plod on and on and never stir a fin; whilst in the open waters above excellent sport was being obtained. My note book told me of this, though I failed to discover any explanation of the fact until after making an exhaustive analysis. From that time I have never missed an opportunity of trying further experiments, and have met with quite sufficient evidence to convince me that this was no mere chance occurrence.

My own theory is that, from the dripping of pine, or juniper, or something else not precisely known to us, an effect of some kind is quickly produced on the fish, and puts them down. We may rest assured that any impure matter which a fall of rain disperses in a river is more harmful than the composition of rain itself. How far a fair artificial sprinkling of chloride of sodium would induce Salmon to rise and take our flies I am not concerned to inquire into; but when Nature herself supplies sea salt by means of rain from the westward ocean, our success in certain neighbourhoods is invariably increased. I say "certain neighbourhoods" from the fact that organic matter exists in the air and rain. In the same way and measure impurities due to budding, as well as to decaying, foliage may do much to cripple or destroy our sport for the time being.

The chief difficulty which I have hitherto met with is my inability to form a fairly approximate idea as to how long it may be before any impurity becomes neutralised. This doubtless could be discovered by chemical auxiliaries, just as it has been ascertained that more sulphates are found inland than by the sea, and that ammoniacal salts are detected in the samples of rain water collected, for instance, in closely inhabited coal districts. In fact, it has been conclusively proved in the North that vegetation ceases when about four grains of acid are found in one gallon of rain water; and, therefore, it is as well for Fishermen not *always* to pin their faith on a good down-fall.

There is much less variation needed in selecting proper flies just after rain than before it.

Fishermen of experience are well aware that we often encounter a rise of water when least expected. One "fresh," sunny day in the North (especially in the months of April and May), and down comes a foot of water, upsetting all one's overnight deliberations and plans. The river has been affected by the melting of snow.

Doctors differ considerably as to the effect of a good dose of snow broth. On one occasion I was requested to arbitrate in the matter, and upon a close examination of the facts and the arguments set forth in writing by the two parties themselves, had to find a verdict in favour of both. The one had formed his opinions from his own experiences of the Dee, the other his of the sister river, the Don. My own knowledge of the peculiarities of these rivers is intimate and of prolonged duration.

I have often met with success on the Dee during a flow of snow broth, but never on the Don, and yet these two rivers empty themselves close to each other.

I may refer here to a curious coincidence which once happened while fishing the Don. There was no snow at the time of any importance. With me sport was at a standstill, whilst the accounts from the Dee were excellent. One day it rained for six or seven hours, but the storm was local and did not extend to the Dee. For several days I watched the state of the weather, and kept up a correspondence with friends in the other district, with the result that I found it varied considerably. Cloudy weather and fogs prevailed with us, while the sun shone brightly on the others. Either of the two former conditions usually tends to quickly lower the temperature of the atmosphere. Even the deposit of dew makes a difference of a few degrees. In my observations I found out that the nature of the soil and the degree to which it is covered by vegetation affects the temperature of the climate, changes it, and spoils sport.

If we carried our thoughts to the sandy deserts of Arabia, we could well imagine that the atmosphere attains a very high temperature owing to the exposed state of the dry ground; but a country overrun with forests, as on Dee-side, is kept comparatively cool, partly by the sun's rays being prevented from reaching the earth, and partly by the abundant evaporation which takes place from living vegetables.

With regard to the statement that temperature is *lowered* by clouds, Fishermen are generally instructed enough to know that the effect is widely different in certain seasons. By intercepting and throwing back the heat which in winter is so abundantly radiated from the earth's surface, clouds tend to preserve a warm temperature.

In summer, the earth receives more heat from the sun that the soil radiates, whilst in cloudy weather the access of the caloric rays to the earth is somewhat obstructed, and our planet is protected from a heat too violent for her needs. The watery areas of the earth are effected under special and highly beneficial conditions, for water being a poor conductor, takes in and gives out heat very slowly—very slowly storing much of it in summer, and very slowly releasing it in winter—with the effect of moderating the cold of the one season and the heat of the other. Thus, too, rivers preserve a much more equable temperature than their banks.

As to the comparatively bad sport on the Don, I am almost convinced that I had hit a clue. In my opinion, the sun was at the bottom of it all, for with me the air was bitterly cold, the water warm. Under those conditions, the sport is never good. But in cold seasons the soil along the valley of the Dee brings more fortunate conditions. It is from 20 to 25 degrees warmer than the surface of the snow above it ; so, of course, the icy chilliness of the water during a thaw is not nearly so perceptible in the one river as in the other.

To resolve the questions which arise from a sudden push of water lessees can erect at a trifling cost, an automatic Water Gauge that registers the exact height of the river they fish. Not once but many times have I made arrangements over night to send friends to that "sure cast," little knowing that in the morning it would be the worst on the whole beat. The unlucky ones would go and thrash away until at length they learnt to the disappointment of all concerned, that the reach had been transformed into barren water, and put altogether out of ply. And, moreover, it has occurred in my own experience to have got up early to make a fly or two for a friend, and afterwards to have directed him to stand on a certain stone beside a stream, cast and bring his rod round and hold it there till the fly fishes on the inner side of the jutting current below—one inch rise in the river or even less, and our joint efforts are vain, for all the "holding" in the world would not cause the fly to cover a Catch of that sort.

All these and other disadvantages are obviated by bringing into use a simple and inexpensive apparatus, which can be made at home and fixed by an angling gillie of ordinary intelligence.

The water gauge is simply a long hollow square box, in which rises and falls the connected corks according to variations in the height of the water. The line, which is of strong gimp, is attached to the corks and runs along on the top of a number of posts, 25 to 35 yards apart, through pulleys. It is also attached to the index plate which rises and falls on the dial in response to the rise and fall of the corks in the box at the riverside. The dial is placed within sight of the windows of your residence.

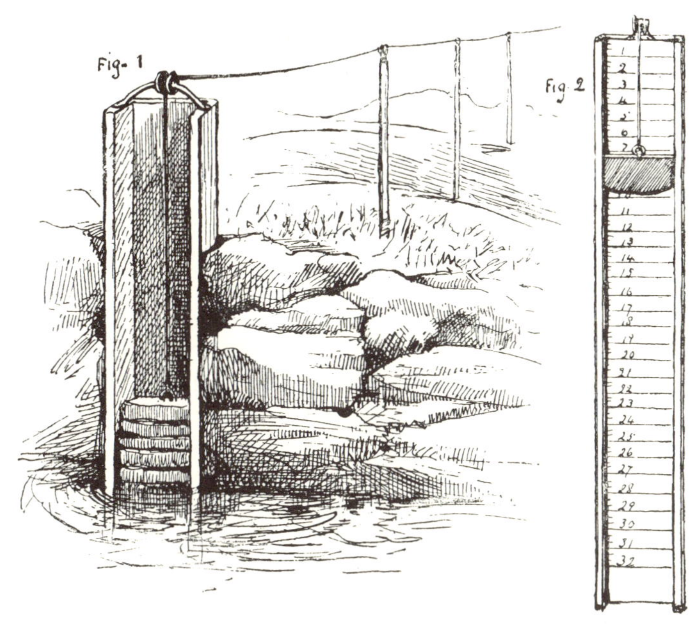

WATER GAUGE.

The box is about 12 feet in length, the inside measurement of which is 12 inches square. It can be put in the water and fixed to the bank; or a hole can be made in the bank for it, and a gully containing a pipe made for the connection. In either case, a hole should be made, so that the box is a little lower than "dead low water" when fixed. The pieces of cork are four in number, 9 inches square and 3 inches thick. These fit on the top of one another, and are fixed together, and weighted at the bottom with layers of lead, the whole to weigh 15 lbs. The gimp is tied to a ring fixed in the middle of the top cork. The box is shown with the front board taken off; the dial, in its natural state. This is merely a fixed upright 7 inch deal, the face of which is painted white: the inches being marked in black figures. Upon each side of this board is fixed a strip of wood, flush with the back and projecting in front, say, $\frac{3}{4}$ of an inch. Upon the front edge of these two strips is nailed another lath, flush with the extreme right and left side of each strip of wood, yet slightly projecting over the face of the dial, and so forming a groove to keep in position the indicating piece of flat lead, which is 5 lbs. in weight. A straight course for the line to play in the pulleys is best, if not indeed necessary. If the pulleys are kept in good working order, the least variation in the height of the water can be detected by glancing at the dial which may be almost any distance in reason from the box in the water.

We will now turn our attention to Flats.

Besides other features of these surgeless reaches to which I will refer presently, Flats always make opportunities for the display of great skill in casting and in killing foul-hooked fish. This is due not only to the smoothness but also to the deepness of the water. Of course, these places vary, but in most cases, unless caused by the wind, the surface is not much ruffled, and unless the fishing is at the head or at the very tail, the water is often too deep to wade, and so in wooded districts a hooked fish cannot be followed up. The general evenness of the *bed of the river* is the distinct feature from which Flats derive their name.

I have constantly noticed in the objectionable change of beat system, which prevails among parties numbering four or five or six, that the "small fish" get fried. The pitiful spectacle presented of a young Angler put down a Flat because it is "his turn," conclusively proves the weakness of the system. Even if he can wade, he cannot command the water with that degree of delicacy about which I would have a word or two to say.

Delicacy, as here used, means not what shopkeepers mean when recommending their fine hooks and lightly dressed flies, but something very different. It has nothing to do with the fly dropping "like thistledown," which in Salmon-fishing is a fad, for the fly should "pop" in, like a falling acorn upon oily waters. The word really denotes the scrupulously light way the *line* should fall, when, in fishing all smooth reaches on calm days, *delicacy* is an indispensable condition of success.

The most effectual means of casting lightly, is to raise the point of the rod by a spring of the wrist just as the line is descending. The very instant the rod is thus handled the point ascends. But this is a knack which requires an immense amount of practice to master.

In writing of Flats, a very much thrashed out controversy crops up and calls to mind many hard struggles with foul-hooked fish. In foul-hooking I have a particularly settled conviction, for there is such a thing as "settled conviction" in piscatory affairs, though the closest observation opens up a long vista of possibilities, and a deal of the non-proven matter must for ever remain mysterious.

Crucial experiments have led me to accept a very good reason for hooking fish foul, and I am not afraid to say that my settled conviction of the subject would take "all the King's horses and all the King's men" to remove. Depend upon this, it happens not from the fly shifting by a sudden sharp curl of water, nor from the method of striking, but from some fault in the fly itself; *it is either too large or is improperly put before the fish*, in most cases.

If he means it, a Salmon will catch a fly in any current easier than a fly is caught by a swallow in a gale of wind; and strike how one will in these reaches, or for that matter, not strike at all, fish are often hooked foul. No, in all smooth waters, a fly cast accidentally *over* fish when the bed of the river is level, or a fly too large or too gaudy, and the chances are they try to kill it with their tail, in which case they often strike the line and get hooked somewhere—not in the mouth. There is indeed, no incident in Salmon-fishing that will more readily convince a man of the importance of studying presentation, light, shade, geological formation, and other local surroundings, than this.

Whatever may be the cause of the dilemma, when his line is run out and the pull-devil pull-baker business (consequent on foul-hooking) sets in, the Angler should resort to certain immediate tactics. Let the reach be what it may, the question of following fish should hardly ever be at all in doubt.*

What is the precise method to adopt in a case of foul-hooking?

There is one golden rule worth noting, and if the fish, hooked in the back or in the belly, can be followed in the water or on the bank it will seldom be lost, provided the Fisherman has a companion. A fairly firm hold should be kept on it till it rises to the surface and lies across the water to be carried down stream by the force of the current. This always occurs when exhaustion sets in. Then, with the rod upright, stand perfectly still and allow the winch to uncoil sufficient line—a hundred yards if necessary—to ensure your being so far above the fish, that in walking on you do not alter its course.

Advance step by step afterwards, never losing the bend of the rod. On arriving at the head of a shallow (frequently found in Salmon rivers) suddenly loosen line, by dropping the point of the rod, when the fish will soon disappear, and as usual face up stream. Should your assistant be without waders, give him the rod and walk into the water well below the fish. Carefully and quietly station yourself, avoiding all dangerous stumbling blocks in the way of big stones coated with muck and moss. As soon as the fish is shown the butt again, its course will direct you to the left or right, and you will be able to use the gaff effectually upon your prize in its floating descent.

If you are alone, in getting in below the fish, you must of course take the rod yourself; but put no pressure on until you are ready with the gaff in hand; then show him the butt in good earnest.

The misfortune of hooking fish in this way is quickly detected by the strange antics they pursue. The fight is usually short, sharp, and severe, the airy somersaults, which would make Blondin sick with envy, are soon exchanged for feeble plunges. In any case, always drop the point of the rod when the Salmon leaps from the water, and bring it back in one movement.

Among other "awkward customers" to deal with in Flats, though less frequently met with, is the "dancer."

* N.B.—Everybody, including proprietors, feels the pinch of hard times, but considering the exorbitant rents, and the small outlay for making a pathway along a wood, or a platform past a deep corner, it is astonishing how tenants bear with easily removed obstructions. Enough is not always done in the interest of Anglers in clearing and making riverside paths, &c.

THE DANCER.

The engraving depicts a memorable fish of about 16 lbs. It is a splendid sight to see these fine fellows get the line taut and fight it out on their tails. This one gave me the hardest tussle I ever had. Sometimes, and, indeed, more often than not, they commence operations by taking across the river, and then sweeping up gently from the water, rest on their tails, and shake their heads in the most violent manner. On these occasions you have once more to break the rule which says, "never let a Salmon have a slack line," for if you fail to do so in good time by dropping the point of the rod, he will break you, as sure as fate.

But do what you may, the odds are very much against success if an abominable snag in the shape of a dead tree is allowed to rest from the shore over the original haunt of the fish half in, half out of water, or if you are debarred from taking him up or down, as I was. You may get the better of him in the open, for in "dancing" he cannot break the tackle when the line is loose, though he will soon make to his corner and claim "foul," and often run foul of the snag. They nearly all do this. After beating mine in the first "round" or two, he did it; and yet he was not happy, for I pulled off a lot of line, switched as much as I could over the water, at least ten yards above the snag, put the point of the rod down on the bed of the river, waited till the sinking slack part had been washed a little below, and then wound up, finding myself in command once again. Not once, but twice did the same remedy bring him up to time. There he would lie and spin round and round on the surface; when all of a sudden, feeling the butt, down-stream he went, "ducks and drakes," over the bough he leapt, back he came to dance in front of me, and—bid me adieu as full of life as ever!

But what about those natural surroundings I was talking of—light and shade and so on?

I have, by the way, really begun to ask myself, with increasing frequency of late, how these things will look in print, disconnected as they are, though as I intended them to be. The arrangement is bad. But the fact remains that, in getting through various topics by the convenient process of division, I have been enabled to bring out the strong points in suitable and fitting places. Had these matters been heaped together many of them might have been easily overlooked. I have written of them as they struck me, and taken care to arrange them in such a way as might give me the prospect of making the whole business clear, intelligible, and easily remembered.

Now of reflection. Side reflection differs materially from that kind of light occasionally produced by white receding rocks high enough to brighten up both sides of the river. If the particular reflector,* whatever its nature be, leans towards the river, a direct glare is cast down close to the mirror, as an elementary study of angles will show. The light, or reflection, is confined to its own side of the river, and is very intense.

This is what we choose to term "side reflection."

Presenting the fly by any of the preceding methods of casting is a hopeless procedure, mere waste of time, and injurious to sport. The Angler must take up a position from which he can pay out the line gradually in a direct line of the fish, and always avoiding sudden effort. As soon as the fly reaches, say, within two yards of the spot, it should be held still for a minute, and then played for no more than another minute.

A degree of uncertainty usually exists with regard to the change fly, for, although fish are extremely sensitive in these resorts and easily frightened away, a second fly should be tried, if not a third. If, however, we are informed by the gillie put to watch the movements of the fish that an "inspection" has been made, our state of uncertainty is considerably reduced. It is not the question of size that should bother us, for all patterns must be very small (No. 6 being considered as the full size), but rather the question of character, colour, and very likely the way the fly should be worked. At all events, we come down immediately in tone, even to using a black body, and we make a thorough change in the style of wing, say, from a built wing to one composed entirely of toppings.

The disposition of the fish to start or move again towards the fly nduces us to mount a pattern having two or three colours in the body, to fish it deeper by the use of shot, and play it in a different manner to that previously adopted.

---

* N.B.—Of course, in speaking of the reflection of an overhanging rock, I have *two reflectors* before me, *e.g.*, the water and the rock. For clearness I shall call the water "mirror" and the object imaged on it the "reflector."

Who, for instance, has not seen a fish seize a fly just as it is being drawn into a strong current from a side eddy—a great secret this in "presentation." The fly cast, say, beyond fish resting on the far side of the current, cannot remain there for long. Do what one may, the intervening stream catches the line, gracefully turns the head of the fly, and gradually increases the pace of it across the catch.

This is a useful lesson to those who are not well versed in presentation.

Where nature fails, art often succeeds. The desirable current is not always there, but the student can, as I have before said, secure the natural and effective movement of the fly, *by working the rod gradually round in front of him.*

However, the Angler fishing alone had better begin operations with a dark silk or Berlin wool body and chance his luck afterwards with the "variegated" body (see Sun fly) made with silks, furs, or chenilles according to the custom prevailing on the river. Silver bodies, black hackles, and plain Mallard wings are very telling when the sun is constantly popping in and out.

The mere brightening up of the water by the sun shining over a bank or a wood upon wet or white rocks which do not throw back rays of light actually into the water, is the signal for decreasing size and increasing gaudiness.

Should the trees overhang and shade the catches on the inner side, a dirty yellow, or a dirty orange body, with a plain hackle at the throat, and with wings composed of Peacock's herl mixed with strands of Golden Pheasant tail, is the kind of fly I invariably use myself.

While directing my attention to Flats, I have learnt that "the sun speaks a language of his own, though no voice breaks the air." To interpret it, we should evoke the whispers of common sense.

Of course, we may strive in vain in our endeavour to collocate all the technical laws which govern the sport, but were a little of the time and thought usually spent in learning the commoner accomplishments of Salmon-fishing bestowed, say, upon the more complex and interesting subjects (for instance, the reflection of light), how many of the so-called "mysteries" would meet with easy explanation, and how much the

Plate 8

Rocke's Grub

The Fairy King

The Mystery

The Little Kelly

St. Bernard

Skirrow's Fancy

Beauly Snow Fly

The Bronze Pirate

pleasure and prosperity of the Angler's life would be heightened and increased.

Besides being very shy, the fish in these places are very sulky when the water is deep; and to render a conflict inevitable, the frequent use of split shot can well be recommended. On these occasions they are, indeed, the greatest labour-saving adjuncts we possess—the amount of sport derived from their employment being far more than commensurate with the labour generally expended without them. And this brings to mind another peculiarity in Salmon that uniformly accompanies the Fisherman on Flats, and is characteristic of them. It may be described as "a fit of the sulks," and nothing more strikingly brings home the utility of patient perseverance and self command than the dexterous delusion and conspicuous conquest of a sulking fish.

I have no record of having killed a 30 pounder in a Flat without first being called upon to cure this tiresome complaint, but of the last thirteen "fits" treated, not one single patient survived to recompense by his presence the pains-taking efforts of another man.

I am still of the opinion that the method adopted resulted in the best "cure" after all. Nor does it require a trained and familiar acquaintance with the handling of our tackle to bring about the desired result.

When all other schemes to release himself have failed, a heavy Salmon seems instinctively prompted to take up his quarters on the bed of the river and there lie, sometimes for hours, still as a mouse. This is called "sulking." There is a belief existing, not only in certain parts of Ireland and Scotland, but also in Wales, that the best means of dealing with this deep-seated policy is to use a "night-cap." I would rather not educate the untutored mind by defining this article, and describing the mode of its application. Suffice it to say that this funnel-shaped scarecrow, though accelerating the battle, maddens the fish by depriving it of the use of the organs of sight, and aggravates it to such an extent that off it will go, at a pace peculiar to the species, against any obstruction in the road—often the opposite bank—when the tackle breaks and the fish retires from sight more dead than alive. It is equally futile to attempt to haul the fish from its haunt; Jumbo himself could not to all seeming have tried the tackle more. But I have moved them by getting below and pulling by the line.

This is known as "hand-lining" a fish. The experiment, however, is not one to recommend the novice to try at any time (except in the absence of the gaff); for it often ends in failure or loss, even with the best of us. Stones and other missiles deserve wholesale condemnation.

The safest and surest remedy is not to disturb the fish in any way whatever, but to put on a good steady strain and bide your time. Get towards him, take up a position that the point of the rod is opposite the tail of the fish and pull sideways, carefully watching the instant he moves for relaxing your efforts.

In this serene situation you patiently sit, and for aught one knows hold your lighted pipe, and a firm grip of the fish simultaneously, till at length it becomes weary and eventually yours.

Beyond the common advantages of other Catches, Flats offer the privilege of successfully running down "travellers." Any observant Angler soon learns for himself that travelling fish almost invariably rest and rise at the very tail of a Flat. Whether the increased aeration of the rapid immediately below works upon them as one would expect, I leave to others to decide for themselves. But we know for a fact that artificial means have been devised, and are used to pump air into bait-cans, such as that exhibited at the "Fisheries," by Mr. Basil Field; and to acquire an idea of the effect of fresh oxygen ascending through the water, as in this instance, during a long day's journey, you may carry baits for coarse fishing, and keep them as fresh and full of life as ever they were.

It is not the mere fact of a Salmon resting and rising in these places to which I would alone call attention, but rather to the ready way a fish will take a fly on reaching them, and to the singular opportunity they afford a recruit to "flesh his maiden sword."

On the tail of a Flat you really may shake up your flies in a hat and choose the first that comes to hand. Of course, I allude only to ordinary standard patterns, and not to "specials" or "exaggerations." And, as to size, here again I should consider that no man would mount a Tay fly, say, on the Lochy or Ness.

Now we come to Rapids; and perhaps the most difficult thing to detect and the easiest to deal with is the "stone-grubber." In any other

Catches, stone grubbing can be immediately recognised; the sensation reminds one of a terrier shaking a rat; but in rapids the action of the water upon the tackle often misleads a man by producing a similar impression. The object of this manœuvre of the fish is to break the hook, by knocking it backwards and forwards against a boulder. Experience

MR. L. J. GRAHAM-CLARKE, AT CRAIGLLYN, WYE.
To show the position for playing a heavy fish in a rapid.

has confirmed the conviction that disaster will follow the application of strain; the line therefore should be, at once, considerably slackened, when the fish will quickly move away. Should you succeed in banking a "grubber" you will find the hook inserted in a bone or very close to one.

It is chiefly owing to this circumstance that I recommended double hooks for these situations. Never once has a "stone-grubber" beaten me when thus appointed. In saying this, I am fully alive to the fact that other authorities will disagree with me. Only yesterday (12th August, 1893), I read an article in a London paper, wherein the writer seemed satisfied of their superiority, but condemned them altogether for use in rapids.

In my opinion, any hook improperly managed will "skirt" or make an objectionable fuss in rapid water. Holland's hooks, made by William Bartleet and Sons, are the least likely to do so, whilst in untutored hands double hooks are certain to "skirt"; and, in rapids, this defect would be noticed directly. But let the reader understand that, the places where the expert himself would be puzzled to use a double-hooked fly correctly, are the very places in which the fish never rest.

Times out of number have I been driven to cast beyond a Salmon lying in the wake of a boulder, and on seeing the fly "skirt" have "mended the cast," lowered the point of the rod, letting it go forward instead of holding it still, and so succeeded in presenting the fly to the fish, in a way, which, at any rate, gave *me* satisfaction. But I take this as a very insignificant detail in comparison with others bearing on the question of Rapids, as, for instance, "garreting." I will briefly explain and deal more fully with the subject in the next chapter.

Rivers are "garreted" (as it is called) for the purpose of forming artificial catches. (The term "catch," so written, differs from a Catch or Cast which may contain several "catches," "lay-byes," or "holds." It denotes a certain spot, or place, in which, according to its dimensions, one or more Salmon will rest for a time as they ascend the river.)

These "garrets" are often constructed with piles shod with iron, boarded in front, and backed up with large stones by way of extra support. The angle at which the piles are driven entirely depends upon the force of water in flood time. For example, if put too slanting, the object desired, which, obviously, is to wash out a portion of the bed of the river below and create a holding place, would be defeated, let the bed of the river be what it may, unless the current is sufficiently strong for the purpose. Much, however, depends upon the bed of the river. If formed of gravel, an angle of 40 degrees might suffice; if of boulders silted up, 50 degrees may be necessary. Again, the length of the garret has to be determined. With a straight flow of water, in the absence of any small bank eddies, five yards, measuring from the outward pile straight across to the bank, is the average distance. But I have hardly ever seen garreting rapids done by any process that led to good results. And although I have seen the experiment tried, it has usually ended in failure, sometimes in disaster.

Artificial Catches, when properly constructed, are quite as useful for angling purposes as those formed by Nature. When improperly made, they not only involve a waste of time and money, but are apt to completely spoil other Casts below them.

There are other means than garreting to make artificial catches. For instance, in gravelly streams, the Salmon, though present, will not rise to flies when the water falls below a certain height. A boulder weighing about 3 cwt. dropped from the stern of a punt into the middle of the current will soon make a sure "rise." Much larger ones are not nearly so efficient. Half a dozen such places could be formed in this way in streams 50 yards in length, but it is desirable to put the boulders in a zig-zag line. Behind each one, for a distance of two and a half to three and a half yards, the gravel will be washed out, and so, of necessity, deepen the water; and, in one or two days, or as soon as each stone gets silted up a little, the fish will take to them.

I have a particular object in view in referring just now to various changes in the beds of rivers, for they sometimes lead to the most fantastic results.

The ancient sites of many towns and villages in Yorkshire, for instance, are now occupied by sandbanks in the sea. Among these the Ravenspur is, perhaps, the most conspicuous example. This seaport town, formerly of such importance that it was a rival to Hull, has been altogether swept away, and nothing is now to be seen of the site it occupied, save extensive sandbanks, which are daily covered by the waves, though still visible when the tide recedes. The coast of Elgin also affords a striking example of the "sand-flood," as it is not improperly termed.

Great alteration is traceable upon some rivers inland, as witness the Spey. Along the valley of this glorious river, once famed for its purity, the geologist meets with many tracts formerly occupied by its waters.

I wonder whether there was any garreting in those days! Be that as it may, whatever may have been the cause in ancient times for any such changes as these, whether by subterranean disturbances or by subsidence, I have with my own eyes seen two of the best pools a man could wish for, silted up and absolutely ruined by an attempt to garret a rapid, and I wish to emphasise this story.

Once while watching some boulders as they thundered down stream in a growing flood, I witnessed a sight never to be forgotten. In less time than it takes to write about it an increasing pile of boulders hitched up in a garret at the head of a rapid and backed up the waters until they struck off at a sharp angle, cutting through the banked up stones alongside, and forming through them a new, navigable channel.

Suddenly, as the river rose, the mass washed away. Two or three days afterwards, the flood having receded, the new watercourse could not be traced, for the bank of stones had assumed its normal condition, and not a vestige of the threatened mischief remained.

If left to themselves, in the absence of obstruction by artificial agency, rapids rarely spoil fishing, or create any mischief in other respects. But it is not too much to say that, in his endeavour to improve the fishing by means of garrets, the inexperienced workman should never be trusted.

The safest places for these constructions are unquestionably those broad reaches frequently met with which have remained for years in an unaltered condition—reaches invariably shallow and barren of fish. And the best spots in them are those in which a huge boulder, raising its head well out of the water, renders the undertaking not only easy, but safe.

One of the most noteworthy schemes for fishing rapids is by that known to me as the "hinged platform." No one will deny that this little stage is simplicity itself and a great convenience. It can either rest upon iron feet, or upon an outstanding rock or boulder, and let down for use and raised afterwards by means of a rope running through a pulley fixed on a tree or on a post at a suitable angle.

In the absence of this contrivance, and in places which, perhaps, are not more than 18 inches in depth, the "Body-belt" provides the only means of fishing wild waters dancing between the rocks in downhill rapids. The sense of safety that always comes in using it inspires one with a feeling of the utmost confidence.

"Upon my word," writes a well-known Fisherman who is just now trying mine, "I feel safer than I ever did in wading before; but I ought to tell you that the first time I tried I was washed off my legs. This was entirely my own fault, as I forgot to follow your directions."

The belt is best made of similar material to that used for saddle girths. It buckles round the waist and fastens in front. A ring is fixed in the centre at the back, through which a fairly strong rope passes, forming a pair of reins. The Angler puts the rope round a tree or a post and lets out rope as he moves down-stream. It is a sure means of support, provided *the Fisherman leans forward*; but if he allows his legs to get in front of him—in other words, if he leans back, the force of the current may wash him "off his legs," as in the instance of my correspondent.

Open rapids can be covered without casting a very long line, as this kind of water generally pursues a course through narrow channels of the river. In fishing the fly, the great secret is to locate oneself as much as possible in front of the "catches," so that the fly may be brought across them at any pace the Angler thinks best. But when, by force of circumstances, he is driven to let the fly travel fast, the size of it should be considerably increased.

Sometimes we encounter narrow fast-running waters shut in between rocks. As a rule, the Catch is situated in the tail of the rapid where the water is usually very deep and "oily" on the surface. Upon such occasions as these, when it is well-known that the fish rise in a perpendicular manner at the fly, the method of presenting it differs from the orthodox fashion. The cast is made in the usual way, but, in playing the fly, instead of the motion of the rod being of a steady backward and forward character, it is a quick up and down movement. The point of the rod vibrates with a rapidity of beat equal to about double that of a man's pulse. It is not held pointing to where the fly fell, but is brought round at a pace corresponding with that of the fly in its course, the up and down movement being continued throughout. This compels the fly to describe an arc of a circle; and if the Angler takes very short steps—no more than twelve inches at a time—the fish lying immediately behind an upright rock are more apt to rise in twenty feet of water as soon as they see the lure thus played than by adopting any other method.

Of course, if a very long line is necessary, the system fails to have any effect upon the fly at all; and to meet the case, the line is seized just in front of the winch and pulled rapidly backwards and forwards while the fly is crossing the water.

We have yet another important matter to bear in mind in connection with fishing places of this latter description. As soon as the fish has taken the fly he does not turn, but rather drops his head and goes down as he came up—perpendicularly. Unless the Angler strikes at once, the fish disappears like a bubble in the palm of one's hand, leaving behind only the damp of disappointment.

I remember accompanying the late Lord L—— to a pool on the Beauly, which I was myself fishing in 1893.

"Well, have you got 'em?" he shouted inquiringly from the top of the rocks to a friend engaged in the "Mare's" Catch.

"No, had five rises though, but missed every one."

"Wind up and wait till I come down," was urged in reply, and that, too, by one of the best Salmon-anglers it has ever been my privilege to meet.

On reaching the bottom and learning how matters stood from "Auld Allan"—a servant with then 40 years or more experience, and who yet lives to relate the story himself—directions were given to strike directly after the rise.

"I never strike my fish, but—"

"Then you'll never catch 'em here, that's certain," Lord L—— remarked in a friendly tone.

But a promise to try the experiment was given, with the result that three Salmon soon lay on the bank before us. Others, I forget how many, were secured afterwards.

For the rest, there is very little that calls for particular notice in rapids. Our attention will now be directed towards matters relating to fishing generally, and of these I purpose dealing first with the question of *striking* Salmon. Let us then ask ourselves once more the object we have in view at the time when a Salmon rises and takes the fly. Our object, surely, is to hook the fish with as little risk as possible.

This branch of our subject is so important that I shall venture to intrude on the reader with various opinions and experiences—my own and those of others. In judging which system to follow, let him examine closely into the principle of it, and let him be guided by the one that best answers the scientific conditions of a rigid test.

The operation of *striking* is conducted somewhat blindfold. What chance, then, would a man have of tearing the flesh of a fish who conducts the operation when holding his line and applying just the same power for a Salmon coming towards him as for one turning down-stream, against the man whose very principle secures for him absolute immunity from all such danger, no matter whether he uses very much power or only just enough?

The reader will form his own estimate of these things. At the same time, I feel bound in these pages to recommend the system I adopt myself from the simple fact that, after years of practice, it has proved by far the most remunerative and economical both in time and tackle.

Much has been said and written of striking Salmon. We have had ardent votaries of no striking, of strong striking, and of modified methods. Of the no strikers I say nothing, considering them out of court, beyond conversion, outside argument, and of that honest perversity of the twelfth juror who damned the other eleven "obstinate asses" who would not agree with him. Of the strong strikers and the moderates, it is, perhaps, best to think that ambiguous language is accountable for most of the differences which separated them during the wordy contests that have filled so many newspaper columns.

In point of fact, I have not observed in practice much difference in the striking manners of my friends, amongst whom are open advocates of the strong and moderate fashion of embedding the hook. What the strong striker practised and advocated as "strong," the moderate striker practised and advocated as "moderate"; and the very mildest-mannered Angler seemed, when he *felt* the fish, to "put the iron in" with as much vigour and bitter purpose as the good fellow who blustered for *strength* in half a dozen sporting papers.

Unless one sees what takes place it is impossible to be certain what a Salmon has done in taking your fly. At least, it is generally impossible to form an exact conclusion, and so act on it as to send your message through rod and line to the hook in his mouth *before you have felt him.* Then is the time to put the barb home. Human nature instructs us to do so, just as instinct tells us to pull up a stumbling horse than leave it to take its chance of falling.

Frankly, I never came across that sweet, gentle creature that hesitated to "raise his rod" at the golden moment when he felt the fish.

Five and forty years ago that fine Irish Angler, "Ephemera," wrote: "My general rule is not to strike at a Salmon until I feel him."

And this is mine, too, with these further conditions, namely, when a fish makes a long rush at a fly and remains stationary; when he takes me on the edge of a sharp-running stream and just wriggles sideways into an eddy; and when he seizes the fly and I know that he comes on with it towards me. On these occasions I never wait for him to turn. No. 1 happens in the Spring of the year in still, bright water; No. 2 occurs in very hot weather; and we meet with No. 3 at any time with a very large fish. In each case it comes to downright skill in striking at the proper moment, for in the next the fish will be gone—not because he breaks the tackle, for if he is not "hit," he will not have had the opportunity of testing it.

In continuing the paragraph, "Ephemera" suggests that every man is nervous at the beginning of the year, and asks the oldest among us whether they do not lose many a fish by their "precipitation in striking."

The question, be it said, was put in those days when the old-fashioned winches were in use, and the dismal practice of holding the line prevailed. In these days such an idea would never enter a man's head. If Anglers, either young or old, are worried with weak nerves, I rather fancy they would err, not so much in proceeding with blind haste, but in using unnecessary strength. And yet any such error as that would, as I say, make no difference whatever under the principle of striking which I uphold, for I have never seen the tackle broken yet or the hooks make much of a tear. Of course, if a man strikes *too* soon, be the principle what it may, his chance would be at a very low premium indeed.

Next comes a very pretty idea which "Ephemera" modestly declines to account for.

"I frequently strike," says he, "and hook fish without, as far as I can conceive, any premeditation or calculation, but almost by instinct. Something—I cannot tell what—tells me that a fish is 'at' me, and consequently I am promptly at him in the sly way he has come at me."

I make a low bow to Ephemera—who, indeed, would not? but as to "cannot tell what," I am strongly of the opinion, he had in mind "that boil," which, breaking the surface yards from one's fly rarely escaped his notice and gave him the hint.

Some authors seem to consider that the most dangerous moment is in striking. This is all very well; but they go on to say that "it requires much patience to use just force enough to bury the barb without tearing the flesh or breaking the gut trace." What better evidence could be offered of the incompleteness of the method originally in vogue? The old form of winch demanded far more caution in the Angler than those at the hand of modern men. I also take exception to the statement, "sometimes I am lucky—sometimes very unlucky." In connection with striking, there is very little room for luck and not as much for argument as people have contrived to make out. Nor do I think it quite fair by the fish for an Angler to fancy himself out of luck when his fly is only *partially* taken; there is a reason for the failure of its attempt to take hold. A Salmon does not miss his aim. The fly from some cause or other has probably made him shy; his inclination has, however, already been tested; and, had the fly been of a different sort, or size, or put in a different way, the fish *might* have taken it into his head, figuratively speaking, to "gobble" it up, instead of "nibbling" at it. How often, under favourable conditions of water, have we not felt that "nip," and merely "rugged" the fish in consequence! Is this, then, bad luck or bad judgment? I hesitate to enumerate those days "when fish are shy," or to blame them for want of boldness, for when the water has settled, I have often but not always found by subsequent trial that the fly was too large or wrongly put. I do not overlook the fact that when Catches are either very high or have fallen below a certain size, fish often rise and touch the fly, yet cannot be made to take it, use what pattern you may.

"I have often landed a fish so slightly hooked," says one gentleman, "that, had I struck, the hold must have given way." Just so, if the writer means "struck with violence,"—but, for all that, by my method of striking, the flesh is never torn, and so the chances in one's favour are inevitably increased.*

Another remarks :—"A fish very often rises at a fly with his mouth wide open, and if he is struck at, the chances are that the fly will be snatched away before he has time to close his mouth on it, which he might have done if the hand had been held steady."

With the aid of binoculars I myself watched the habits of Salmon in this respect for many years. Sometimes they came with a rush, at other times quite gently. In the former case, what I saw would be of no practical value here, for as a matter of fact I saw next to nothing ; but I have *never once seen a fish come slowly* with his mouth shut, or fail to close his mouth on taking the fly.

Precipitation in striking has already been discussed.

In placing upon record some unusual success on the Tweed, another writer observes :—"For two hours I never saw so many fish hooked and lost. But the Angler was somewhat successful, as he caught four, 15½ lbs., 16½ lbs., 19½ lbs., and 21½ lbs. in weight. It is the system I am anxious to write in praise of."

The "system" evidently meant the system of striking; and I fail to see where the praise comes in, with such an acknowledgment of fish lost.

Next I read :—"Many a time have I seen my fly drop out of the fish's mouth, the moment he was gaffed."

How, I would ask, can a fly *drop* out, after the usual battle, unless the flesh is torn, or, the barb broken?

I hope I am not wearying the reader by these quotations and opinions, my object is purely to instruct, or rather to convince the novice as to the

* N.B.—A Frenchman wrote :—"There are clowns who kiss their sweethearts with brutality a gallant gentleman will kiss his foe with delicacy."

value of the method which I adopt myself; and I think the explanations given of these cases, emanating from men of whom one or two have fished almost as long as I have, will tend to further that end. One gentleman considers it to be "a very bad habit" to strike a Salmon at any time. It is a curious fact, but his is not the only individual case in which I have had the opportunity of directly judging for myself. "Halloa!" I once said to my friend whom I had been closely watching unperceived. "You hit him pretty hard that time; whatever you *think* you do, if you do not strike I never yet saw the man who does." "Bless me," said he, "who thought of seeing you! Ah, ah! come down here and I'll show you something as soon as I have this fellow on shore." I went, to see my greatest opponent fishing with *my winch and a double hooked fly*. How mellow that whisky of his tasted!

Let us pass to the next opinion which runs:—"When striking from the winch—especially when fishing with large flies, if the winch is not a very stiff one (which to me is an abomination)—a sufficient strain on the line cannot, in my opinion, be available to fix the point of the hook over the barb; and when striking with the line tightly grasped between the hand and the reel, the sudden jerk and strain on the line is apt to leave the fly in the fish's mouth, or smash the top of the rod; also the fly will be often snatched away before the fish has had time to take hold of it, which may scare him to such a degree that he will not rise again."

I can scarcely keep from my mind the idea that the writer, in this instance, was joking. Still, here is the judgment of a successful Angler, and I shall say no more than sufficient to place my experience of these matters along with his and others for the reader's consideration. I need not institute a comparison between a stiff and a free running winch just now, for this, together with the crucial and exhaustive test of the particular strain "available to fix the point of the hook over the barb," must obviously form part of the material to work upon, in presently explaining my own ideas of the best methods of striking. But with regard to the fly being left in the fish's mouth—well, this is just one reason that induced me to work out that method. Of a different order is the following address, which strikes the key note of the new method and raises a point in the argument of the utmost importance. "By attending to Mr. Kelson's instructions," says one who knows the advantage of the method, by long practice, "I find it absolutely impossible to break the gut or line, or strike too hard. The strike should be a long, firm, steady pull, but not a jerk. Trout, grilse, sewin, and other species of the *salmonidæ*, will instantly reject an artificial fly unless struck, and *my impression is, Salmon will do the same.*"

Then the Editor, himself an enthusiastic Fisherman, takes up the cudgels, and amongst other matters of my method gratuitously remarked :—"It is an infinitely better plan than striking with the line held fast—a number of Anglers have thanked us for suggesting the system."

Now, in this contradictory business there must be a right and a wrong. In the opinion of a few, the practice of striking is a mistake altogether. Others insist they lose more fish when the practice is ignored, and are satisfied that it is an imperative necessity. And, whilst many complain bitterly of the losses sustained by the old methods of holding the line, they yet sing praises in favour of the new, by which they meet with neither failure nor loss of tackle.

In the light of these facts, it would appear there are two sets of Anglers, whose opinions upon this vital question are widely divergent ; and although I have in the past pages frankly expressed my own views, it is well, in such a volume as this, to ventilate the views of opponents. It is evident that one side wishes you to believe that it is unnecessary to strike at all, and that if you do, you will lose tackle ; but it does not say how many fish get away by leaving them to hook themselves. The other side tell you the fish *must* be struck, that if not, many will drop the fly after taking it, and that if you adopt the new method you never break the tackle or tear the flesh of the fish, and so get many more to the gaff.

The former school I know get some fish ; the latter, three times as many. But in the very constitutions of these two sides there is an infinite variety. What is wholesome in fishing and what is the reverse, are two different things, and must be estimated accordingly. The "pull," for instance, and the subject of presentation, which, as foreign ingredients were poison to one side, is food to the other. Not a tittle of evidence have we from that man who can say :—"I have tried Kelson's plan, it's all humbug and I'll prove it." Anglers must not suffer from off-hand decisions, any more than from belief in the old fetish, which, despite the losses and failures of the vast majority, a few of the surviving ancients keep alive. It is a pity that all the facts concerning the failures and successes of each side are not honestly tabled; and that it is not satisfactorily settled what constitutes a strike and what does not. Obviously in such a matter as this, sound practical knowledge is worth propagation.

Truth, be it said, is established not so much by what men say as by what they prove; but still, I should like to call attention to an early experience of my own in view of briefly pointing out to novices the mistaken zeal of devotees to the old system and showing the real value of the new.

In the autumn 1882, when my Patent Lever Winch was first tried, I managed to get with it no fewer than ninety-one Salmon without a single one having its flesh torn at the hold.

Do not such results as these serve to prove that with this winch the *tear* does not take place at the moment of striking, and, provided subsequent operations are decently performed, that it never occurs at all? However, by adopting the method made easy by this winch, I have reduced in a remarkable degree the proportion of fish that used to escape my "iron" gripe.

At this point I should like to ask one question :—Has it not happened to you and to your friend, in point of fact to all who traipse up and down a Salmon river, to be startled by that well-known "tug" when least expected, when all hope, as it were, had been dead within you? In one flash, while the thoughts are wandering, you saw, or rather felt, that it was too late to strike and likewise knew that you had missed a chance! What do you say to that! But never mind, let it pass. We all know that what is past help is past grieving for.

By this time the reader will have formed a pretty true estimate of my ideas, all of which, I need hardly say, are based on similar experiences to those just recorded. They shall be carefully explained after bringing forward one matter which, being the worst enemy to our cause, must not be overlooked.

I admit to the full that, where there is no principle of personal benefit opposing it, the voice of the people interested in Angling questions ought to prevail. But the difficulty that faced and still faces us in the solution of this great problem is to clear the atmosphere of certain influences arising from the filmy foundation of guesswork or business interests. If we can do this—it is all I intend to say on the point—we may be very sure that the opinions of authorised men will meet with warmer fervour in Angling circles than has yet been accorded to them.

Now, as a general rule, the safest and surest way of securing a fish and, at the same time, of avoiding the infliction of such a wound as will render the hold of the hook uncertain, is, in my judgment, to strike from the Lever Winch *in all cases* in which the hook used does not exceed 2/0 in size. That is my opinion. But as individual opinion may or may not count for much, let us take an illustration with which many old hands are familiar from prolonged practice themselves.

We have, for instance, two noted rivers—the Lochy and the Ness—on which the very smallest double-hook flies are used. On both these rivers it is the practice to *strike*. Then we have other waters, on which the custom prevails of first using these tiny flies, not on Salmon, but on Trout tackle. What is the result in each case? With the Salmon tackle, Anglers strike and get their fair average of fish, while, on the other hand, striking with fine drawn gut is altogether impracticable. If a man strikes with it, the fish breaks "everything" instantly. The Angler has, of necessity, to run his chance of the fish getting hooked, *and his chance is a very poor one five times in six.*

Striking from the winch is to let the line have free play between the winch and the hook. In other words, the line is not held by the fingers as was the original practice during the operation. This method of striking can only be achieved by the use of a proper winch, the lever of which the Angler can regulate at his will. For rapid waters, the lever should be so adjusted that the line will not overrun itself when drawn out swiftly by the hand. For quieter currents it should be set somewhat tighter—so arranged that, in the hands of the most severe critic, the winch could not be said to be "stiff." It requires very little practice to secure the desired degree of the pressure of the lever, and that is the only precaution needed.

As already mentioned, it is of no importance should the Fisherman strike a little hard, for the reel-plate will revolve when the hook or hooks have taken hold, and so prevent any breakage of tackle. He would do best, perhaps, not to be misled by the term strike to *jerk* the rod, but, in elevating it, to give a short, upward spring of the wrist.

When the Angler is compelled to use a hook in excess of size 2/0 he must hold the line in slow-running waters, and strike from his fingers, in order to drive in the hook over the barb.

The reason why I recommend striking from the winch where it is practicable to do so, is that the force exerted is far better regulated by the resistance of the properly-adjusted lever than it can be even by an expert's muscles. Upon numberless occasions have I noticed that, bar accidents in playing, the hooks remain intact. In playing, sometimes a fish is too severely handled; the line may be hitched up in a "snag"; the fish may run down a weir; but the flesh is never torn, provided no inordinate pressure is put on at dangerous intervals. The reader will better understand this presently.

By the method I have recommended, a Salmon, when fairly hooked, is hardly ever lost; it either gets off at once, which shows it has been merely "pricked," or is brought to bank barring other accidents over which the Angler has no control. No man, for instance, can help heavy fish running up-stream, and sometimes it is impossible to keep pace with them. Only the other day I had one quite a hundred yards above me; but I took good care to give him his head. Had he turned and come full-swing down the river and passed me—here is the point—the chances are the line would have caught up among the boulders. In such circumstances the hooks would hardly remain intact.

I have now only to remind the novice of one other fact. He will remember that, in presenting the fly to the fish, the rod is to be at a certain angle down-stream during the process, for if the rod is held up in the air, he cannot make that "long, firm, steady" strike, which would assuredly imbed the hook without tearing the flesh of the Salmon, or even that of the tender-mouthed grilse.

But it is one thing to hook a Salmon, and quite another to get it. How, then, should we proceed in that direction?

Playing a fish is one of the delights of an Angler's experience. It calls for patience, coolness, activity, and keen perception.

Gaffing a fish when it is exhausted is exceedingly simple, and no part of our business requires less practice. We will take these subjects together.

The first thing to be done on hooking either a Salmon or grilse which keeps below the surface of the water is to hold the rod in its raised position, and while so doing, to slightly loosen the lever of the winch. This is the work of a moment, and so easy in itself that all instruction is dispensed with in this book.

The next thing to be done is to get on shore (if wading) as quickly as possible and to keep in command as much as possible. By this I mean, never to allow the fish to get away far up-stream* above you; always to follow him down-stream; and in the event of his taking across the water, to station yourself a little above him, holding the rod high in the air in order to avoid the line from bellying too much in the strong current.

It is not always on hooking a Salmon that one can immediately form an idea of its weight. A large fish, for instance, will reserve its strength for a time; and even for the space of several minutes will appear little better than an inanimate substance. But the strain of the rod, though moderate in degree at first, soon tells, and the fish will give vent to its fury in grand impetuous runs and bursts. On the other hand, a small Salmon will often make off hurriedly down-stream, and lead you to suppose he is "that monster" which you have been so anxious to catch.

But it would be idle to speculate as to the precise treatment that may be required in either case; the Angler is towed along by events and deals with facts as they present themselves. Rest assured there will be plenty of matter for consideration, and probably I am not far wrong in asserting that the first cause for anxiety will proceed from "the leap for life." In this instance, however, the Angler already understands the absolute necessity of slackening line by dropping the rod point as quickly as possible, and instantly recovering it when the plunge or somersault is

* N.B.—Although turning a fish's head down-stream that he may be choked quickly is an advantage to be got best when he is above the Angler, dangers resulting from that position are so grave and numerous that I cannot recommend it being sought for.

over. He is also prepared for a "fit of the sulks," as I have termed it elsewhere, as well as for a "stone-grubber" and a "dancer."

Perhaps the chances of success are more remote in the case of a Salmon which, having run up or down stream, makes directly towards the Angler. In these circumstances the object is to recover slack line. Every available precaution should be taken in this, especially at those Catches where the bed of the river is rendered foul by rocks or boulders. Sometimes I hasten towards the "slack," so as to wind in line as fast as possible. If, however, the ground on land or in water is shallow and free from obstruction, it is better to walk back into the field, straight away from the fish, and reel up with all possible speed. The next dangerous moment in one's endeavour to prevent the flesh being torn comes when the fish starts off again, puts his head down and his tail up, making good use of it by "smacking" the line as he goes. Held lightly, and he will soon give up this "kicking."

Let me deal with another source of danger. It so happens, and not unfrequently either, that, manage a wild fish how one may, the line will catch in something or other quite on the bed of the river. I am talking now of a fish running down-stream. The plan is to get above the unlucky spot, letting out line, and the moment the run terminates, with the upper hand holding the rod and line, pull quickly from the winch a few yards, raise the rod, and switch the line out beyond the mischief, when the chances are that you will very soon find yourself in command again. It is only too well known that some people will stand and pull at the part caught up, and the best advice I can think of to give is that classical hint vouchsafed to persons on the brink of matrimony—"Don't."

The one great thing to bear in mind is "*to be easy with him in his frantic movements*," and to show him the butt, putting on pressure gradually, when the usual signals of distress exhibit themselves. And should circumstances prohibit you at any time from following your fish while the line on the winch is running short, to fearlessly and suddenly drop the point of the rod; for remember the more you pull at "a runaway horse" the more he "gallops."

The student will not fail to remember this expedient in the case of a fish showing signs of taking down a fall or a weir, or making for a snag.

Although *gaffing* an exhausted fish is an extremely simple business, in this, as in all other matters, there are many ways, of which one is undeniably the best.

The motto I adopt is that of the poacher, for, short and simple as it is, it contains the whole philosophy of the matter—"Gaff him and get him." From that man of metal and determination I learnt nearly all that can be learnt. He *makes* opportunity rather than takes it, and not without immediate advantage to himself. As a gillie he is slow to act when haste is not imperative, but swift and prompt on emergency.

Of the many ways advocated, the usual one directs you to "wait and put the gaff in the shoulder of the fish," but exception must be taken to this notion, if only by reason of the frequent disappointments it inflicts upon Anglers. No good purpose can be served by invariably waiting for such a favourable opportunity. Such advice seems to me to be an elaborate practical joke. As soon as the hook has lost its hold and the fish wriggles away from sight and danger, there shall you behold the man *who waits*, and a pretty object he is truly when he has had his chance and lost it, and stands contemplating vacancy with a philosophic gaze!

Nevertheless, *Prudence* must be the watch-word of the gaffer in attendance. For instance, he must be most careful to avoid too close acquaintanceship between the gaff and the fishing line. He must keep out of sight of the fighting fish. He must finally plant himself on a favourable spot where the deed may be most safely accomplished, and, without delay stoop or sit down, holding the gaff deep down in the water, *for it matters not one jot whether the gaff be used from below or above the fish.*

The preliminaries over, the duty of the Angler is not to haul the tired fish directly towards the gillie, but to bring it broadside on, and to gently lower the point of the rod at the very moment "that bold stroke, which should never fail," is given.

At that very moment, the expert gillie will reveal to spectators the one great secret of ultimate success, which is this. The instant the gaff is inserted, *the wrist must be turned* to prevent the fish taking undue liberties. If it is heading towards the bank the back of the gaffer's hand is sharply turned towards *the head of the fish*; if heading *from* the bank, the back of the hand is as sharply turned *towards its tail* and then the gaff holds hard and fast. And, with the remark that the fish should be immediately dragged *in* the water and not lifted *out* of it, but little more need be said on the subject.

We have, however, yet to consider the *modus operandi* of the unattended Angler. To this particular class, I myself belong, when lumbago (which offers considerable impediment to free action) does not trouble me.

My two-foot-two gaff is all I require, though sometimes, but not often, I find occasion for the other joints belonging to it. The ring (seen in the illustration) is hooked on to a swivel, which is sewn on to the top of the waders under the left elbow.

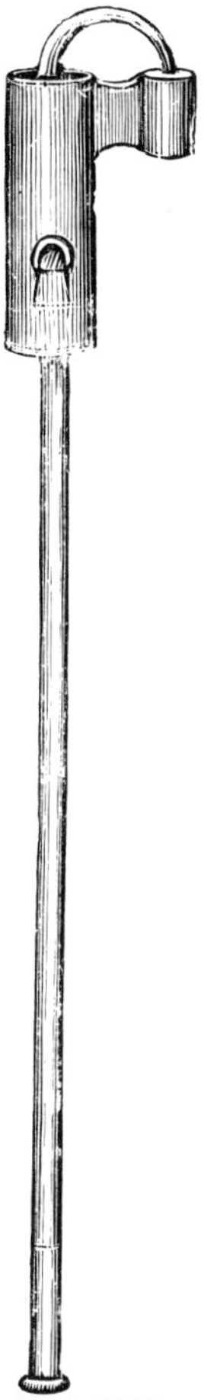

In my opinion, this is by far the best contrivance for carrying the gaff. Here we have a double piece of *thick* leather, forming a sheath $6\frac{1}{2}$ inches long, $4\frac{1}{2}$ broad at the head, the two sides of which are closely and firmly sewn together. The face is a hollow tube (for the point of the gaff) about the size of a two-shilling piece, into which is fitted a champagne cork enlarged in bulk, by previous soaking in water. A tack is fixed through the leather and into the cork on each side of the tube, out of the line of the gaff-point, to keep the cork firmly in place. There is the gaff and the $6\frac{1}{2}$ in. leather socket through which the handle passes. At bottom is a button with a slot across its head. This button is made of steel or brass to fit into steel or brass sockets which are fixed at each end of the thin malacca handle. Steel is decidedly the most reliable and the most durable. For the sake of balance it is necessary to attach the little "dee" (a sort of half hoop, as used in dog collars, and in shape like the letter D), so as to measure $2\frac{3}{4}$ inches from the top of its round head to the bottom of the leather sheath. A piece of leather is passed through the white metal "dee,"

THE GAFF.

folded, and sewn to the sheath in a way that allows it to have free play in the fold. The straight side of the metal "dee" which I use measures $\frac{3}{4}$ inch. The leather sheath is stitched not at the back part of the socket but in front, facing the cork, and in continuation of the stitching between the socket and cork. The gaff and sheath may be obtained at Winchester, by applying to G. Holland. But after a long bout of fishing, in summer when every ounce weighs a pound, when days are long and rivers low, it is a treat to carry a gaff that weighs no more than your watch—or, perhaps, even your purse. And so I use the "Summer Gaff," which is made on the same principle and is also supplied to Anglers by Hancock & Co.; and by Farlow & Co.

For convenience in gaffing from high banks, I have two short extra joints which, when screwed together, measure in all 5 feet. But in wading, these are quite unnecessary; and once only, in several years of office, has the third joint been put into requisition.

I really fail to understand why "so much practice,"—to quote from many well-known authorities—"is essential to the making of a good gaffer." I found it as easy to gaff my first Salmon when a boy as I did my last towards the close of the past year.

I do not deny that a little skill is needed, first to bring the Salmon to the gaff, and then for the Fisherman himself to fix him and take him ashore in dignified fashion. He should be careful not to wind in *too* much line. The rod should not be bending down over the fish, but held well up above it, *so that the point can be lowered with effect if the struggle be resumed.* After such experience with two or perhaps three fish, what is there to learn? I really do not know.

The Angler will soon find the advantage of not standing in very shallow water to secure his fish,* and of dropping the point of the rod when the gaff takes hold. He will, moreover, soon learn to feel as much at home with the fish in gaffing it as in playing it.

It would be ridiculous to assert than a man can gaff his own fish in as short a time as his gillie for him; but being stationed well in the

* N.B.—So short a length of line is obviously needed to hold the fish under the rod, and so often will the fish make from there a little *détour* before it is all over with him, that unless the "treble" is married to the line (as described elsewhere), so that the jointure runs freely through the rod rings, the fish will often reap the benefit.

water, it is sometimes curious how quickly he is enabled to perform the operation for himself, especially when he can raise the head of

CORRECT METHOD.

the fish doing nothing a little *out of water*, and so prevent it from seeing him. From the bank the operation takes longer single-handed.

As most of us know, the gaff is prohibited at certain seasons, and the net takes its place. The one I have is made of silk, and came from Garden's establishment in Aberdeen. But I will describe and illustrate a more recent invention in the next chapter.

There is no good excuse why the Angler should be bothered with a

INCORRECT METHOD.

net in Springtime, and there is still less justification for depriving him of the gaff. Undoubtedly the gaff is "too much" for an old kelt which can hardly "put one leg before the other"—too much for nine in ten of them. *So is the net.* Kelts fight hard, and rarely rally after a good set-to, even when "tailed." So much the better for all the good they *may* do, as distinct from all the harm they *will* do. I never gaff them when I can avoid it, but I always take the gaff when the law permits, for, in my opinion, notwithstanding the prejudices of many precious reformers, we have nothing to supersede it; and I am not afraid to add that there is no one thing in Salmon-fishing whereof the uses to human life are yet thoroughly understood. Facts, however, clearly point to the inference that the "instrument of satisfaction" is *not* productive of the cruelty people would have us believe; for, on breaking away in his final struggle for life, a fresh-run fish never "keeps the wound green." Even in the very next pool, on the very next day, he will rise as readily as ever and take the fly he wants. (See exceptional case mentioned on p. 382.)

I hate cruelty to animals, so do all true sportsmen; and, deeply as all humane hearts would deplore the infliction of unnecessary pain to the fish, the present method of "getting and securing" by means of the gaff, leaves in my mind little to be desired in the matter alike of humanity, suitability, and economy of time. If the fish suffer much, which is questionable, for they are cold blooded creatures, is it not rather in depriving them of their native element? But against that same, a very big contra account is to be framed, and the student of angling can quite depend on my vote for both *catching* and *gaffing* when he can.

However, another weapon has recently been introduced, and of this *Land and Water* says:—

"We commend to the notice of our readers Crawshay's improved patent fish lander, of which the sole manufacturers are Messrs. Holbrow & Co., 40, Duke Street, St. James's. Some of the special advantages the inventor claims, are the following:—(1) The fish is not damaged as with a gaff, so that no mistake can possibly be made with a kelt. (2) It is much easier to use than a gaff, which latter instrument inevitably requires a certain amount of practice. (3) The fish once snared can be carried anywhere by the tail over sand or high rocks, and has no power to kick. (4) This lander is far superior to any net, for the man who is fishing can use it himself as easily as a gaff, and there is nothing for the tackle to get entangled in, as with a net. This is an especial desideratum as regards prawn and minnow fishing, and would save much vexation where pike have to be got rid of in all cases. (5) It can be carried like a gaff, and is also made to screw into any landing net handle. These are a few of the advantages of Crawshay's patent improved fish lander.

"Slip the noose over the fish's tail, *behind* the dorsal fin, not in front of it, and a sharp jerk upwards to the full length of the wire secures the fish."

How to wade is a subject upon which I desire to say a few words.

Wading requires much practice ; courage is to be desired ; but a good deal may be done by rule. Some Anglers stick at nothing ; others look askance at the most simple waters. The bravest, however, may run into danger unforeseen.

In my youth, if I may say so, I was a strong wader and never consulted the interests of "Number one." But now I am prepared with an Alpenstock, for, like other seniors, I am compelled to reduce these matters to the humble level of personal safety. It was only a few years since, that I had a very narrow escape—one which comes back in my dreams. To the question, "Well, what have you done?" "*Done?*" I replied to my friend on returning home that evening, "I've had a ducking, smashed my rod, lost a fish, and nearly lost my life as well!"

It happened in this way.

I had left my friend to perambulate open pools, and made tracks down river for a cast over a favoured spot, which invariably held a fish. Oak trees spreading their boughs, compelling one to wade out upon a huge flat rock, some three yards from shore, fringed the water. A previous experience reminded me of the difficulty in reaching the rock, owing to the strength of the water. On arriving at the Catch, fancying the water too high, I "threw out a feeler," by trying my luck in waders only. Although the water came no higher than my knees, it splashed above my shoulders; but still I went to the rock and back without being "taken in." So I dressed, and, with rod in hand this time, soon set foot on terra-firma and began operations with a rather gaudy Grub. After the third cast, up went the rod and down went the fish with about thirty yards of line, no more. It meant an hour's work to remain where I was, for, though the fish was not large, the force of the water put all chance of bringing it to the gaff out of the question ; therefore, I waited for a favourable opportunity and made for the shore. Just at the critical moment, splash, dash—that spirit-stirring sight and sound—the Salmon shot up river, and checked me to such a extent that my foot missed its aim and in I went. In the twinkling of an eye, I saw the perilous position facing me. The waters dashed under a huge rock and took me with them. My rod hitting the head of it snapped in two as though it were only a lucifer match, and left me engulfed beneath. Fortunately, I went legs first and was able to take breath now and again as the waters receded. At last by a supreme effort I kicked myself out, and coming breast first across the head of the rock, scrambled up to the top of it, and, breathless and beaten, stepped over the dry boulders below, and reached land more dead than alive. Two gentlemen fishing a little lower down came to my assistance, and, disarranging my battle array, I, looking like our parents before the Fall, ran in amongst the heather and into a perfect glow. Deep draughts of Highland air and whisky soon put me on my legs again ; and after a merry laughing and chaffing time, I went more soberly to work, and felt none the worse for a good ducking and a good drink.

Our learning is just one of those pleasures we can never exhaust; the very practice of our vocation gives us strength to dare and to endure ; and occasionally the greatest craftiness can be traced back to the poorest beginnings in wading over the roughest track to the "seat of war."

Some profit, perhaps, may be drawn from the incident recorded. It is, however, manifestly impossible for any novice to follow in safety the footprints of others.

Take, for instance, your big, black-browed, lusty Fisher-fellow, up to every wrinkle, and what chance have you in competition with him? Not that he is really web-footed, you know, but this sturdy don, this amphibious professor, spends the best part of his life breast high in water. Of course, you have no chance at all, whatever be your height and strength ; yet even a giant could not support himself as easily, nor make such headway as a weak-knee'd but practised dwarf—he (the giant) being ignorant of the business, and relying solely upon his strength.

Much may depend upon the material and make of your waders and brogues. I find "Sateen" the best material for the former, and get mine made by the North British Rubber Co. For years I have used the largest hob-nails, and I carry an "iron foot" for convenience in knocking the nails in or out. This useful adjunct was bought at Moody's, Queen Street, Ramsgate. But there are better nails than these for very slippery districts, though they soon wear down. They are made of steel, square headed, filed on the face crossways ; the four corners being somewhat pointed, after the fashion of an ice nail. They screw into the sole with nearly half-inch projecting. I used to make these myself, and found I could stand firmly on almost any rock.

Many prefer boots to shoes. I much prefer the latter, and get them made with soles three-quarters of an inch thick by Cording, of Piccadilly. The Norwegian "Kimagas" he makes are fashionable at the present time. The forepart of these wading boots is constructed of one piece of material, built so high that all pressure on the feet is avoided.

To this must be added the further consideration that from ill-health, accident, or advance of years, many Anglers are incapacitated from wading. A really comfortable leather boot, watertight, is such an indispensable article that I never lose an opportunity of recommending the "Wye Boot," which is made by Hatton Brothers, of Hereford. Mine have been in wear since July, 1885 (nine seasons), and are still soft and sound. I dress them with Griffin's Preservative (Reading) and use them only when fishing from the bank. In dry, hot weather I wear the Highland brogues, made at Aberdeen by Lorimer and Son. Nothing, in my opinion, could be more comfortable.

Not the least important item among other matters in wading is "to keep ourselves dry," and so long as we do not trip or stoop, there is little to fear on this score. Nor need the student be alarmed by the common report which is current in regard to swimming in waders. I have been out of my depth many a time, and, except that the pace was naturally impeded, I have been fortunate enough never once to be troubled by the sensation of *my head going down and my legs coming up.*

In crossing a ford, the impetus of the water generally varies; in one moment it may be pressing us hard, while in the next, yet in the same spot, it is comparatively easy to stand against. The directions here are very simple to follow. You cannot take too short steps if the current runs fast, and before each one, firmly plant the Alpenstock in front, down-stream, somewhat in advance. A little presence of mind is worth any amount of muscle.

The next rule to be studied is *to dig one foot in before moving the other.* Press the foot firmly down and force it as it were while so doing to the right and then to the left to "dig" the nails in, when you will finally ascertain that they will not give way; then, and not until then, you raise the hind foot.

Always keep the legs fairly wide apart; this will give you a firmer balance; and never on any consideration face or turn your back directly up-stream, unless you are certain you can do so with impunity.

In getting back up-stream from deep water, take short steps sideways. Step over, or on one side of boulders, do not tread on them if you can possibly avoid it.

Constantly look up river in order to be prepared for any floating debris. And remember the one great secret in the case of quick-sand or gravel, namely, always to clear away the material with the gaff *behind* you and take your foot out *heel first.*

It is generally believed that wading is injurious to health, but I am convinced this depends upon circumstances. In my opinion, the early spring is not detrimental to health, provided the Angler so dresses as not to feel the cold water in the least degree.

He may require, besides flannel drawers, long stockings reaching to the thigh, and having straps at top and bottom. The upper straps button to the trousers under the waistcoat; the lower ones fixed on each side of the stockings—fit under the feet and so prevent any working up the leg. No; it is in the height of summer that a wader suffers, unless he constantly takes the precaution of airing his waders. Too strict a regimen would undoubtedly be wearisome; but, in this case, if the damp, which escapes freely from our bodies in warm weather, is forced back upon the pores of the skin, it is far from pleasant, anything but wholesome, and *may be* very injurious to health.

While upon this subject, I may be allowed to add my experience in regard to the Anglers fishing dress. I need not enter into particulars for a complete outfit, but lightness for summer, and warmth for spring and autumn, are the chief characteristics to be studied.

The proper get-up for fishing, nowadays, is very different from what it was in times gone by, when any old morning coat was brought out for the purpose. We were satisfied then by tucking the tails inside the waders and wearing the braces outside. But this plan prevented ventilation, and had the effect of almost doubling the work.

Twenty years ago, I introduced into use a short jacket to wear outside both waders and braces; but it was not perfected until Rice Brothers, of Bond Street, took the matter in hand. The original coat was a comfort in many ways, but it still hampered us in casting, which the new one does not. Perhaps any coat would show creases when the arms are raised, but the pleats put in front and behind the improved garment are so well arranged, that they open and shut, like a concertina, with each motion of the wearer, who is perfectly free and easy in any position taken up. The results are decidedly satisfactory.

Perhaps my favourite fishing jacket is of homsepun—a material to be had in various patterns by applying to Miles, of Hanover Street, Bond Street.

A perfect forest of hands will, at any rate, be held up in favour of wearing the wading braces *underneath*, thereby rendering the Angler more at liberty for all arm and muscular action. The Angler will please himself as to length, I have mine reaching over the waders about 1½ inches. He would scarcely credit the difference between the restriction of the old plan and freedom of the new. I use the musculine pronoun, but "he" is very often of the gentler sex. Ladies delight in Salmon-fishing after the fatigue of London gaieties, and hardly ever give it up when once the taste is acquired. But it would be no easy task for me to write a description of ladies' costume, which would make the heart of woman glad.

"The Princess of Wales and her daughters," says the *Daily Telegraph*, "are enthusiastic and skilful wielders of the Salmon rod."

"Their Royal Highnesses believe in wearing light, warm, tweed dresses for fishing, made of the natural homespun, which retains its natural capacity for resisting rain, the oil not being extracted from the wool before it is woven. Gowns made with skirts to the ankle, loosely fitting coats and blouses, are the kind of garments which these Royal ladies usually wear for fishing, with stout Balmoral boots made with low broad heels, and soft felt or tweed hats to match their dresses.

A more elaborate get-up for fishing consists of a short skirt of tweed bound deeply round the hem with porpoise hide, and worn over knickerbockers. This is made so that it can be buttoned right up, forming a sort of fishwife skirt, and furnished with a big pocket for fly-book and tackle. The coat is of tweed, with lapels and cuffs of porpoise hide, and it is bound with this leather-like substance and furnished with many pockets; for the ardent Fisherwoman likes to have everything she may require at hand, and yet cannot be hampered with much impedimenta, while the attendant gillie's many duties necessitate his being left fairly free handed. If it is necessary to wade, so as to cast over a favourite hole, waterproof over-all fishing boots can be put on; but, as a rule, this is not found needful; and few ladies use them. A high-legged pair of porpoise-hide boots and thick woollen stockings are usually deemed sufficient, as, if a Fisherwoman must get wet, she will soon walk herself dry again. When a Salmon is hooked, the excitement of playing the fish, humouring him, and gradually exhausting him, until he can be brought near his fate, in the shape of the murderous gaff, wielded by the skilful gillie, is an experience of the most absorbing description, and many a fair Fisherwoman has been known to cry from disappointment when her finny prey has jerked away the cast and flies and been lost to her for ever. In thinking out a suitable dress for fishing, it is always well to remember that a few very hot hours may be experienced, though these can seldom be propitious for the sport. It is, therefore, well to wear a thin blouse under the warm tweed coat, so that the latter can be handed over to the gillie when extra exertion or the sun's rays induce too great warmth. If the skirt is not of a nature to loop up and form a large pouch, a belt with a satchel is found useful for a long day. The luncheon must be easily portable, and is usually confided to the attendant, but most women, knowing the strain that such continued exertion imposes, carry nourishment in a compressed form, furnishing their pouches or satchels with frame-food tablets, or meat lozenges, or such things as they most approve for the purpose, besides a small flask of sherry or claret in their own possession, as it would be awkward to want food or drink on one side of a stream with the attendant carrying it on the other. For loch fishing, a waterproof skirt and cape are often most useful, as there the exertion is confined to casting, and showers must be defied. It would be bad, too, to have to wait to dry without keeping up the heat of the body by exercise. The danger of an unporous waterproof is in putting it on over slightly moist clothes, and so driving the damp in, and also in wearing it, while walking, and preventing necessary exhalation from the body. Many people have the tweeds which

THE KELSON COAT.

they wear for fishing slightly waterproofed without interfering with the ventilating quality of the material; but there is no doubt that the natural wet-resisting element in the wool of the sheep is the best, and homespuns undyed, and, as far as possible, in their oily condition, are the safest wear when exercise has to be taken. It should be remembered that, for this pursuit, nothing is so safe to put on as wool, and that even the cool blouse, which is pleasant for hot hours, should be of thin flannel."

My own waterproof over-jacket is made by Field, of Piccadilly, London. It is about two inches longer than the under-jacket. The cloth consists of a light-brown Scotch tweed, thoroughly waterproof. The jacket is ventilated across the back by means of a cape which gives freedom to the arms for casting. False cuffs are provided to prevent rain-water running up the wrists, and there are two large inside pockets. In weight, it is very light, yet the coat lasts for several seasons.

I have often heard complaints made, and not without just cause, of men's wading socks. I ask for nothing better than a sock made of the wool called "abb." It is sold at the Marine Stores, 34, York Street, Ramsgate, and is very thick and durable. I generally get 2 lbs. at a time, and send it to the Steward, Grangegorman Prison, Dublin, together with a pattern ; this amount of material is sufficient for three pairs of socks, the cost of which in the aggregate is about 1/3 per pair. They last for years.

GLOSSARY OF TERMS AND EXPRESSIONS.

Maiden pools are Catches not previously fished on the day in question.

Fresh days are mild days.

Inspection is a term used when a fish has followed, or been stirred by a fly.

Presentation, presenting the fly to the fish.

Hand-lining, playing a fish by holding the line.

Catch. A Catch is a pool, stream, flat, or rapid ; but a catch (with a small c) is one of the number of actual lay-byes in the Catch.

Oily waters. The surface of the water smooth.

The Pull. See illustration and explanation, page 35.

CHAPTER VIII.

MISCELLANEOUS.

SILKWORM GUT.

ALTHOUGH to-day forgotten, one, William Hay, who represented the ancient town of Seaford in the House of Commons in the year 1734, deserves our remembrance for introducing Silkworm Gut into this country. What it cost then I do not know, but the question of price in these days need not be seriously considered. The investment of a little extra money in the best sample invariably brings its own reward. I get mine at Ramsbottom's establishment, Market Street, Manchester.

But although Fishermen are grievously conscious of the present depression in the trade and entertain fears, not altogether unfounded, of the supply in future,* yet very few understand the several processes by which the silkworm is developed, or by what methods the gut is produced. This of itself offers occasion for a few particulars, which may be of interest, before pronouncing upon the respective qualities of gut, its choice and management.

When we come to consider that the luscious leaf of the mulberry is the staple food of the silkworm, it is not surprising that the insects thrive most in localities where the trees grow best. In the province of

* I think this depression would pass away if young mulberry trees were forced under glass to bring forth their leaves earlier in the season than those out of doors. The season for them is later in the South than it used to be.

Murcia mulberry trees are innumerable. So thoroughly does the Spanish climate and soil suit them, that for richness and abundance of tender and succulent foliage they cannot be surpassed.

MR. SAMUEL ALLCOCK'S MANUFACTORY AT MURCIA.

Looking from the Cathedral tower in the town of Murcia (the capital of the province) the eye surveys miles of country closely dotted with a countless number of little houses surrounded by plantations of mulberry trees. The inhabitants, for the most part, devote their time to the rearing of silkworms, and, comparatively speaking, angling interests are of minor importance to the "farmers." Murcia, however, more than holds her own in the production of Salmon gut, nor is the interest of the Fisherman entirely confined to this "garden" of Spain, which, in round numbers, is sixteen miles in length by eight in breadth.

Sericulture is pursued in many foreign countries. China, Japan, Sicily, and the United States alike boast their silkworm manufactories, the product of which, however, so far as silkworm gut is concerned, fails to reach the standard of excellence usually needed for a good fight with a fifteen pound fresh-run fish unless the rod is extremely lissom.

Of the various silk producing moths the *Bombyx mori* best serves Anglers. But, by a somewhat strange coincidence, the best results obtained in Murcia are not from home-bred hatchings, but from eggs, first imported into the South of France, and, after development, sent back to Spain.

The selection of eggs is almost a business of itself, though great consideration is extended to every item of detail during incubation, After the selection is made the eggs are *placed* at the end of the month of February, but are immersed beforehand for three or four hours in water at about the temperature of 50 degrees Fahr. They are spread on a cloth separately, there to remain for about a week in a dry, well-ventilated apartment. The temperature of this room during the first day is 60 degrees, during the second 62, the third 66, the fourth 68, and from the fifth never higher than 70 degrees. With this attention the eggs gradually darken in appearance, and the little "black-a-moors" come to life in seven or eight days. To keep the rooms specially sweet and clean, and the floors sprinkled with water to lay the dust before sweeping, are the indispensable conditions of the success of the undertaking.

The various stages of the silkworm from the eggs to the silk sack may be best understood by the accompanying illustrations.

1. Female moth, which lays about 200 eggs.
2. Grub—three days old.
3. Worm—seven days old.
4. Worm—fourteen days old.

5. Worm—twenty-one days old.
6. Worm—Thirty days old.
7. Worm—Forty-two days old, and ripe for drawing or spinning.
8. Gut sack, there being two in each worm.

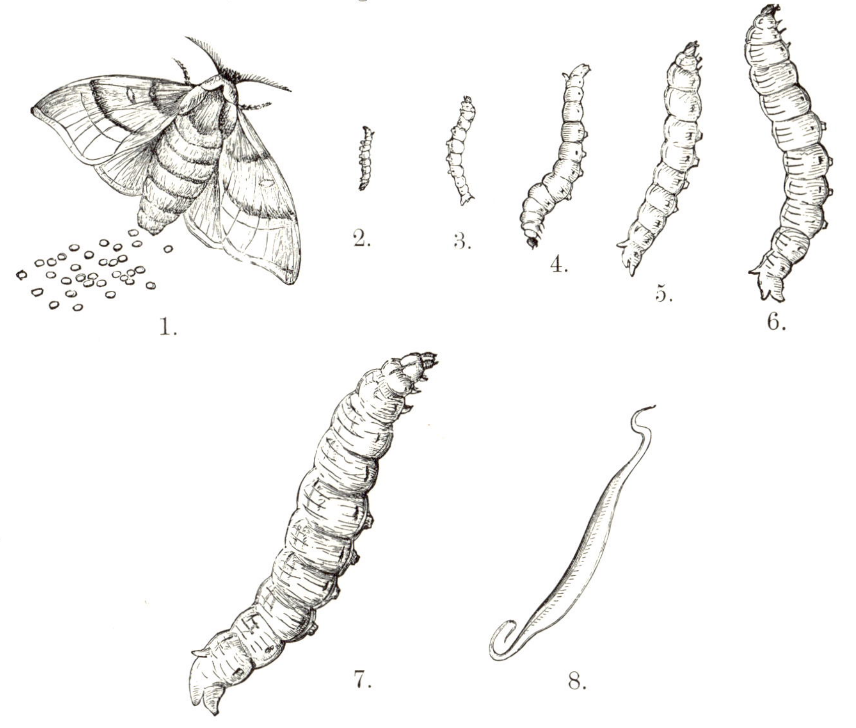

THE SILK-WORM.

The grub is fed upon fresh unfermented mulberry leaves, gathered and conveyed daily in clean baskets. The leaves are cut up with a sharp knife and well scattered *over* the insects. In three days, these grubs, which are protected from any great change in temperature, become dormant, and awake after four days' rest, when they are fed more abundantly. Having now cast their first coat, they are from that time called worms; but they again become dormant. In fourteen days they eat whole leaves voraciously, and sleep again. When three weeks old, the worm takes its fourth and final sleep. It eats enormously, and, after casting its fourth skin, becomes restless, and soon seeks shelter for the purpose of spinning.

When quite ready to spin (not an hour before or after), the worms are picked up and thrown into a tub containing a strong mixture of vinegar and water. They die instantly, and are allowed to remain in this "pickle" for about twelve hours, so as to give a consistency to the silk bags.

On taking them out of the "pickle," the worms are broken in half, and the gut sacks carefully removed. The strength of the "pickle" regulates the thickness of gut. Strong mixtures render the gut short and thick; with weak mixtures, the gut is longer and thinner. If too strong, the gut "pulls out" into crooked and lumpy strands.

When the gut is pulled out—a process simply managed by taking hold of each end and stretching it as far as it will go—it is thrown down upon the floor, when the extreme ends begin to curl up. Each strand is covered with a thin coat called "carne." In a few days the gut is collected, washed in pure water, and hung up to dry in rooms where a current of air passes through freely. When thoroughly dry, the strands are tied in bundles from 5,000 to 10,000, sold by weight to the merchants who then remove the "carne" by a certain process discovered and made known by Morris Carswell, the wholesale manufacturer of the Salmon lines bearing my name.

The bundles, each of which contain one-third *estriada* (spurious pieces), are undone, and carefully examined before the polishing process takes place. The spurious pieces are or ought to be separated from the superior quality, which is easily detected by the practised observer. It is finally assorted, with due regard to both roundness and thickness, and tied up in "hundreds" or "hanks."

The proportion of the different grades of the thicknesses varies from year to year. For enumerating them, to begin with the thinnest, there is Refina, Fina, Regular, Padron second, Padron first, Marana, Double-thick Marana, Imperial, and Hebra.

Many and many a man has been deceived by his own estimate of the quality and value of his packages. Only by a very accurate knowledge of what the low grades will realise, together with the faculty of close, general averaging of each season's products, can the purchaser feel at all confident of making a profit over the transaction.

Having been frequently asked for particulars, I have entered upon

A STORE ROOM.—STANDARD WORKS, REDDITCH.

these brief details in view of meeting a long felt want; but, perhaps, the few following simple rules, which may be safely observed by the Angler, who buys for himself, will not be the least interesting to the general reader.

Gut depends for its value in the market on length and quality. Twelve-inch gut is worth quite 15 per cent. more than that measuring eleven inches; eight inch strands realise about half the price. But in Salmon fishing, give me *quality*, be the length what it may.

The quality of the gut is determined chiefly by its freshness, colour, and roundness. Fresh samples are detected by the general appearance of the rough, frizzled ends. That is to say the gut may be said to be new so long as the ends are *not parched* and so long as they maintain *a clean, clear, white look about them.*

With regard to the colour of new gut, we seek for a pure, pearly white, and of very lustrous appearance, *without the faintest sign of yellow thrown in.*

Roundness is, of course, determined by the eye and touch. By passing the thumb and middle finger up and down a strand, any roughness or unevenness will instantly be felt.

The best gut, however, is no more the best of gut than the best cream is the best of cream. That is to say, an ordinary hank of fairly good gut contains 15 per cent. of rough strands of unequal thickness; whilst the "best selected" is not only free from all rubbish, but made up of silky strands without a flaw, picked from the choicest parcels. The test best calculated to tell the novice good gut, though somewhat severe, is to tie a single knot in a strand, which, if old and dry, will split or break asunder.

I have tried various stains, and find none surpass that commonly known as a smoky-blue. This can be obtained by first soaking the gut in cold, soft water, and afterwards immersing it for an hour or so in a tumbler of water, having one teaspoonful of Stevens's blue-black ink stirred with it. But the sooner it is put away the better, for light and air cripple gut considerably. The sun will soon bring out "flecks" or light spots and spoil it altogether.

It is indelibly impressed on my mind that the best way to preserve gut, before use, is to roll it up tightly in fresh wash-leather, tied round and round with strong string. By this means of protection it will last good and remain serviceable for many long years.

Before knotting Salmon gut for use, the strands should remain in soft water for eight or ten hours.

In use it is not desirable to roll up the length of single gut and put it away for the night. Detach it from the treble, give the whole length a good coating of mutton fat, rubbed on first from one end and then from the other, and hang it to a pin by its loop. With this attention, a yard of single will last good for three months hard wear, provided it is not frayed by rocks or other obstacles.

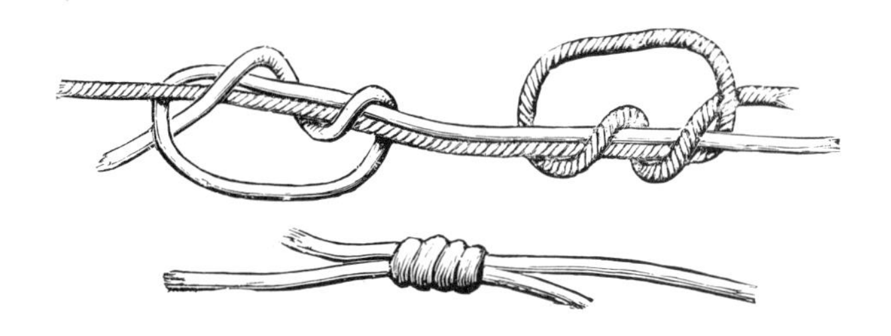

KNOTTING SINGLE STRANDS OF GUT TOGETHER.

Of the various methods of making up "casts" or "traces," I find the following principle of knotting the best:—

Lay the ends together (pointing right and left) between the left forefinger and thumb.

It may be described thus:—Bend left strand back as a loop, and place under left forefinger and thumb behind the strands therein held, and bringing the extreme end out below the left thumb and finger. Pass end over the strands and through the loop. Repeat this, and, then holding this end of the left strand and the right strand in the right forefinger and thumb, draw the left strand with the left forefinger and thumb, *but not tight.*

Turn the work round, left to right, and go through the same process with the other strand.

Finally pull the strands moderately tight to bring the knots together, by one short, sharp tug; but *do not pull the short ends.* Cut off waste.

KNOT FOR ATTACHING GUT TO FLY LOOP.

This is easily learnt, and practised with two bits of string, say 3-in. and 8-in. long respectively.

Make the short bit into a loop, and take it between left forefinger and the thumb, holding the loop to the right. Then, with one end of the 8-in. bit in right forefinger and thumb, follow this diagram.

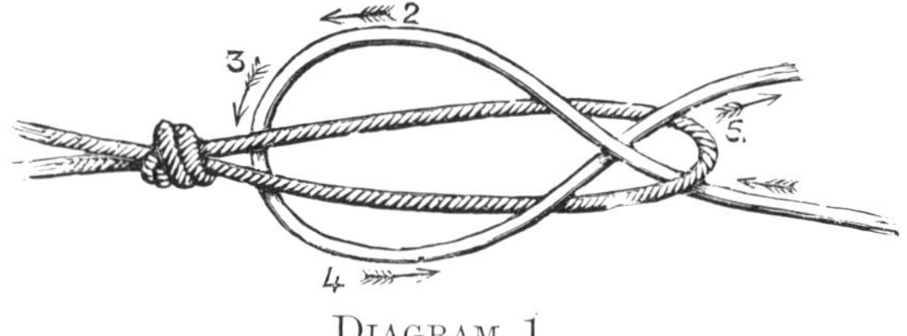

DIAGRAM 1.

The end of the white cord having been passed through the dark cord loop in the course and succession marked by the arrows, 1, 2, 3, 4, 5, represents the first stage completed.

In the second stage, the object is to get (see diagram 2) A over and round B, and then in between the white loop and dark loop at A.

This is best done by keeping the point of the left forefinger under the white loop at the arrow 2, and by taking hold of B end at the arrow 1. Now put B end under and round, and bring it up towards you, while pushing the end A with the right forefinger into its position as specified, so that it lies on the fork of the dark loop, as shown in diagram 2.

DIAGRAM 2. (Showing work upside down.)

The knot is seen here as turned over and now ready to be drawn taut. Hold the end A with the dark loop by the left forefinger and thumb (do not turn the fly over), and pull tight the end B; but while doing so push the end A towards the knot as it tightens so as to have none of it to cut off.

This knot is based on rational principles; amongst other advantages, observe :—

(1) The part at *a* acts as a pad and saves wear on gut loop.

(2) The knot is easily undone. Hold end B close up to loop and

push it to loosen the tie. If any difficulty arises, which is not likely with good gut, draw out end A, and the whole falls loose.

(3) By facing tailwards the end A gathers no substance floating on the water, such as leaves, &c. It is manifest that this knot is absolutely secure from slipping or self-cutting; and that a little practice will soon teach ready adjustment.

TWISTING GUT FOR LOOPS OF FLIES.

In twisting gut for loops, use an ordinary twisting machine with the metal pendants about one inch apart. Cut a piece of soft wood into a pear shape one inch in length, three quarters of an inch in diameter, and well pointed. Make three grooves along its side, equidistant, one for each strand of gut to ride in as the work proceeds. Screw the machine to a mantel-piece, and knot on the three lengths of gut, which should have been soaking in soft, cold water for six hours. Hook on the conical lead weight sold with the machine to the loosest of the three strands of gut (which have been knotted together) at the bottom. Now place the "pear" point upwards about one inch from the bottom in between the strands. Hold the "pear" in one hand, and with the other hand turn

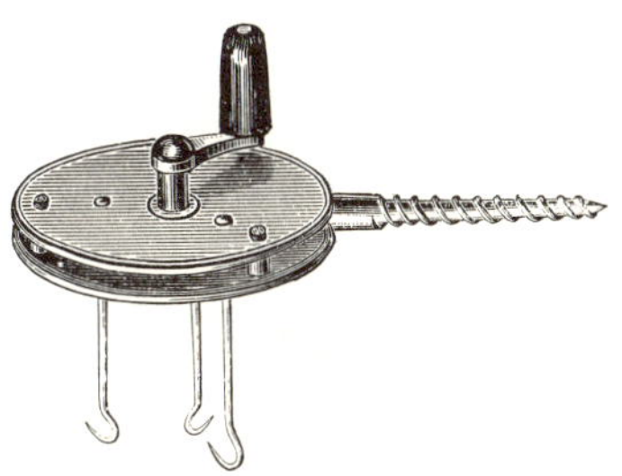

GUT TWISTING ENGINE.

the handle of the machine eight times; then steadily guide the "pear" to the top, turning away all the time. If the "pear" is moved up too soon or too quickly the twist will be loose. If it is not moved quickly enough the gut will break. On reaching the top, quickly take out the "pear," catch hold of the weight to prevent untwisting, and with the fingers give it a few extra spins; the effect of which has to be regulated along the whole length by holding the twisted gut between the finger and thumb, and passing them somewhat firmly up and down the gut at the time. Catch hold of each end of the twisted gut, stretch it and double it. If not wanted for immediate use, it should be packed away in new wash-leather. The tighter the gut can be twisted the better.

SPLICING MACHINE.

I know of no method of cutting the two ends of the joints of a rod, so that they shall exactly overlap each other, equal to that afforded by a

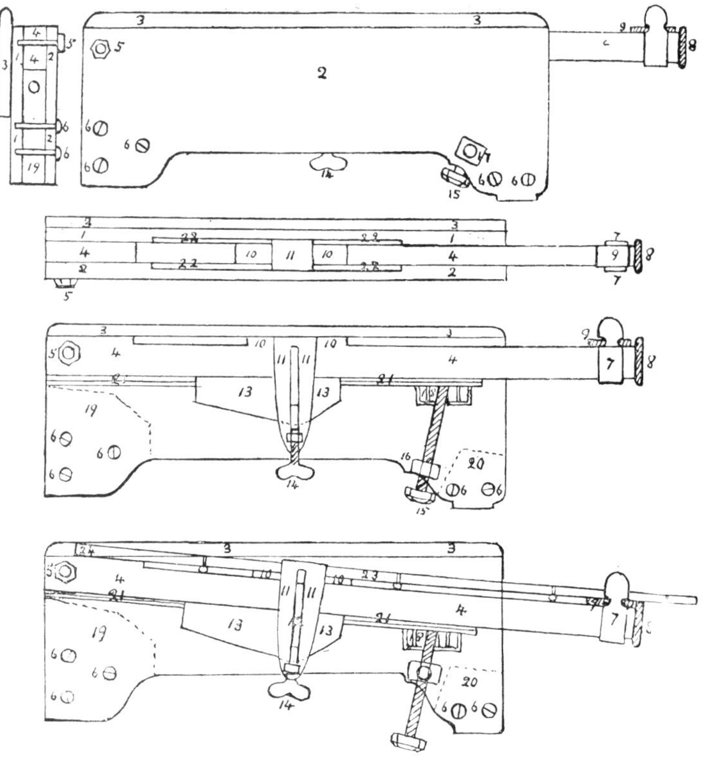

SPLICING MACHINE.

certain splicing machine. The chief merit of the apparatus lies in the fact that an amateur, with but a modest acquaintance of a plane, can scarcely fail to make a splice free from imperfection.

EXPLANATION.

1 and 2.—Parallel side pieces made of oak. (Fig. 1 and end piece.)

3.—Ledge to guide plane.

4.—Rectangular movable arm, made of oak with vertical lever motion on the axis numbered 5.

5.—Iron bolt forming the axis to arm, numbered 4.

6.—Screw through the side pieces and oak blocks, 19, 20.

7.—Iron plates each side. Guides forming extra fixtures for rod.

8.—Finish to end of oak arm. Not essential.

9.—Small fixed block of wood forming adjustment.

10.—Movable strip for same purpose.

11.—Top and side pieces of iron clamp, with vertical motion.

12.—Iron guide for vertical motion, fixed to side pieces. Fig. 4.

13.—Iron cheeks carrying the clamping arrangement, and sliding in the groove, 21.

14.—Thumb-screw passing through cross piece with its extremity working against the under-surface of the rectangular arm, 4. This screw fixes the clamp in any required position. Figs. 3 and 4.

15.—Screw for raising and depressing the movable rectangular arm, 4.

16.—Rocking nut to give the necessary play to the screw. Figs. 1 and 4.

17.—Iron plate and axis of rocking nut. Figs. 1 and 4.

18.—Nut with circular motion, fixed under movable arm and holding the end of the screw, 15.

19 and 20.—Oak blocks holding the side pieces (see end view) an equal distance apart.

21.—Recess or ledge in which the cheeks of the clamp slide.

22.—Recess to admit of the clamp sliding on the rectangular arm. Fig. 2.

23.—Rod in position.

24.—Portion to be planed off. When the movable arm (4) has been adjusted to the required angle, it is evident that corresponding surfaces may be obtained with perfect accuracy for two, or as many more splice-joints that may be wanted. I find a "Jack" plane best suited to start with, and a "Trying" plane for the finishing strokes. Their cutting edges must be of the exact width of the movable arm (4) and they must be centred so as to travel just clear of the side pieces (1) and (2).

THE FRAIL.

In this part of one's outfit the needs of the Salmon-fisher differ from those of the Trout fisher. The latter can without inconvenience carry a small basket slung over the shoulder; the former requires the free use of his arms, and so deposits his kit upon the bank. Anything in the shape of bag, basket or gaff, slung over the shoulders, hampers the movement of the arms, and at times may be a source of danger.

The best basket for Salmon fishing is the frail. In this everything, fish included, can be carried with ease and comfort. The leather pad,

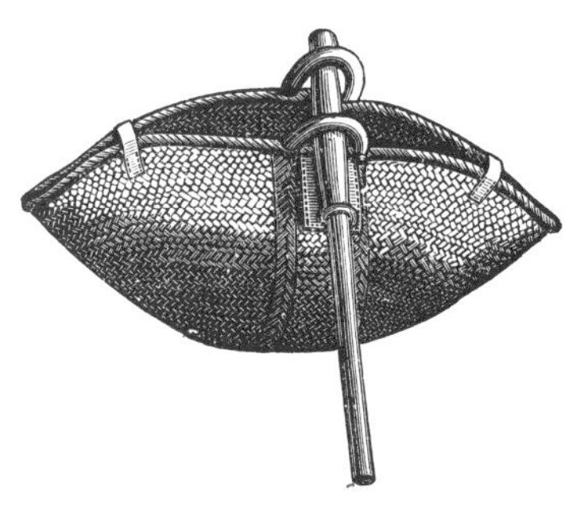

THE FRAIL.

stuffed with horsehair, rests on the shoulder and is effectual in preventing soreness or even pain.

In such a basket I once carried no fewer than six Salmon over a mile, and without it I must have lost my train or left the fish behind.

The frail is usually made of rushes, without lining, and can be kept clean and sweet by a free use of the sponge. I prefer to use it with a lining and have a very large pocket made at the back to carry fly books, flask and mid-day meal. The fish are wrapt in thin waterproof cloth, or in ferns, long grass, or rushes. In packing it, the soft articles such as socks and waders should be put on the side next the back of the carrier; brogues, gaff, etc., on the far side.

The frail is not durable, but it is cheap. The leather straps and pad last for years, and can easily be removed from an old to a new basket. It will be found that heavy weights can be carried in a frail with less inconvenience than in any bag slung over the shoulders.

An excellent method of carrying a fish is to string it. The process is simple and effective, and one I usually adopt when fishing near home.

The string is first tied together to form a loop. One end is passed under the gill-cover, then out of mouth at the lower corner, over the nose, in at the mouth at the opposite corner and under the far side gill. The other end is then passed up through this end, under gills, and after a loop is formed quite at the other end it is passed over, around tail and pulled taut.

THE "QUICKSURE" LANDING NET.

At about the time the "Summer Gaff" was introduced for me by Hancock & Co., a convenient net, highly patronised by ladies, was put on the market by the same firm. It is especially useful during the Grilse season. *Land and Water* says :—

"We have frequently noticed that many landing nets now in the market seem rather got up for sale than to be of practical and lasting service to Anglers. A very common fault is that the net is attached to the landing ring by cord of insufficient strength, and imperfectly waterproofed; consequently the net is liable to ravel up on the ring, and frequent repairs undertaken in the hurry of

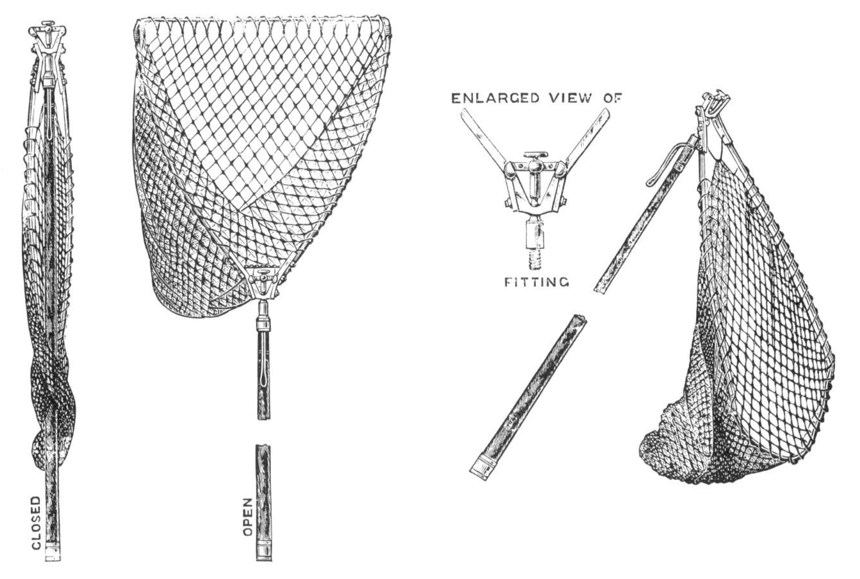

business by the riverside do not improve the appearance or serviceable qualities of the implement. We could multiply faults common to many landing nets. Sometimes the ring is weak and constantly losing shape, or screws drop out and are lost, hinges get out of gear, and the whole affair is a constant source of worry to its owner.

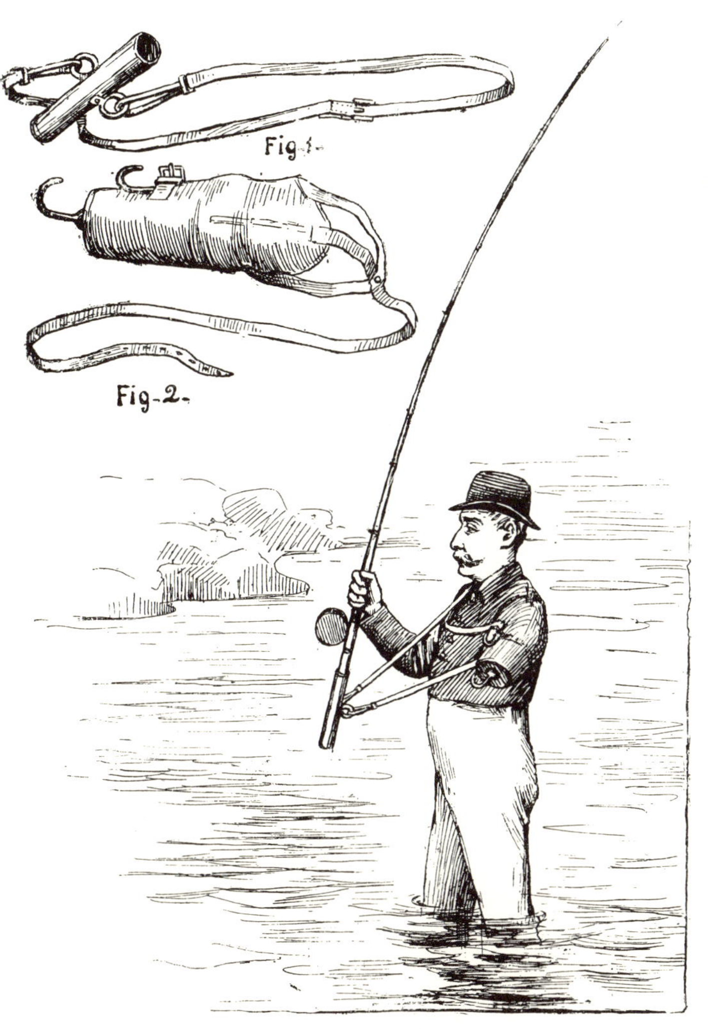

THE NECKLACE. (See next page.)

"Messrs. Hancock & Co., of 4, Pall Mall Place, St. James', have patented a new automatic lock-fast fitting, of which we need give no lengthened description, the construction being sufficiently apparent from the accompanying illustrations. The workmanship of the whole implement is of high class, and there is little risk that it will get out of order if subjected to ordinary fair treatment. The net itself is made of durable material, and has the further advantage of being of a good size. For Salmon and Grilse the handle is made Malacca or other cane."

THE "NECKLACE" FOR ONE-ARMED FISHERMEN.

This contrivance is the only one known to me for the use of those Anglers who have unfortunately been deprived of one arm. The "necklace" with its socket is admirably adapted for casting right or left handed, and gives the Angler supreme control over a fish. It demands but the least acquaintance for complete appreciation.

In examining the sling and its appurtenances, which are represented in Figs. 1 and 2, it will be observed that the necklace is provided with a socket wherein the butt of the rod rests. By a slight downward pressure in casting, the line is sent out almost as far and as easily as in the ordinary way with two hands. The strap fastened over the shoulder is buckled to suit the desired length. The article shown in Fig. 2 points to the convenience afforded for holding Salmon. It fits on to the stump of the amputated arm. The rod rests in the lower arm-hook while "playing" a fish; in "butting" him the rod is placed in the upper hook, which enables the Angler, by means of extra leverage, to put on sufficient pressure for the purpose.

BOXES AND GARRETS FOR BARREN WATERS.

The following letter of mine, written at Carlogie House, on the Dee, appeared in the *Field* on July 27th, 1895, and will, I think, explain all that is wanted:—

"Although one often comes across worthy owners of Salmon rivers, who are not aware of the advantages offered in the improvements of their beats, the day must come when they will exercise their wits and make the endeavour to deal with barren stretches beyond tails of pools. Better luck, however, has fallen to our lot here. In dealing with such places, there are two ways of procedure—the one is by Boxing, the other by Garreting. In my opinion (and I speak from constant

MR. J. C. HASLAM, OF CARLOGIE.

observation and not a little practical experience), by far the better and safer of these two schemes is the Box. The Box is preferable, because the Garret, built at almost any angle from the bank itself, is not unfrequently injurious, if not altogether ruinous, to pools on the opposite side, as well as to others below on the near side. Some Garrets and many Boxes, which I have in mind, have done and are doing an incalculable amount of good to landlords and tenants alike. Those which I have recently made here are put in singularly suitable quarters, and require no more than one snow-water flood to ensure a couple of high-water catches, perhaps second to none for sport on the whole estate.

"The way I usually make a Box is easily described. In shape it is a sort of triangle, and, as I suppose the whole world knows, the Box faces upstream. The two sides are constructed of 12 ft. planks, 2 in. thick, measuring 11 in. at the broad and 9 in. at the narrow end, so that the height of the Box in front is 2 ft. 3 in., and at the back 2 ft. 9 in. The back boards are of similar material, but not tapered. There is a post at front, and one at each corner at back. These posts, 7 in. in diameter, and pointed, are 5 ft. 6 in. in length, so that when the top part of them—damaged in driving—is sawn off, they will be at the height desired. Good, strong old larch is a serviceable wood. The one in front is the first to fix. It is driven into the gravel pretty much as far as it will go—say, a little over 2 ft. When this is done, it is advisable first to place the other two into position, and take a close inspection from a point well above or well below, in order to decide that the Box shall ultimately face straight with the stream. Perhaps it should here be said that the whole of the materials ought to be at hand before operations begin. The river, for instance, may rise too soon for one's liking, and level unprotected work to the ground. Apart from the materials quoted above, all that is required is comprised in the following list, viz., five 4 in. posts, a plank, 8 in. wide, 2 in. thick; a 2 ft. 4 in. strip of iron sheeting, 8 in. wide, having holes drilled on both sides at every 3 in.; three other iron strips, 2 ft. 6 in. long, 3 in. broad, drilled in the same way; and about fifteen tons of boulders, together with some smaller stones to pack them all firmly in the Box level with the top. Some Boxes are required to be higher.

"Before fixing the side planks to the strong front and back posts, the gravel should be somewhat levelled for the edge of the bottom board to rest fairly flush on the river bed, and the planks themselves bevelled off at their inner end edges so as to leave them when nailed together in front with a head-end or nose, say, not more than a thickness of ½ in. Of course, these are fixed as closely as they will go at the front of the head post. The other end of the planks may temporarily extend a trifle beyond the back posts, and be sawn off flush at a later stage. The side boards, resting upon each other, are nailed with 5½ in. nails. When they are fixed, the tail boarding commences. But these latter planks are nailed to the front of the back posts, so as to provide extra support; they are also bevelled at the two ends, so as to fit in tight. The

MR. R. W. COOKE-TAYLOR, AT CARLOGIE.

next thing to do is to place a head-stone inside the Box. The one used here is a tapering stone (with which this neighbourhood abounds), 5 ft. 3 in. in length. Its point is about $2\frac{1}{2}$ in. through, its foot about 15 in. in diameter both ways. A slot to receive the point is cut into the top of the post which has already been reduced. By the use of a chisel the stone can be made to bed into the slot. But before placing it, a firm foundation for its foot should be made in the gravel, and a slanting flat stone put to back up with. If this sort of head-stone is not to be procured, a good, strong larch post might serve the purpose, but, in this district, where thousands of tons of ice wend their way seawards in winter, strength is of infinite importance.

"After getting in the stone, the space underneath it is packed closely with well-fitting boulders, and the small open part between the post and the point or nose of the boards jammed with little stones. The five smaller posts are now driven into the ground—three inside the Box at the middle part of the sides and back, and the two others outside the Box at back, midway between the inside centre one and the two corners. These are all likewise firmly nailed, and then the 6 in. plank is let into the top side planks, so as to butt against the two middle posts. A platform is now made, upon which the boulders are wheeled, and tipped into the box. As each barrow load comes, a little cautious packing of the stones is desirable. When the box is thus filled, the work is completed by fixing the 2 ft. 4 in. piece of sheeting upright round the nose of the box and nailing to the planks on each side. The 2 ft. 6 in. strips of iron are nailed thus, one over a thick piece of well-fitting plank, previously put flush with the top of the sides against the headpost (this strip is bent over and down the sides before the hammer at that part is used), and the two others round the two outer back posts are put at the middle of the top board. The cost of this construction, provided the landlord supplies the wood from his saw mill and allows the boulders in the neighbourhood to be gathered, should not exceed 30s.

"There is a little fresh to add concerning the situation of these Boxes; but it is not easy to describe with exactness the safe and sure place that can be depended upon. It may, however, be taken that the tail end of a pool or catch, which gradually gets shallower and has a gravelly bed, over which the water, at any height, flows fairly straight with the bank, is as good a spot as one might wish for. But the Box must be within thirty yards of the catch itself, or the fish will not linger long in its wake. Mine here is twenty-four feet from the front post to the bank. To make the job yet more enticing, a boulder, weighing about four hundredweight, should be bedded into the gravel below. If this is put at a spot about the place where the two streams meet, it will remain. These out-flowing streams (it may be said for the uninitiated) are formed by the current striking the box, and they will probably join each other not farther distant than from thirty to thirty-five yards down-stream. Properly set, this boulder which, like the suspicion of onion in a salad, animates the whole, and gives the merest angling

MISS KELSON AND HER GILLIE, AT CARLOGIE.

novice a sight at once relishing, causes a wash, deepens the gravel behind it (as in the case of the Box), into which hole the stone will eventually bed itself, and never move again. Should the Box fail to meet one's expectations, it can be removed; but this could hardly be the result in such places with even the most moderate luck. If it should prove effective, several other Boxes might be put below it at intervals of fifty yards, or thereabouts. A constant and watchful oversight of these Boxes is needed in flood time; for, the encroachment of trees and whatnot—the very presence of which will tear the whole thing away—must be cleared.

"Garreting, as I have hinted, is a dangerous experiment, and has been known to do immense damage to the river and its banks. It is to be hoped that no delusions may be entertained on that head. Nature, nevertheless, occasionally furnishes a corner as suitable for Garrets as a reach for Boxes. Still, these places should be studied diligently by thoroughly practical men, and all the work determined upon executed under their control. The great thing to look out for is an immense boulder weighing about two tons, to which an outer post can be fixed if necessary. If, however, this boulder is of suitable shape, or even made suitable, it can be bored for bolts, in which case the post is not wanted. The next item of importance at places where the current flows rapidly consists of a few other well-bedded boulders of long standing lying within a few yards up-stream. They protect the garret, and, it should be added, are imperative agents where the river has a very sharp descent. For boring such a boulder, which makes the Garret unique of its kind, a quarryman's boring-mall and a couple of jumpers serve the purpose well. The mall, by which name it is commonly known, is merely an iron hammer of about 7 lb. in weight, having a handle 7 in. long. A jumper is a sort of cold chisel; one should be 18 in. in length, the other 9 in., and both at least 1½ in. in diameter. In boring, the jumper is slightly turned about by the hand holding it with every stroke of the hammer. Only by this means can the hole be cut round. In ten minutes a hole an inch deep can thus be made even into a mongrel stone, and then it is best for the jumper to carry a shangie. This is made of straw, or, say, a dozen stalks of long, coarse grass, first twisted into rope fashion, and then coiled twice round the jumper, carefully taken off, and itself tied in and out with string. When pruned, this shangie serves as a sort of collar. Put at the mouth of the hole, for the jumper to pass through when working, it answers a double purpose. In the first place, it can be dipped into water to keep the stone wet and the tool cool, in which case the operation of boring is facilitated; and in the second place, the powdered stone, instead of nearly blinding you, sticks to the jumper, and is withdrawn as the work progresses. It is a mongrel (six yards from the bank) to which the two horizontal supports put here for the front paling are bolted. The water running fast, the angle is made extra sharp. The two larch poles fixed to carry the paling are 8 yards long and 12 in. in diameter at the centre portion of them. They are made fast to a tree, or may be a strong post in the bank, and bolted to the stone, one placed a short distance below the other. A strong, upright post is fixed behind them at the middle part, that is to say, inside the Garret. From about midway up the post another larch log, knotched in, slants a little downward and butts against the bank some twelve yards below. The paling selected here is also of larch. These planks are 5 ft. 6 in. long and 2 in. thick. They are nailed upright to the poles close to each other in front, so as to make a smooth face.

"The large boulder is 4 ft. 3 in. high at the outer corner, and the paling is sawn evenly off 1 ft. higher than it. One large log bolted to the boulder about 2 ft. from the bed of the river butts the bank sixteen yards down-stream. It suffices to protect the stones inside the Garret. As an extra support, another log butts against the middle part of the boulder with its other end against the bank. When so much of the work is done, the Garret is packed with boulders and stones from the top of the paling to the level of the log in the rear; and then cartloads of gravel put on the surface and washed in. So it will be seen that in this instance the highest part of the construction is in front."

HOW TO RE-SHAPE FEATHERS.

Into a basin of boiling water immerse the bent feather and let it remain for ten minutes. Then, taking it by the root, put it on a fine linen towel, and with a soft rough towel twisted round the forefinger smooth the fibres, which will readily yield and resume their original form. Allow time to dry.

TO BLEACH FEATHERS.

Immerse the feather in Hydrogen Peroxide, and to quicken operations, add one teaspoonful of Liquid Ammonia to one pint.

FLY-DRESSING BOXES.

I use three. One, the size of an ordinary little japanned cash box, has room in the lid for a hackle book, and seals' furs. There is only one tray; and it carries hooks, tinsels, scissors and other implements. Beneath this tray, which rests on projecting pieces of tin at the four corners, and measures one inch in depth, I keep a temporary stock of feathers, in about a two-inch space; but I only use this box on occasions when paying a short visit from one river to another.

A second case of mine, made by Bambridge (Eton), is of oak, covered with leather. This one holds a much larger stock of materials, and is quite enough for a spring, a summer, or an autumn outing.

A third one, made by Rollason (Hatton Garden, London), has seven trays and is of japanned tin, covered also in leather. The lower tray has no partitions, and is three and a half inches deep. It is stocked with parchment parcels of all kinds of feathers, such as Turkey, Bustard, etc., also a set of tinsels in a tin air-tight box, fitting along the back. Above these rests a hackle book, that just fits the tray. The second tray, three inches deep, has one partition in the centre lengthways. On one side I keep Pheasants' tails and Peacocks' wings; while the opposite compartment holds dyed Swan. The third tray, two and a half inches deep, has one partition lengthways and one crossways. The fourth is two inches deep. The fifth and sixth, one and a half inches deep and still more divided; whilst the top tray, with a right and left lid, is partitioned for every sized hook on right side, and with one narrow partition on the left to hold tinsels and fly-making materials. The lid of the box is two inches in depth, and holds a cardboard box divided into separate compartments for Seals' furs, as well as a parchment-book for special feathers. These are held in by two revolving buttons at each end fixed to the box. With this kind of box, properly stocked, the Angler should be able to dress every sort of standard or nondescript pattern of the day.

THE ROUND JAPANNED BOX FOR DOUBLE-HOOKED FLIES.

Forrest's (Kelso) round japanned tin box is what I use for the

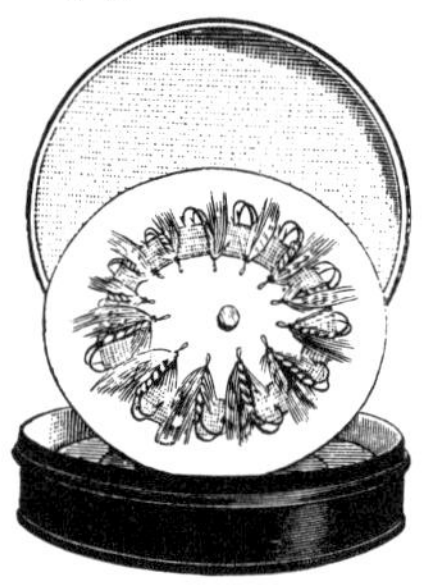

double-hook flies. It has cork circles mounted on round cards, each circle holding from ten to twenty flies according to size.

This firm also supply Anglers with a fly-box (devised by Malloch),

made of steel, covered with tin, to carry single-hook flies. The flies hook in springs made of German silver, each one having a spring for itself.

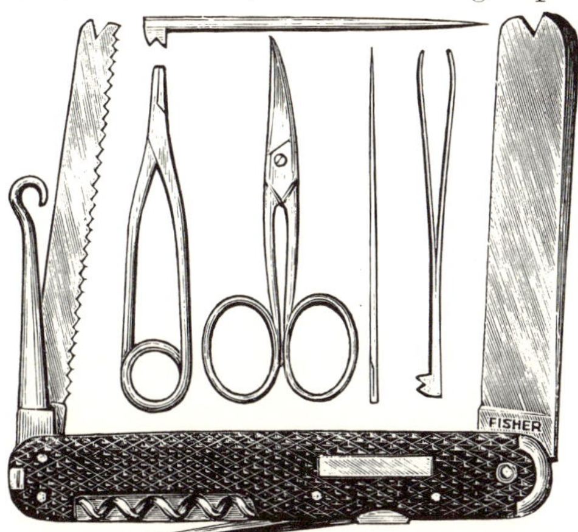

THE FISHERMAN'S KNIFE AND FLY DRESSING SCISSORS.

A good knife is often useful and sometimes indispensable. The one engraved was made for me by Fisher, in the Strand. The needle has a slit at the end for threading prawns. The scissors represent those I use and have recommended in former chapters.

AN APPURTENANCE TO RENDER VISIBLE LOST ARTICLES LYING ON THE BED OF A RIVER.

Paint the inside of a pail black, remove the wooden bottom, and tack a "petticoat" round the end. Put the mouth of the pail just under the surface of the water, and, with his head hidden by the petticoat, the man, looking through this appurtenance, can see the smallest article in the deepest water.

TO WATERPROOF FELT HATS.

I hardly ever wear anything else, but the so-called "bowler." To me they are the most comfortable. Apply two coats of size and when dry two coats of Acme Black.

AN ANTIDOTE FOR MIDGES AND MOSQUITO'S.

Two ounces pine tar, two of castor oil, one ounce pennyroyal. Heat and mix. Apply several times to the face and hands until a sort of varnish is formed. It is a sure preventive, easily washes off, leaves the skin sweet and clean, and is quite harmless.

GRIFFIN'S LEATHER PRESERVATIVE.

This compound makes leather of all kinds soft, pliable and waterproof. It penetrates the material and prevents it from cracking. Brown leather brogues, boots or covers of fly boxes should be rubbed briskly with a cloth, after the application, till they are polished. Blacking can be used afterwards on black leather. This preservative is free from the objections which can be taken to several other compositions. (251, Oxford Road, Reading.)

CURE FOR STICKY LINES.

Tie up the line in one length to two posts, and with a piece of leather rub yard by yard. During that process spin the line backwards and forwards. Now rub the line with a linen pad damped in spirits of wine. Then put into a one-ounce bottle one teaspoonful of copal varnish and fill nearly to the top with spirits of wine. Shake the bottle well against the ball of the right forefinger, and, still spinning, apply the polish, using the thumb and forefinger, to about four inches. Repeat this quickly, and when, say, sixteen inches have been thus treated, continue the spinning and rub (with the same fingers) the length wetted, up and down, three or four times, leaving off as soon as any decided stickiness is felt. The line will be fit to use on the following day. The mixture must be freshly made; it will not keep.

SPECIMEN FISH.

I have often been asked to give an opinion on the question of "setting up" Salmon. Some people like them "stuffed," others have a "cast" taken, but this entails the necessity of parting with the fish.

My plan now, is to place the Salmon on a sheet of paper and with a lead pencil carefully draw the correct outline, make notes of any details for the artist, and send them to Farlow, who will return you a copy of the fish carved and painted in wood.

IN CONCLUSION.

Recollecting the many friendships made, it has often seemed to me in writing these pages that life has a value beyond the wholesome acquirement of business knowledge and habits of official work. It has many times struck me, as well as others, that this value is found in those nobler pursuits which teach us to become masters of ourselves, and qualify us for promoting the welfare and happiness of our fellow-creatures. One authority after another has pronounced the most competent judgment in favour of this view. Their verdict has never been challenged; and if "there is no vocation that claims for its contingent a finer race of men than Angling—level-headed Britons whose lives are superior to those of lower fortune more by the graceful exercise of generous qualities than for their immediate possessions," it is quite certain that no sport has gained favour with fashionable folk so fast as Salmon fishing. Surely business and sport are not incompatible. Surely there is more wisdom and more benefit in combining them than some people like to believe. Life has time enough for both, and its enjoyment is increased by the union. That being so, the sentiments with which the author of this book hopes to be regarded by all who pursue Salmon fishing enthusiastically, and by those who swim only with the stream, are such, perhaps, as it would take a real enthusiast to understand and appreciate. To others, even to that vast multitude in the outer world who, with special delight, estimate our pursuit merely as a light and infectious recreation, the enthusiasm itself can scarcely be intelligible. But the view by our recruits, taken as they find their brain ceases to perform its work efficiently when the heart's work is imperfectly done, is a different one altogether. They study the subject and soon declare that difficulties at the riverside may often be surmounted by indomitable energy, unfailing punctuality, and intelligent reasoning. Afterwards, with the exercise of other attributes not always combined in one individuality, such as absolute self-confidence ("for they can conquer who believe they can"), tenacity of purpose, equability of temper, and a generous and elegant hospitality to colleagues with whom they come into contact, these recruits concentrate their ideas; and, thinking of it all as an art, in which the degrees of attainable excellence are practically infinite, and the attainment of supreme excellence extremely rare, eagerly contest every inch of ground for promotion in our ranks. Finally, they acquire a train of thoughts that engender thought—thoughts that shed a gleam of light on the more obscure problems, and without a shadow of doubt give permanence to the enchantment of every day life. The question whether experts are born or made is, like any such query, hardly necessary to discuss. Prevailing opinion has it that skilled performers are *always* made. How else could it be? Skill at the riverside, or at the fly-table, never came, nor ever will come to us by any road than that of practice. And yet the result of *devotion* is to produce, for one and all alike, a well-marked type of character entirely different from that developed by the love of any other sport or pastime. As to the element of *luck*—well, there is some luck in every branch of sport; and though absence of skill and want of method are too often fitting substitutes for "bad luck," it is not good for our too enslaved votaries to persevere wholly apart from it. Bad luck invariably precedes good luck, and it is better it should go first than last. A word may be said of *chance*. Salmon fishing abounds with chances, as none have known better or avowed more freely than its greatest masters. The mere accidental tug of a Salmon, for instance, symbolises the recognition of the fact. Then with regard to *blunders*—not uncommonly set down as "accidents"—brought about by want of judgment, by any and every conceivable way inclusive of that modest contempt for apparently sound advice—one is naturally inclined to the belief that men who are invariably unlucky are wanting in those very qualities that command success.

But while recalling to mind those many friendships made and thinking of all these things, it was not likely that, having the interests of our juniors at heart, I should pass over unnoticed the many friendships broken by the "busybodies." The trouble occasionally brought about by a deal of unsolicited advice, usually given with intense emphasis to beginners, by people hardly qualified to express an opinion at all, led me, against my will, to point out in these pages the "badge" to know them by. And I should like to wind up by saying, with equal honesty of intention, that few men have done more harm to the rising generation of Anglers than those who are commonly thought to do the least. If, however, one final suggestion may be made, it would probably flow best in the following words of Seneca:—"LET NO MAN PRESUME TO GIVE ADVICE TO OTHERS, THAT HAS NOT FIRST GIVEN GOOD COUNSEL TO HIMSELF."

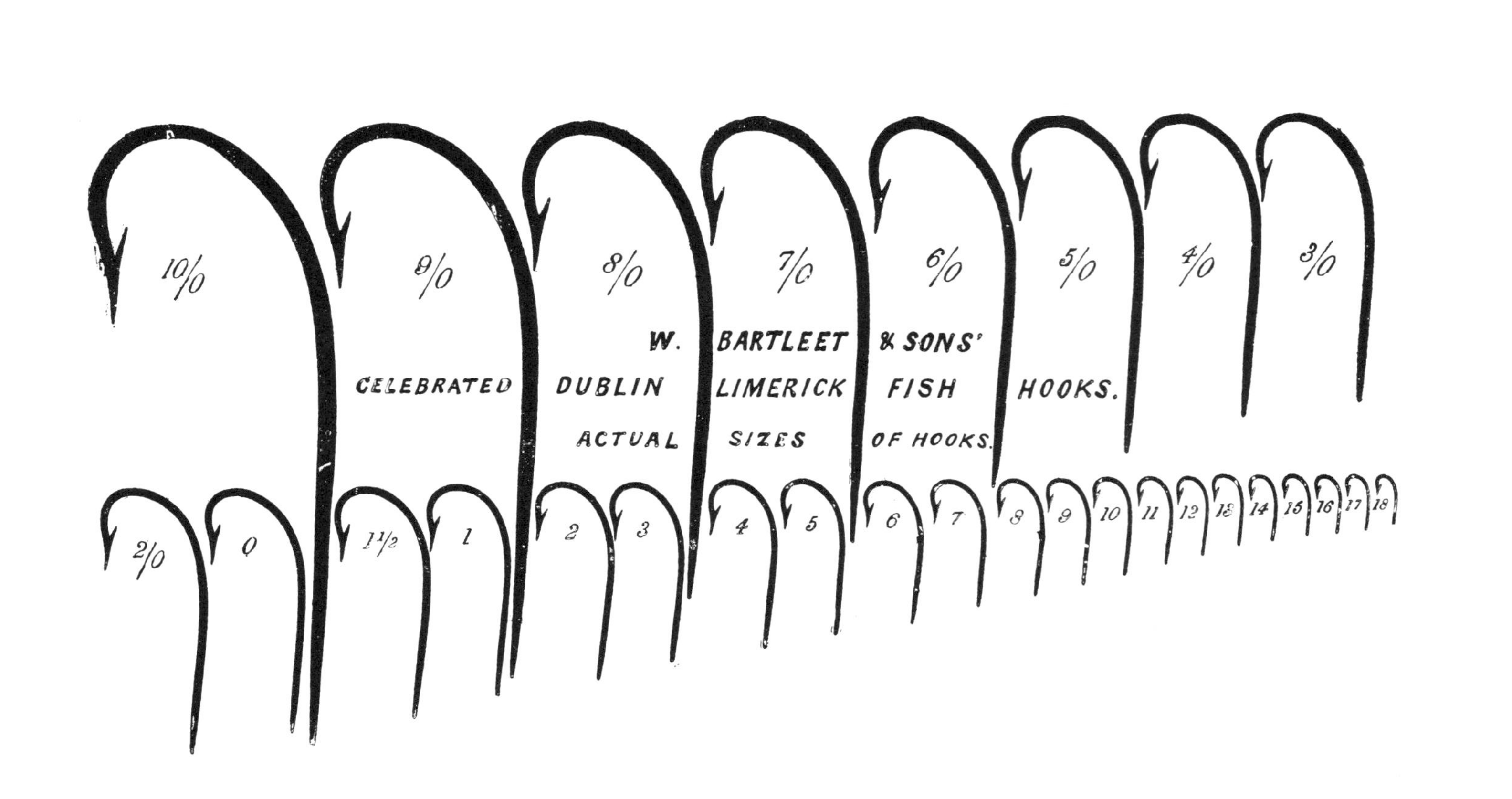

10/0
9/0
8/0
7/0
6/0
5/0
4/0
3/0
W. BARTLEET & SONS'
CELEBRATED DUBLIN LIMERICK FISH HOOKS.
ACTUAL SIZES OF HOOKS.
2/0
0
1 1/2
1
2
3
4
5
6
7
8
9
10
11
12
13
14
15
16
17
18

TABLE SHOWING THE LIMITS OF THE FISHERY DISTRICTS OF ENGLAND AND WALES; THE CLOSE SEASONS; THE RATE OF ROD LICENCE DUTY FOR SALMON, INCLUDING TROUT; AND THE NAMES AND ADDRESSES OF THE CHAIRMEN AND CLERKS OF THE SEVERAL BOARDS OF CONSERVATORS.

Name of District.
In order of Coast
from N.W. to N.E.

1. Eden.

LIMITS OF DISTRICT.

The Eden below Kirkby Stephen and its estuary and tributaries (except the Caldew above Hawksdale Bridge, the Petterill above Wreay Bridge, the Eamont and Lowther above their junction, the Irthing above the boundary of Northumberland, and the Croglin); the English half of the Solway and sea between lines drawn true S. from Sark Foot to Rockcliff Marsh and true W.N.W. from the northern boundary of Seaton; the coast between such lines; and all rivers flowing into such part of the sea and Solway (except the Esk and Sark above Sark Foot).

ANNUAL CLOSE SEASON FOR SALMON.
(All dates inclusive.)

Except in the cases marked below, the Annual Close Season in England and Wales is:—

*NETS, &c.—From 1st September to 1st February.

RODS—From 2nd November to 1st February.

NETS, &c.—In the Solway Firth, from Old Sandsfield downwards, 10th September to 10th February.

RODS—16th November to 15th February.

PERIOD DURING WHICH GAFF IS ALLOWED IN CONNECTION WITH ROD AND LINE. (EXCEPT IN THOSE CASES WHERE ITS USE IS LEGAL THROUGHOUT THE WHOLE ANGLING SEASON.)

1st July to 15th November.

ROD LICENCE DUTY.
Salmon (including Trout and Char).

Season, whole district, £1 1s.; above Armathwaite Bay, 10s.; in Irthing, Wampool, and Waver, 5s.; week, 5s.; Single-handed rod, used in Duke of Devonshire's socage water, season, 5s.

* The Annual Close Season for puts and putchers is from 1st September to 1st May.

Name of District. In order of Coast from N.W. to N.E.	
1. Eden—*continued.*	NAME AND ADDRESS OF CHAIRMAN AND CLERK OF BOARD OF CONSERVATORS. Chairman—F. PARKER, Fremington, Penrith. Clerk—J. B. SLATER, Court Square, Carlisle.
2. Derwent.	LIMITS OF DISTRICT. The Derwent and its estuary and tributaries (except the St. John's Beck above a point 100 yards below the junction of Mill Gill, and Naddle Beck above Roughow Bridge); all rivers flowing into the sea between North Head Lighthouse and the northern boundary of Seaton; the coast between these points; and the sea for three miles seaward. ANNUAL CLOSE SEASON FOR SALMON. (All dates inclusive.) NETS, &c.—15th September to 10th March. RODS—15th November to 10th March. The GAFF (see River Eden)—1st July to 14th November. ROD LICENCE DUTY. Salmon (including Trout and Char). Whole district season, £1; ditto, to 5th September, 10s.; ditto, month, 10s.; week, 5s.; any part except river Derwent below Ouse Bridge, season, 10s.; ditto, month, 5s.; ditto, week, 2s. 6d. Chairman—W. FLETCHER, Brigham Hill, Carlisle. Clerk—T. C. BURN, Rosemont, Papcastle, Cockermouth.
3. West Cumberland.	LIMITS OF DISTRICT. The Mite, Esk, Irt, and Calder; and the Ehen below the Weir at the foot of Ennerdale; their estuaries and tributaries; the coast, and all rivers flowing into the sea, between Haverigg Point and North Head Lighthouse, and the sea for three miles seaward. ANNUAL CLOSE SEASON FOR SALMON. (All dates inclusive.) NETS, &c.—15th September to 31st March. RODS—14th November to 10th March. The GAFF (see River Eden)—1st July to 1st November.

Name of District. In order of Coast from N.W. to N.E.	
3. West Cumberland—*continued.*	ROD LICENCE DUTY. Salmon (including Trout and Char). Season, 15s.; week, 5s.; day, 2s. Chairman—ROBERT JEFFERSON, Rothersyke, Egremont, Cumberland. Clerk—J. WEBSTER, 102, Scotch Street, Whitehaven.
4. Kent.	LIMITS OF DISTRICT. The coast and territorial sea between lines drawn (1) true W.S.W. from Haverigg Point, and (2) S.W. from N. boundary of Wharton till it bisects a line from the S.W. point of Walney Island to Rossall Point; all rivers (with their tributaries and estuaries) flowing thereinto. ANNUAL CLOSE SEASON FOR SALMON. (All dates inclusive.) NETS, &c.—15th September to 31st March. RODS—15th November to 31st March. The GAFF (see River Eden)—2nd June to 31st October. ROD LICENCE DUTY. Salmon (including Trout and Char). Season, 10s.; week, 5s. Chairman—JOHN FELL, Flanhow, Ulverston. Clerk—S. H. JACKSON, Heaning Wood, Ulverston.
5. Lune.	LIMITS OF DISTRICT. The Lune, Wyre, Keer, and Cocker, and their tributaries; so much of Morecambe Bay as lies south of the S. limit of Kent District; the coast as far as Blackpool. ANNUAL CLOSE SEASON FOR SALMON. (All dates inclusive.) NETS, &c.—Tidal, 8th September to 1st March; upper, 15th September to 1st March. RODS—15th November to 1st March. The GAFF is used throughout the whole Angling season. ROD LICENCE DUTY. Salmon (including Trout and Char). Whole District, £1; in Wyre, Keer, Cocker, Conder, Wenning, Greta and tributaries, 5s. Chairman—T. F. FENWICK, Burrow Hall, Kirkby Lonsdale. Clerk—W. T. SHARP, 30, Cable Street, Lancaster.

Name of District. In order of Coast from N.W. to N.E.	
6. Ribble.	**Limits of District.** The coast and territorial sea between lines drawn due west from (1) Blackpool, and (2) Formby New Church Tower; all rivers (with their tributaries and estuaries) flowing thereinto. **Annual Close Season for Salmon.** (All dates inclusive.) Nets, &c.—1st September to 1st February. Rods—2nd November to 1st February. The Gaff (see River Eden)—1st May to 1st November. **Rod Licence Duty.** Salmon (including Trout and Char). Season, £1. Chairman—R. J. Aspinall, Standen Hall, Clitheroe. Clerk—T. J. Backhouse, 27, Victoria Street, Blackburn.
7. Dee.	**Limits of District.** The coast and territorial sea between lines drawn (1) from New Brighton to the Rock Lighthouse and thence through the Bar Lightship, and (2) from Meliden Parish Church though the West Hoyle Spit Buoy; all rivers (with their tributaries and estuaries) flowing thereinto. **Annual Close Season for Salmon.** (All dates inclusive.) Nets, &c.—1st September to 31st March. Rods—2nd November to 31st March. The Gaff is used throughout the whole season. **Rod Licence Duty.** Salmon (including Trout and Char). Season, £1; week, 10s.; day, 5s. Chairman—The Duke of Westminster, K.G., Eaton Hall, Chester. Clerk—Henry Jolliffe, 13, St. John Street, Chester.
8. Elwy and Clwyd.	**Limits of District.** The coast and territorial sea between lines drawn from (1) the tower of Meliden Parish Church through the West Hoyle Spit Buoy, and (2) true N. from the Colwyn Bay Railway Station at Rhôs Bay; all rivers (with their tributaries and estuaries) flowing thereinto.

Name of District. In order of Coast from N.W. to N.E.	
8. Elwy and Clwyd—*continued.*	ANNUAL CLOSE SEASON FOR SALMON. (All dates inclusive.) NETS, &c.—15th September to 15th May. RODS—15th November to 15th May. The GAFF is used throughout the whole season. ROD LICENCE DUTY. Salmon (including Trout and Char). Season, £1. Chairman—Colonel C. S. MAINWARING, Galltfaenan, Tretnant. Clerk—H. F. BIRLEY, The Mount, St. Asaph.
9. Conway.	LIMITS OF DISTRICT. The coast and territorial sea between lines drawn (1) true N. from Colwyn Bay Railway Station at Rhôs Bay, and (2) true N. by E. from the E. bank of the River Aber at the Lavan Sands; all rivers (with their tributaries and estuaries) flowing thereinto. ANNUAL CLOSE SEASON FOR SALMON. (All dates inclusive.) NETS, &c.—15th September to 30th April. RODS—15th November to 30th April. The GAFF (see River Eden)—1st May to 31st October. ROD LICENCE DUTY. Salmon (including Trout and Char). Season, £1; month, 10s.; week, 3s.; day, 1s. Chairman—J. BLACKWALL, Hendre, Llanrwst. Clerk—C. T. ALLARD, Bodgwynedd, Llanrwst.
10. Seiont.	LIMITS OF DISTRICT. The Seiont, Gwrfai, and Llyfni, and their tributaries; all rivers in Carnarvonshire flowing into the sea between the Ferry Causeway at Garth Point and Llanaelhaiarn Point; all rivers in Anglesea flowing into the sea between the Ferry Causeway at Garth and Twyn-y-Parc Point; the coast between those points respectively; and the Menai Straits south and west of the Ferry Causeway.

Name of District. In order of Coast from N.W. to N.E.	
10. Seiont—*continued.*	ANNUAL CLOSE SEASON FOR SALMON. (All dates inclusive.) NETS, &c.—15th September to 1st March. RODS—15th November to 1st March. The GAFF (see River Eden)—2nd March to 1st November. ROD LICENCE DUTY. Salmon (including Trout and Char). Whole district season, £1 1s.; month, 10s. 6d.; week, 5s.; day, 2s. 6d. Rivers Cefni, Braint, and Llyfni, season, 10s. 6d. Chairman—Captain N. P. STEWART, Bryntirion, Bangor. Clerk—J. T. ROBERTS, Marino, Carnarvon.
11. Dwyfach.	LIMITS OF DISTRICT. The Dwyfach and its estuary and tributaries; the coast, and all rivers flowing into the sea between Llanaelhaiarn Point and Criccieth; and the sea for three miles round. ANNUAL CLOSE SEASON FOR SALMON. (All dates inclusive.) NETS, &c.—15th September to 1st March. RODS—15th November to 1st March. The GAFF is used throughout the whole season. ROD LICENCE DUTY. Salmon (including Trout and Char). Season, £1 1s. Chairman—H. J. ELLIS NANNEY, Gwynfryn, Criccieth. Clerk—T. ROBERTS, Portmadoc.
12. Dovey.	LIMITS OF DISTRICT. The Dovey, Mawddach, and Glaslyn, and their tributaries; all rivers flowing into the sea between Criccieth and the south side of the stream at Cynvelin; and the coast between those points. ANNUAL CLOSE SEASON FOR SALMON. (All dates inclusive.) NETS, &c.—1st September to 1st February. RODS—15th November to 14th February. The GAFF is used throughout the whole season.

Name of District, In order of Coast from N.W. to N.E.	
12. Dovey—*continued.*	ROD LICENCE DUTY. Salmon (including Trout and Char). Season, 10s.; month, 5s.; week, 2s. 6d.; day, 1s. Chairman—C. R. WILLIAMS, Dolmelynllyn, near Dolgelly. Clerk—W. R. DAVIES, Dolgelly.
13. Ayron.	LIMITS OF DISTRICT. All rivers with their estuaries and tributaries, and the coast between Carreg Tipog and New Quay Head; and the sea for three miles seaward. ANNUAL CLOSE SEASON FOR SALMON. (All dates inclusive.) NETS, &c.—1st September to 1st February. RODS—15th November to 14th February. The GAFF is used throughout the whole season. ROD LICENCE DUTY. Salmon (including Trout and Char). Season, £1; four weeks, 10s.; fortnight, 5s. Chairman—JOHN EVANS, 1, Alban Square, Aberayron, R.S.O., Cardiganshire. Clerk—E. LIMA JONES, 5, Bridge Street, Aberayron, R.S.O., South Wales.
14. Teify.	LIMITS OF DISTRICT. All rivers, with their estuaries and tributaries, and the coast, between New Quay Head and Dinas Head, and the sea for three miles seaward. ANNUAL CLOSE SEASON FOR SALMON. (All dates inclusive.) NETS, &c.—1st September to 1st February. RODS—20th October to 1st February. The GAFF is used throughout the whole season. ROD LICENCE DUTY. Salmon (including Trout and Char). Season, £1; month, for non-residents in districts, 10s. 6d.; fortnight, ditto, 5s. Chairman—H. W. T. HOWELL, Glaspant, Newcastle Emlyn. Clerk—H. W. Howell, 13, Alban Square, Aberayron, R.S.O., South Wales.

Name of District. In order of Coast from N.W. to N.E.	
15. Cleddy.	**LIMITS OF DISTRICT.** The East and West Cleddy and their estuaries and tributaries; all rivers between Dinas Head and St. Govin's Head; and the coast between these points. **ANNUAL CLOSE SEASON FOR SALMON.** (All dates inclusive.) *NETS, &c.—15th September to 15th March. RODS—1st November to 1st February. The GAFF is used throughout the whole season. **ROD LICENCE DUTY.** Salmon (including Trout and Char). Season, 10s. 6d. Chairman—R. CARROW, Johnston Hall, Haverfordwest. Clerk—R. T. P. WILLIAMS, Haverfordwest.
16. Towy, Loughor, and Taff.	**LIMITS OF DISTRICT.** The Towy, Loughor, and Taff, and their estuaries and tributaries; the coast, and all rivers flowing into the sea, between St. Govin's Head and Worm's Head; and the sea for three miles seaward. **ANNUAL CLOSE SEASON FOR SALMON.** (All dates inclusive.) * NETS, &c.—In the sea between Carmarthen Bar and St. Govin's Head, 1st September to 30th April; rest of district, 1st September to 15th March. RODS—2nd November to 15th March. The GAFF is used throughout the whole season. **ROD LICENCE DUTY.** Salmon (including Trout and Char). Season, £1 1s. Chairman—T. JENKINS, The Friary, Carmarthen. Clerk—W. M. GRIFFITHS, St. Mary Street, Carmarthen.

* The Annual Close Season for puts and putchers is from 1st September to 1st May.

Name of District. In order of Coast from N.W. to N.E.

---

17. Ogmore and Ewenny.

LIMITS OF DISTRICT.

The Ogmore and Ewenny and their estuaries and tributaries; the coast, and all rivers flowing into the sea, between the breakwater at Porthcawl and Cold Knap; and the sea for three miles seaward.

ANNUAL CLOSE SEASON FOR SALMON.

(All dates inclusive.)

NETS, &c.—15th September to 30th April.
RODS—15th November to 30th April.
The GAFF is used throughout the whole Season.

ROD LICENCE DUTY.

Salmon (including Trout and Char).

Season, £1 1s.; month, 10s. 6d.

Chairman—C. P. DAVIES, Cae Court, Bridgend.
Clerk—S. H. STOCKWOOD, Bridgend, Glamorganshire.

---

18. Taff and Ely.

LIMITS OF DISTRICT.

The Taff and Ely with their estuaries and tributaries; the coast, and all rivers flowing into the sea, between Cold Knap and the east end of Bute Dock; and the sea for three miles seaward.

ANNUAL CLOSE SEASON FOR SALMON.

(All dates inclusive.)

NETS, &c.—31st August to 30th April.
RODS—15th November to 30th April.
The GAFF (see River Eden)—1st June to 1st November.

ROD LICENCE DUTY.

Salmon (including Trout and Char).

Season, 10s. 6d.

Chairman—HENRY LEWIS, Greenmeadow, near Cardiff.
Clerk—GEO. E. HALLIDAY, 19, Duke Street, Cardiff.

---

19. Rhymney.

LIMITS OF DISTRICT.

The Rhymney and its estuary and tributaries; the coast and the northern half of the Bristol Channel between the east end of Bute Dock and Ty-ton-y-Pill; and all rivers flowing into the same.

Name of District. In order of Coast from N.W. to N.E.	
19. Rhymney-*continued.*	ANNUAL CLOSE SEASON FOR SALMON. (All dates inclusive.) NETS, &c.—1st September to 1st April. RODS—2nd November to 1st April. The GAFF (see River Eden)—1st May to 1st November. ROD LICENCE DUTY. Salmon (including Trout and Char). Season, 10s. 6d. Chairman—R. W. KENNARD, Llwyndû, Abergavenny. Clerk—Colonel LYNE, Westgate Chambers, Newport, Monmouth.
20. Usk and Ebbw.	LIMITS OF DISTRICT. The Usk and Ebbw and their tributaries; and the northern half of the estuary of the Severn between Ty-ton-y-Pill and Collister Pill. ANNUAL CLOSE SEASON FOR SALMON. (All dates inclusive.) NETS, &c.—1st September to 1st April. RODS—2nd November to 1st April. The GAFF is used below a line drawn from the north boundary of the district along the eastern watershed of the Honddu to Llanvaes Bridge at Brecon, and thence along the eastern watershed of the Tarell to the south boundary of the district, 1st May to 1st November; other parts of district, 1st May to 1st September. ROD LICENCE DUTY. Salmon (including Trout and Char). Season, £1. Chairman—Colonel CHAS. LYNE, Brynhyfryd, Newport, Monmouth. Clerk—HORACE S. LYNE, Westgate Chambers, Newport, Monmouth.
21. Wye.	LIMITS OF DISTRICT. The Wye and its estuary and tributaries; and the northern half of the estuary of the Severn between Collister Pill and Lydney Pill. ANNUAL CLOSE SEASON FOR SALMON. (All dates inclusive.) NETS, &c.—1st September to 1st February. RODS—2nd November to 1st February. The GAFF (see River Eden)—15th March to 1st November.

Name of District. In order of Coast from N.W. to N.E.	
21. Wye—*continued.*	ROD LICENCE DUTY. Salmon (including Trout and Char). In Wye below Llanwrthwl Bridge and other parts of district below Builth Bridge, £1; elsewhere, 10s. Chairman—The DUKE OF BEAUFORD, K.G., Badminton, Wilts. Clerk—E. OWEN, Builth, R.S.O., Brecon.
22. Severn.	LIMITS OF DISTRICT. The estuary of the Severn above Lydney Pill; the Somersetshire half of the estuary between Clapton Pill and Avon Battery; the Severn and tributaries (except the Avon so far as it lies in Warwickshire); all streams with their estuaries and tributaries flowing into the portion of the estuary above defined. ANNUAL CLOSE SEASON FOR SALMON. (All dates inclusive.) NETS, &c.—In Borough of Shrewsbury, 1st September to 15th June. RODS—2nd November to 1st February. The GAFF is used throughout the whole angling season. ROD LICENCE DUTY. Salmon (including Trout and Char). Season, 10s. Chairman—J. W. WILLIS, Bund, 15, Old Square, Lincoln's Inn, W.C. Clerk—J. STALLARD, Junior, Pierpoint Street, Worcester.
23. Avon, Brue, and Parret.	LIMITS OF DISTRICT. The Avon, Brue, and Parret; their estuaries and tributaries; all streams flowing into the sea between Avon Battery and the boundary of Devon and Somerset; and the coast between those points. ANNUAL CLOSE SEASON FOR SALMON. (All dates inclusive.) NETS, &c.—1st September to 1st February. RODS.—2nd November to 1st February. The GAFF is used throughout the whole angling season. ROD LICENCE DUTY. Salmon (including Trout and Char). Season, 7s. 6d. Chairman—H. D. SKRINE, Claverton Manor, near Bath. Clerk—T. FOSTER-BARHAM, Castle Street, Bridgwater, Somerset.

Name of District. In order of Coast from N.W. to N.E.	
24. Taw and Torridge.	LIMITS OF DISTRICT. The Taw and Torridge and their estuaries and tributaries in Devonshire; the north coast of Devonshire; and all rivers in Devonshire flowing into the sea adjoining. ANNUAL CLOSE SEASON FOR SALMON. (All dates inclusive.) NETS, &c.—21st September to 30th April. RODS—16th November to 31st March. The GAFF (see River Eden)—1st June to 15th November. ROD LICENCE DUTY. Salmon (including Trout and Char). Season, £1 1s. Chairman—Sir W. R. WILLIAMS, Bart., Upcott House, Barnstaple. Clerk—W. H. TOLLER, Barnstaple.
25. Camel.	LIMITS OF DISTRICT. The coast and territorial sea between lines drawn due west from (1) the W. boundary of Devon, (2) Peel Point; all rivers (with their tributaries and estuaries) flowing thereinto. ANNUAL CLOSE SEASON FOR SALMON. (All dates inclusive.) NETS, &c.—1st November to 4th April. RODS—1st December to 30th April. The GAFF is used throughout the whole Angling Season. ROD LICENCE DUTY. Salmon (including Trout and Char). Season, 10s. Chairman—J. J. E. VENNING, Ker Street, Devonport. Clerk—J. R. COLLINS, Fore Street, Bodmin.
26. Fowey.	LIMITS OF DISTRICT. The coast and territorial sea between lines drawn (1) due west from Peel Point, and (2) due south from Rame Head; all rivers (with their tributaries and estuaries) flowing thereinto.

Name of District. In order of Coast from N.W. to N.E.	
26. Fowey—*continued.*	ANNUAL CLOSE SEASON FOR SALMON. (All dates inclusive.) NETS, &c.—Below Lostwithiel Bridge, 1st November to 4th April. RODS—Between Lostwithiel Bridge and a line drawn from north end of Penquite Wood to St. Winnow Point, 1st December to 30th April; other parts of district, 1st December to 4th April. ROD LICENCE DUTY. Salmon (including Trout and Char). Season, 10s. Chairman—R. FOSTER, Lanwithan, Lostwithiel. Clerk—W. PEASE, Jun., Lostwithiel.
27. Tamar and Plym.	LIMITS OF DISTRICT. The coast and territorial sea between lines drawn true south from (1) Rame Head, and (2) Stoke Point; all rivers (with their tributaries and estuaries) flowing thereinto. ANNUAL CLOSE SEASON FOR SALMON. (All dates inclusive.) NETS, &c.—1st September to 1st February. RODS—2nd November to 1st February. ROD LICENCE DUTY. Salmon (including Trout and Char). Season, 7s. 6d. Chairman—Captain R. C. COODE, Polapit, Tamar, Launceston. Clerk—W. W. MATHEWS, Tavistock.
28. Avon. (Devon.)	LIMITS OF DISTRICT. The coast and territorial sea between lines drawn (1) true S. from Stoke Point, and (2) true E. from Start Point; all rivers (with their tributaries and estuaries) flowing thereinto. ANNUAL CLOSE SEASON FOR SALMON. (All dates inclusive.) * NETS, &c.—In the Erme, 30th September to 4th April; rest of district 30th September to 1st May. RODS—In the Erme, 30th November to 4th April; rest of district, 30th November to 1st May. The GAFF (see River Eden)—1st April to 30th September. * The Annual Close Season for puts and putchers is from 1st September to 1st May.

Name of District. In order of Coast from N.W. to N.E.	
28. Avon. (Devon.)—*continued.*	ROD LICENCE DUTY. Salmon (including Trout and Char). Season, £1. Chairman—F. J. CORNISH-BOWDEN, Black Hall, Ivybridge. Clerk—W. BEER, Kingsbridge.
29. Dart.	LIMITS OF DISTRICT. The coast and territorial sea between lines drawn true E. from (1) Start Point, and (2) Hope's Nose; all rivers (with their tributaries and estuaries) flowing therinto. ANNUAL CLOSE SEASON FOR SALMON. (All dates inclusive.) NETS, &c.—1st September to 1st March. RODS—2nd November to 1st March. The GAFF (see River Eden)—2nd April to 31st October. ROD LICENCE DUTY. Salmon (including Trout and Char). Season, £1; week, 7s. 6d. Chairman—Hon. R. DAWSON, Holne Park, Ashburton. Clerk—A. PIKE, Clifton Villa, Bridgetown, Totnes.
30. Teign.	LIMITS OF DISTRICT. The coast and territorial sea between lines drawn (1) true E. from Hope's Nose, and (2) true S.E. from the shore near Dawlish, through the Clerk Rock; all rivers (with their tributaries and estuaries) flowing thereinto. ANNUAL CLOSE SEASON FOR SALMON. (All dates inclusive.) NETS, &c.—1st September to 2nd March. RODS—1st November to 2nd March. The GAFF (see River Eden)—1st May to 1st September. ROD LICENCE DUTY. Salmon (including Trout and Char). Season, £1; month, 5s.; week, 2s. 6d.; day, 2s. Chairman—LORD CLIFFORD, Ugbrook Park, Chudleigh. Clerk—SID. HACKER, Newton Abbot.

Name of District.
In order of Coast
from N.W. to N.E.

---

31. Exe.

LIMITS OF DISTRICT.

The Esk and its estuary and tributaries, all rivers flowing into the sea between Clerk Rock and first headland west of Ottermouth; and the coast between those points.

ANNUAL CLOSE SEASON FOR SALMON.
(All dates inclusive.)

NETS, &c.—1st September to 1st March.
RODS—2nd November to 1st March.
The GAFF (see River Eden)—1st May to 30th September.

ROD LICENCE DUTY.
Salmon (including Trout and Char).

Season, £1.

Chairman—J. E. C. WALKEY, Ide, near Exeter.
Clerk—B. J. FORD, 25, Southernhay, Exeter.

---

32. Otter.

LIMITS OF DISTRICT.

The Otter and its estuary and tributaries; all rivers flowing into the sea between first headland west of Ottermouth and Beer Head; and the coast between those points.

ANNUAL CLOSE SEASON FOR SALMON.
(All dates inclusive.)

NETS, &c.—1st September to 1st February.
RODS—2nd November to 1st February.
The GAFF is used throughout the whole Angling Season.

ROD LICENCE DUTY.
Salmon (including Trout and Char).

Season, £1.

---

33. Axe.

LIMITS OF DISTRICT.

The Axe and it estuary and tributaries; all rivers flowing into the sea between Beer Head and Portland Bill; and the coast between those points.

ANNUAL CLOSE SEASON FOR SALMON.
(All dates inclusive.)

NETS, &c.—20th September to 30th April.
RODS—20th November to 30th April.
The GAFF is used throughout the whole Angling Season.

Name of District. In order of Coast from N.W. to N.E.	
23. Axe—*continued.*	ROD LICENCE DUTY. Salmon (including Trout and Char). Season, 10s. Chairman—W. H. B. KNIGHT, Cloakham House, Axminster. Clerk—W. FORWARD, Axminster.
34. Frome.	LIMITS OF DISTRICT. The Frome and its estuary and tributaries; all rivers flowing into the sea between Portland Bill and the west boundary of Hants; and the coast between those points. ANNUAL CLOSE SEASON FOR SALMON. (All dates inclusive.) NETS, &c.—1st September to 1st February. RODS—2nd November to 1st February. The GAFF is used throughout the whole Angling Season. ROD LICENCE DUTY. Salmon (including Trout and Char). Season, £1. Chairman—W. M. CALCRAFT, Rempstone Hall, Corfe Castle. Clerk—P. E. L. BUDGE, Wareham.
35. Avon and Stour.	LIMITS OF DISTRICT. The Avon and Stour and their tributaries in Hants, Dorset, and Wilts; their estuaries; all rivers between the west boundary of Hants and Hurst Castle Lighthouse; and the coast between those points. ANNUAL CLOSE SEASON FOR SALMON. (All dates inclusive.) * NETS, &c.—31st July to 1st February. RODS—2nd October to 1st February. The GAFF is used throughout the whole Angling Season. ROD LICENCE DUTY. Salmon (including Trout and Char). Season, £1. Chairman—Hon. E. B. PORTMAN, 46, Cadogan Place, London, S.W. Clerk—R. D. SHARP, Christchurch.

* The Annual Close Season for puts and putchers is from 1st September to 1st May.

Name of District. In order of Coast from N.W. to N.E.	
36. Ouse. (Sussex.)	LIMITS OF DISTRICT. The Ouse and its estuary and tributaries ; the coast, and all rivers flowing into the sea, between Portobello Coastguard Station and Seaford Head Signal House ; and the sea for 3 miles seaward. ANNUAL CLOSE SEASON FOR SALMON. (All dates inclusive.) NETS, &c.—1st September to 1st April. RODS—1st November to 1st April. The GAFF is used throughout the whole Angling Season. ROD LICENCE DUTY. Salmon (including Trout and Char). Season, 5s. Chairman—JAMES H. SCLATER, Newick Park, Newick, Lewes. Clerk—F. HOLMAN, 86, High Street, Lewes.
37. Stour. (Canterbury.)	LIMITS OF DISTRICT. The Stour and its estuary and tributaries ; all rivers flowing into the sea between the north and south Forelands ; and the coast between those points. ANNUAL CLOSE SEASON FOR SALMON. (All dates inclusive.) NETS, &c.—1st September to 1st May. RODS—2nd November to 1st May. The GAFF is used throughout the whole Angling Season. ROD LICENCE DUTY. Salmon (including Trout and Char). Season, £1. Chairman— Clerk—M. KINGSFORD, Canterbury.
38. Trent.	ANNUAL CLOSE SEASON FOR SALMON. (All dates inclusive.) NETS, &c.—1st September to 1st February. RODS—2nd November to 1st February. The GAFF is used throughout the whole Angling Season.

Name of District. In order of Coast from N.W. to N.E.	
38. Trent—*continued.*	ROD LICENCE DUTY. Salmon (including Trout and Char). Season, 10s. Chairman—Sir CHARLES WOLSELEY, Bart., Wolseley Hall, Stafford. Clerk—C. K. EDDOWES, 13, St. Mary's Gate, Derby.
39. Yorkshire	LIMITS OF DISTRICT. The Yorks half of the Humber; all rivers in Yorks, with their tributaries flowing into the Seine; the coast, and the sea for 3 miles seaward, between Spurn Head, and the north side of Thorney Beck; all rivers in Yorks flowing into the sea between those points. ANNUAL CLOSE SEASON FOR SALMON. (All dates inclusive.) NETS, &c.—1st September to 1st February. RODS—16th November to last day of February. The GAFF (see River Eden)—1st May to 1st November. ROD LICENCE DUTY. Salmon (including Trout and Char). Season, £1. Chairman—Capt. the Hon. CECIL DUNCOMBE, The Grange, Nawton, York. Clerk—J. H. PHILLIPS, 22, Albemarle Crescent, Scarborough.
40. Esk. (Yorks.)	LIMITS OF DISTRICT. The Esk and its estuary and tributaries; the coast, and all rivers flowing into the sea, between the north side of Thorney Beck and the south side of Skinningrove Beck; and the sea for 3 miles seaward. ANNUAL CLOSE SEASON FOR SALMON. (All dates inclusive.) NETS, &c.—1st September to 1st February. RODS—2nd November to 1st February. The GAFF is used throughout the whole Angling Season. ROD LICENCE DUTY. Salmon (including Trout and Char). Season, 10s.; month, 5s.; day, 2s. 6d. (Monthly and day licences are not to extend beyond 30th June.) Chairman—Lieut.-Col. J. W. RICHARDSON, The Hall, Sneaton, Whitby. Clerk—W. BROWN, The Sawmills, Whitby.

Name of District. in order of Coast from N.W. to N.E.

41. Tees.

LIMITS OF DISTRICT.

The coast and territorial sea between lines drawn seawards from (1) the south side of Skinningrove Beck, and (2) the north side of the stream near Hardwick Hall; and all rivers (with their tributaries and estuaries) flowing thereinto.

ANNUAL CLOSE SEASON FOR SALMON.
(All dates inclusive.)

NETS, &c.—1st September to 1st February.
RODS—2nd November to 1st February.
The GAFF is used throughout the whole Angling Season.

ROD LICENCE DUTY.
Salmon (including Trout and Char).

Season, £1.

Chairman—Rt. Hon. J. LOWTHER, M.P., 59, Grosvenor Street, London, S.W.
Clerk—M. B. DODDS, Stockton-on-Tees.

---

42. Wear.

LIMITS OF DISTRICT.

The Wear and its estuary and tributaries; the coast, and all rivers flowing into the sea, between the north side of the stream near Hardwick Hall and Souter Point; and the sea for three miles seaward.

ANNUAL CLOSE SEASON FOR SALMON.
(All dates inclusive.)

NETS, &c.—1st September to 1st February.
RODS—2nd November to 1st February.
The GAFF is used throughout the Season.

ROD LICENCE DUTY.
Salmon (including Trout and Char).

Season, 5s.

Chairman—Colonel T. C. MCKENZIE, The Cedars, Sunderland
Clerk—WM. HALCRO, 52, John Street, Sunderland.

---

43. Tyne.

LIMITS OF DISTRICT.

The Tyne and its estuary and tributaries; all rivers flowing into the sea between Souter Point and Crag Point; and the coast, and the sea for three miles seaward, between Souter Point and Newbiggin Point.

Name of District In order of Coast. from N.W. to N.E.	
43. Tyne—*continued.*	**Annual Close Season for Salmon.** (All dates inclusive.) Nets, &c.—1st September to 1st February. Rods—2nd November to 1st February. The Gaff is used throughout the whole season. **Rod Licence Duty.** Salmon (including Trout and Char). Whole district, £1; in South Tyne, above Warden Dam, 5s.; in Reedwater and North Tyne, above junction of Reed and Tyne, 10s.; in Reed above Old Bridge, 5s. Chairman—J. M. Ridley, Walwick Hall, Humshaugh, Northumberland. Clerk—R Gibson, Hexham.
44. Coquet.	**Limits of District.** The Coquet and its tributaries; and all rivers flowing into the sea between a point of two miles north of Coquet mouth and a point seven miles south of Coquet mouth; and the coast, and the sea for three miles seaward, between Newbiggin Point and Hawick Burn mouth. **Annual Close Season for Salmon.** (All dates inclusive.) Nets, &c.—15th September to 25th March. Rods—1st November to 31st January. The Gaff (see River Eden)—1st February to 30th September. **Rod Licence Duty.** Salmon (including Trout and Char). Season, 5s. Chairman—Rev. R. Burdon, Heddon-on-the-Wall, Northumberland. Clerk—C. Percy, Alnwick.

SALMON FISHING IN THE UNITED KINGDOM.

ANNUAL CLOSE SEASONS FOR FISHING FOR SALMON OTHERWISE THAN BY ROD AND LINE, AS APPOINTED UP TO THE 31ST JULY, 1893.

ENGLAND AND WALES.

The Statutory Annual Close Season for fishing for Salmon, otherwise than by Rod and Line, in England and Wales, is from SEPTEMBER 1st to FEBRUARY 1st, except in those cases where this Close Season has been altered as follows :—

Name of District.	Close Season for Nets. (All days inclusive.)
Avon and Stour (Hants)	July 31st to February 1st.
Avon and Erme (Devon) (River Erme only)	September 30th to April 4th.
Avon (rest of district)	September 30th to May 1st.
Axe	September 20th to April 30th.
Camel	November 1st to April 4th.
Cleddy	September 15th to March 15th.
Clwyd and Elwy	September 15th to May 15th.
Conway	September 15th to April 30th.
Coquet	September 15th to March 25th.
Cumberland, West (Ehen, Calder, Irt, Esk, Mite)...	September 15th to March 31st.
Dart	September 1st to March 1st.
Dee	September 1st to March 31st.
Derwent (Cumberland)	September 15th to March 10th.
Dovey, Mawddach, and Glaslyn	September 14th to April 30th.
Dwyfach	September 15th to March 1st.
Eden, in the Solway, from Old Sandsfield downwards only	September 10th to February 10th.
Exe	September 1st to March 1st.
Fowey (below Lostwithiel Bridge only) ...	November 1st to April 4th.
Kent, Leven, Duddon, Bela, Winster ...	September 15th to March 31st.
Lune (in tidal waters)	September 8th to March 1st.
Lune (in upper waters)	September 15th to March 1st.

ENGLAND AND WALES—*continued.*

Name of District.	Close Season for Nets. (All days inclusive.)
Ogmore and Ewenny	September 15th to April 30th.
Ouse (Sussex)	September 1st to April 1st.
Rhymney	September 1st to April 1st.
Seiont, Gwrfai, and Llyfni...	September 15th to March 1st.
Severn (in the Borough of Shrewsbury only)...	September 1st to June 15th.
Stour (Canterbury)...	September 1st to May 1st.
Taff and Ely	August 31st to April 30th.
Taw and Torridge	September 21st to April 30th.
Teign	September 1st to March 2nd.
Towy, Loughor and Taf (in the sea between Carmarthen Bar and St. Govin's Head)	September 1st to April 30th.
Towy, Loughor, and Taf (in other parts of the district)	September 1st to March 15th.
Usk and Ebbw	September 1st to April 1st.

IRELAND.

Name of District.	* Close Season for Tidal Nets. (All days inclusive.)
Achill Island	September 1st to February 15th.
Annagassan	August 20th to February 11th.
Ballisodare	September 14th to March 3rd.
Ballycastle (County Mayo)...	August 13th to March 15th.
Ballycroy Rivers	September 1st to February 15th.
Ballynahinch	August 16th to January 31st.
Bandon	August 16th to last day in February.
Bann...	August 20th to February 3rd.
Bantry Bay Rivers	October 1st to April 30th.
Barrow	August 16th to January 31st.
Blackwater	August 1st to January 31st.
Boyne	August 5th to February 11th.
Buncrana	September 15th to April 14th.
Bundrowes	August 20th to last day in February.
Burrishoole	September 1st to February 15th.
Bush...	August 20th to March 16th.
Carragh	August 1st to January 16th.

* In a few instances in Ireland, the season for fresh water netting differs from the tidal netting.

IRELAND—*continued.*

Name of District.	* Close Season for Tidal Nets. (All days inclusive.)
Carrownisky...	September 16th to June 30th.
Cashla or Costello	August 16th to January 31st.
Cashen	September 1st to May 31st.
Clifden	September 1st to February 15th.
Clohane	September 16th to March 31st.
Crumlin	August 16th to January 31st.
Dawros or Kylemore	September 1st to February 15th.
Dee	August 20th to February 11th.
Deel or Askeaton	Prohibited.
Delphi	September 1st to February 15th.
Doohulla	August 16th to January 31st.
Doonbeg	September 16th to April 30th.
Drumcliffe	August 20th to February 3rd.
Easkey	September 1st to May 31st.
Ennistymon or Lahinch	September 16th to April 30th.
Erriff	September 1st to February 15th.
Erne	August 20th to last day in February.
Eske	September 18th to March 31st.
Fane	October 1st to April 30th.
Fergus	August 1st to February 11th.
Foyle	September 1st to April 14th.
Galway	September 1st to February 15th.
Glen of Teelin	August 20th to last day in February.
Glenamoy	September 16th to April 30th.
Glenarm	August 20th to March 16th.
Glendun	August 20th to March 16th.
Glyde	August 20th to February 11th.
Grange	August 20th to February 3rd.
Gweebarra	October 1st to March 31st.
Gweedore	August 20th to February 3rd.
Ilen	October 1st to April 30th.
Inny	October 1st to April 30th.
Inver (County Galway)	August 16th to January 31st.
Kenmare Bay Rivers	September 16th to March 31st.
Kilcolgan	August 16th to January 31st.
Laune (County Kerry)	August 1st to January 16th.
Leanane	August 20th to February 3rd.
Lee	August 16th to January 31st.

* In a few instances in Ireland, the season for fresh water netting differs from the tidal netting.

IRELAND—*continued.*

Name of District.	* Close Season for Tidal Nets. (All days inclusive.)
Liffey	... August 16th to January 31st.
Lough Neagh	... August 20th to last day in February.
Louisburgh	... September 16th to June 30th.
Maigue	... July 17th to January 31st.
Maine (County Kerry)	... September 16th to April 30th.
Moy	... August 13th to March 15th.
Moyour	... September 1st to February 15th.
Mulcaire	... August 1st to February 11th.
Munhim	... September 1st to February 15th.
Newport	... September 1st to March 19th.
Nore...	... August 16th to January 31st.
Owenea (Glenties)	... September 1st to May 31st.
Owengarve	... September 1st to February 15th.
Owenmore (County Mayo)... ...	... September 1st to February 15th.
Palmerston	... September 1st to May 31st.
Roe	... September 1st to April 14th.
Screeb	... August 16th to January 31st.
Shannon	... August 1st to February 11th.
Slaney	... September 30th to March 31st.
Sligo...	... July 16th to December 31st.
Spiddal	... August 16th to January 31st.
Suir	... August 16th to January 31st.
Waterville	... July 16th to December 31st.

SCOTLAND.

The Annual Close Season for fishing for Salmon, otherwise than by Rod and Line, in Scotland, is from August 27th to February 10th, except in the following Districts:—

Name of District.	Close Season for Nets. (All days inclusive.)
Add	September 1st to February 15th.
Drummachloy or Glenmore (Isle of Bute)...	
Eckaig	
Esk, North	
Esk, South	
Fyne, Shira, and Aray (Lock Fyne) ...	
Ruel...	

* In a few instances in Ireland, the season for fresh water netting differs from the tidal netting.

SCOTLAND—*continued.*

Name of District.	Close Season for Nets. (All days inclusive.)
Annan	September 10th to February 24th.
Bervie	
Carradale (Cantyre)	
Clayburn, Finnis Bay, Avennan-Gesen, Strathgravat, North Lacastile, Scalladale, and Mawrig (East Harris)	
Fincastle, Meaveg, Ballanachist, South Lacastile, Borve, and Obb (West Harris)	
Fleet (Kirkcudbright)	
Fleet (Sutherland)	
Girvan	September 10th to February 24th.
Howmore	
Inner (Jura)...	
Iorsa (Arran)	
Irvine and Garnock	
Laggan and Sorn (Islay)	
Luce	
Mullanageren, Horasary, and Loch-na-Ciste (North Uist)	
Nith...	
Orkney Islands (River from Loch of Stenness, &c.)	
Shetland Islands (River of Sandwater, &c.)	
Stinchar	
Ugie...	
Urr	
Ythan	
Tweed	September 15th to February 14th.

TABLE SHOWING THE CLOSE SEASONS FOR SALMON AND TROUT IN THE DIFFERENT DISTRICTS IN IRELAND AT DATE OCTOBER, 1893.

No. and Name of District.	
1. Dublin.	**Boundary of District.** Skerries to Wicklow. **Tidal.** Between Howth and Dalkey Island, between 15th August and 1st February; between Dalkey Island and Wicklow Head, between 30th September and 1st April; for remainder of District, between 15th September and 4th March. **Fresh Water.** Same as Tidal, save between Dalkey Island and Wicklow Head (exclusive of Bray River), which is between 15th August and 1st April; and, save also in Bray River, which is between 30th September and 1st April. **Angling with Cross Lines.** Same as Nets in Fresh Water. **Angling with Single Rod and Line.** Between 31st October and 1st February, save Broadmeadow Water and Ward Rivers, between 14th October and 1st February. **Date of Last Change.** 15th October, 1874; 21st July, 1882; 27th January, 1883; 4th September, 1893. **Principal Rivers in District.** Liffey, Bray, Vartry.
2. Wexford.	**Boundary of District.** Wicklow to Kiln Bay, east of Bannow Bay. **Tidal.** Between 15th September to 20th April, save in River Slaney, which is between 29th September and 1st April.

<table>
<tr><th>No. and Name of District.</th><th></th></tr>
<tr><td>2.
Wexford—
continued.</td><td>FRESH WATER.
Between 15th September and 20th April.
ANGLING WITH CROSS LINES.
Same as for Nets in Fresh Water.
ANGLING WITH SINGLE ROD AND LINE.
Between 30th September and 15th March, save River Slaney and tributaries, between 14th September and 16th February.
DATE OF LAST CHANGE.
26th December, 1873; 2nd October, 1882; 24th December, 1888.
PRINCIPAL RIVERS IN DISTRICT.
Slaney, Courtown, Inch, Urrin, Boro.</td></tr>
<tr><td>3.
Water-ford.</td><td>BOUNDARY OF DISTRICT.
Kiln Bay to Helvick Head.
TIDAL.
Between 15th August and 1st February.
FRESH WATER.
Same as Tidal.
ANGLING WITH CROSS LINES.
Same as for Nets in Fresh Water.
ANGLING WITH SINGLE ROD AND LINE.
Between 30th September and 1st February, save River Suir and tributaries, between 15th October and 1st February.
DATE OF LAST CHANGE.
12th November, 1874; 17th February, 1883.
PRINCIPAL RIVERS IN DISTRICT.
Suir, Nore, and Barrow.</td></tr>
<tr><td>4.
Lismore.</td><td>BOUNDARY OF DISTRICT.
Helvick Head to Ballycotton.
TIDAL.
Between 31st July and 1st February.</td></tr>
</table>

No. and Name of District.	
4. Lismore—*continued.*	**Fresh Water.** Same as Tidal. **Angling with Cross Lines.** Same as for Nets in Fresh Water. **Angling with Single Rod and Line.** Between 30th September and 1st February. **Date of Last Change.** 8th September, 1893. **Principal Rivers in District.** Blackwater.
5. Cork.	**Boundary of District.** Ballycotton Head to Galley Head. **Tidal.** From Ballycotton to Barry's Head, between 15th August and 1st February; and from Barry's Head to Galley Head (save in Bandon and Argideen Rivers) between 15th August and 15th February; for Bandon, between 15th August and 1st March; and for Argideen, between 31st August and 1st March. **Fresh Water.** Same as Tidal. **Angling with Cross Lines.** Same as for Nets in Fresh Water. **Angling with Single Rod and Line.** From Ballycotton to Barry's Head, between 12th October and 1st February; and from Barry's Head to Galley Head, between 12th October and 15th February, save in the Argideen River, which is between the 31st October and 15th February. **Date of Last Change.** 20th September, 1875; 14th December, 1881; 6th April, 1889. **Principal Rivers in District.** Lee, Bandon, Argideen.

No. and Name of District.	
6[1]. Skibbereen.	**Boundary of District.** Galley Head to Mizen Head. **Tidal.** Between 30th September and 1st May. **Fresh Water.** Same as Tidal. **Angling with Cross Lines.** Same as for Nets in Fresh Water. **Angling with Single Rod and Line.** Between 31st October and 1st February. **Date of Last Change.** 17th June, 1891. **Principal Rivers in District.** Ilen.
6[2]. Bantry.	**Boundary of District.** Mizen Head to Crow Head. **Tidal.** Between 30th September and 1st May. **Fresh Water.** Same as Tidal. **Angling with Cross Lines.** Same as for Nets in Fresh Water. **Angling with Single Rod and Line.** Between 31st October and 17th March. **Date of Last Change.** 29th January, 1873. **Principal Rivers in District.** Glengariffe, Snave, &c.

No. and Name of District.	
6[3] Kenmare.	BOUNDARY OF DISTRICT. Crow Head to Lamb Head. TIDAL. Between 15th September and 1st April. FRESH WATER. Same as Tidal. ANGLING WITH CROSS LINES. Same as for Nets in Fresh Water. ANGLING WITH SINGLE ROD AND LINE. Between 31st October and 1st April. DATE OF LAST CHANGE. 7th February, 1856; 14th November, 1882. PRINCIPAL RIVERS IN DISTRICT. Blackwater, Roughty, Cloonee, Sneem.
7. Killarney.	BOUNDARY OF DISTRICT. Lamb Head to Dunmore Head, including Blaskets. TIDAL. Between Dunmore Head and Canglass Point, embracing the Blasket Island, the sea and sea coast between these points, and all lakes and rivers and their tributaries running into the sea between said points, save the rivers Maine, Laune, Carragh, and Rosbehy or Behy, and their lakes and tributaries between 31st August and 1st May. In River Maine and its tributaries, between 15th September and 1st May. In Rivers Laune, Carragh, and Rosbehy or Behy, and their lakes and tributaries, between 31st July and 17th January. Between Canglass Point and Bolus Head, embracing the islands and sea and coast between these points, and all lakes and rivers and their tributaries running into the sea between said points, between 15th September and 1st June. Between Bolûs Head and Lamb Head, embracing the islands and sea and coasts between these points, and all lakes and rivers and their

No. and Name of District.

7. Killarney *continued.*

tributaries running into the sea between these two points, save the River Inny and the Waterville or Currane River and their tributaries, between 31st July and 1st May.

In the River Inny and its tributaries, between 30th September and 1st May.

In Waterville or Currane River and its tributaries, and all lakes running into said river, between 15th July and 1st January.

Fresh Water.

Same as Tidal.

Angling with Cross Lines.

Same as for Nets in Fresh Water.

Angling with Single Rod and Line.

Between Dunmore Head and Inch Point, and embracing all lakes and all rivers and their tributaries running into the sea between those points, between 31st October and 1st April.

Between Inch Point and Canglass Point, and including all lakes and all rivers and their tributaries flowing into the sea between those points, save the River Maine and its tributaries, between 15th October and 1st February.

In River Maine and its tributaries between 31st October and 1st April.

Between Canglass Point and Bolus Head, and embracing all lakes and rivers and their tributaries flowing into the sea between those points, between 15th September and 1st June.

Between Bolus Head and Lamb Head, and embracing all lakes and rivers and their tributaries flowing into the sea between those points, between 15th October and 1st February.

Date of Last Change.

27th September, 1889.

Principal Rivers in District.

Inny, Roshehy, Currane, Balencia, Maine, Laune, Caragh.

No. and Name of District.	
8. Limerick.	**Boundary of District.** Dunmore to Hags Head. **Tidal.** Between 31st July and 12th February, save Rivers Cashen and Maigue, and tributaries, and save between Kerry Head and Dunmore Head, and between Loop Head and Hag's Head, and all rivers running into the sea between those points. For River Cashen (down to its mouth) and tributaries, between 31st August and 1st June. For Maigue River, between 16th July and 1st February. Between Dunmore Head and Kerry Head, and all rivers flowing into the sea between those points, between 15th September and 1st April. Between Loop Head and Hag's Head, and all rivers running into the sea between those points, between 15th September and 1st May. **Fresh Water.** Same as Tidal. **Angling with Cross Lines.** Same as for Nets in Fresh Water. **Angling with Single Rod and Line.** Between 30th September and 1st February, save in that part situated in the County Westmeath, the waters of which flow into Lough Ree and the River Shannon, and save in Lough Sheelin; save Shannon, Feale, Geale, and Cashen, save in Mulcair River, and save in all rivers running into the sea, between Loop Head and Hag's Head, and between Dunmore Head and Kerry Head, and save also in Rivers Owenmore and Feohanagh, in the County of Kerry, which are situated between Dunmore Head and Kerry Head. For Rivers Shannon and Mulcair between 31st October and 1st February following. For Feale, Geale, and Cashen and tributaries, between 31st October and 1st May; between Loop Head and Hag's Head, between 30th September and 1st March and between Dunmore Head and Kerry

No. and Name of District.	
8. Limerick—*continued.*	Head (save in the Rivers Owenmore and Feohanagh), between 30th September and 1st April. For Owenmore and Feohanagh, situated between Dunmore Head and Kerry Head, between 31st October and 1st May. For that part of the Limerick district, situated in the County of Westmeath, the waters of which flow into Lough Ree and River Shannon, and for Lough Sheelin, between 30th September and 1st March. DATE OF LAST CHANGE. 13th October, 1874; 17th September, 1878; 27th August, 1879; 19th August, 1882; 8th September, 1885; 27th August, 1889; 14th September, 1889; 18th January, 1893. PRINCIPAL RIVERS IN DISTRICT. Shannon, Deel, Fergus, Doonbeg, Cashen, Maigue, &c.
9[1]. Galway.	BOUNDARY OF DISTRICT. Hag's Head to Sea Point of boundary between Townlands of Keeraunnagark South and Banraghbaun South S.E. of Cashla Coastguard Station. TIDAL. Between 15th August and 1st February, save in Corrib or Galway, which is between 31st August and 16th February. FRESH WATER. Same as Tidal. ANGLING WITH CROSS LINES. Same as for Nets in Fresh Water. ANGLING WITH SINGLE ROD AND LINE. Between 15th October and 1st February, save Spiddal and Crumlin, which is between 31st October and 1st February; and save Oughterard and tributaries, which is between 30th September and 1st February. DATE OF LAST CHANGE. 26th December, 1871; 23rd October, 1876; 20th August, 1878; 10th July, 1879; 27th January, 1887. PRINCIPAL RIVERS IN DISTRICT. Corrib, Spiddle, Crumlin, Oughterard, &c.

No. and Name of District.	
9[2]. Connemara.	BOUNDARY OF DISTRICT. Sea point of boundary between Townlands of Keeraunnagark South and Banraghbaun South, S.E. of Cashla Coastguard Station to Slyne Head. TIDAL. Between 15th August and 1st February. FRESH WATER. Same as Tidal. ANGLING WITH CROSS LINES. Same as for Nets in Fresh Water. ANGLING WITH SINGLE ROD AND LINE. Between 15th October and 1st February, save Doohulla, Cashla, Ballinahinch, Screeb, and Inver, which is between 31st October and 1st February. DATE OF LAST CHANGE. 26th December, 1871; 17th September, 1877; 20th August, 1878. PRINCIPAL RIVERS IN DISTRICT. Cashla, Doohulla, Inver, Screeb, Ballinahinch, Gowla, &c.
10[1]. Ballinakill.	BOUNDARY OF DISTRICT. Slyne Head to Pigeon Point. TIDAL. Between 31st August and 16th February, save in Louisburgh and Carrownisky Rivers and estuaries. For Louisburgh and Carrownisky Rivers and estuaries, between 15th September and 1st July. FRESH WATER. Same as Tidal. ANGLING WITH CROSS LINES. Same as for Nets in Fresh Water. ANGLING WITH SINGLE ROD AND LINE. Between 31st October and 1st February, save in Carrownisky River—between 31st October and 1st July; and save Louisburgh River and tributaries, between 31st October and 1st June. DATE OF LAST CHANGE. 1st June, 1872; 20th December, 1880. PRINCIPAL RIVERS IN DISTRICT. Erriff, Dauross, Louisburgh, Carrownisky.

No. and Name of District.	
10². Bangor.	**BOUNDARY OF DISTRICT.** Pigeon Point to Benwee Head. **TIDAL.** Between 31st August and 16th February, save in Newport and Glenamoy, Burrishoole and Owengarve Rivers and estuaries; for Newport River and estuary 31st August and 20th March; Glenamoy River and estuary, 15th September and 1st May; Burrishoole and Owengarve River and estuaries, 31st August and 16th February. **FRESH WATER.** Same as Tidal. **ANGLING WITH CROSS LINES.** Same as for Nets in Fresh Water. **ANGLING WITH SINGLE ROD AND LINE.** Between 30th September and 1st May, save in Owenmore and Munhim, which is between 30th September and 1st February; and save in Burrishoole, between 31st October and 1st February; and save Owengarve and Glenamoy, between 31st October and 1st May; and save Owenduff or Ballycroy, and Ballyveeny and Owenduff, and all rivers in Achill Island, between 31st October and 1st February. **DATE OF LAST CHANGE.** 1st June, 1872; 7th October, 1875; 5th December, 1876. **PRINCIPAL RIVERS IN DISTRICT.** Newport, Owenmore, Burrishoole, Owengarve, Glenamoy, Ballycroy.
11. Ballina.	**BOUNDARY OF DISTRICT.** Benwee to Coonamore. **TIDAL.** Between 12th August and 16th March, save Palmerston and Easkey Rivers, which is between 31st August and 1st June. **FRESH WATER.** Between 31st July and 1st February, save Palmerston and Easkey Rivers, which is between 31st August and 1st June.

No. and Name of District.	
11. Ballina—*continued.*	**ANGLING WITH CROSS LINES.** Same as for Nets in Fresh Water. **ANGLING WITH SINGLE ROD AND LINE.** Between 15th September and 1st February, save Cloonaghmore or Palmerston River and tributaries which is (in Tidal) between 31st October and 1st February (upper) between 31st October and 1st June; and save Easkey River and tributaries, which is between 31st October and 1st February. **DATE OF LAST CHANGE.** 19th December, 1870; 10th July, 1877; 25th January, 1881. **PRINCIPAL RIVERS IN DISTRICT.** Moy, Easkey, Cloonaghmore.
12. Sligo.	**BOUNDARY OF DISTRICT.** Coonamore to Mullaghmore. **TIDAL.** Between 19th August and 4th February, save in Sligo River and its estuary, which is between 15th July and 1st January; and save also in Ballisodare River and its estuary, which is between 13th September and 4th March. **FRESH WATER.** Between 19th August and 4th February, save Sligo River, which is between 31st July and 16th January; and save also in Ballisodare River and its estuary, which is between 13th September and 4th March. **ANGLING WITH CROSS LINES.** Same as for Nets in Fresh Water. **ANGLING WITH SINGLE ROD AND LINE.** 13th September and 1st February, save in Brumcliffe River and Glencar Lake, between 19th October and 1st February; and in Grange River between 31st October and 1st February; and save also in the Tidal parts of the Sligo or Garvogue River, which is between 15th July and 1st January.

No. and Name of District.	
12. Sligo—*continued.*	**Date of Last Change.** 24th April, 1871; 27th September, 1877; 30th January, 1886; 11th October, 1886; 9th June, 1893. **Principal Rivers in District.** Sligo, Ballisodare, Brumcliffe.
13. Ballyshannon.	**Boundary of District.** Mullaghmore to Rossan. **Tidal.** Between 19th August and 1st March, save River Eske and tributaries, which is between 17th September and 1st April. Between 19th August and 4th February for Tidal and for one mile above tideway, save Crana or Buncrana and Gweebarra Rivers, Trawbreaga Bay, and Owenea and Owentocker Rivers. **Fresh Water.** Same as Tidal, save Bundrowes, which is between 31st July and 1st February. **Angling with Cross Lines.** Same as for Nets in Fresh Water. **Angling with Single Rod and Line.** Between 9th October and 1st March, save Bunduff, Bundrowes, and Erne Rivers and tributaries; Bunduff River, 30th September and 1st February; Bundrowes, 30th September and 1st February; and Erne River, 30th September and 1st March. **Date of Last Change.** 24th November, 1871; 26th June, 1875; 3rd December, 1884; 31st October, 1891. **Principal Rivers in District.** Glen, Inver, Eske, Bunduff, Dundrowes, Erne.

No. and Name of District.

14. Letterkenny.

BOUNDARY OF DISTRICT.

Rossan to Malin Head.

TIDAL.

For Crana or Buncrana River, between 14th September and 15th April; for Gweebarra, between 30th September and 1st April.

For Trawbreaga Bay, between 30th September and 1st July.

For Owenea and Owentocker Rivers, between 31st August and 1st June.

FRESH WATER.

Between 19th August and 1st March; Crana or Buncrana River, Lennon and Gweebarra Rivers, same as Tidal for these rivers; Owenea and Owentocker Rivers, between 19th August and 1st June.

ANGLING WITH CROSS LINES.

Same as for Nets in Fresh Water.

ANGLING WITH SINGLE ROD AND LINE.

Between 1st November and 1st February, save in Crana or Buncrana, between 31st October and 1st March; and Owenea and Owentocker rivers between 30th September and 1st April.

DATE OF LAST CHANGE.

2nd September, 1857; 28th February, 1874; 25th November, 1874; 21st March, 1876; 3rd August, 1885; 26th August, 1885.

PRINCIPAL RIVERS IN DISTRICT.

Lennon, Gweedore, Gweebarra, Buncrana.

15[1]. Londonderry.

BOUNDARY OF DISTRICT.

Malin to Downhill boundary.

TIDAL.

Between 31st August and 15th April.

FRESH WATER.

Same as Tidal.

ANGLING WITH CROSS LINES.

Same as for Nets in Fresh Water.

No. and Name of District.	
15[1]. London-derry—*continued.*	ANGLING WITH SINGLE ROD AND LINE. Between 10th October and 1st April, save in the Culduff, which is between 15th October and 1st March. DATE OF LAST CHANGE. 27th January, 1862; 19th July, 1877; 30th December, 1880; 18th April, 1890. PRINCIPAL RIVERS IN DISTRICT. Foyle, Roe.
15[2]. Coleraime.	BOUNDARY OF DISTRICT. Downhill Boundary to Portrush. TIDAL. Between 19th August and 4th February. FRESH WATER. Between 19th August and 1st March. ANGLING WITH CROSS LINES. Same as for Nets in Fresh Water. ANGLING WITH SINGLE ROD AND LINE. Between 19th October and 16th March, save Rivers Bann, Maine, Sixmile-water, Moyola, and Ballinderry, between 31st October and 1st March. DATE OF LAST CHANGE. 15th December, 1856; 31st March, 1871; 23rd August, 1875; 15th January, 1876. PRINCIPAL RIVERS IN DISTRICT. Bann.
16. Bally-castle.	BOUNDARY OF DISTRICT. Portrush to Donaghadee. TIDAL. Between 19th August and 17th March. FRESH WATER. Same as Tidal.

No. and Name of District.

---

16. Bally-castle—*continued.*

ANGLING WITH CROSS LINES.

Same as for Nets in Fresh Water.

ANGLING WITH SINGLE ROD AND LINE.

Between 31st October and 1st February, save in the Bush River, which is between 30th September and 1st February.

DATE OF LAST CHANGE.

23rd July, 1890.

PRINCIPAL RIVERS IN DISTRICT.

Ballycastle, Glenarm, Bush, Glendun.

17[2]. Dundalk.

BOUNDARY OF DISTRICT.

Donaghadee to Clogher Head.

TIDAL.

Between Ballaghan Point in Co. Louth, and Donaghadee in Co. Down, embracing all lakes and rivers and their tributaries flowing into the sea between said points, between 15th September and 1st April.

Between Clogher Head and the northern boundary of the mouth of the River Annagassan, Co. Louth, embracing all lakes and rivers, and their tributaries flowing into the sea between said points, between 19th August and 12th February.

From the northern boundary of the mouth of the River Annagassan to Ballaghan Point, and embracing all lakes and rivers and their tributaries flowing into the sea between said points between 30th September and 1st May following.

FRESH WATER.

Between Ballaghan Point in Co. Louth, and Donaghadee in Co. Down, embracing all lakes and rivers, and their tributaries flowing into the sea between said points, between 15th September and 1st April.

Between Clogher Head and the southern boundary of the mouth of the River Annagassan, Co. Louth, embracing all lakes and rivers and their tributaries flowing into the sea between said points, between 19th August and 1st April.

From the northern boundary of the mouth of the River Annagassan to Ballaghan Point, Co. Louth, embracing all lakes and rivers, and

No. and Name of District.

17[2]. Dundalk—*continued.*

their tributaries flowing into the sea between said points, between 30th September and 1st May.

In the Annagassan, Glyde, and Dee Rivers and their tributaries, 19th August and 12th February.

Angling with Cross Lines.

Same as for Nets in Fresh Water.

Angling with Single Rod and Line.

In the Upper or Fresh Waters between Clogher Head and the northern boundary of the Mouth of the River Annagassan, and embracing all lakes and all rivers and their tributaries flowing into the sea between said points, 30th September and 1st February.

In the Upper or Fresh Waters between the northern boundary of the mouth of the River Annagassan and Ballaghan Point, and embracing all lakes and all rivers and their tributaries flowing into the sea between said points, between 30th September and 1st May.

In the Upper or Fresh Waters between Ballaghan Point and Donaghadee, between 31st October and 1st March.

In any Tidal Waters between Clogher Head and the northern boundary of the mouth of the Annagassan River between 19th August and 12th February.

In any Tidal Waters between the northern boundary of the mouth of the Annagassan and Ballaghan Point, between 30th September and 1st May.

In any Tidal Waters between Ballaghan Point and Donaghadee, between 31st October and 1st March.

Date of Last Change.

30th October, 1880; 13th December, 1888; 18th November, 1892.

Principal Rivers in District.

Fane, Annagassan, Glyde, Dee.

17[1]. Drogheda.

Boundary of District.

Clogher Head to Skerries.

Tidal.

Between 4th August and 12th February.

No. and Name of District.

17[1]. Drogheda-*continued.*

FRESH WATER.

Same as Tidal.

ANGLING WITH CROSS LINES.

Same as for Nets in Fresh Water.

ANGLING WITH SINGLE ROD AND LINE.

Between 15th September and 12th February.

DATE OF LAST CHANGE.

1st October, 1888 ; 6th December, 1892.

PRINCIPAL RIVERS IN DISTRICT.

Boyne.

NOTE.—Pollen Fishing by Trammel Nets in Lough Neagh between 1st November and 31st January, both days inclusive.

NOTE.—The 21st Section of the 26th and 27th Vic. C. 114, requires there shall not be fewer than 168 days Close Season in each Fishery.

WEEKLY CLOSE SEASON.—By the 20th Section of the 26th and 27th Vic. C. 114, no Salmon or Trout shall be fished for or taken in any way, except by Single Rod and Line, between six of the clock on Saturday morning, and six of the clock on the succeeding Monday morning.

† Close Season for the capture of Eels by means of any Coghill, Eel, or other Net or Basket work in the eye, gap, or sluice of any Eel or other weir, between the 10th January and 1st July, save in the River Shannon, which is between 31st January and 1st July, and in all other rivers in the Limerick District between 31st December and 1st July in year following, and save in Drogheda District, which is between 30th November and 1st July, and save in the Coleraine District, which is between 10th January and 1st June in each year, and save also in Corrib or Galway River, which is between the 10th February and 1st July in each year.

ANNUAL CLOSE TIME APPLICABLE TO THE SCOTCH SALMON RIVERS.

N.B.—Observe that, in the following List, the days fixing the commencement and termination of the Annual Close Time and of the extension of Time for Rod-fishing are, in all cases, inclusive.

Name of River.	Annual Close Time. (Both days inclusive.)	Extension of Time for Rod-fishing. (Both days inclusive.)
Add	Sept. 1 to Feb. 15	Sept. 1 to Oct. 31
Aline	Aug. 27 to Feb. 10	Aug. 27 to Oct. 31
Alness	Aug. 27 to Feb. 10	Aug. 27 to Oct. 31
Annan	Sept. 10 to Feb. 24	Sept. 10 to Nov. 15
Applecross	Aug. 27 to Feb. 10	Aug. 27 to Oct. 31
Arnisdale (Loch Hourn)	Aug. 27 to Feb. 10	Aug. 27 to Oct. 31
Awe	Aug. 27 to Feb. 10	Aug. 27 to Oct. 31
Aylort (Kinloch)	Aug. 27 to Feb. 10	Aug. 27 to Oct. 31
Ayr	Aug. 27 to Feb. 10	Aug. 27 to Oct. 31
Baa and Glencoilleadar	Aug. 27 to Feb. 10	Aug. 27 to Oct. 31
Badachro and Kerry (Gairloch) ...	Aug. 27 to Feb. 10	Aug. 27 to Oct. 31
Balgay and Shieldag	Aug. 27 to Feb. 10	Aug. 27 to Oct. 31
Beauly	Aug. 27 to Feb. 10	Aug. 27 to Oct. 15
Berriedale	Aug. 27 to Feb. 10	Aug. 27 to Oct. 31
Bervie	Sept. 10 to Feb. 24	Sept. 10 to Oct. 31
Bladenoch	Aug. 27 to Feb. 10	Aug. 27 to Oct. 31
Broom	Aug. 27 to Feb. 10	Aug. 27 to Oct. 31
Brora	Aug. 27 to Feb. 10	Aug. 27 to Oct. 31
Carradale (in Cantyre)	Sept. 10 to Feb. 24	Sept. 10 to Oct. 31
Carron	Aug. 27 to Feb. 10	Aug. 27 to Oct. 31
Clayburn, Finnisbay, Avennan-Geren, Strathgravat, North Lacastile, Scalladale, and Mawrig (East Harris)	Sept. 10 to Feb. 24	Sept. 10 to Oct. 31
Clyde and Leven	Aug. 27 to Feb. 10	Aug. 27 to Oct. 31
Conon	Aug. 27 to Feb. 10	Aug. 27 to Oct. 31
Cree	Aug. 27 to Feb. 10	Aug. 27 to Oct. 31
Creed or Stornoway, and Laxay (Island of Lews)	Aug. 27 to Feb. 10	Aug. 27 to Oct. 31
Creran (Loch Creran)...	Aug. 27 to Feb. 10	Aug. 27 to Oct. 31

Name of River.	Annual Close Time. (Both days inclusive.)	Extension of Time for Rod-fishing. (Both days inclusive.)
Crowe and Shiel (Loch Duich) ...	Aug. 27 to Feb. 10	Aug. 27 to Oct. 31
Dee (Aberdeenshire)	Aug. 27 to Feb. 10	Aug. 27 to Oct. 31
Dee (Kirkcudbright)	Aug. 27 to Feb. 10	Aug. 27 to Oct. 31
Deveron	Aug. 27 to Feb. 10	Aug. 27 to Oct. 31
Don	Aug. 27 to Feb. 10	Aug. 27 to Oct. 31
Doon	Aug. 27 to Feb. 10	Aug 27 to Oct. 31
Drummachloy or Glenmore (Isle of Bute)	Sept. 1 to Feb. 15	Sept. 1 to Oct. 15
Dunbeath	Aug. 27 to Feb. 10	Aug. 27 to Oct. 15
Earn	Aug. 27 to Feb. 10	Aug. 27 to Oct. 31
Eckaig	Sept. 1 to Feb. 15	Sept. 1 to Oct. 31
Esk, North	Sept. 1 to Feb. 15	Sept. 1 to Oct. 31
Esk, South	Sept. 1 to Feb. 15	Sept. 1 to Oct. 31
Ewe	Aug. 27 to Feb. 10	Aug. 27 to Oct. 31
Fincastle, Meaveg, Ballanachist, South Lacastile, Borve, and Obb (West Harris)	Sept 10. to Feb. 24	Sept. 10 to Oct. 31
Findhorn	Aug. 27 to Feb. 10	Aug. 27 to Oct. 10
Fleet (Sutherlandshire)	Sept. 10 to Feb. 24	Sept. 10 to Oct. 31
Fleet (Kirkcudbrightshire)	Sept. 10 to Feb. 24	Sept. 10 to Oct. 31
Forss	Aug. 27 to Feb. 10	Aug. 27 to Oct. 31
Forth	Aug. 27 to Feb. 10	Aug. 27 to Oct. 31
Fyne, Shira, and Aray (Loch Fyne)...	Sept. 1 to Feb. 15	Sept. 1 to Oct. 31
Girvan	Sept. 10 to Feb 24	Sept. 10 to Oct. 31
Glenelg	Aug. 27 to Feb. 10	Aug. 27 to Oct. 31
Gour	Aug. 27 to Feb. 10	Aug. 27 to Oct. 31
Greiss, Laxdale, or Thunga	Aug. 27 to Feb. 10	Aug. 27 to Oct. 31
Grudie or Dionard	Aug. 27 to Feb. 10	Aug. 27 to Oct. 31
Gruinard and Little Gruinard ...	Aug. 27 to Feb. 10	Aug. 27 to Oct. 31
Halladale, Strathy, Naver, and Borgie	Aug. 27 to Feb. 10	Close time for Rod-fishing, Oct. 1 to Jan. 10
Helmsdale	Aug. 27 to Feb. 10	Close time for Rod-fishing, Oct. 1 to Jan. 10
Hope and Polla or Strathbeg ...	Aug. 27 to Feb. 10	Jan. 11 to Feb. 10 and Aug. 27 to Sept. 10

Name of River.	Annual Close Time. (Both dates inclusive.)	Extension of Time for Rod-fishing. (Both dates inclusive.)
Howmore	Sept. 10 to Feb. 24	Sept. 10 to Oct. 31
Inchard	Aug. 27 to Feb. 10	Aug. 27 to Oct. 31
Inner (in Jura)	Sept. 10 to Feb. 24	Sept. 10 to Oct. 31
Inver	Aug. 27 to Feb. 10	Aug. 27 to Oct. 31
Iorsa (in Arran)	Sept. 10 to Feb. 24	Sept. 10 to Oct. 31
Irvine and Garnock	Sept. 10 to Feb. 24	Sept. 10 to Oct. 31
Kennart	Aug. 27 to Feb. 10	Aug. 27 to Oct. 31
Kilchoan or Inverie (Loch Nevis) ...	Aug. 27 to Feb. 10	Aug. 27 to Oct. 31
Kinloch (Kyle of Tongue)	Aug. 27 to Feb. 10	Aug. 27 to Oct. 31
Kirkaig	Aug. 27 to Feb. 10	Aug. 27 to Oct. 31
Kishorn	Aug. 27 to Feb. 10	Aug. 27 to Oct. 31
Kyle of Sutherland	Aug. 27 to Feb. 10	Aug. 27 to Oct. 15
Laggan and Sorn (Island of Islay) ...	Sept. 10 to Feb. 24	Sept. 10 to Oct. 31
Laxford	Aug. 27 to Feb. 10	Aug. 27 to Oct. 31
Leven	Aug. 27 to Feb. 10	Aug. 27 to Oct. 31
Little Loch Broom	Aug. 27 to Feb. 10	Aug. 27 to Oct. 31
Lochy	Aug. 27 to Feb. 10	Aug. 27 to Oct. 31
Loch Duich	Aug 27 to Feb. 10	Aug. 27 to Oct. 31
Loch Luing	Aug. 27 to Feb. 10	Aug. 27 to Oct. 31
Loch Roag	Aug. 27 to Feb. 10	Aug. 27 to Oct. 31
Lossie	Aug. 27 to Feb. 10	Aug. 27 to Oct. 31
Luce	Sept. 10 to Feb. 24	Sept. 10 to Oct. 31
Lussa (Island of Mull)	Aug. 27 to Feb. 10	Aug. 27 to Oct. 31
Moidart	Aug. 27 to Feb. 10	Aug. 27 to Oct. 31
Morar	Aug. 27 to Feb. 10	Aug. 27 to Oct. 31
Mullanageren, Horasary, and Loch-na-Ciste (North Uist)	Sept. 10 to Feb. 24	Sept. 10 to Oct. 31
Nairn	Aug. 27 to Feb. 10	Aug. 27 to Oct. 31
Nell, Feochan, and Euchar	Aug. 27 to Feb. 10	Aug. 27 to Oct. 31
Ness	Aug. 27 to Feb. 10	Aug. 27 to Oct. 15
Nith	Sept. 10 to Feb. 24	Sept. 10 to Nov. 15
Orkney Islands (River from Loch of Stenness, &c.)	Sept. 10 to Feb. 24	Sept. 10 to Oct. 31
Ormsary (Loch Killisport, Loch Head, and Stornaway Mull of Cantire)	Aug. 27 to Feb. 10	Aug. 27 to Oct. 31
Penygowan or Glenforsa and Aros ...	Aug. 27 to Feb. 10	Aug. 27 to Oct. 31

Name of River.	Annual Close Time. (Both dates inclusive.)	Extension of Time for Rod-fishing. (Both dates inclusive.)
Resort	Aug. 27 to Feb. 10	Aug. 27 to Oct. 31
Ruel	Sept. 1 to Feb. 15	Sept. 1 to Oct. 31
Sanda	Aug. 27 to Feb. 10	Aug. 27 to Oct. 31
Scaddle	Aug. 27 to Feb. 10	Aug. 27 to Oct. 31
Shetland Islands (River of Sandwater, &c.)	Sept. 10 to Feb. 24	Feb. 1 to Feb. 24 and Sept. 10 to Nov. 15
Shiel (Loch Shiel)	Aug. 27 to Feb. 10	Aug. 27 to Oct. 31
Sligachan, Broadford, and Portree (Isle of Skye)	Aug. 27 to Feb. 10	Aug. 27 to Oct. 31
Snizort, Orley, Oze, and Drynoch (Isle of Skye)	Aug. 27 to Feb. 10	Aug. 27 to Oct. 31
Spey	Aug. 27 to Feb. 10	Aug. 27 to Oct. 15
Stinchar	Sept. 10 to Feb. 24	Sept. 10 to Nov. 15
Tay	Aug. 27 to Feb. 10	Jan. 15 to Feb. 10 and Aug. 27 to Oct. 15
Thurso	Aug. 27 to Feb. 10	Jan. 11 to Feb. 10 and Aug. 27 to Sept. 14
Torridon, Balgay, and Shieldag ...	Aug. 27 to Feb. 10	Aug. 27 to Oct. 31
Ugie	Sept. 10 to Feb. 24	Sept. 10 to Oct. 31
Ullapool (Loch Broom)	Aug. 27 to Feb. 10	Aug. 27 to Oct. 31
Urr	Sept. 10 to Feb. 24	Sept. 10 to Nov. 30
Wick	Aug. 27 to Feb. 10	Aug. 27 to Oct. 31
Ythan	Sept. 10 to Feb. 24	Sept. 10 to Oct. 31